Women
in the
West

Series Editors
Sandra L. Myres   Elliott W. West   Julie Roy Jeffrey

The Women in the West series is designed to reflect the extraordinary range of new research into the contributions made by women to the westward movement and to the subsequent development of western North America. Maxine Benson's finely crafted biography of Martha Maxwell marks an auspicious beginning for this series.

Based on many years of research in public and private collections and depositories, Benson's work illuminates the little-known but important career of a remarkable woman. Naturalist, museologist, and artist, Maxwell pioneered in a number of fields new for women in addition to carrying out the traditional roles of wife and mother. Her complex character and personality reflected many of the conflicting ideas about woman's place and woman's role in nineteenth-century society. And her tragic and lonely death revealed something of the price she paid for daring to be different.

Like that of other accomplished women of her era, Maxwell's fame did not keep pace with the significant influence she had on her profession. Thanks to Maxine Benson, Martha Maxwell has been restored to her deserved place in the history of the West and of the nation.

In this portrait, probably made around the time of the Centennial, Martha Maxwell was photographed with a palette as well as a gun, both emblematic of her chosen life. Courtesy Colorado Historical Society, Denver.

Maxine Benson

MARTHA MAXWELL,
Rocky Mountain Naturalist

University of Nebraska Press
Lincoln and London

Portions of this work have previously been published as "Centennial Naturalist: Martha Maxwell, 1831–1881," in *A Taste of the West: Essays in Honor of Robert G. Athearn,* edited by Duane A. Smith (Boulder: Pruett Publishing Co., 1983), 17–31, and "Colorado Celebrates the Centennial, 1876," *The Colorado Magazine* 53 (Spring 1976):185–99. Grateful acknowledgment is made for their use.

Library of Congress Cataloging-in-Publication Data
Benson, Maxine.
Martha Maxwell, Rocky Mountain naturalist.
Bibliography: p.
Includes index.
1. Maxwell, Martha, 1831–1881.
2. Mammals—Rocky Mountains
Region—Collection and
preservation. 3. Birds—Rocky
Mountains Region—Collection
and preservation. 4. Naturalists—
Colorado—Biography.
5. Taxidermists—Colorado—
Biography. I. Title.
QH31.M36B46   1986   508'.092'4 [B]   86–6936
ISBN 0-8032-1192-9

*To my parents and Ben
and to
Martha's great-granddaughter
Cornelia Scott Chapin*

Contents

Illustrations

Mrs. Maxwell is the woman who made a collection of
animals of Colorado, procuring herself, either by
shooting, poisoning, trapping, buying, or soliciting
from her acquaintances, specimens of almost every kind
of living creature found in that region, skinning,
stuffing, or in other ways preserving them.

*Taxidermy, as a fine art, subservient
to science,* became the work of her life.
On the Plains

Preface

"See; there she is!" cried one visitor to the Philadelphia Exposition. "Just think! she killed all them animals," echoed another. "There, that's her!"[1] All during that hot centennial summer of 1876, throngs of people pushed and shoved their way into the Kansas-Colorado Building, eager to catch a glimpse of the small, dark-haired woman responsible for creating the display of bears, deer, and various other mammals cavorting over a "Rocky Mountain" landscape. Curious, skeptical, friendly—on and on they came, until even the policemen stationed at the entrance and exit of the building were hard-pressed to maintain control, so intent were the fairgoers on seeing for themselves the "modern Diana" who had come all the way from the wilds of Colorado.

Innately shy and reserved, the object of this attention struggled to accommodate the tourists and reporters anxious to find out who she was and how and why such a seemingly delicate, feminine woman had managed not only to shoot but, yes, actually to stuff the specimens on display. Two years later at least some of the answers were provided in a small book entitled *On the Plains, and Among the Peaks; or, How Mrs. Maxwell Made Her Natural History Collection*, written by Martha Maxwell's half-sister Mary (with considerable assistance from the subject herself). In a little over two hundred pages, the volume recounted Martha's adventures in collecting the birds and mammals of the Rocky Mountain region and mounting them in displays resembling their natural habitats.[2]

A century later, as Americans celebrated the Bicentennial of the United States and Coloradans marked their own statehood Centennial, articles appeared on the nation's one-hundredth-birthday observance—the buildings, the ceremonies, the personalities. One participant who intrigued several writers was Martha Maxwell, and from the pages of the *American West* to the volume entitled *The Women* in the Time-Life series The Old West, readers were introduced to her via photographs showing her attired in a hunting costume with bloomers, complete with rifle, or posing among her specimens.[3]

For my part, although I had grown up in Boulder, Colorado, just a few blocks from the site of Martha Maxwell's first Rocky Mountain Museum and from her home at the mouth of Boulder Canyon, I knew little of her, save for the brown-and-white-checked hunting outfit on display in the local historical society museum, to which an aged newspaper clipping about her had been pinned. Not until I began preparing my own article about Colorado's participation in the Philadelphia Centennial did I discover *On the Plains* as well as the numerous stereographic views of her Colorado and Centennial exhibits. Colorful and dramatic, these sources began to bring Martha Maxwell to life, and I devoted several pages of my article to her.[4]

Here the matter might have rested, however, save for a serendipitous telephone call. One day in 1976 while I was in my office at the Colorado Historical Society, I picked up the receiver and began answering a question about a display of portraits of Colorado women mounted for the Centennial-Bicentennial observance. The question was not one that normally would have come to me, but I did know of the exhibit and began giving directions. During the conversation the woman at the other end of the line mentioned that she had a particular interest in one of the subjects, Martha Maxwell. "I am her great-granddaughter," she confided. With mounting excitement I explained that I had recently been writing an article in which her great-grandmother figured prominently, and we quickly turned the discussion to her.

Thus I became acquainted with Cornelia Scott Chapin, and in future conversations I discovered that considerably more material about Martha Maxwell existed than had previously been known. Still in the hands of the family were hundreds of letters as well as other material such as photographs, reminiscences, and newspaper clippings. Mrs. Chapin generously presented this collection to the Colorado Historical Society, and I determined to continue my research and attempt to write a biography of Martha Maxwell.

First, however, it was necessary to organize the papers, which had arrived in typical disarray. As I read the letters between Martha and her husband James, her half-sister Mary, and her daughter Mabel, I began to see the project as one that promised for the first time to permit a full and detailed examination of her life. The letters and accompanying material revealed a fascinating story, one that in a novel would scarcely be credible. Born in 1831 in Pennsylvania, Martha moved with her family first to Illinois and then to Wisconsin; in rapid succession she attended two coeducational colleges during the early 1850s (Oberlin and Lawrence University); married James Maxwell, a widower twenty years her senior with six children, in 1854; had a child of her own in 1857; traveled overland with her husband to the Colorado gold fields in 1860; had a chance encounter with a German taxidermist that determined her lifework; returned to Wisconsin without her husband in 1862; entered a health institute (now the Battle Creek Sanitarium) and then took her daughter to the new temperance settlement of Vineland, New Jersey; rejoined her husband (under some pressure) and accompanied him back to Colorado in 1868; began obtaining and mounting the birds and mammals of Colorado and made a collection that was sold to Shaw's Garden in St. Louis in 1870; constructed habitat displays and opened her own Rocky Mountain Museum in Boulder in 1874, moving it to Denver in early 1876; transported her exhibit to Philadelphia for the Centennial, where she achieved international renown; became the subject of a book; had a subspecies of owl named for her by a Smithsonian ornithologist; and spent the remaining years until her death in 1881 exhibiting her collection on the East Coast, while her husband stayed in Colorado.

In addition to recounting the details of Martha Maxwell's remarkable life, this book attempts in the process to explore the several themes that were a part of that life. Martha was a woman who had a strong interest in learning and in intellectual development, as well as a commitment to achieving reform in many areas, particularly feminism and women's rights. Combining these traits with artistic abilities and a love of nature, *"taxidermy, as a fine art, subservient to science,* became the work of her life," as her sister phrased it in *On the Plains.*[5] By showing "what a woman could do," she thought to advance the feminist ideals to which she became increasingly committed. Although she gained considerable fame during her lifetime with her museums in Boulder and Denver and her Centennial exhibit, her achievements were largely unacknowledged and even forgotten afterward. This study attempts to place Martha Maxwell in perspective as "a pioneer" in the art of habitat grouping, as University of Colorado Museum Curator Junius Henderson once termed her, and to indicate her contributions to the development of the habitat displays that are now a common feature of natural history museums.[6] It also explores the underlying reasons why she sought this unusual path for self-fulfillment and examines the costs she paid, especially in the relationships with her husband and daughter.

The mother-daughter relationship between Martha and Mabel indeed constitutes another major theme of this book. In recent years, Carroll Smith-Rosenberg has described an eighteenth- and nineteenth-century "female world of love and ritual" in which women—mothers, daughters, sisters, friends— formed bonds that lasted through life.[7] "At the heart of this world," she writes, "lay intense devotion and identification between mothers and daughters." In this harmonious sphere, "mother-daughter bonding served as the model for subsequent relations with other women." In Smith-Rosenberg's view, this model held true until approximately the last third of the nineteenth century, when young women began attending college in larger numbers and more alternatives to marriage opened up. Now conflict between the generations began to "mar this unself-conscious intimacy," as daughters increasingly rejected the domestic and circumscribed lives their mothers had lived.[8]

The story of Martha Maxwell and her daughter Mabel permits an examination of an interesting variation on this theme.

While Martha's lifetime relationship with her half-sister Mary affords a classic example of the female bonding of which Smith-Rosenberg writes, her relationship with her daughter is almost a mirror image of the mother-daughter model she describes. In this instance, it was the college-educated, feminist mother who sought her own fulfillment outside the traditional confines of domesticity and the daughter, similarly college-educated, who looked for hers *within* it. Although the generational conflict and the rejection remained the same, the issues were exactly reversed.

Certainly abundant material is available to document these themes. In addition to the manuscript collection there is, of course, Mary's book *On the Plains*, which can be used (and I have so used it) on at least two levels. First, the volume is a source of factual information about Martha Maxwell, for which it is in the main accurate and capable of independent verification, the details presented in colorful, highly quotable prose. It also indicates to some degree how Martha Maxwell viewed herself, and how she wished to be perceived by others.

In addition, Martha's daughter, Mabel Maxwell Brace, provided yet another perspective in her memoir, *Thanks to Abigail*, published in 1948 when she was ninety years old (she lived to be almost one hundred).[9] Here were Mabel's memories of her childhood, recounted so many years later as clearly and vividly as if the events had happened yesterday.

Thus, for not a few episodes in Martha Maxwell's life, three separate yet converging sources are available: a letter to or from Martha, a section in *On the Plains*, and a passage written by Mabel in *Thanks to Abigail*. Not to be overlooked are the numerous reminiscences and notes Mary jotted down over the course of her long life (she too lived to be nearly one hundred). Much information would have been lost had it not been for Mary's burning desire to preserve accounts of Martha's accomplishments in the belief that sometime, someone would find them of value. Mary herself published a good deal in addition to *On the Plains*, and I often thought of her as a coauthor, the two of us separated by the years but united in a common endeavor.

During the process of research and writing, when people

asked what this book was "about," I usually replied that it was the story of a mid-nineteenth-century woman naturalist-taxidermist who gained fame at the Philadelphia Centennial Exposition. Of course, now I know that the book is "about" that and about many other things as well—about mothers and daughters and sisters, about the struggle of a woman to come to terms with both marriage and motherhood and her own desire for self-fulfillment, about museums and habitat groups, feminism, the Colorado gold rush, education for women, and a whole host of other topics. Most of all, though, it is about Martha herself. I hope those who read this book will enjoy making her acquaintance.

Acknowledgments

I thank all those who contributed in so many ways to my research during the past nine years. William E. Bigglestone and Gertrude Jacob of the Oberlin College Archives assisted with early Oberlin history. Timmie (Mrs. E. Geoffrey) Cullen, St. Louis, Missouri, Martha Maxwell's great-great-granddaughter, generously allowed me access to the Maxwell family documents in her possession, as did her father, Harold B. Scott, Palm Beach, Florida. Nijole Etzwiler, then president of the Sauk County Historical Society, drove me around the sites in Baraboo, Wisconsin, associated with Martha Maxwell's life there and facilitated the use of the society's collections. Joseph Ewan, Tulane University, New Orleans, offered encouragement and assisted with an elusive identification. Marion Jenkinson Mengel, University of Kansas Museum, Lawrence, helped me understand ornithological nomenclature. Laurence T. Paddock, editor of the Boulder *Daily Camera*, helped greatly with access to materials on early Boulder history. Hugo G. Rodeck, who directed the University of Colorado Museum for many years, donated significant materials to the Maxwell Papers at the Colorado Historical Society. Others who assisted in important ways were Marcia Bonta, Tyrone, Pennsylvania; Gretchen Boyd, Boulder, Colorado; Donald Jackson, Colorado Springs, Colorado; and H. Lee Scamehorn, University of Colorado, Boulder, Colorado.

I am grateful also to Carol M. Spawn and Mark Robbins, Academy of Natural Sciences, Philadelphia, Pennsylvania; Michael Husband and Rita Alter, Boulder Historical Society and

Museum, Boulder, Colorado; Lois Anderton, Boulder Public Library, Boulder, Colorado; Gary Kurutz, California State Library, Sacramento; Stanley Lombardo, Classics Department, University of Kansas, Lawrence; Judy Heberling, Diane Rabson, Alice Sharp, Amy Vigil, and especially Catherine Engel and Mary Winnell, Colorado Historical Society, Denver; Frederic Athearn, Colorado State Office, Bureau of Land Management, U.S. Department of the Interior, Denver; Eleanor Gehres, Bonnie Hardwick, Augie Mastrogiuseppe, and Fred Yonce, Western History Department, Denver Public Library; Nancy Markham and Bette D. Peters, Four Mile Historic Park, Denver, Colorado; Carol J. Butts, Lawrence University Archives, Appleton, Wisconsin; Barbara L. Mykrantz, Missouri Botanical Garden, St. Louis; William A. Deiss and Susan A. Blum, Smithsonian Institution Archives, Washington, D.C.; and John A Brennan and Cassandra M. Volpe, Western Historical Collections, University of Colorado Libraries, Boulder.

I thank also staff members of the following institutions: Amon Carter Museum, Fort Worth, Texas; Appleton Public Library, Appleton, Wisconsin; Bancroft Library, University of California, Berkeley; Battle Creek Sanitarium Hospital, Battle Creek, Michigan; Baraboo Public Library, Baraboo, Wisconsin; Bentley Historical Library, University of Michigan, Ann Arbor; Historical Society of Pennsylvania, Philadelphia; History of Medicine Division, National Institutes of Health, National Library of Medicine, Bethesda, Maryland; Illinois State Historical Library, Springfield; Local History Collection, Willard Library, Battle Creek, Michigan; Long Island Historical Society, Brooklyn, New York; Massachusetts Historical Society, Boston; Philadelphia City Archives, Philadelphia, Pennsylvania; Saratoga Springs Public Library, Saratoga Springs, New York; State Historical Society of Wisconsin, Madison; and the interlibrary loan departments of the Denver Public Library and the Kansas State Library, Topeka.

Several readers contributed many helpful comments and corrections as the manuscript was being refined. Glenda Riley, University of Northern Iowa, Cedar Falls, and Sandra Myres, University of Texas at Arlington, generously shared their extensive knowledge of western women's history and made numerous important suggestions. Their early encouragement meant more than I can say. Michael J. Brodhead, University of Nevada, Reno, and Marianne Ainley, McGill University, Montreal, Quebec, furnished significant clarifications and friendly support, as did Robert W. Richmond, Kansas State Historical Society, Topeka; Jane Valentine Barker, Boulder, Colorado, and Hugo G. Rodeck and Sally Lewis Rodeck, Northglenn, Colorado. W. E. Bigglestone, Oberlin College Archives, helped with chapter 2 on Oberlin, as did Liston E. Leyendecker, Colorado State University, Fort Collins, with chapter 4 on Colorado mining.

Lastly, but most importantly, I thank my parents for emotional and financial support and for making all the other family sacrifices necessary while I worked on this project. And I thank especially Cornelia Scott Chapin, for without her generous gift of the collection and her willingness to let me tell Martha's story the way I saw it, there would be no book.

1

A Naturalist's Childhood

Not far from the site of her later success at the Philadelphia Centennial Exposition, Martha Ann Dartt grew up in north-central Pennsylvania in an area abounding in wildlife and un-spoiled natural beauty. From earliest childhood she was drawn to the woods and to the animals who lived there, storing up impressions that would last throughout a lifetime of adventure in the Rocky Mountains and beyond. Here her innate interests were nurtured and defined as were many of her personal characteristics, for as her daughter later wrote, Martha was born into a family of women who had for generations displayed "prodigious energy, tenacity of purpose, and a fierce independence of judgment."[1] Shaping the direction of Martha's life and work, these influences can first be discerned in the few shadowy fragments of information remaining from that early Pennsylvania childhood.

When Martha was a little girl, she had a small yellow duckling that followed her around like a puppy. Along with the hens, dogs, and other animals of the household, it was her constant companion and faithful friend. Indeed, one of her most vivid childhood memories was of a spring day when the lazy stream near her home became a raging torrent, carrying with it everything in its path. As Martha stood on the bank and watched in horror, her little duck plunged into the current and was swept downstream. "She would at times appear in sight, then disappear for some time & then could be seen again struggling for the shour," Martha recalled later. At last the duckling disappeared, and Martha watched for her in vain until darkness came. "My heart was in great anguish. I cried untill Mother made me stop for fear it would make me sick." All she could do now was to pray to God to save the duck, her mother told her, and this she did "with all the sincerity and fervor of a person whose last earthly friend was in the place of that duck." Happily, her prayers were answered, and the next morning, when she went to look for her pet, she discovered it safe in a hollow stump some distance downstream.[2]

Martha also became acquainted with the wild animals who lived near her home through long walks in the forest with her grandmother, a free-spirited and strong-minded old lady named Abigail Sanford. Indeed, in later years Martha often looked back on these excursions and credited Abigail with sparking her interest in natural history. For example, responding in 1878 to an editor's query about her "early associations," she mused that when she was a small child, "those rambles in the woods with Grandmother among the rocks, birds and squirrels had perhapse something to do with fixing my natural tastes."[3]

Martha and her grandmother also reportedly studied the specimens they had found during the long winter evenings.[4] Still surviving as a tangible reminder of those early years is a small paperbound booklet published in Cooperstown, New York, in 1839. Entitled *Natural History of Quadrupeds; for the Edification & Amusement of Youth*, it bears the inscription "Martha Ann Dartt's Book" penned in a childish hand inside the cover.[5]

Abigail Sanford influenced her granddaughter in other ways as well, communicating to her the traits of independence and single-mindedness (which sometimes became obstinacy and stubbornness) that were to prove to be such important factors in Martha's life and work. Born Abigail Wooster in Milford, Connecticut, in 1780, she married Jared Sanford, also a Connecticut native, in 1803. Both could trace their roots back to the earliest days of colonial settlement, Abigail to an ancestor who had come to America in 1622, and Jared to the immigrant Thomas Sanford, who had arrived in the early 1630s. After their marriage the couple settled in Prospect, where Jared tilled the rocky Connecticut soil and plied his trade as a shoemaker. Between 1805 and 1817 they became the parents of four daughters, Amy (1805), Asenath (1809), Abigail (1815), and Araminta (1817), and three sons, Jared (1807), Joseph (1811), and James (1813); all except Abigail survived childhood.[6]

As the Sanford children reached adolescence and young adulthood, they began the first steps on a westward journey that would be repeated by untold numbers of Americans seeking better opportunities on the frontier. By the late 1820s young Jared had obtained a millsite in Dartt's Settlement in Charleston Township, Tioga County, Pennsylvania. Taking its name from the Tioga River, the major stream flowing through the heavily timbered and rolling countryside, the county was located on the New York state line in north-central Pennsylvania. The first white settlers had arrived in Charleston Township, situated squarely in the middle of the county, early in the nineteenth century, founding clusters of homes they called Cherry Flats or Shumway Hill or Dartt's Settlement.[7] Here, in this wild and beautiful land, Jared Sanford began manufacturing wooden casks at his millsite; soon his brothers Joseph and James arrived, as did sisters Amy and Asenath.[8]

Amy Sanford, in fact, had been away from her parents' home for some time, attending school in Litchfield and then apprenticing to become a tailor, an occupation that was regarded as neither uncommon nor unusual for women.[9] Writing in 1817, in *Sketches of America*, Henry B. Fearon commented that tailoring was "a variable business, sometimes good employment, often not, it is a good deal in the hands of women."[10] From Connecticut Amy had gone to New Marlborough, Massachusetts, where she engaged in tailoring for about a year, and then to Pennsylvania.[11] There she apparently opened a shop in the county seat of Wellsboro, a short distance from Dartt's Settlement, with the help of her younger sister Asenath.[12]

With most of their family in Pennsylvania, it was natural for Jared and Abigail, along with their youngest daughter Araminta, to join them. It is here, in Dartt's Settlement, that one is able to catch the first glimpses of Abigail's personality and qualities of mind and character. If some women regretted leaving their friends and homes to journey westward, even to be with other members of their families, Abigail seems not only to have accepted but to have relished the opportunity. Homesick and unhappy, Jared soon returned to Prospect, but it is perhaps indicative of her view of the marriage, as well as the state of her mind, that Abigail steadfastly refused to accompany him, and for several years no amount of entreaty or persuasion could induce her to reconsider.

That she remained in Pennsylvania was certainly not because of lack of effort or desire on Jared's part. "You Shall have the deed of the whole if you will," he promised her on one occasion, "and We Can Live Comfortable and happy together while we live in religion. I do not think we had ought to Live apart."[13] Asking his children to intercede for him, he painted a glowing picture of his "Corn and potatoes and beans and peas and beats and Carrots and turnips and good whortleberries and some bilberries and some Millit," modestly concluding that overall he had "the pleasantist place in Prospect."[14]

Alas, all was to no avail. Joseph informed him that "Mother declares that she will not go their at all," and Amy concurred, reporting that "Jared says that mother uterly refuses to go to Connecticut."[15] Furthermore, said his son-in-law Spencer Dartt, "all reasonings, arguements, and entreaties . . . are useless and worse than useless for by them we incur her displeasure although done in a most friendly manner." Truly, he stated, "She will do as she pleases regardles of friends or foes."[16] This being the case, both Amy and Joseph thought that their father was better off without her. Although Joseph agreed that it would be "disagreeable and lonesome" for him to live alone, "Yet I have reason to beleive you will live more agreeable than you would with her if she should go contrary to her own mind. . . ."[17]

Jared Sanford's son-in-law Spencer Dartt, who found himself in the midst of this tempest, had become a member of the family through his marriage to Amy Sanford on June 25, 1830. Born in Vermont in 1808 (and thus three years younger than Amy), he was the fifth of nine children of Justus Dartt, Jr., and his first wife, Polly Sperry, and a descendant of Richard Dart, who had come to Connecticut in the early 1660s.[18] Shortly after Spencer's birth the family moved to New York and then to Pennsylvania, where Justus Dartt, Sr., Spencer's grandfather, founded Dartt's Settlement in 1811.[19] A Revolutionary War veteran who served as a colonel in the Vermont militia, the senior Justus Dartt was the all-around "first citizen" of the community and was characterized by his granddaughter-in-law Amy as "not only a very efficient, forceful character but also very courtly and dignified."[20]

When Spencer Dartt was about eleven years old his mother died, and he lived thereafter with his Aunt Irene Wilson, his father's childless sister.[21] It was to Aunt Wilson's home in Dartt's Settlement that the newlywed Spencer and Amy Dartt moved following their wedding, and it was here that just over a year later, on July 21, 1831, they welcomed their only child, a daughter they named Martha Ann.[22]

Within a short time after Martha's birth the family moved to a home of their own on Spencer's farm about a mile from Aunt Wilson's.[23] Yet all was not well in the young household, for Amy had become an invalid, remaining incapacitated to one degree or another for the next five years.[24] Few clues survive as to the specific nature or origin of her illness, although Spencer did write to his father-in-law on one occasion that Amy "has been confined to her bed and room 22 weeks unable to walk or sit up but a very little; some of the time she has been very low not able to speak a loud word for ten days. . . ."[25] Such symptoms invite the conjecture that Amy may have been suffering from hysteria, a chronic ailment that one scholar has recently termed "one of the classic diseases of the nineteenth century."[26] The symptoms of hysteria could range from paralysis, numbness, pain, and depression to the "hysterical fit," and moreover could change, alter, and then reappear within the same patient. "Its symptoms are so varied and obscure, so contradictory and changeable," wrote one doctor of the period, "and if by chance several of them, or even a single one be relieved, numerous others almost immediately spring into existence."[27] If Amy was in fact a hysteric, it is impossible to determine from the limited evidence precisely why she may have thus taken to her bed, although it has been theorized that nineteenth-century women often became hysterics to escape from situations with which they could no longer cope, or with which they were dissatisfied.[28] Whether Amy may have been responding through illness to the demands of motherhood or the loss of her role as a self-supporting businesswoman (or both) can only be surmised.

Despite her illness, Amy apparently was able to give her daughter Martha some attention and rudimentary education during her early years. "She taught me to read spell knit and sew," Martha remembered later. "I know [I] have a small work pocket which I completed the day I was 3 years old."[29] Yet the sight of her mother lying in her bed month after month, or stretched out in the long red wooden cradle that had been carved especially for her, must have profoundly affected Martha's early development, making it even more natural (and necessary) for her to form a deep attachment to her vigorous grandmother Abigail.[30]

When the little girl was just two and one-half years old she suffered an even more profound blow when her father succumbed on December 14, 1833, to the scarlet fever he had contracted while caring for a brother's two children.[31] Martha herself, also ill with the disease, survived. "This to my mother was a most afflicting providence," as Martha noted years later. "My father, being naturally of a kind disposition and influenced by the meak and quiet spirit of the gospell was to her, more than all the earth beside."[32] Thus widowed, ill, and alone, Amy moved back to Aunt Wilson's with her daughter, facing what must have seemed a bleak and uncertain future.

The next two years passed relatively quietly, so far as the surviving records indicate, with Amy occasionally improving, then relapsing again. Early in 1835, for example, she commented in a letter to her brother James, who by then had left Pennsylvania for Michigan, that her "general health is rather better than when you left but not as good as it was 3 months ago [for] by walking a little too far I brought on my old complaint again and am unable to walk at all now."[33]

This being the case, Abigail decided that strong measures were necessary, and despite her earlier reservations, late in 1835 she bundled up her daughter and set off for Prospect in the hope that familiar surroundings would speed Amy's recuperation. Although Amy had originally planned to take Martha with her, she was so feeble that she had to ride lying down in a bed, and thus she concluded reluctantly to leave her daughter behind in Pennsylvania. The anguish of their parting left an indelible impression on the four-year-old little girl, who years later recalled the "day of sorrow" when her mother departed. "It was quite early in the morning, before I had risen from my bed that she told me she thought that I had not better go," Martha remembered. "It was a sad disappointment [and] the tears flowed freely for awhile."[34]

After a journey of some three weeks Amy and Abigail arrived at their old home in Prospect, where Jared was, as might be expected, overjoyed to see them. Although she was not as well as when she had left Pennsylvania, Amy told her sister Asenath, she was eating salt crackers and oysters which "relish[ed] and agree[d] with" her stomach, and she hoped to improve. Her father, she added, was going to get her some crutches, and she expected to walk soon.[35] Meanwhile, Martha had been left with her paternal grandfather, but she "soon became discontented" and returned again to Aunt Wilson's. Finally, a full year after her mother and grandmother had gone away, Martha was told that Amy was returning to Pennsylvania. She had just sat down to dinner, she recalled, "but that intelligence was my meat and drink . . . for my apetite fled away." After days of anxious waiting at last she saw the carriage drive up, and once again she was in her mother's arms.[36]

At first Martha and Amy again lived with Aunt Wilson (Grandmother Abigail had remained for a time in Prospect), although they were later able to return to the farm left by Spencer. Amy, much improved in health, took care of the livestock, with her daughter's help, while Martha attended school. Martha grew close to her mother again and later remembered a summer during this period as "the happiest one I ever enjoyed."[37] Yet while Martha did have at least one playmate who later recalled that they "waded the brook, roamed over orchard & playgrounds, & were like sisters together,"[38] the picture of her early childhood that emerges most clearly is that of a lonely, only child who often turned either to her aged grandmother or to animals for solace.

All that changed when Martha was ten years old, for on

November 21, 1841, Amy married Josiah Dartt, her late husband Spencer's first cousin.[39] Although Martha would later call Josiah "about the *best* Stepfather than any body ever had," initially she was "very much displeased" at this alteration in her circumstances, apparently fearing the loss of her mother's companionship that she had earlier experienced through absence or illness.[40] Yet Josiah was destined to play a critical role in Martha's development, not only as a much-loved father but as a teacher who by example and encouragement helped to guide her lifelong quest for knowledge.

Josiah Dartt was, in fact, exactly as close to his stepdaughter in age as he was to his wife. Born on August 29, 1818, he was thirteen years older than Martha, and thirteen years younger than Amy.[41] This rather striking disparity in age between the thirty-six-year-old Amy and her twenty-three-year-old second husband seems never to have been commented upon, nor to have been a factor either in the happiness of their union or in the problems that they would have from time to time. Nor did it leave Josiah a relatively young widower, for despite her protracted and recurring illnesses, Amy ended up outliving him by fully twenty years.

What, then, had drawn this rather unlikely couple together? Josiah, well educated as a surveyor and civil engineer in the Wellsboro Academy, was by all accounts a man of intellect and intelligence, if somewhat inclined to live in an ivory tower.[42] Amy, no less intelligent, had been determined and independent enough to leave home at an early age and maintain a successful tailoring business prior to her first marriage to Spencer Dartt. Indeed, although she suffered occasionally from ill health, her "greatest charm," according to her second daughter Mary, was her "intensity and vivacity," which overshadowed even her "delicate and refined" face and figure.[43]

The spirited Amy and the scholarly Josiah, however, probably would not have contemplated matrimony at all had it not been for the strongest bond of all: religion. Representative of what one historian has aptly characterized as "a supremely religious society working feverishly to become even more so,"[44] Amy and Josiah had apparently concluded that their mutual interest in religion was sufficient to overcome any differences they had in age or temperament. Originally influenced, according to family tradition, by the Calvinistic exhortations of Lyman Beecher while she was attending school in Litchfield, Amy had since joined forces with the Methodists after moving to Pennsylvania. Always, said Mary, "to those who were religiously interested she was in closest sympathy."[45] Josiah, although trained as an engineer, had also studied for the ministry and dreamed of traveling to Oregon as a missionary. Thus deciding that theirs was a union made in heaven, they married.[46]

A little more than a year after their marriage, Josiah and Amy's first daughter, Mary Emma, was born on December 10, 1842.[47] Now Martha had someone to look after and to play with, a sister who would become her closest confidant and friend as the years went by. Indeed, Mary wrote toward the end of her life that Martha had "fairly idolized" her, adding that this did not surprise her, "for previous to my birth her only companions had been grown people and pets. . . ."[48] Initially, however, Mary's birth was more of a burden than a pleasure for Martha, for Amy was again plagued with ill health, perhaps in a recurrence of the hysteria that had afflicted her earlier, and Martha consequently had to take over most of the care of the new baby and the household. It was, she later concluded, "a *very* hard winter."[49]

Neither illness nor the birth of a new baby, however, diminished the dreams that Amy and Josiah harbored to minister to the Indians in Oregon, dreams that would have been nurtured by accounts of the first Methodist missionaries, who had settled there in 1834, and of the noted Presbyterian Marcus Whitman, who had arrived two years later. Adventurous frontiersmen and homesteaders had followed, drawn by glowing reports that portrayed Oregon as a promised land of abundance and plenty. Soon the "Oregon fever" was raging as Americans in increasing numbers set their sights on Oregon or on the equally magical land of California and turned their wagons westward along the Oregon Trail.[50] By the late summer of 1844, Amy and Josiah had concluded to join them.[51] Their decision to go west seems to have been a completely mutual one; it was, moreover, the very foundation of their relationship. Far from being a "reluctant pioneer," as some historians have termed the women who went west, even as her mother Abigail, Amy may have been the more determined of the two when it came to deeds, rather than dreams.[52] As Sandra Myres has written in *Westering Women*, "for some women the principal motivation for going West was not family desires or economic betterment but an answer to a religious calling to minister to the Indians."[53]

Since it was obviously too late to reach Oregon before the weather made travel impossible, the Dartts planned to spend the winter in northern Illinois at Byron, where Amy's brothers, Joseph and Jared, had settled, and then complete the journey the next year.[54] Undeterred by the fact that Amy was pregnant (as were perhaps twenty percent of women who went west), they loaded their two covered wagons with the necessary supplies and set out in September with Martha, just turned thirteen, and Mary, not quite two.[55] The party also included Grandmother Abigail, who had again been living in Pennsylvania; this time, though, apparently she was rejoining her husband instead of leaving him, for the evidence suggests that he was living in Illinois with his sons.[56]

By mid-October the Dartts had arrived at Joseph Sanford's home in Byron. "We went by land & lived in our wagons night and day," Martha recalled later. "I never enjoyed five weeks better I think."[57] Scarcely two months later, on December 2, 1844, Martha's second half-sister, Sarah Elizabeth, was born.[58] Once again, Martha evidently had to assume many of the household responsibilities; for example, several years later, writing in her diary on Sarah's seventh birthday, she commented on how different her life was presently, in comparison with the days in Illinois when she had "the whole care of the family on my hands together with an aged grandfather & an infant Sister."[59]

After Sarah was born the Dartts continued to live with Joseph Sanford, looking forward to the day when they might continue their journey to Oregon. However, they had not counted on contracting the ague, the malarial "chills and fever" that was the common scourge of frontier communities. The disease left its victims weak and depleted, often for months, and by February of 1845, the Dartts had concluded after their bout with the debilitating illness that it would be impossible for them to go on to Oregon. Yet neither could they return to the home they had given up in Pennsylvania, and so, in an effort to find a place that was free of the ague and to recuperate, they decided to try Wisconsin, where another of Amy's brothers, James Sanford, had located.[60]

After spending several years as a Methodist circuit rider in Michigan, James Sanford had come to the Wisconsin frontier early in 1841, joining other westering Americans and European immigrants who envisioned a rosy future tilling the abundant, fertile soil. Enormous quantities of public land were available, and so many moved to Wisconsin to take advantage of the opportunity that in just the five years between 1842 and 1847, the population grew from slightly under 45,000 to more than 200,000, an increase of almost 375 percent.[61] As a Wisconsin historian notes, one is likely to think of the westward expansion of the 1840s and 1850s only in terms of the pioneers who traveled to California or Texas or Oregon (even as the Dartts had originally planned), minimizing the impact of the migration from New England and Europe into the Great Lakes states. "Romance may be on the side of the Oregon Trail," he observes, "but census figures favor the Erie Canal."[62]

James Sanford had settled at Middleton, just west of the capital of Madison, where he had gained a measure of local fame for raising the first wheat and bringing in the first sheep.[63] By early 1845 he had just moved into a new, frame house, and he generously offered his sister's family the use of his vacated log cabin for as long as they wished. "And that," said Mary, "is how our family became citizens of Wisconsin."[64]

For about a year the Dartts lived on James Sanford's farm before moving to their own land that Josiah had purchased at Cross Plains, a few miles west of Middleton.[65] They put up a log house and planted some crops, but in order to have sufficient grass to winter their stock they had to drive them to a claim that Josiah had preempted some twelve miles distant at Simpson's Creek.[66] Here Josiah built a log hut for the family to live in during the winter, and it was here that Amy observed, probably not for the first time, that her intellectual husband was not cut out for farming. As Mary told the story later, on one occasion Josiah had stacked hay for the cattle "and the cattle ate from the stacks—a very shift-less way to have them to do, and one that annoyed mother very much." Eventually one of the herd was buried by a haystack that had collapsed after having been eaten through to the middle. Amy hurried to the rescue, and "with a pitch-fork and her hands, frantically worked at the hay. . . . She got air to him so that he lived until father came home."[67]

Amy's reservations about living on a farm, whether at Simpson's Creek or Cross Plains, were strengthened after the family survived a winter at Simpson's Creek when they were snowed in for weeks at a time, marooned in the ten-by-twelve-foot log cabin that had only a door on one side and a tiny window in the end.[68] For the children it was a lark and an adventure. "That snow lay on the ground all winter!" Mary marveled. "Only once during the winter did any human being come to us!"[69] Amy, however, felt more keenly the effects of isolation; for her, said Mary later, "it was a journey, spiritually, through the 'Valley of the Shadow of Death.' "[70]

The situation during that winter might have been even more unbearable, however, if Martha had been there along with Josiah and Amy and the two little girls. As it was, in order to attend school she had been sent in September 1847 to live with her Uncle Joseph, who by that time was operating a store in Shullsburg, in southwestern Wisconsin. Working for her board, she stayed during the winter and went home early in March of the next year.[71]

After surviving the winter at Simpson's Creek, Amy concluded that she wanted no more of farming, at least for the time being, and she persuaded Josiah to dispose of both properties and go on to Baraboo, where Joseph Sanford had just established another general merchandise store.[72] Years later the trip some forty miles north from Cross Plains still remained vivid in Mary's mind. "We were going every mile into a still newer region of Wisconsin. The roads were new and in many places were made of poles cut of varying lengths and laid close together over the mud," she recalled. Once their wagon became stuck at a spot where the wooden planks had worn through. Luckily, two men happened by and helped place fence rails under the wagon so they could continue.[73]

Apparently without further mishap, the Dartts proceeded past scenic Devil's Lake and across the rugged Baraboo Bluffs to Baraboo. Then a village of perhaps three hundred persons, Baraboo had grown up on both sides of the Baraboo River, where less than ten years earlier the first settlers had established the water-powers that provided the economic livelihood of the area. S. A. Dwinnell, who visited Baraboo in May 1848, about the same time that the Dartts arrived, later recalled his first impressions. "There were . . . a dozen to a score of dwellings, mostly small, on the south side. The river was crossed by a bridge. On the north side ran a street parallel with the river, upon which were two or three stores and several houses." Baraboo had recently been made the county seat, wresting the honor from Prairie du Sac, and there was also a new courthouse as well as a small hotel. "Besides these, there were a few board shanties occupied by families. The village site was covered with a sparse growth of small oaks."[74]

Here in Baraboo Josiah Dartt began working for Joseph Sanford, while the family lived in a house adjoining the Sanford store. Joseph had added on a living room for them, which Amy furnished with a carpet and a table and stand brought from Pennsylvania; the whole, thought Mary, was "quite cozy." In the evenings, after she and Martha had returned from school and Josiah had closed the store, Mary recalled that her father would take out his flute and play for them. "He did it very well. Both he and Mattie sang well, and one or two young men with good voices used to drop in to make up a quartet. Their singing I remember as being among my pleasantest memories."[75]

Some of Mary's memories of her family's early life in Baraboo were not so happy, however, for within a year or so of their arrival her mother again was taken ill, and again the oldest sister Martha assumed the household duties and the care of the younger children.[76] Clearly, though, this time Amy's illness seems to have been created by a spiritual frenzy that according to Mary "confined her to her bed and seemed to affect her mind in a peculiar way."[77] She thought that she saw visions, which were "all of a religious nature and to her 'dying day' they influenced her. She thinks the second coming of the Savior is at hand and every one must prepare to meet him."[78] (It takes no great stretch of the imagination, however, to find Amy's symptoms consistent with the hysteria she seems to have exhibited earlier.) Thus having gone from the theology of Lyman Beecher to Methodism, Amy was well on her way to embracing the precepts of the Adventists, which she did with the same fervor and intensity that marked all of her religious beliefs.[79]

Meanwhile, Josiah Dartt was finding the mercantile business as uncongenial as farming, and within three years or so after the family arrived in Baraboo he decided to take up surveying, which he had studied in the Wellsboro Academy.[80] Better suited to activities that were cerebral rather than manual, Martha's stepfather was committed to the lifelong pursuit of learning. "In regard to myself," he told her on one occasion, "I believe . . . that my stock of useful knowledge is considerably increased every year, & I expect during life & not only so but to all eternity to continue to expand in intellect & increase in useful knowledge."[81] Apparently Josiah had an extensive library, and when he furnished his surveying office, he expended a considerable sum on books that ranged from Greek and Latin lexicons to "a new history of 637 pages" to add to those already in his collection.[82]

"Father had a knack for telling us the most wonderful historical events so they grew into our lives," said Mary in describing scenes from her childhood that undoubtedly were similar to Martha's experiences as well.[83] Mary recalled that often in the evenings she and the youngest daughter Sarah Elizabeth, or "Lizzie," as she was called, were placed in their beds while Amy sewed and Josiah read aloud. "We children were supposed to be asleep, but far from it! I, at least, followed his voice through the contents of the weekly paper, . . . through the contents of several books which I do not recall. . . ."[84] As Mary indicated, Josiah's interests encompassed current affairs as well as history, and he read the *New York Tribune* and discussed politics with his children until, Mary said, "I was better posted on the issues of the times than I have ever been since."[85]

With his intellectual interests and concern for learning, Josiah Dartt was anxious for Martha to continue her schooling, confiding to her on one occasion that it was "the great desire of my heart—that you might get a good education."[86] How to accomplish this objective was not apparent, however, until the Congregational minister in Baraboo, Rev. Warren Cochran, proposed a solution. Despite the fact that the Dartts were not Congregationalists they had become friendly with Cochran, who was described by one early settler as a man of "strong physical powers, a towering intellect and a benevolent heart" and thus a congenial companion for Josiah Dartt.[87] Recognizing Martha's desire and potential, Cochran, a graduate of Oberlin College, suggested that she attend the Ohio school.[88] Martha agreed enthusiastically, and somehow Josiah and Amy managed to gather enough money to make the dream a reality.

In addition to providing the emotional and financial support necessary to send her to college, Martha's family also engaged a dressmaker to make a "trousseau" so that she could depart in style. Because there was no millinery store in Baraboo the dressmaker also fashioned a bonnet. "It had a stiff pasteboard foundation and was covered with a soft queer-woven blue and white silk with folds of the same for trimming!" Mary remembered. "We thought Mattie looked lovely in the new things but when she had them on we were a bit awed and rushed to her when they were removed to kiss her and cling to her with a vague feeling of impending separation."[89]

Thus outfitted, Martha Dartt said good-bye to her mother and stepfather and two little half-sisters. That she did not typify what women were (or were expected to be) is obvious, for at mid-century the Cult of True Womanhood was in full flower, carrying the idea that women should be pious, pure, submissive, and domestic, regarding marriage and motherhood as their highest calling and the home as their proper sphere.[90] Certainly Martha had been brought up to be both pious and pure, but nowhere is there any indication that she also was expected to be either submissive or domestic, in the sense of living her life only in the home and through a husband and children. Both her grandmother and her mother were strong-minded women, and submissive is not a word that would have been applied to either. Furthermore, her stepfather Josiah Dartt consistently encouraged Martha to pursue knowledge and to live up to her highest potential; while never ruling out marriage or motherhood for her, neither did he assume that either was necessary for her happiness and fulfillment. "My daily prayer," he told her on one occasion, "is that you may be blessed & prospered that you may be an ornament to the institution of which you are permitted to be a member—an example to your Sex—a blessing to the church—& be abundantly useful to the world."[91] Certainly Martha intended to try. Closing one chapter of her life and beginning another, she left Baraboo in late April 1851 for Oberlin.

2

Learning and Reform

As Martha Maxwell prepared to enroll in Oberlin, she was part of a small, though significant and increasing, minority of American women who had access to any sort of advanced schooling. Between 1790 and 1850, educational opportunities for women had expanded dramatically, a response to such factors as the growing consensus that mothers of future citizens should be well educated and the growing need to educate teachers, especially for the western frontier settlements. These were the years that saw the founding of colleges, academies, and seminaries throughout the country, including such influential female institutions as Emma Willard's Troy Female Seminary (1821), Catharine Beecher's Hartford Female Seminary (1823), and Mary Lyon's Mount Holyoke Female Seminary (1837).[1]

The coeducational Oberlin College, opened in 1833, provided an alternative as well as a model for later schools. It also provided the setting for what may have been the happiest period in Martha Maxwell's life. Here she was free to study from morning until night, to participate in the variety of college clubs and organizations, to see and hear the politicians and entertainers who appeared before the students and faculty. Thriving in the rich intellectual and social milieu, she found opportunities in abundance that augmented and intensified her commitment to learning and reform, two themes that with variations formed the basis for much of her life and work.

Along with the colony of Oberlin, carved out of land in the Western Reserve of northern Ohio, Oberlin College had been founded by Congregationalists and Presbyterians intent on creating a Christian community and school in the wilderness. Heavily influenced by the tenets of the renowned revivalist Charles Grandison Finney, who had arrived in 1835 as professor of theology and who later served as president, Oberlin aimed primarily to educate the ministers and teachers who would then be sent out to diffuse "useful science, sound morality, and pure religion, among the growing multitudes of the Mississippi Valley."[2] Blacks were admitted on an equal basis, and a manual labor system was instituted so that students could help pay for their educations. Coupling revivalism with reform, Oberlin to one degree or another embraced and furthered a number of mid-nineteenth-century millennial crusades, from abolition and temperance to various dietary and health regimens. Although by the time Martha arrived the most radical period of Oberlin's development had passed, "Oberlinism" could still conjure up visions either of farsighted reform or dangerous extremism among its supporters and detractors.[3]

Oberlin, moreover, had been the first school in the nation to admit women to regular college classes along with men (1837), and the first to grant women the A.B. degree (1841). Yet it seems clear today that coeducation was embraced less out of a belief in the equality of women than because of a desire to provide domestic support and a congenial atmosphere for the young men who were being educated as ministers and missionaries. Although they sat beside men in the classroom, women otherwise played a traditional role in the institution, taking care of the usual female tasks of washing, cooking, and cleaning while the men worked outdoors on the college farm.[4] An Oberlin education did, however, provide women who wished to advance the cause of their sex the means to do so. As Anne Firor Scott has pointed out in her discussion of the Troy Female Seminary, one important factor contributing to the spread of feminism in the nineteenth century was "a dramatic increase in the number of well-educated women."[5] Early Oberlin graduates who became prominent in the women's movement, for example, included Lucy Stone, who with her husband Henry Blackwell later founded the American Woman Suffrage Association, and Antoinette Brown, ordained by the Congregational church in 1853 as the nation's first woman minister.[6] In 1862, Mary Jane Patterson became the first black woman to receive an A.B. degree from an American college.[7]

Feminists such as Lucy Stone and Antoinette Brown were in the minority, however. A number of Oberlin women in the early years entered the school intent on preparing to evangelize the world as teachers or missionaries (within the framework of marriage) or as wives of young ministers.[8] Many others, like Martha Dartt, came to Oberlin mainly to gain a good education at a reasonable cost.

In another way Martha was typical of most Oberlin students, male or female, because even before she enrolled in the school, she faced a journey from home that was at best long and tedious and at worst, downright dangerous. In 1851 those who came from the East (New York and New England accounted for the largest number of out-of-state students during this period) used a variety of means—canal boat, steamboat, railroad, stagecoach—to travel to Cleveland. Here they took the Cleveland, Columbus and Cincinnati Railroad, which had been completed in mid-1850, to Wellington, where carriages awaited to transport them the final nine miles to Oberlin. Although few students in the early 1850s came to Oberlin from the West, most who did, like Martha, also had to make their way to Cleveland for the final connections to the village.[9]

Martha began the trip to Oberlin from Baraboo, apparently by wagon, on Tuesday, April 22, 1851, accompanied by four male passengers. All went well the first day, and the group spent the night in a private home. However, the man driving the team of horses, one Fowler, whipped the animals and did not feed them, abusing them to the point that they could go no farther. Thus stranded, the travelers made other arrangements to ride with a teamster who happened along in an empty wagon. Meanwhile, Fowler caught up with them and offered to fulfill his promise to take them as far as Milwaukee if they would ride all night. "I told him I did not want to ride with any man who would abuse a horse as he abused his," replied Martha, saying she thought it best to continue with the other man. She did agree, however, to pay Fowler for the trip as far as she had gone with him, but when he told her that would be two dollars, she countered that the sum was too much, especially considering the difficulty he had caused them. Instead, she offered him fifty cents, but he told her he would have the two dollars or nothing. "Very well," said Martha and gave him nothing.

Without further difficulty, Martha went on to Fort Atkinson and then to Whitewater, finally arriving in Milwaukee at 3:00 a.m. on Saturday. Taking a steamer from Milwaukee across Lake Michigan, she arrived at New Buffalo, the western terminus of the Michigan Central Railroad, at 9:00 Saturday evening. She then rode the train all night across Michigan, arriving in Detroit about 11:00 a.m. on Sunday. There she had to wait until Monday evening for a boat to take her across Lake Erie to Cleveland, where she arrived at 7:00 a.m. on Tuesday after a rough, turbulent voyage. She then took the train to Wellington and the stage to Oberlin, arriving on Tuesday, April 29, about 3:00 p.m., a full week after she had left home. Despite the problems she had encountered, all in all she had managed well. "I had no trouble for want of company," she assured her parents, "for I found friends all along who were ready to assist me."[10]

Arriving in Oberlin, Martha deemed it much "handsomer" than she had expected, a minority view among students who often found the small town to be dull and uninteresting, particularly in contrast to their eastern homes, with streets that were either dusty or overflowing with mud.[11] Fewer than two thousand persons lived in the village in the early 1850s, which then as now centered around the square where the college buildings were located. "It was a small College village, lately hewn from the forest with ungraded and unpaved streets," recalled Oliver L. Spaulding, a student who also came to Oberlin in 1851. "The College was the town. All business, social and religious interests centered in the College and were dominated by it."[12]

Centrally located in the college square (which for many years was called Tappan Square) was the four-story Tappan Hall, completed in 1836 and used as a men's dormitory. Passing through this building was the main walkway across campus.[13] To the north was the First Congregational Church, the only building at the college that still remains from Martha's time. With the capacity of some two thousand persons (fourteen hundred seated, with the rest crowding in), it was the setting for public exercises such as commencement as well as for the church services where Finney preached.[14]

South of Tappan Hall, and commonly known as the Boarding House, was the first Ladies' Hall, where Martha was given a room on the second floor. A three-story frame building, with two wings extending south, the hall accommodated sixty students and included a dining room for both sexes which seated two hundred. Considered the first college dormitory for women in the United States, it was replaced by the second (brick) Ladies' Hall in 1865.[15]

Once settled in her room, Martha then enrolled in the Young Ladies' Preparatory Department for the term beginning on the fourth Wednesday in May, signing up for Andrews and Stoddard's Latin Grammar and Reader, Colburn's Arithmetic, and Greenleaf's Arithmetic.[16] The Young Ladies' Preparatory Department was one of several in the college, the others being the Theological, Collegiate, Teachers', Preparatory, and Young Ladies' departments. A substantial number (241) of the 571 students recorded for the 1851–52 school year were women, 89 of whom were in the Young Ladies' Preparatory Department and 144 in the Young Ladies' Department.[17] All women students were part of the Female Department, which was presided over by the principal and the Ladies' Board.

Oberlin students during this period ranged widely in age, from those as young as eleven in the Preparatory Department to the older, married men in their twenties in the Theological Department. The average age was about nineteen, just a year younger than Martha.[18] Antoinette Brown had also been twenty when she had arrived in 1846, while Lucy Stone was twenty-five when she began her studies at Oberlin. (Stone had attended other institutions, however, including Mount Holyoke.)[19] Yet Josiah Dartt was afraid that his stepdaughter would be "tempted to despondency & discouragement" at the thought that she was too old to pursue her studies. "Thousands of instances might be cited where men have commenced their literary career at an advanced age & have excelled," he reminded her, citing the contributions of Socrates, Cato, Plutarch, Boccaccio, Franklin, and others. "But you are young—in the opinion of Some of the most eminent Scholars of the present day—quite young enough for what you have undertaken. So that this is no reason at all why you Should not Succeed."[20]

Josiah also encouraged Martha to overcome other problems that he perceived might trouble her. "Another thing that has often hindered you," he continued, "is, that you are Slow to learn. Here as before I might cite numerous instances to Show that the greatest lights that have ever shone upon the world have had to contend with the Same difficulty. The most beautiful & useful minerals generally lie under much rubbish." He was aware, he told her, that she would "meet with many a difficulty, & pass many a trying hour, but it is a rule that seldom has an exception, that, 'that which is worth the most, costs us the most.' "[21]

After receiving this advice, Martha hastened to reassure her stepfather. While it was true, she told him, that there were younger students who were more advanced than she, there were also much older students in her own classes, "& instead of feeling discouraged by the attainments of others, I feel encouraged." Also, while she admitted that "I do not learn as easily as many others . . . I can take as few studies at a time as I please, & if it takes me longer than most others to go through a course of study, I shall have learned so much more patience and perseverance." However, she concluded that "I have as many studies and get my lessons as well as almost any others, in the classes."[22]

Martha also investigated the opportunities available for work, for the lack of money was an ever-present fact of life in the Dartt family. The manual labor system, a central feature of the Oberlin way of life, provided an opportunity for students to earn part of the costs of their educations. In the beginning, each student was *required* to work four hours per day. By the time Martha arrived, however, the college was advising that women not attempt "to do more than defray about half the expense of their board."[23] Tuition was twelve dollars per year, incidental expenses one dollar per year, room rent in Ladies' Hall seven to ten cents per week, and board one dollar per week. In all, the college estimated in 1851 that the annual expenses of an economical Oberlin student would not exceed eighty-five dollars.[24]

To earn even a part of this sum herself would be a help to her family, but she told her parents that because so many students wanted to work she could only get about an hour per day, at a wage of four, or more likely, three cents per hour. "You need not feer, that my miserly disposition will tempt me to neglect my books for the sake of geting rich at this rate," she assured them.[25] Despite their financial problems, both Amy and Josiah supported her decision. "If you cannot get but 4 cents an hour for washing unless you need the exersise we dont wish you to do it," Amy advised her daughter. "We sent you there to improve your mind and we wish to have you persue that course which will best secure that end."[26] Similarly, Josiah cautioned her to remember that "we sent you there to study—not to work—Do not lift your finger to do the first thing more than is necessary for your health & comfort."[27]

Soon Martha began to settle into the Oberlin routine. Virtually all aspects of a woman student's life were governed by the twenty-two *Laws and Regulations of the Female Department*, which specified the daily round of activities.[28] These rules, according to historian Keith Melder, owed much to the influence of the Ipswich Female Seminary in Massachusetts, where the early women principals of the Female Department had studied. That school "was governed by a rigid schedule which left no time for idleness and scarcely any choice of activities," he observes, and although Oberlin was noted for coeducation, there too the routine for women "followed the principles of separation and inequality between the sexes derived from the regulations and disciplinary practices at Ipswich Seminary."[29]

At Oberlin, the "young ladies" were required to attend evening prayers at the chapel, morning prayers at "their respective boarding places," the weekly religious lectures, and church twice on Sunday. There were prescribed study hours, varying slightly from winter to summer, and the students had to be in their rooms in the evenings, although exceptions were made for attendance at night meetings.[30] Even outdoors the activities of the women were governed by the college; indeed, the rules specified that "no young lady who does not reside with her parents will be allowed to walk in the fields or woods without special permission from the Principal."[31] During vacations the regulations were relaxed somewhat, or as Martha neatly summed it up, "we can do pretty much as we are a mind to, if we are a mind to do about right."[32] All failures to follow the "laws and regulations" were recorded by the principal of the Female Department and read before the faculty and the Ladies' Board at the end of each term, "in order that a just estimate may be formed of the diligence, progress and general deportment of each lady connected with the Institution."[33]

Martha was not at all unhappy with the structure and orderliness at Oberlin, telling her mother approvingly that she would be "greatly pleased to see the perfect harmony which prevails here in the dispatch of business, especially in the Hall. Each one knows her place and expects to fill it."[34] More than twenty years later, however, she took a less wide-eyed look back at the Oberlin way of life. "I tried . . . to realize the fact, so often repeated in our hearing, that Oberlin was treading on forbidden ground when admitting ladies to its collage walls," she told her daughter Mabel, "and that our conduct would be taken as a precedent by all literary institutions, and that our conduct might more closely seal the doors of many collages whose thresholds were sacred to masculine footsteps." She was glad, she concluded, "that my bad behaviour did not blast womans hopes in this direction, and that it is becoming fashionable to extend equal educational advantage to men & women. . . ."[35]

For the most part, though, Martha was delighted with Oberlin. "There is perhaps as little aristocracy here as any place in the world," she told Amy and Josiah on one occasion, commenting that "all the fault I can find with the people is they are many of them quite dressey."[36] Moreover, she reveled in the opportunities available for learning that had suddenly opened up to her. Truly, she told her parents, she possessed "a contented mind which you know 'is a continual feast.' "[37]

Yet despite her overall happiness with the college, Martha soon came face-to-face with policies that discriminated against women even at Oberlin. On August 26 the commencement exercises, featuring essays read by the graduates, were held for the nine women who had completed the course in the Young Ladies' Department.[38] The next day the Collegiate Department graduated twelve students, including three women, but as Martha told her parents incredulously, "their pieces were *read by the Proff.* the propriety or necesity of this *I* could not see."[39] As she had discovered, although those graduating from the Young Ladies' Department were permitted to read their own essays, those receiving degrees from the four-year collegiate program were not. Thus while Oberlin was advanced in many ways, the college nonetheless adhered to the proscription against female "public speaking" that was not uncommon even at mid-century.[40] In protest against this policy, Lucy Stone had refused to write any essay at all when she was a candidate for the A.B. degree in 1847, and not until 1858 did the first woman college graduate at Oberlin read her own essay at commencement.[41] More than twenty years later Martha still recalled this evidence of discrimination, commenting to her daughter that the practice of not allowing the women to present their papers had "seemed a great injustice" to her.[42]

The August commencement marked the end of Martha's first term at Oberlin, and she was happy to write home that her teachers had given her high marks for her work. The grading system, she told her parents, involved each teacher keeping "an account of the conduct of each member of his class and a strict account of the manor that each one recites." These reports were given weekly to the principal of the Female Department, Mary Sumner Hopkins, who generally did not speak to the students about their marks "unless they are bad." Martha naturally was pleased, therefore, when Hopkins singled her out for praise on several separate occasions. Once, when they met in a hallway, the principal laid a gentle hand on her shoulder, saying "Miss Dartt, your reports were *very* good to-day." Another time, as Martha was coming in to breakfast with a book in her hand, she commented that "it is not to be wondered at that your reports are so good. —you study before breakfast." And several days later, as they were both doing their ironing, Hopkins informed her that her reports "were about the best that were given in."[43]

Such encouragement was a boon, of course, to Martha's

sometimes shaky self-confidence, although she remarked that she did not feel that her reports were "any *better* than my class-mates generaly & I wonder why they think so."[44] Receiving good marks at Oberlin also conferred higher rewards than simply self-satisfaction, as Martha accurately observed. "Mrs. Hopkins says the established reputation of a good Scholar is a great help to a student here, and why should it not be—for upon *this* and *piety*, as the chief cornerstones do they base their estimate of a person's worth."[45]

Even at Oberlin, however, there was much more to college life than the prescribed daily round of classes and chapel, and when her studies were done, Martha filled the remaining hours with social activities, clubs, meetings, and lectures. About a month after Martha arrived at Oberlin, the anniversaries of the two men's literary societies were celebrated in observances that were among the major events of the college year. Oberlin men could join either the Union Society (later Phi Delta) or the Young Men's Lyceum, which became Phi Kappa Pi. Both were founded in 1839; the Union members generally were younger than those who belonged to the Lyceum. In 1851 the Union marked its anniversary on June 30 in the chapel of Colonial Hall, a men's dormitory located to the west of Ladies' Hall, followed the next day by the Lyceum.[46] Thus Martha found herself, along with the other women students, fashioning the traditional decorations of hemlock bows and flowers for the chapel. The Union Society celebration, she told her parents, featured "a number of excellent pices spoken & a number of beautiful pieces [of] music," while the chapel for the Lyceum observance was "fixed more beautiful-ly than any thing I had ever before imagined."[47]

Impromptu parties and sleighrides also were part of the Oberlin social scene. On one occasion just after Christmas, the women in Ladies' Hall collected a pail of butternuts, a gallon of molasses, and some sugar and made "quite a respectable quanti-ty of excellent candy," Martha told her parents. They immediate-ly invited some young men over to share it with them, and for about two hours that evening some forty young people "met in the sitting-room, where the evening was spent *very* pleasantly." Although other parties in the village had been planned further ahead of time, Martha was "quite sure that ours was excelled by none of them."[48]

A winter sleighride a few days later, however, was less successful. A four-horse sleigh had been hired for the occasion, but it was not strong enough to bear the weight of twenty-two students, and consequently it broke down a few miles from Oberlin. Cold, tired, and hungry, the students were forced to walk home, straggling into the Ladies' Hall about eight o'clock in the evening.[49]

Oberlin also gave Martha the opportunity to continue her interest in singing through membership in the choir, founded in 1837 as the Oberlin Musical Association. Coeducational and social as well as musical and religious in nature, the weekly choir meetings were extremely popular with the students.[50] In order to join the choir, however, it was necessary to pass an audition, an obstacle that the shy Martha struggled valiantly to overcome. When it was time for her to be examined, she related in her diary, "the number present was large, and I had to sing my part alone before those & worse than this, before the Prof. of music and several others of nearly the same class." The ordeal, she observed, was "truly embarrassing."[51] Nonetheless, she was admitted and several months later sang with the group when it presented the first oratorio performed at Oberlin.[52]

In addition to singing in the choir, Martha also taught Sunday school, participated in the Young Ladies' Literary Society (the female counterpart of the Young Men's Lyceum and the Union Society), and worked in the Oberlin Female Moral Reform Society.[53] Founded in 1835, the Oberlin society became one of the largest and most active of the groups (more than 250 in 1837) that were allied with the New York (later American) Female Moral Reform Society. Continuing through the 1850s, the Oberlin group enthusiastically battled against impure thought, dress, and action, although by that time the emphasis both nationally and locally had shifted to charitable work on behalf of destitute women.[54]

Very much imbued with the reform sentiments of antebellum America, Martha indeed could have found no more congenial atmosphere than the Oberlin College of the 1850s. Along with her activities in the Female Moral Reform Society, for example, she found an antitobacco pledge in a Cleveland newspaper and sent it home for all to sign, telling her family that it "advocates my sentiments *exactly*."[55] She also read the copies of the *Fonetic Advocat* that her stepfather sent her and pursued phonetic spelling to the extent of purchasing a reader and a class book.[56] "I am an advokat of fonetic spelling," she declared upon arriving at Oberlin, "& no mor kar much a bout the old wa."[57] (After reading Martha's correspondence, one is tempted to observe that *never* in her life did she "kar much a bout the old wa.")

Along with all of this, Martha reported that she had opportunities to hear lecturers such as Ohio Congressman Joshua R. Giddings, who spoke on "Slavery and poloticks"[58] and missionary George Thompson, who discoursed "upon the manors, wants, & character of the Affricans."[59] The famed singing Hutchinson Family presented a concert shortly after Martha arrived at Oberlin; she estimated that over one thousand persons were present and thought that the "music & mimicing surpassed any thing I ever heard of."[60] Small wonder, then, that Martha exclaimed to her parents on one occasion that she occupied her time "so completely that I hardly dare commence a letter for fear that it will never get finished or, if it should, that no one save myself will be able to decipher its contents."[61]

Despite her immersion into the social and cultural life of Oberlin, Martha never lost sight of the fact that she was in college to get an education. Enrolled initially in the Young Ladies' Preparatory Department, she was giving serious thought to her overall plan of study as her first term drew to a close. "I can take the young ladies course and include the studies that [are] in the scientific cours if I choose," she told her parents, "or take a regular scientific course, which I rather think would be preferable, although there are but very few ladies in it." Principal Hopkins pointed out to her that it made "but very little difference which course I take, as they are very nearly alike," and in fact the various curricula were chosen from a single set of classes.[62] For example, the same course might be taken as part of the work of the Collegiate, the Teachers', and the Young Ladies' departments. From 1850 to 1858 the four-year Scientific Course was offered along with the Classical Course in the Collegiate Department, whose enrollment, of course, was predominantly male. Those who successfully completed the Scientific Course were awarded the A.B., while those who finished the Young Ladies' Course received diplomas.[63]

Although the early Oberlin records are incomplete, it appears that Martha spent two terms in the Young Ladies' Preparatory Department before the beginning of the winter term on December 2, 1851.[64] Many students used the long winter break (from the fourth Wednesday of November to the fourth Wednesday of February) to teach in rural schools and thus earn money for their educations. Others, like Martha, remained on campus, where "winter school" was held in the college buildings and taught by the college teachers. The classes, which were offered at the preparatory level, were not a regular part of Oberlin College.[65] This term she took Willson's American History, algebra, "Analysis and Parsing," and Latin, which she thought especially hard. "I think that I never attempted to learn any thing more difficult than this," she lamented to her parents.[66]

By the time spring came in 1852, Martha was in the middle of her fourth term at Oberlin, and Josiah Dartt reminded her that "the time of birds and flowers—that time in which above all others you delight" was now at hand. "Bear in mind that though it be duty to *study*, yet it is not duty be *all study*," he told her. "We should make good use of the season so peculiarly adapted to the relaxation & expansion of mind & the restoration of the elasticity of spirits which is apt to become so worn down by the labors of the ballance of the year."[67] Martha admitted that she found "studying rather irksome business this pleasant spring weather, still I am getting along tolerably well."[68]

Yet even as Josiah Dartt was encouraging Martha in her studies, he was proposing a change that would radically alter her future plans. "What say you," he inquired casually, "to leaving Oberlin next fall, & going to Pennsylvania to make your visit, & returning here, so as to start with us for Oregon next spring[?]"[69] It had been eight years since the Dartt family had set out from Pennsylvania bound as missionaries for Oregon; this time, though, the principal motivation was economic, for Josiah realized that Oregon would have greater opportunities for surveying than Wisconsin, where much of the government surveying work had been completed. He still retained a good deal of his missionary fervor, however. "If I have any *calling*," he mused, "it appears to be that of assisting to lay the foundations of morals in Society & this, it might seem, was the reason of our moving so often into new places." Truly, he told Martha, "we are by no means to look only to our own good but be assured that where we can be most useful there (if we are what we should be) we shall receive the most real benefit."[70]

Martha immediately bombarded her stepfather with questions about the proposed journey. "Are you in *earnest* about going there next Spring?" she asked. "If I go shall I be obliged to relinquish my literary pursuits entirely, or, only for a short time? Can I do as much good by going their now, as I could do somewhere else, after staying here a while longer? Or, is life so short and uncertain that with the slight qualifications for a sphere of usefulness, which I now possess, I shall be likely to accomplish more good by leaving this place in the fall, than by spending a greater length of time in . . . *preparing* for usefulness[?]" Finally, she cried, "am I prepared to take my place in *that* country, or *any other*, as a *woman* of the *nineteenth century*?"[71]

Josiah took pains to reassure Martha, telling her that her education came first and that it was not for him to say when she should leave Oberlin. "You ought to stay there (if you have not already accomplished it) till you shall have acquired such a love for mental & moral culture, such a desire for the acquisition of useful knowledge & such a habit of intellectual training, that no ordinary circumstances will prevent your continuing to improve down to the end of life."[72] Elaborating on this theme several months later, he analyzed the choices facing her as follows:

Should you leave Oberlin next fall & not expect to return
it would a good thing for you to teach school next
winter—and such an one, to, if practicable as will call
into exercise a knowledge of all the branches of learning
that you have studied; but should you conclude in the
fall, to continue your studies there, our best scholars
say, you ought to *rest* this winter—

"Ne mens ipsa necessum
   Intestimun habeat cunctis in rebus agundis
   Et devicta quiasi, cogatur fene, patique"
But should we go to Oregon next Spring you will have a
fair opportunity for relaxation &
   "Praesentiorum conspicere Deum
   Per invias rupes, fera per juga
         Clivoque praemptos, sonantes
         Inter aquas, nemosumque noctern"[73]

Martha therefore continued her studies at Oberlin through
the spring and summer of 1852. The records show that during the
summer term she took botany, which was part of the second-year
work for students in both the Scientific Course and the Young
Ladies' Department, and that she signed up for geometry, Biblical antiquities, and Taylor's Manual of History for the term com-
mencing in August.[74] Josiah heartily approved of her choices,
telling her that mathematics "is such good discipline for the
mind" and urging her to "take in at one view not only one but a
dozen of Euclids deepest propositions—Deep—Close—Protracted investigation." He also encouraged her to take more
courses in history and the natural sciences if she had the opportunity. "You know I love to study and especially to study nature," he reminded her, "& I think there is no branch of study
except the Scriptures that so tends to lead the mind up to the
great Source of wisdom & goodness as the works of nature as
brought to view in the natural Sciences."[75]

Yet even as Josiah was encouraging his stepdaughter in her
studies, it was becoming increasingly apparent that Martha
might have to return to Baraboo, not because of the proposed
Oregon trip but because no money was left to pay her expenses.
Money, of course, had always been something of a problem, but
in the beginning Josiah had been able to scrape together what she
needed without too much difficulty. This he always did willingly
and gladly, urging her on one occasion not to hesitate to ask for
money, for "it is as freely given as the air you breathe," and on
another telling her that he considered it "a privilege to do anything in my power to assist you."[76]

By March 1852, however, he informed her that "times are exceedingly hard," and the next month he wrote that he was having difficulty collecting the money that he had earned.[77] Several months later her mother told her that Josiah not only could not collect what was his due, but that he had borrowed to the hilt, and she enclosed a dollar that she herself had saved.[78] In September Martha was able to obtain a scholarship to pay her tuition, and Josiah sent her fifty dollars received from one of his debtors, but it was obvious that the long-term outlook was bleak.[79] "I have tried to borrow—I never saw such hard times. It has afflicted me almost to despair that I could not raise the money for you before," Josiah wrote. "I have tried every honest way I knew of but all to no purpose, till, by the blessing of providence, I was able to collect this. When this is gone I do not know where the next will come from but if we try to do the will of God I trust he will provide."[80]

One last alternative remained, and that was to sell the land in Pennsylvania that Martha and her mother had inherited from Spencer Dartt and use the proceeds to pay for her education. Josiah had been attempting to complete such a transaction since the summer of 1851, but the proposed deals had always fallen through.[81] Martha was loath to give up this ray of hope and asked her stepfather in September to consider "other arrangements" with regard to the land. "I am very ansious to persue my studies here untill I have completed the Ladies course," she wrote, "and in order to procure the necessary means (without taxing you too heavily) . . . I very much desire that the place should be sold."[82]

Unhappily, it became apparent soon after that Josiah's resources would be exhausted before the land could be sold. Thus Martha departed from Oberlin around the first of October in 1852.[83] For something over a year she had been immersed in a world that had given full rein to her interests and abilities, and she hated to leave it. Like her stepfather, she loved learning for its own sake and had done well in her studies, preparing herself, she hoped, to take her place as "a *woman* of the *nineteenth century*." She also took part in a wide range of Oberlin activities and enjoyed the fellowship afforded by the coeducational college, remarking on one occasion "how much more pleasant, animating, & beneficial for students of both sexes to be educated together, and to associate together."[84] There were some problems, of course, for Martha clearly saw, and did not in the least approve of, the subtle forms of discrimination against women at Oberlin. And, like college students in all times and places, she had difficulty with her roommates, commenting that her patience had been "exceedingly tried with each one of them at different times."[85] Yet for Martha the positive aspects of her Oberlin experience far outweighed the bad, and the depth of her unhappiness at leaving is apparent in a diary entry she penned some months later, when she at last saw no possibility of returning. "Oberlin, O! how has fancy-winged hope sunk like a leaden wait to the bottom of deep waters of my heart. But shall I murmur and repine? No! I will not. For the greatest good frequently results from apparant misfortune."[86] With such a combination of despair and faith in the future, Martha resolutely left Oberlin and returned to Baraboo.

Marriage and Reform

Once more in Baraboo, Martha began to contemplate her future, searching for a way to remain involved in education even though the possibility of further study at Oberlin had been foreclosed for the moment. While she could not have anticipated the dramatic changes the coming months would bring—marriage, especially to James Maxwell, evidently was the farthest thing from her mind—in many ways her life would proceed in the directions established in childhood and strengthened at Oberlin. Intellectual development and a commitment to reform were the benchmarks along this continuum, as would become apparent again in Baraboo.

For the time being, Martha decided that teaching school offered the most attractive possibilities. One of the few professions open to women at mid-century, teaching allowed women to function in their traditional sphere and provide a needed service while preparing for their ultimate responsibilities as wives and mothers.[1] Teachers especially were needed on the frontier; as Polly Welts Kaufman has shown, in the decade following 1846, some six hundred single women heeded the call of Catharine Beecher and the National Board of Popular Education to bring education and Protestant evangelical religion to the West.[2]

For Martha Maxwell, already on the Wisconsin frontier, the prospect of teaching was not unpleasant; in fact, she had written to her family while still at Oberlin, asking their opinion if she obtained a school near home in the fall. Even if she returned to Oberlin, she told them, the experience would be beneficial, for "those persons who have taught school succeed better in their studies than those who have not."[3] For herself, then, Martha saw teaching primarily as an activity that would contribute to her own education, in addition to providing a much-needed means of livelihood. Within about a month of her arrival, she submitted herself for examination and in due course received a teaching certificate from the Township of Brooklyn in which Baraboo was then located.[4] A few days afterward, in mid-November 1852, she met her first class of seven students.[5]

For the next few months Martha taught school near Baraboo and boarded with various families during the week.[6] Yet she had by no means given up hope of returning to Oberlin and completing her studies. By the spring of 1853, however, the possibility that she could ever go to college again seemed remote indeed, for it was apparently at this time that she contributed the money gained through the sale of the Pennsylvania land toward the purchase of the family's new home. The price was low because the owner was anxious to leave for Oregon, and when the Dartts inspected the property they could scarcely contain their enthusiasm. Located in the Devil's Lake area south of Baraboo near a place called the "Pewit's Nest," the farm was set amidst "picturesque scenery and [had] wonderful trees on it [and] a white frame house and a beautiful spring of water," Mary later recalled.[7] Since coming to Baraboo the Dartts had been living in quarters provided by Joseph Sanford, and therefore it was small wonder that, in Mary's words, "we went and all lost our hearts to the 'Peewits Nest.' "[8] Sacrificing her own dreams, Martha used her inheritance so that the whole family could realize their dream of owning the home.[9]

Only a few months later, then, it must have seemed nothing less than a miracle to Martha when James A. Maxwell, a prominent Baraboo businessman, asked her to accompany his two oldest children to the new Lawrence University in Appleton, Wisconsin. Although not a great deal older than sixteen-year-old Emma and James P., aged fourteen, Martha was to serve as a companion and chaperone, and in return, Maxwell would pay her expenses.[10] Just over forty, Maxwell and his father, Col. James Maxwell, had been among the earliest Baraboo pioneers, coming from Walworth County and before that from New England by way of Indiana and Illinois. With business interests that ranged at various times from mills and a waterpower on the Baraboo River to a general store on the village square, the Maxwells were one of the leading families of Baraboo.[11] Recently, James A. Maxwell had been left a widower when his consumptive wife, Susan Clark Maxwell, died.[12] In addition to Emma and James P., Maxwell also had the care of Charles Alonzo (Lon), twelve; Caroline (Carrie), ten; Ellen (Nellie), eight; and Augusta (Gussie), six.[13]

Martha, Emma, and James arrived in Appleton in time for the fall term at Lawrence, which began on August 25, 1853.[14] Situated on a bluff high above the Fox River in an area of northern Wisconsin that had been settled only recently, the Methodist school had been founded with the aid of a ten-thousand-dollar grant from Boston merchant and philanthropist Amos Lawrence. The college opened in 1849 in one rudimentary frame structure which housed the chapel, recitation rooms, and living quarters for both students and faculty. In June 1853 the first president, Rev. Edward Cooke, was inaugurated and the cornerstone was laid for Main Hall, a graceful building constructed of local gray stone that remains the heart of the university today.[15]

From the beginning both men and women were admitted to Lawrence, although initially no collegiate classes were formed because of the lack of students with the necessary preparation. By the fall of 1853, however, the school planned to organize college classes for the first time, although it appears that such classes may not have begun until the following year.[16] The curriculum was similar to that of Oberlin, with a Preparatory Department and a Collegiate Department (primarily for men) that offered a Classical Course, leading to the Bachelor of Arts degree, and a Scientific Course, which led to the degree Bachelor of Science and English Literature. In the Female Collegiate Department the three-year course of study (with the same requirements for admission as the Classical Course) culminated in the Lady Baccalaureate of Arts degree. However, as the catalog pointed out, "any lady can take the full four years classical course if she prefers it."[17]

For her first term Martha registered in the Preparatory Department for algebra, natural philosophy, and drawing.[18] James Maxwell urged her to take music lessons as well. "Don't hesitate a moment on acct. of the expense," he told her, encouraging her much as had Josiah Dartt. "If you have *time*, & a *desire*, Commence."[19] Although initially Martha felt that she was too busy, the records show that she did enroll in music for the second term, along with natural philosophy, drawing, and bookkeeping.[20]

In addition to attending her classes, Martha also joined the Young Ladies Mutual Improvement Association, as did Emma, and apparently worked on *The Casket*, a literary journal established by the women early in 1854.[21] Despite her naturally shy personality and the fact that she attended Lawrence only for a short time, Martha evidently made a lasting impression on at least some of her classmates. Years later Francena Kellogg Buck, who was graduated with the first class in 1857, recalled Martha as one of the students from that period "who achieved reputations of which the rest were proud." Buck did admit to some surprise at the fame and attention Martha attracted at the Centennial, for when they were in school together, she wrote, "Miss Dart wore no badge of 'genius' on her sleeve and no knowledge of her slumbering talent came to us."[22]

With her studies, organizations, and responsibilities toward Emma and James, Martha had little time to think of anything else. Yet soon she was being asked to consider a question of the greatest importance, the answer to which could alter the course of her life forever. Not long after she and the Maxwells arrived in Appleton, Martha received a lengthy letter from James Maxwell containing certain assertions and inquiries. "It is both my *interest* and my *inclination* to marry again when the *proper* time comes round," he informed her, "provided, it brings with it an *arrangement* with a *suitable person*." It was difficult, he pointed out, to find such a person; initially it must be settled whether or not there was "a reciprocity feeling, of *good, warm, heart* affection, if not, then we need go no further, for without I could not consent to marry, no not even Queen Victoria, for without it, there can be *no* connubial bliss." Also to be considered, he continued, were disparities in religion, education, "or anything else, or all combined, as to be likely to prove too strong for the ties of affection."

Having discussed the requirements for marriage, James then went on to "propose a little talk" with Martha. "I like you," he said, "not because I think you handsome, above many, neither because I think you have gifts or graces, natural or acquired above many, but because I think you have *good, warm, affections*, with a sound judgement and discretion, to govern you in their *direction* and *bestowment*. . . ." Mindful of the differences in their ages, he then considered and dismissed any possible obstacles to their union. "In circumstances I can see, *really*, but little difference we are both Probationers & shall have to account for our behaviour here—as to dollars & cents they are not to be taken into account, for they may fly away, as to *Family* or Blood, we both belong to the *Human Family*, and our blood is probably much of a color." Continuing in this manner, he told her that "in education the disparity is not so great, I think, as to prove much of a barrier, unless you should improve faster than I am looking." As for religion, the differences were probably even less, while "in our *affections* I cant say how we should compare, however I think I will give mine, for yours."

In conclusion, James surmised that Martha probably had given no thought to the matters he had discussed, although he confessed that the question of marriage had been on his mind since he first had asked her to accompany James and Emma to Appleton. "And yet I would not have you think, that the thought prompted me in aught I have done, in relation to your going there to School," he assured her, "for I think I should have done all I did, and perhaps more had I have had no such thought, therefore you are under no obligation in the matter to the *particular* thought spoken of, and will feel yourself perfectly free, in your answer, to follow the promptings of your own feelings & the dictates of your Judgement, the which, if you fully do, you will much oblige me, be it as it may."[23]

A month later, however, James had not heard from Martha, and he was beginning to worry. Had the letter miscarried, he inquired? If so, he would write again; if not, "why then, I suppose I shall hear from it in your own good time."[24] A short while later he received a response that alleviated his anxiety to some extent. Emma and James were fine, Martha reported, and as for the other matter, she had "only been presuming" on the privilege to take her time in replying to him, as she had been "very much surprised at the sentiment" in the letter. At first she thought that "the indescretion manifest in the choice of person to whome you make the proposition is a sufficient reason why the proposal should not be accepted," but she later concluded that he was not being indiscreet, merely overestimating her abilities. "Think you that I am capable of bearing the responsibilities of *Mother* in a family like yours? As you very justly conclude I 'have neither gifts or graces above many,' but I think that I should *need* to have were I to enter this responsible situation, for I know of *no* one of my age, who is, (in my opinion) capable of filling it."[25]

Martha assured James that although she would not be influenced by a sense of obligation toward him, she was afraid of making the wrong decision, "for it would be a poor way to compensate you for your kindness to allow myself to be placed in a relation to you which might, I fear, secure to you misery instead of happiness." She would not be able to reach a definite conclusion, however, without speaking to her mother, "as I always consider *one* word from *her* upon such a subject worth more than *all my* musings."[26]

James was immensely relieved, although he had not doubted that his letter "would be received *kindly* & answered respectfully. . . ." But after reading her response he still could not determine what Martha's *"personal individual feelings"* were toward him. Moreover, he asked, after she talked with her mother, "how shall I know whether I am indebted to *your* 'musings' or *hers*, for the answer, to *your* want of Affection or *hers* for a negative?" Referring to his initial letter, he reminded her that "I esteem the *feelings* or *affections* the *ground work* upon which all negotiations of this character should be based." If both were not satisfied, then they could drop the matter "without the aid or knowledge of friends," but if they decided to proceed, they could consult with others concerned and, barring negative judgments from them, "undertake to prosecute lifes journey together understandingly. . . ."[27]

Apparently the matter was decided over the Christmas holidays, for on New Year's Day James wrote to Martha that he had decided to break his habit of treating his rheumatism with liberal doses of brandy, for there was no better time than the present, "being aided, you know . . . by a counter excitement, attendant upon the wooing & winning of the hand and Heart, I expect—of a 'fair Lady,' or rather I would say of a *good* little Body." Asking what she thought of being married at the close of the winter term, he inquired if she needed more money or anything else to conclude such arrangements. "Remember Martha! be *free* spoken & tell *all* that is in thine heart, so shall it be *well* with thee!"[28]

Martha agreed that it would be a good idea to marry at the end of the term, although when they first began talking of marriage she had had no idea of leaving school so soon. "But after giving more thought to the subject," she continued, "I conclude *not* that I do not need to apply myself to my books longer, for there are many branches of science, of which I have long desired a knowledge and of which I am still entirely ignorant, but that my ignorance of those branches will effect you about as much as it will me so that if you do not complain perhapse I ought not to." Appleton, she thought, was "as appropriate a place as any other" for the event.[29]

The matter thus having been settled between them, James then proceeded to obtain the consent, or at least the acquiescence, of Martha's family. Concurrent with obtaining the permission of the Dartts, it was also necessary to make the proper arrangements with respect to Martha's property. The Pewit's Nest farm, apparently, had been deeded to Martha (in exchange for the Pennsylvania land she had contributed to the purchase), and Josiah expected to complete the payments on it in February. After that some portion on which he and Martha could agree could be deeded to him. James was concerned that all of this should be taken care of before the marriage so that his children would have no claim on her assets, come what may. Moreover, if he should meet with business reverses in the future, they would have something on which to fall back.[30]

With the younger members of both families it was a somewhat different matter. Mary Dartt was not happy at all at the prospect of losing her older sister, whom she called "the idol of my heart," to matrimony.[31] As for Emma, Martha reported that she had said on one occasion that "if you ever marry *any body*, she will not live at home another day, nor will she receive any assistance from you whatever, so for aught I see if you marry you must necessarily marry a Miss *Nobody* if in so doing you wish to pleas Em."[32] While James was sorry to hear of Emma's feelings and hoped that she would someday come to accept their union, he was also certain that nothing could mar their prospects for future happiness "so long as *we* are *right*, So long as all is *right* between us. . . ."[33]

James had, of course, gained some insight into the matrimonial state, and he tried to reassure Martha and to give her some idea of his hopes and expectations, cautioning her as well against the common pitfalls of marriage. "Matrimony, my dear girl, is a *duet*," he explained, "in which there is always more or less discord, at least until the parties learn to *harmonize*, until the characters modulate themselves to each other."[34]

For her part, Martha was understandably worried about her abilities "when the experiment is to begin for me what is but an experiment—the launching of my frail bark upon an unknown sea." Much more than her own happiness was at stake, but she was consoled by the thought that she would be "accompanyed on this voyage by one who has been upon the sea before, and is acquainted to some extent with its dangers."[35] Fully cognizant of the dangers as well, James was nonetheless certain that they would be as "*happy* as *mortals can be*, provided that while we are made *one* in flesh, we also become *one* in *heart*, in *mind*, in *Spirit*, *One* in our *aims* & *purposes*, *one* in our *hopes* & *fears*, and *Joys* and *Sorrows*." Truly, he exclaimed, "if ours is an *unhappy* match! O how *bitter* will be my *disappointment*; & I suppose yours would be no less so. . . ."[36]

Thus with reasonably equal measures of faith, hope, apprehension, and perhaps even love, James A. Maxwell and Martha Ann Dartt were married in Appleton on March 30, 1854, by the Reverend Edward Cooke, the president of Lawrence University.[37] A few days later the newlyweds arrived at the Dartt home, where a dramatic scene occurred that remained etched in

Mary Dartt's mind forever. Several letters addressed to Martha were waiting for her. "One she seized and opened & read with a face growing white," Mary recalled. "I was watching her & shall never forget her face as she crushed it into her pocket and moved away like one in a dream." Not until many years later did Mary learn the true dimensions of Martha's horror. According to Mary, Martha had had an "understanding" with a fellow student at Oberlin and had written to him after she returned home, but had received no response in return. Therefore "she had concluded he did not care for her & was so blue over it she felt quite desperate & that nothing mattered much what she did. If all her friends wanted her to marry Mr. Maxwell she would better do so." The letter she read shortly after her wedding described what had happened. "For some unexplained reason," Mary related, "her letters had reached him but none of his had come to her. In this one he had told her of his love for her & begged her to continue to write him & to let him hope that soon he could claim her for life!"[38]

Nothing survives that gives a clue to the identity of Martha's suitor, although Mary said once that he was a divinity student at Oberlin.[39] Martha's diary contains references only to letters sent to "friend H." or "friend F." from Baraboo. Her extant correspondence also offers no evidence of the romance, nor do her letters to James Maxwell indicate that she had reservations about their marriage except those concerning her schooling or the assumption of her responsibilities as stepmother to the Maxwell children. In fact, as their courtship developed, Martha seemed to have become quite affectionate toward James, telling him early in 1854, for example, that she wished "not only *this* year, but for *many* years, as much happiness as you crave for me, and even more if it could be."[40] Yet if the story is true, and there is no reason to believe that it is not, it does offer perhaps one explanation for the ultimate collapse of the Maxwell union. One can speculate also that the crushing disappointment was a factor that caused Martha to channel all of her energy and emotion into her work, to the detriment of her marriage and her family.

In any event, at the age of twenty-two Martha Dartt was now Mrs. James A. Maxwell and the stepmother of the six Maxwell children. If she were distraught over the recent turn of events, certainly the scene she found at the Maxwell home would not have lifted her spirits. According to her sister Mary, the place was in "great disorder" and the children in a "sad condition," especially Gussie, the youngest. "I hesitate to write of her condition," Mary confided many years later. "It would seem incredible in this day among people who claimed to be respectable, but Mattie's horror was too real for me to forget & her cautions to us made too deep an impression." Martha brought Gussie with her when she visited her sisters several weeks after her marriage. "She was six & very pretty," Mary recalled, "but her hands & head were covered with half healed sores & Mattie said the other children were in varying degrees likewise afflicted—due to itch & lice to put it bluntly. She had cleaned & bathed & doctored ever since she entered the house."[41]

Even without such problems, Martha now had charge of a household that would tax the energy and endurance of a woman with twice her age and experience. Along with Lon and the three youngest Maxwell daughters, James's father, Colonel Maxwell, lived with them, as did the hired man. Sometimes, recalled Mary, there was a woman to help out, "but not often." If that was not enough, "there were always Methodist ministers visiting there if there were any extra ones in town."[42]

Methodism, in fact, was a dominating influence in the Maxwell family, and Mary later painted a vivid picture of one aspect of the daily routine, giving a glimpse into that long-ago household. "Mr. Maxwell always had family prayers before breakfast in the dining room," wrote Mary. "We all sat around the outside [of] the room. He usually passed us each a bible & hymnal & he told us the chapt[er] & we looked it up with speed & the reading began with him & followed to the right each reading a verse." Then they all found the hymn that was to be sung, and "he pitched the tune with a tuning fork & led off." Afterward they all knelt while Maxwell prayed. Then "one of the girls collected the book[s] while Mattie rushed into the kitchen & took breakfast from the range & put it on the table!"[43]

Despite her difficult domestic situation, like her mother and grandmother Martha was certainly no doormat, nor apparently was she reticent about speaking up for what she wanted. For example, she soon found that the Maxwell house in Baraboo was, in Mary's words, "shabby & uncomfortable" and not fit for the family. James also owned a farm at the edge of town, and Martha suggested that he erect a barn on the property in which they could live while awaiting the completion of the new house she encouraged him to build. One side of the property was "heavily wooded with maples oaks & elms in true Wis. style," as Mary described it, and Martha chose the site for the residence with care, "back far enough from the street so there was a wide tree dotted lawn about it & a drive up circled in front of the barn back to the street." Ultimately the "pretty Gothic house" built by the Maxwells became, said Mary, "the showplace of Baraboo."[44]

Martha also continued her activist ways in Baraboo after her marriage. She had not been raised, after all, to be only a wife and mother—quite the contrary. Like most women at mid-century, however, she would not have escaped such powerful socializing influences as *Godey's Lady's Book* and the countless other periodicals that described and prescribed the home as women's proper sphere. In order to protect and preserve that sphere, however, increasingly women were becoming active outside of it—in benevolence, in temperance, in moral reform. Activism bred independence, and a few women went beyond religious, charitable, and humanitarian concerns to take on more political causes such as abolition (a moral reform as well) and woman suffrage, in the process changing both themselves and their society and moving away from the home.[45]

Martha Maxwell likely was drawn to reform principally by the example of her family, with its tradition of strong-minded women going back beyond her grandmother Abigail. She had as well the influence of her mother and stepfather and their desire to work as missionaries in Oregon. If she sometimes thought herself shy, she also had a steely determination, and once she made up her mind, nothing could dissuade her. This heritage, coupled with her educational experiences at Oberlin, was more than sufficient to propel her into her own life of activism.

If Martha was always sympathetic to the reforms of the day, whether championing the rights of women graduates to read their commencement essays at Oberlin, working with the Oberlin Female Moral Reform Society, campaigning against smoking, or advocating phonetic spelling, she was especially committed to temperance. In the spring of 1854, after the death of a man blamed on "hard drinking" at the Brick Tavern, she and other women of the town determined to take matters into their own hands. Resolving themselves into a secret society, they led a raid on the tavern on May 15, opening bottle after bottle and allowing the liquor to drain out onto the floor. They then proceeded to enact similar scenes in other Baraboo bars.[46] As many as sixty women may have taken part in what became known as the "Whiskey War of 1854"; Martha and five other leaders were taken before a justice of the peace at Lower Sauk and later before a circuit court judge, fined, and set free. Ultimately their husbands or fathers agreed to pay damages to the barkeepers in restitution.[47] Thus in Baraboo, as in other eastern and midwestern towns in the 1850s, temperance advocacy was being manifested increasingly in such political, "vigilante" episodes. The movement also was becoming a seedbed which produced many of those who took leadership roles in the post–Civil War woman suffrage movement.[48] For Martha Maxwell, clearly in the most active minority of women who smashed whiskey bottles to demonstrate their revulsion against drink, the "Whiskey War" was but one more logical step on the road to reform.

Not surprisingly, Martha was also in the forefront of the Baraboo citizens who banded together to support the Free-State forces in Kansas, then a battleground to determine whether slavery or freedom would prevail in the new territory. In 1856 they met in the Methodist Episcopal Church and organized themselves into a Kansas League Auxiliary to the Wisconsin Kansas Aid Society. Chaired by James A. Maxwell, the meeting heard a lecture on the geography, agriculture, mineral resources, and "present perilous condition of the Free State inhabitants" which culminated in a plea for material aid. Six men, including Maxwell, and one woman, Martha Maxwell, each agreed to furnish the money to purchase one Sharp's rifle for the use of the "Free Kansas Emigrants."[49]

Occasionally Martha also turned her attention to traditional endeavors in the woman's sphere, apparently pursuing such activities with the determination and quest for excellence that would be evident throughout her life. For example, in 1856 she won awards at the Sauk County Agricultural Society Fair for the best cage and lot of canary birds and the best collection of house plants and in 1859 for the best bouquet of flowers, workbasket, and pincushion.[50]

Thus Martha's life in Baraboo during the 1850s, although considerably burdened with domestic cares, was not without its satisfactions and fulfillment. And at least one of her problems was alleviated when Emma Maxwell, by then evidently reconciled to her father's marriage, returned from Lawrence and married Howard Potter in the family home on October 15, 1856.[51] Yet something was missing from Martha's life: a child of her own. As with everything else she did, Martha was determined that if she were going to become a mother, she would do it the right way. Her husband's former brother-in-law, Judge James A. Clark, contributed to the cause by giving her literature, in her sister Mary's words, "of the most advanced kind of hygiene & breeding all forms of life in the most perfect ways," and she convinced her husband "to live so as to attain the highest point of physical perfection."[52] The result of this dedication, daughter Mabel, who was born on November 17, 1857, recalled the circumstances of her birth more bluntly. "Indeed, the steel-willed Martha so dominated her husband that she denied him both tobacco and liquor for one year prior to the conception of her child," Mabel wrote in her autobiography. "For Martha wanted a superior product. I was the result."[53]

While Martha was thus occupied James Maxwell continued to take a leading role in Baraboo, which by the mid-1850s had grown into a town of some two thousand inhabitants.[54] At various times his activities ranged from serving as a Sauk County Supervisor and representing Baraboo at the Republican State Convention to reading the Declaration of Independence at the Baraboo Fourth of July celebration in 1856. A staunch Methodist, as has been seen, he was elected president of both the Baraboo Sabbath Union, to promote the observance of the Sabbath, and the Sauk County Union Bible Society.[55] Moreover, since mid-1854 he had been a member of the Board of Trustees of Lawrence University.[56]

Yet like so many others in the late 1850s, James Maxwell was going broke, a victim of his own good nature and faulty judgment as well as of the depressed economic conditions in the country following the Panic of 1857. Easygoing and popular as well as influential, Maxwell had signed many notes and in general was not prepared for financial reverses.[57] The warning signs had been apparent at least as early as 1854, when he wrote to Martha that he had sold his old farm in Walworth County for three thousand dollars, using the money "mostly in the payments of debts & they are not all paid yet."[58] By 1857 notices of sheriff's sales naming Maxwell and others began appearing in the Baraboo newspaper, and it appears that he eventually lost his mill and virtually all of his other properties.[59]

Just as Maxwell's financial situation seemed the bleakest, however, a ray of light promised salvation. "Ho! For Pike's Peak!" headlined the *Baraboo Republic* early in 1859. "In common with every other locality, this neighborhood is in danger of losing many citizens to the Pike's Peak fever," the paper continued, estimating that at least forty residents were planning to start westward in the spring.[60] "Later News from Pike's Peak! Gold in still Greater abundance! Immense Emmigration!" proclaimed the *Republic* a month later as the great rush of 1859 to the gold fields began.[61] Despite reports a few months later from those who turned back, denouncing the whole thing as a hoax and a humbug, the lure of quick and easy riches continued to draw the adventurous, the ambitious, the desperate. By early 1860 James Maxwell had made up his mind. Like thousands of his contemporaries, he would seek his fortune at Pikes Peak.

Thus as the new year began Martha Maxwell faced momentous changes in her life. The past decade had seen her grow from a schoolgirl into a married woman with a daughter and six stepchildren, in the process surviving a deep personal disappointment. Primarily concerned with these domestic responsibilities, she nonetheless continued her interest in and commitment to activism and reform in Baraboo. Now she was preparing to leave everything behind to accompany her husband on a journey full of risk and hope; there seemed little doubt, however, that she would prove more than equal to the challenges that awaited on the Rocky Mountain frontier.

4

Working in the Gold Fields

Although she might not have realized it at the time, as Martha Maxwell prepared to leave Baraboo with her husband for the trip across the plains, she was also taking the first steps in a personal journey that would eventually lead her far beyond the familiar confines of home and family in Baraboo. Once in the mountains she would find ample opportunity to demonstrate the independence, industriousness, and ambition that were so much a part of her character as she made her way in the thriving and turbulent frontier society. Every step that she took beyond Baraboo, however, led her farther away from her daughter Mabel, the physical barrier creating a psychological one that was never quite to heal. Nonetheless, in 1860 Martha and James Maxwell were doing what they thought best for everyone, and one late-winter day they turned their wagon westward toward a new land and a new life.

For centuries the central Rocky Mountains had hidden their riches of gold and silver amidst craggy peaks and towering canyons. To be sure, there had been occasional reports from Spanish explorers such as Juan Rivera in the mid-seventeenth century, or from fur trappers like James Purcell early in the nineteenth century, who claimed to have found outcroppings of the precious metals and gold nuggets shimmering in the icy streams. Yet the first great gold rush was not to the area that became Colorado but to California, recently won from Mexico, as thousands of Forty-niners rushed westward along the Oregon and California trails, unaware that they were bypassing equally good opportunities to strike it rich.

A few California-bound argonauts did stop briefly in the Rockies, however, and later they remembered the "color" they had seen there. The news of such discoveries reinforced William Green Russell's suspicions that gold could be found along the Front Range, and after spending several years mining in California, the former Georgian and his brothers decided to look for it in earnest. Prospecting along Cherry Creek and Ralston Creek, the Russells finally hit pay dirt along Dry Creek (in present Englewood) in the summer of 1858. Other parties also made exciting discoveries that year, and the reports of easy riches spread like wildfire. By the spring of 1859 the "Rush to the Rockies" was in full swing, as gold seekers congregated in the "jumping-off" towns of Westport or Omaha or Leavenworth and set out for the Pikes Peak country some seven hundred miles distant. Following trails along the Platte and the Arkansas rivers, or along the more central Smoky Hill and Republican River routes, they streamed westward by covered wagon, by mule train, or even on foot.

Reaching the base of the mountains, the Fifty-niners found shelter and supplies in Auraria and Denver City, "instant cities" of hastily built cabins and rude tents that had sprung up at the confluence of Cherry Creek and the South Platte River. From there the argonauts spread out into the mountains, expecting easy pickings and immediate wealth. On and on they came, perhaps fifty thousand, perhaps more, and for many optimism turned to despair as reality failed to match expectation. Turning around and heading home, they painted signs on their wagons warning newcomers to go back or get busted.

Yet during that first part of 1859 some continued their lonely search, and for a few, determination and luck paid off. George Jackson, a former California miner, struck paydirt along Chicago Creek near present Idaho Springs, while not far away, John H. Gregory found gold at present Central City in the gulch that would bear his name. Along with news of similar finds near Boulder, these discoveries kept the rush alive. Further credibility was added when the respected and widely read journalists Henry Vil-

lard, Albert D. Richardson, and Horace Greeley visited the Gregory diggings in June and sent back generally favorable reports to
the "states." Although some of the Fifty-niners would continue
to go back, now many others would stay and seek their fortunes
on the Rocky Mountain frontier.[1]

As 1859 dawned in Baraboo the situation was no different
from that in hundreds of other midwestern and eastern towns
when the first reports from Pikes Peak began to find their way
into the local press. "Accounts of the gold discoveries continue to
flow in," stated the *Baraboo Republic* on January 27, "for the most
part corroborating the accounts previously received." Although
cautioning that the gold rush might not prove to be an "El Dorado
for all who travel thither," still the paper thought that Pikes Peak
"*may* prove better remunerative to the masses" than other areas.
"There is little, if any, abatement in the 'fever' in this neighborhood, and we here [*sic*] of some new victims nearly every day. We
expect soon to hear that some have reached the convalescent
stage."[2]

Throughout 1859 the newspaper kept Baraboo citizens
apprised of the latest developments in the Rockies, reporting on
the weekly departures of would-be gold seekers as well as on the
return of those who pronounced that they had been "hum-
bugged."[3] A year later the exodus was still continuing, prompt-
ing the editors to worry on occasion that the rush might be taking
Baraboo's most productive citizens. On March 8, 1860, the paper
noted "every exchange we take up now has a paragraph stating
that numbers of its citizens are going to Pike's Peak, so we must
be in the fashion." About twenty had started from Baraboo that
spring, and about a score more were preparing to follow. "We
hope it may suit them so well," said the *Republic*, "as to bring
them home in a year or two with their 'pockets full of rocks.' "[4]

Certainly that was the hope of James and Martha Maxwell,
who were among those who set out from Baraboo to Pikes Peak
early in 1860. "One dozen of our citizens, including our well-
known and highly respected townsman, JAS. A. MAXWELL, Esq.,
and his wife, started last Tuesday morning [February 21] for the
Pike's Peak region, via Dubuque," reported the *Baraboo Republic*

on February 23. "They take with them their own teams, and go, most of them, with the intention of 'hoeing their own row' in the mines."[5]

Because their daughter Mabel was not yet three years old, James and Martha judged her far too young to accompany them on the long and perhaps dangerous journey, and they left her in the care of her maternal grandmother, Amy Dartt, and Martha's two half-sisters, Mary and Sarah Elizabeth. Thus, just as Martha's own mother had left her, at almost exactly the same age, when she traveled from Pennsylvania to Connecticut, so did Martha leave her own daughter a generation later. Evidently, however, Amy did not approve of the separation, for Mary informed Martha a few months later that "Mamma thinks you are losing what to you would be the most interesting portion of May's life when her little mind first begins to develop its self."[6]

Any problems were far in the future, however, when Martha and James left Baraboo for Pikes Peak. They were accompanied by James Maxwell Clark, a son of Judge Clark, and at least three other young men identified as David Brown, Edward Palmer, and John Day; Martha was the only woman among them.[7] James P. Maxwell, who had been graduated from Lawrence University in 1859, left by train with his aunt, Caroline Maxwell Estabrook, who had been visiting in Baraboo; he would go with her as far as her home in Omaha and then join his father's group there.[8] According to J. Max Clark (or Mac, as he was often called), the party had six months' worth of supplies in their wagons, including about twenty bushels of potatoes and onions.[9]

On March 14, some three weeks after James and Martha and their companions had left Baraboo, they arrived in Omaha by way of Anamosa and Cedar Rapids, Iowa. A few days earlier Martha had written to her family in Baraboo to reassure them and give them some idea of her situation:

> If you wish to know where I am, just imagine you see
> me seated on a wooden pail instead of a chair beside me
> a writing desk composed of first, a trunk for the base
> next a pail for the stand and, last a tinpan bottomside up
> for the top . . . . at my left hand is situated a conglomer-
> ate mass of household or (tenthold) utensels and provi-

sions such as Potatoes & Salt, bread & water, Soap &
Sugar, Saluratus & acid, Apple Sauce & dried beaf,
Buckwheat flour & molasses, Eggs & butter, etc. and behind me a Prairie chicken is stewing sleepily on the
stove.[10]

As Martha implied in this letter and in another written several days later, most of the time the trip thus far had been neither
particularly arduous nor uncomfortable, considering the circumstances. Although the roads had been bad during the first
week, she said, since then they had been "just as good as anyone
could wish." For food, in addition to the provisions she mentioned, "during the latter part of our journey we have had all the
wild ducks & hens that we could dispose of—have lived sump-
tuously all the way." Moreover, she told them, even though she
was the only woman along, cooking was no hardship, "for David
generaly gets breakfast sometimes washes the dishes and is as
handy as a girl. I consider myself fortunate in having him in the
company." The other men also helped, she added, "so that it all
goes off nice."[11] Even their sleeping arrangements, she wrote,
left little to be desired. "We partition off a bedroom with a sheet,
put 6 or 8 inches of hay or straw to lay our beding on, which
makes as good a bed as one need ask for, and we sleep as sweetly
as we could at home."[12]

In fact, their only real difficulty had occurred when Martha
had had an accident when one of the front axletrees broke off
while she was at the reins. Even this was no problem, she assured
her family. "I sugested to James that I considered him capable of
facing any immergency and had no doubt the thing would be
fixed up without much delay. 'And you are not going to try to
mend the matter by sheding a pint or so of tears?' he answered.
Of course I replyed in the negative, for you know I've but little
faith in that remedy." Presumably James did indeed fix the
wagon, and without delay. Outside of this incident, and the fact
that the tent had once blown down, Martha concluded that "our
journey has been very *tame* but very pleasant withall most of the
way."[13]

After spending about two weeks in Omaha the Maxwell party resumed the journey across the plains on April 4; James P. had

not yet caught up with them but did arrive somewhat later.[14] By April 13 they were encamped in the vicinity of Fort Kearny on the Platte River where, as Martha explained to her mother, travelers were not allowed to camp within two miles of the fort.[15]

From Fort Kearny the Maxwell party continued to travel along the banks of the Platte, which like many overlanders Martha found uninteresting. "I doubt whether any river, or any country for the same distance presents less variety. . . ," she wrote to her sisters. "The river broad, shallow, still, full of Islands & sandbars without timber most of the way with low bare banks, and only in two or three instances have I heard its waters ripple after going to bed."[16] Newlywed Mollie Dorsey Sanford, who was traveling from Nebraska City to search for Pikes Peak gold with her husband Byron and reached Fort Kearny a few weeks after the Maxwells, termed the Platte a "low sluggish stream" and the scenery "monotonous."[17] And Samuel Mallory of Danbury, Connecticut, who was taking a quartz mill to the mines, pronounced it "the most peculiar river I ever saw. It is about a mile wide and runs with a rapid current, yet I can wade across it at any place, and I have not seen a place yet where it is four feet deep."[18]

Even if the scenery was monotonous, however, Pikes Peakers along the Platte in the spring of 1860 had plenty of company, and many of them remarked on the sheer numbers of persons streaming westward. "It did not look like a barren wilderness to see so many teams camped and men walking around and traveling all toward the land of gold," wrote fellow Wisconsinite George T. Clark on May 14.[19] Similarly, journalist Albert Richardson, making a return trip to the mines, noted on June 5 that while he and his party were stopping for breakfast more than two hundred wagons passed them by. "The valley of the Platte, as far as we can see, is white with 'prairie schooners,' " he observed.[20] Mollie Dorsey Sanford agreed. "Emigration is immense," she wrote on April 26. "We hear that 70,000 persons have already passed this route going west."[21]

In addition to their fellow argonauts, the Pikes Peakers were likely to encounter Indians, whom Martha found more interesting than the scenery. Observing them with a scientific curiosity, she told her sisters that her party had seen four different tribes of Indians; "they interest me much. Their manner of conversing by signs, their orniments &c &c amuse me vastly." Once, she said, an Indian had even "proposed buying me, or swaping three ponys for me." Although such trades are a standard component of many reminiscences, where in the retelling they often were greatly exaggerated (or even invented), Martha certainly had no reason to embellish the incident in the letter she wrote to her sisters soon afterward. Perhaps she even should have accepted the offer, she mused. "You see I'm just beginning to be appreciated—had better favor the trade, and turn Squaw had I not?"[22]

Martha and the Maxwell party were fortunate that their dealings with the Indians were so pleasant, for by 1860 the natives were a growing threat to those who were making the overland crossing. Dispossessed of their traditional hunting lands, they had begun more and more to confront rather than to aid the seemingly never-ending tide of westward-bound immigrants and settlers. "Houses are geting quite common," Martha reported to her sisters on May 6, "nearly every patch of firtle bottomland is fenced or about to be. This I think is not right for it must interfere very much with the Indians depriving them of their hunting ground and particularly of pasturage for their ponys. I anticipate a remonstrance on their part before long."[23] Just four years later, Indian-white conflict on the Colorado plains erupted in the bloody and still controversial battle at Sand Creek.

The Maxwell party continued without incident, however, and after many seemingly endless days along the Platte, they were finally able to discern the faint outlines of the Rocky Mountains, still far in the distance. Like countless other travelers before and since, Martha would not soon forget her first glimpse of the Rockies. "I thought that I could imagine something how Columbus felt when he discovered America," she wrote, "as after a months monotonous journying over a sea of land, we saw looming up silvery and beautiful in the robes of eternal white the objects of our search. . . . They appear more & more magnificent each day. I have seen nothing except Niagra which can compair with them in grandeur." [24]

As the Maxwell party approached the end of the journey,

Martha concluded that all in all the trip "has been a very interesting one. The very vastness of the extent of nothing (almost) fur-
nishes ample room for the exercise of the imagination. . . ."[25]
Although some women may have crossed the plains reluctantly,
bound for Oregon or California or Pikes Peak, like her mother
and grandmother, Martha was neither frightened nor unwilling
to go west, despite the need to leave her daughter behind. Indeed, she seems to have approached the whole as an adventure
with a combination of scientific curiosity and unbounded enthusiasm, embracing rather than fearing what the future might hold
in store. Little did she realize that her adventures were only beginning.

On May 7 the Maxwell party had arrived in Denver, which in
a year had grown from a few clusters of rude log cabins to a thriving, bustling settlement that was already taking on an air of
permanence and stability.[26] The first brick structure had been
erected in the fall of 1859, and more were appearing by the spring
of 1860. Later in the year the census taker counted 4,749 persons
in Denver (which had merged with Auraria in April), but these
figures did not begin to take into account the thousands of prospectors who were constantly passing through and picking up
supplies before heading into the mountains. "Denver is growing
like Jonah's gourd," wrote Albert Richardson on June 12, "and all
the mountains within two hundred miles of here are literally
swarming with people."[27] Whereas the population had been
overwhelmingly male the year before, now there were women
and their children, who brought with them the need for churches
and schools as well as their Victorian cultural and social values. If
there were also saloons by the dozen, in addition to the prosti-
tutes, gamblers, murderers, and other lowlifes associated with a
frontier community, there were also unmistakable signs that
Denver was becoming "civilized."[28]

Although some newcomers still found Denver "an exceedingly primitive town," as Lavinia Porter did in the summer
of 1860[29], others like Martha Maxwell were more favorably impressed. "This is quite a city," she told her sisters. "Seems more
business like than any place that I have seen for years."[30]
Richardson concurred, commenting on the "activity and that in-

describable air which pervades a young metropolis" and calling Denver "the most *live* town west of St. Louis."[31] Mollie Dorsey Sanford also approved of what she saw. "I like the looks of the place," she wrote on June 26. "Everybody seems glad to welcome the coming pilgrims, as we are called, anybody from 'back in the States.' "[32]

In Denver the members of the Maxwell party were greeted by James's son Lon, who had walked down from Mountain City, having arrived in the gold fields the year before. The group stayed in Denver only for a short time, going on to Golden, where they camped overnight, and then into the mountains, where they joined the thousands of other prospectors in the mining camps clustered around Central City.[33] Several distinct settlements had grown up around the site of John Gregory's 1859 discovery. The one closest to that find was known as Mountain City, while southwest, up in Nevada Gulch, another took the name of Nevada, Nevada City, or Nevadaville. Between them, and so termed because of its central location, was Central City, while just below Mountain City the town of Black Hawk developed at the intersection of Gregory Gulch and North Clear Creek.[34]

Even before the Maxwell party left Denver, Martha had made arrangements to go into business in the mining district, motivated not only by the desire to make money and to have some degree of independence, but also to prove wrong those who had tried to discourage her from accompanying the prospectors. "You know some of my Baraboo friends were inclined to laugh at me for coming out here," she reminded her sisters, "saying that it was no place for a woman and that I would be only a bill of expence & a bother."[35] In Denver Martha had found a woman named Mary Cawker, who had arrived on April 17, 1860, and decided to go into partnership with her. A widow in her late forties with two teenage children, Cawker had lived at one time in Milwaukee and Appleton, Wisconsin, and she and Martha had evidently known each other before coming to the mines.[36]

For one hundred dollars the two women bought a 40' by 100' lot, described as being "situated on the West side of Spring Gulch on the New Nevada Road," along with almost enough hewn logs for a house.[37] Because only a few sawmills had been built in the vicinity and finished lumber was both scarce and expensive, they spent an additional thirty dollars for hauling more lumber from some fifteen miles away. In order to get the whole "house shape," Martha told her mother, they gave the job for fifty dollars to James Maxwell.[38] This was not the last time that Martha would conclude such a business arrangement with her husband. After the Centennial, for example, one of her disputes with the Colorado commissioners concerned the fact that she claimed reimbursement for her husband's services in helping her pack. One of the commissioners, adhering reportedly to the doctrine that "a man and his wife are one," opined that her husband's compensation should be considered simply as part of the allowance paid to her. "I would not work for my husband for nothing," she is quoted as having responded, "and I would not ask him to work for me without pay."[39]

By the first part of June the house, which Martha termed "a kind of boarding and eating establishment," was ready. Two stories high, with dimensions of 18' by 20', it had one room above and another room and bedroom below.[40] The women were still waiting for glass for the windows, which Lon had been instructed to buy in Omaha on his next trip for provisions, and the structure did not yet have a proper roof. However, as Martha pointed out, "with our tent spread with one end against a door in the side of the house (the end stands next [to] the road), the other end opens handy to the oven, this makes us a firstrate kitchen, so you see we are very nicely fixed, vastly more so than most of our neighbours." Martha and Mary Cawker then hung out a sign that said "washing," and as Martha told her mother, "I'm trying to make what I can in every laudible way. Washing, baking, mending &c. &c." In two weeks, she reported, she made about thirty-five dollars from selling pies and washing.[41]

Such work was typical of that done by women in mining towns that were dominated by men, as recent studies have shown. Summarizing the literature, historian Susan Armitage points out that the "job opportunities for women were very few and specific—they were domestic or sexual. The spectrum ranged from the respectable 'private' housewife, followed by a range of domestic jobs (domestic servant, cook, laundress) to the semisexual, semidomestic jobs (waitress, bargirl, etc.) ending with the bad 'public' woman—the prostitute."[42]

Despite her success, Martha feared that her prosperity was short-lived. "Since then scores of women have got here, some are washing very cheap, so that we shall not do much more of that business." In fact, although women were still scarce in the mining district (the ratio of men to women in the area around Central City at the time has been estimated as seven to one), certainly more were living there than had been the year before.[43]

By mid-August Martha had sold her interest in the house to Mary Cawker, who shortly afterward acquired the Four Mile House on Cherry Creek near Denver, which she ran as a tavern and stage stop until 1864.[44] Martha then became involved in building another, this time on her own in Nevada City on the north side of Main Street adjoining the Idaho Hall. For the land, most of the material for a two-story house 22' by 40', and some of the carpenter work, she was to pay a man named A. J. Edwards $350 one year from the date of the agreement plus fifteen percent interest. Although Martha thought that the deal might not be a very good transaction in the "states," she was convinced that "it will help us much."[45] By comparison, a month earlier Samuel Mallory had contracted to have an 18' by 24' house built in Nevada City. When completed he expected it to cost about $500.[46] Again, James Maxwell, assisted by his son Jim and David Brown, put up the body of the house, this time to pay off $100 that Martha had given to Mary Cawker on his account.[47]

Even though James was helping to put up the two houses, most of the time he was engaged in what was, after all, the reason he had come to the mountains: prospecting. Along with his sons James and Lon, Mac Clark, and David Brown, he worked in Lump Gulch, about ten miles north of Mountain City, coming home about once a week.[48] Like many others, however, the men found that looking for gold was far from a sure thing, as the surface placers were almost played out by the summer of 1860, leaving only the deep lode deposits of precious metals. As Martha told her family on August 20, "When James & the boys commenced mining they worked in the Gulsh among the ice (for the ground was still frozen in spots) mud & water, but they did not find gold enough to pay expences so they concluded to prospect for Lode claims." Although they did find several, she added, they still had not made their expenses.[49]

Martha also was involved in claim acquisition. "I am securing claims too," she told her sisters, "which may be valuable some day but I place little dependence upon them at present."[50] Other women were hoping to find properties; some were taking claims next to those of their husbands to protect their spouses' properties, much as women later took homestead land in their own names to add to the family farm.[51] For example, John and Mary Stone took adjoining claims on the Washington Lode; Elizabeth and H. J. Christ took numbers sixteen and seventeen west of discovery on the Pennsylvania Lode; and Margaret and William James took numbers seven and eight west of discovery on the Mountain Lode.[52] On the other hand, Hannah Griffen, Eliza Wemple, Isabella Rice, Elizabeth Kimball, Mary Marshall, and Elizabeth Smith are all examples of women who seem to have made claims independently.[53] Martha herself estimated later that she had about twenty claims in all; one was on the Kansas Lode, which James, Jim, and Lon Maxwell and Mac Clark had also claimed, and three others were on lodes which various members of the Baraboo group also claimed.[54] Although the records are incomplete, it appears that the rest of Martha's claims were made on her own.[55] Given Martha's passion for independence and for keeping her financial arrangements apart from those of her husband, it is probable that most of her claims were separate from his.

All in all, however, it was not an easy way to make a living. Hard work and more of it was the rule, and it did not take long to discover the fact. "A man must have capital, work hard, and be exceedingly lucky, or come short of success," Hiram Johnson wrote from Nevada Gulch on July 18. "I tell you, of all the places I ever saw, this is entirely the worst place for a gentleman of leisure."[56] Samuel Mallory thought that "a large number come here with less than a cent in their pockets, and when here are too lazy (or constitutionally tired) to work; and I am decidedly of the opinion that the latter class have no business in these mountains, for of all poor creatures here, a lazy man is the poorest."[57]

Martha, of course, was not planning to give up, although she acknowledged the difficulties to her sisters. "You know that I am blessed with a pretty strong hang-on-it-ive trait of charactor and so is James consequently we expect to accomplish the object for which we came, sooner or later as we are blessed with prosperity. . . ."[58]

Despite the hard work and the lack of money, life in the mining district did have some compensations. The mountains surrounding the camps were awesome, and when Martha and James took a walk one day they hiked to the summit of Bald Mountain; Martha thought the view was "both beautiful and sublime." Then, too, her health was "never better," although all of the men had been felled by the "summer complaint." Martha attributed her good health to her "manner of living," for, she told her sisters, "I carry out my principles of diet so far as I am able."[59]

By October many who had arrived a few months earlier with high hopes had decided to join the ranks of the "go-backers." Even in August, Martha commented, "people are daily starting for the states some disgusted with every thing and every body more especially themselves. . . ."[60] Not surprisingly, Martha found her business suffering because of the exodus and the fact that little paper money was circulating.[61] A correspondent writing from Mountain City on October 14 concurred, telling readers of the *Rocky Mountain News* that "times are very dull and money very hard to catch or collect" and noting that there were not now "quite as many families or lady inhabitants" as there had been a few months previously.[62] Yet neither Martha nor James thought of giving up at this point, even though the Baraboo party still was making nothing in mining, and she asked to borrow one hundred dollars from her family, assuring them she would repay the money at fifteen percent interest.[63]

Nonetheless, by early 1861 Martha was doing well enough to buy a "ranch claim" some ten miles downstream from Denver on the Platte River.[64] A one-room log cabin was located on it, and Martha initially sent Mac Clark down from the mountains to live there. By late May or early June, however, he had left to join the Union Army, and James Maxwell then lived on the "Maxwell Ranche," as they called it, long enough to comply with the settlement requirements. After that Lon Maxwell and two friends occupied the place occasionally.[65]

A year after their arrival in Colorado, Martha and James continued their attempts to make a living, and a life, in the mines and on the ranch. Not only were they staying in Colorado, but they had been joined by friends and relatives from Baraboo, including Martha's stepfather, Josiah Dartt; James's youngest daughter from his first marriage, Gussie; and Baraboo physician Charles Cowles. (James had gone back to Baraboo and had accompanied the party to Colorado.)[66] Such "kinship networks" played an important role in western migration as family and friends joined those who had gone before, even as Martha and James had followed Lon Maxwell to the gold fields.[67] At one point Martha had wanted her daughter to come out with the group but had decided the trip would not be advisable, telling her mother and sisters that she was "afraid to trust any one but you or myself to bring her."[68] Yet it takes little imagination to wonder how four-year-old Mabel felt when her father came back to Wisconsin, without her mother, only to leave again while taking another daughter with him to Colorado.

While the men prospected in Lump Gulch and elsewhere (although the scientific Josiah seems to have devoted most of his attention to collecting "a very exclusive herborium," as his stepdaughter termed it)[69], Martha worked from dawn to dusk washing, cleaning, and cooking at her boardinghouse. Of them all, however, she may have been the most successful. Remembering how her Baraboo friends (and perhaps James) had laughed at her, she early on decided to keep strict accounts. "So far I have made more than all the rest of our folks put togather," she told her sisters in August 1860, "but they *expect* every day to strike a fortune and then they say I'll have to give in. I tell them that a *small* sure thing is better than a *great* uncertainty."[70] By June 1861, she toted up the accounts again and described the results to her mother and sisters:

You know I have had a curiosity to know how much I, individually, can make in this country. Well James and I figured up the other day I giving him credit for all the provisions etc. which I have had with the usual amount of freight on the same & twelve percent interest on the whole amount, also interest upon the value of all labor performed by himself & the boys Dave & Jim & giving me credit for their board etc. when they have not done chores enough to pay. After all debts & demands of any kind are payed I have invested in this property ranch & claims $1583.35. all of which has been made by *hard work* and close management. & I suppose that in the present state of affairs it would be impossible to sell for half the original cost of my claims of which I have about 20, may be worth as many fortunes and they may not all be worth one cent, but it will be rather strange if there are not some good ones among them.[71]

Thus it seemed that Martha's hard work and sacrifice were beginning to achieve results. And, despite the demands of her business, occasionally there was time for other activities. For example, the Nevada correspondent to the *Rocky Mountain News* reported on March 4, 1861, that "a fine social party was given on Tuesday evening last in Mrs. Maxwell's hall. . . . Everything went of[f] in splendid style. The management was good, music excellent, and the supper got up in her own best style by the charming hostess."[72] The next month the noted actor John Langrishe and his company gave a performance, "The Lady of Lyon," in Maxwell's Hall.[73]

Martha also continued her strong interest in temperance, joining the Good Templars' lodge that had been established in Nevada City in August 1860 as a charter member and serving as an officer in 1861. Organized in New York in 1851, the temperance group, often found in the West, had both men and women members and treated women equally with respect to voting and officeholding. The organization supported woman suffrage as well.[74]

Then there was the Fourth of July, one of the year's two major holidays in a mining camp. Nationalistic and patriotic, mid-nineteenth-century Americans celebrated Independence Day in grand style. The observance in Nevada City in 1861, as Martha described it to Mary, was typical, the flavor all the more intense as war threatened to tear the country apart. Martha and Gussie dressed up in identical outfits featuring aprons "embodying our national colors the shirt of red and white stripes and a blue bib holding 13 stars," she wrote. "These were highly complimented and I think are really *pretty.*" The "eatables" (ice cream and canned fruit) were excellent, she went on. Fireworks, picnics, and a parade with musicians playing "Hail Columbia" and "Yankee Doodle" rounded out the activities, and a party was held that night in her hall that brought in about sixty-five dollars, "about two thirds of which was clear gain, that is leaving out of the question a good deal [of] hard work & loss of sleep."[75] All in all, everyone had a grand time.

A few months later, however, the Maxwells' life in Nevada City came to a temporary halt when a great fire, that common and almost inevitable scourge of the mining camp, destroyed much of the settlement. According to one report, the flames began above Nevada City in the timber; by the time the conflagration was all over, some fifty houses and about sixty thousand dollars' worth of property had been destroyed.[76] The boardinghouse was lost and the family's belongings consumed; Martha especially regretted losing her copy of *Proverbial Philosophy*, a gift to her many years before.[77]

After the fire the Maxwells went first to Lump Gulch, where James P. had a cabin on a placer claim that he owned.[78] Martha and James, with the help of friends, also built a barn and "hay yard" on the lot that had been burned over, then sold it to Edwards, from whom she had bought the property, for four dollars.[79] In the middle of December they left Nevada City for the ranch, where more bad luck awaited them. They found three men in their "shantee" who were "claiming the ranch & declaring that they would not give it up." Fortunately, James and Martha were able to stay with neighbors, and a week or so later an arbitration hearing awarded the claim to them.[80]

Although they returned briefly to Nevada City to settle their affairs, James and Martha spent most of the spring and summer of 1862 on the ranch. Two years had elapsed since they had set out from Baraboo, and if they had not met with absolute failure, neither had they found overwhelming success in Colorado. They had managed to build a house on the ranch, however, and when

James's sister Caroline Estabrook came out for a visit in the summer of 1862, she thought that the "ranch is very pretty, and their house very comfortable. . . ." Yet life was no easier; both James and Martha worked round the clock trying to wrest a living from the land. Caroline thought that her brother was "breaking down fast," but he would not give up, always hoping that the crops next year would be better. As for Martha, Caroline reported to her father, Colonel Maxwell, back in Baraboo that she would be happy to stay on the ranch "if she only had little May with her for company—it must be awful lonesome for her, in the house all day long, with no one to speak to, only at meal time. She is very thin, and works hard."[81]

Clearly, by this time the hard work, coupled with the separation from her daughter, seemed to be taking its toll on Martha. Mabel was growing from a toddler into an independent little girl; as Mary commented to Martha in September of 1862, "she is getting so large I cant believe she is the same person she was a year ago. . . . I shall have to stop calling her my *little* pet before long."[82] Thus it was perhaps with relief as well as concern that Martha learned that her mother was apparently seriously ill in Wisconsin, and that it would be necessary for her to return. Amy Dartt was, in fact, so sick that the family had begun to despair of her recovery, and Mabel had had to live with her half-sister, Emma, and Howard Potter for the last five months.[83] Mary had borne the brunt of her mother's care, and by late September 1862, she confided to Martha that "confinement, constant care, and anxiety are beginning to have there effect upon my own health somewhat and I have been almost sick for the past week."[84]

Martha's stepfather Josiah had returned home to Baraboo in December 1861, after some nine months in Colorado, and by the fall of 1862 Martha concluded that the family circumstances made it necessary for her to go home as well. Thus in late November, the *Baraboo Republic* informed its readers that "Mrs. Jas. A. Maxwell, of Denver, Colorado Territory" had returned "on a winter visit, probably."[85]

By that time it had been more than two and one-half years since Martha had seen her daughter, and when she arrived in Wisconsin she found that Mabel was calling her grandmother

Amy "mother" and did not know Martha.[86] Indeed, whatever the price Martha had paid, the long separation seems ultimately to have been far more costly for Mabel, and more damaging. Often in later life she spoke of her hunger for the maternal affection she felt she had been denied and had had to seek elsewhere. "There was always grandmother," she confided in her autobiography. "Her surface was austere and rigid, her discipline inflexible, but underneath was a heart of such tenderness that she was the greatest love of my life. That is the pitiful penalty which separation brought not only to me but, I believe, to my mother as well."[87]

Indeed, Martha's life in Colorado during the period 1860–62 foreshadowed both the professional success and the personal difficulties she would experience later. She had demonstrated, not for the first time, her capacity for hard labor, as well as the single-minded quality she once described as "a pretty strong hang-on-it-ive trait of charactor." She also showed that she placed a high premium on independence, especially in financial affairs. These attributes had brought her at least a measure of success on the frontier, yet she had sacrificed being with her daughter for such a lengthy period that the seeds were sown for a lifetime of recriminations and regrets. For the present, however, Martha was home in Baraboo, and mother and daughter were reunited.

Taxidermy and Reform

Martha's years in Wisconsin following her return from Colorado were fruitful and productive in many ways but trying and discouraging in others. During this period (1862–67) she began work in earnest as a taxidermist, and she also reinforced her active commitment to reform. But although she was reunited with her daughter, she was separated from her husband (practically, if not legally), and the passing years only emphasized the distance that seemed to be growing between them. Finally, whatever personal torment she was undergoing took its toll and she entered a sanitarium, but she soon emerged even more committed to her favorite reform, temperance. Taxidermy and reform, then, are the major themes of this part of her life, which saw also the beginning of the end of her marriage to James Maxwell.

When Martha returned to Baraboo the Dartt family was once again living at Joseph Sanford's brick house so that Mary and Sarah Elizabeth could attend school in town.[1] At the time Baraboo had two institutions that were typical of the academies and institutes established throughout the country to provide educational opportunities at the secondary level.[2] The Baraboo Female Seminary, founded in the late 1850s, followed in the tradition of the movement led by Catharine Beecher; from 1859 to 1863, in fact, the principal was Mary E. Mortimer, who had been associated with Beecher's Milwaukee Female College.[3] James Maxwell had served as a director of the seminary before he went to Colorado, and Mary Dartt had lived with Martha and attended the school briefly in 1859.[4] Baraboo also supported the coeducational

Baraboo Collegiate Institute. It was less expensive than the semi-nary, and since money was always a factor to be considered, the Dartts had decided to send the girls there.[5]

The institute had grown out of a school begun in 1854 by the Reverend Warren Cochran, the minister who had encouraged Martha to go to Oberlin.[6] In 1861 Prof. E. F. Hobart, a graduate of Beloit College, took over as principal, and he and his wife, in the words of the *Baraboo Republic*, "infused new life into the Colle-giate Institution."[7] By mid-century both coeducational and women's institutions were reflecting and contributing to the popular interest in science, as manifested by attendance at lec-tures on botany or geology, the collection of specimens, and the formation of local societies, and Hobart drew up a curriculum that placed more emphasis on the natural sciences and less on the classics.[8] He also took the natural history "cabinet" that had been in the courthouse and made it available to all of the natural his-tory classes in Baraboo.[9]

Hobart also was a firm believer in teaching by example and illustration. "Teaching to be good must be live and real," he observed on one occasion. "It must not be confined to the narrow limits of the text book."[10] Later, Mary Dartt remembered how the professor "had the art of imparting his enthusiasm to his schol-ars, and many of them count as among the pleasantest recollec-tions of their lives the memory of the long rambles over hills and beside streams, in which they were invited to join him for the study of nature from his stand-point of loving admiration."[11] Thus it was not long before Hobart decided that the institute needed a collection of mounted birds and mammals. "We must have a Department of Zoology; can't some of you young ladies, who have more skilful fingers than I, assist me in putting up some birds?" he asked.[12]

Although both Sarah Elizabeth and Mary declined, they sug-gested that their older sister Martha would be happy to help the professor. According to Mary, the girls were sure that Martha would be interested because she had attempted to learn the rudi-ments of taxidermy at the Maxwell Ranche in Colorado a year or so earlier. As Mary told the story later in *On the Plains*, when Martha had returned to the ranch, one of the claim jumpers she found was a German who had a number of mounted birds in his possession. Martha was fascinated by the specimens, the first she had ever seen, and had asked him to teach her the process. He agreed to give her lessons at ten dollars apiece, after making her promise not to practice taxidermy in Denver.

When Martha came back the next day, however, eager to begin work, she found that the German had changed his mind "because she was a woman!" As Mary related the conversation later, the German declined to keep the bargain because he was afraid of the competition: "Vimen is besser as men mit den hands in shmall verks. Ven you know dis pisness you makes de pirds and peasts so quicker as I; you leave me no more verk at all! Es is besser for me I keeps vat I knows mit mineself!" Although Martha repeatedly assured him that she wanted to learn the art "only for her own gratification," he would not relent.

This was not the end of the story, however. As noted earlier, the Maxwells were awarded the claim at an arbitration hearing. But the German made no move to leave the premises, and so Martha decided to take matters into her own hands. Mary described the ultimate resolution of the conflict:

> Possession in those days was *ten* points in the law. Mrs. Maxwell had no idea of surrender, and keeping watch of the disputed cabin from a neighboring ranch, made a raid upon it one day during his absence. Withdrawing the staple, which held his padlock, from the door-frame, she entered, and carefully gathering up his earthly effects, removed them to a convenient point on the plains, where she left them in a neat pile to await his further disposition, while she proceeded to adjust things to her own mind in the recovered domicile!
>
> Among his possessions were not the birds she had seen—those he had already sold—but others in an early stage of preparation. Of them she felt at liberty to make a critical examination, and gather an idea of the materials he used in stuffing them, if nothing more.[13]

Who was this mysterious German taxidermist who apparently stimulated Martha to embark on her lifetime vocation? When Martha described the claim-jumping incident in her letter of

January 1, 1862, she made no mention of him, saying only that three men were in the house "declaring that they would not give it up." However, just two men, David Wood and Thomas Rease, were named as the parties contesting Martha's claim; perhaps the third person was the German who left the scene after having been summarily displaced.[14] In any event, toward the end of Martha's account there is a telling phrase that lends credence to the substance, if not the details, of the encounter. Enclosing one dollar in stamps, Martha asked her family to send her a book on "instruction in the fine arts" that she had left in Mabel's bureau. "I wish," she said, "to learn how to preserve birds & other animal curiosities in this country."[15]

Martha's entrance into the field of taxidermy thus was a logical outgrowth of her abiding interest in art and natural history, apparently stimulated first by an encounter of some sort in Colorado and later by the request of Professor Hobart. For most of the next two decades she would become more and more immersed in collecting and mounting specimens, presenting them in public exhibitions, and continuing serious scientific study, demonstrating time and again "what a woman can do."

Here in Baraboo, then, Martha Maxwell really began work as a taxidermist; little more than a decade later her accomplishments would be available for all to see in Philadelphia. In the beginning, though, she needed a good deal of assistance, and she asked a Mr. Ogden of Baraboo, who had mounted some birds, for help. For about two years she worked for the institute, assisting the professor in mounting "over a score" of birds and mammals in that time, according to Felger.[16] As Mary commented, however, the collection never grew to be very large because the school had few financial resources to devote to the project and because neither Martha nor the professor "had a surplus of elegant leisure which they could donate to it."[17]

By the spring of 1865 Martha had even less leisure, as she and Mabel moved from the Pewit's Nest home of the Dartts to the Maxwell home. There she had her hands full overseeing the fluctuating Maxwell household, which besides herself and Mabel usually included Colonel Maxwell and the three youngest daughters by James's first marriage, Ellen, Carrie, and Gussie.

Yet in addition to her family responsibilities and her work at the institute, Martha also found time to continue her active involvement in the community. For example, in July 1863 she was elected secretary of the Loyal Women's League of Baraboo, an organization which then counted well over two hundred members. Proposing "to continue its work of diffusing through the public mind an intelligent interest in the great moral questions of the day," the league was then cooperating with the National Loyal Women's League to gather signatures for a petition urging Congress to "pass an act of universal emancipation." The group also worked with the Sanitary Commission of Baraboo to furnish aid to Union soldiers.[18] Thus in Baraboo, as throughout the Union, women like Martha Maxwell were finding ways to participate actively in national affairs, laying further groundwork for the expanded roles they would assume after the Civil War.[19] For Martha, a veteran of the Baraboo Whiskey War of 1854, such activism was a natural manifestation of her deeply held beliefs. As she had demonstrated before and would again, she was not one to sit on the sidelines when it came to "the great moral questions of the day."

All the while James remained in Colorado, except for a short trip now and then back to Baraboo. Whether because of circumstances or rather by design (perhaps a bit of both), the Maxwells' separation stretched into one, then two, then three years. During this period James and his son Jim became involved in a variety of business endeavors both in the Central City–Black Hawk area and just over the mountains in Boulder, a thriving supply center for the mines. Along with Nelson K. Smith and Clinton M. Tyler, who had been partners in a hardware and cutlery business in Baraboo, they were active in starting sawmills in Black Hawk and at the junction of Boulder and Four Mile creeks, shipping lumber as far away as Cheyenne, and in spearheading the construction of a wagon road up Boulder Canyon.[20] James A. Maxwell also bought cattle on the plains and drove them back to Colorado for Smith and Tyler.[21] After 1863, however, the Maxwells no longer had the ranch, for it was sold, at least in part to provide funds for James to invest in his partnerships with Smith and Tyler.[22] (These business dealings were really all in the family, for Jim Maxwell married Smith's daughter Francelia in 1863, and Tyler was married to Smith's daughter Emma.)[23]

Meanwhile, back in Baraboo life went on, and the young people grew up and went out on their own. Two of James's daughters, Ellen and Carrie, married early in 1865, while later that year Martha's half-sisters Mary and Sarah were graduated from the Baraboo Collegiate Institute.[24] By this time it had been almost three years since Martha had left James in Colorado to return to Baraboo, and there was little indication that she planned to return anytime soon, although Colonel Maxwell did tell James that Martha would rather live in "that country" than in Baraboo.[25] Yet, although few letters between James and Martha survive from this period, there are some hints as early as 1864 that all might not be well with the marriage. "If I am not to you all I ought to be," James wrote to Martha on April 17, "it is not because I do not hope & long & try to be."[26] For her part, it is not known what Martha was thinking, but clearly, she had made no move to return to Colorado since 1862, and in fact she gave every indication of settling down in Baraboo. Actions, in this case, were speaking at least as loudly as words.

In addition, by 1866 Martha was in poor health, apparently worn out (and no wonder) from caring for James's first family, his father, and her own daughter Mabel. After the two Maxwell girls married, Martha and Mabel had gone back to live with Amy and Josiah Dartt, while the Colonel and Gussie traveled to Colorado for an extended visit. By the fall of 1866 even living with her mother had not restored Martha's health, and thus she decided to enter the new sanitarium that had recently opened in Battle Creek, Michigan.[27]

As in the case of her mother's various illnesses, it is tempting to speculate that there were psychological as well as physical reasons for Martha's failing health—an unhappy marriage, resentment over the burdens of her stepchildren, growing frustration about the lack of opportunity for self-fulfillment. As Barbara Berg has written, "Few women consciously expressed the wish to 'flee' or escape from a life they found unbearable, but thousands of nineteenth-century females fell victim to this particular form of psychoneurosis. Manifesting itself in disabling symptoms, this illness gave women no choice but to retreat from their daily routines."[28] One who did so was Harriet Beecher Stowe, who had undergone a crisis in her own life similar to Martha Maxwell's in the late 1840s. Partially paralyzed, she had left husband, children, and aged mother-in-law and entered a Vermont water-cure sanitarium, where she remained for a year. Only after Calvin Stowe apparently assured her that she could continue her writing did she return home; soon thereafter she wrote *Uncle Tom's Cabin.*[29]

Whether Martha and James would similarly resolve their difficulties remained to be seen. For the present, Martha sought help at the Western Health Reform Institute, later known as the world-famous Battle Creek Sanitarium, which had opened in September 1866 under the auspices of the Adventists. In the beginning, patients stayed in a two-story, frame cottage which soon was bursting at the seams with those seeking relief from health problems. By December 1866, for example, the institute's monthly publication, the *Health Reformer,* was reporting that patients had arrived from Canada, Vermont, Rhode Island, New York, Ohio, Indiana, Michigan, Illinois, Wisconsin, and Iowa.[30] The treatment given, emphasizing the popular "water cure" in which water was applied to the body by various means, called for patients to follow a diet of vegetables, grains, and fruits. "No Drugs whatever will be administered;" one advertisement further explained, "but only such means employed as Nature can best use in her recuperative work, such as Water, Air, Light, Heat, Food, Sleep, Rest, Recreation, &c."[31]

Given the beliefs that Martha and her mother Amy, a devout Adventist, had long espoused, the program at the institute would have been quite familiar and congenial to Martha's way of thinking. While she was in the Colorado gold fields, for example, she had attempted to carry out her "principles of diet" so far as she was able, inquiring at one time if her copy of the *Water-Cure Journal* had been delivered safely to her sisters at home.[32] As for Amy, she was a fervent believer in such regimens after her bouts of illness. "O how thankful I am for the health reform," she had exclaimed to Martha on one occasion in 1852.[33]

Martha remained at Battle Creek from September 1866 to the

spring of 1867.[34] Sometime during her stay, according to Mary, she took a job as a nurse-companion to a woman in order to earn money. By March 1867 she was able to inform her family that "my health is better now than when I last wrote, but I am able only to pay my way, and I know I don't do that all the time." The institute, she wrote, was "crowded to overflowing," but she was thoroughly enjoying the way of life; she told her family that if she could only send them some of the apples, peaches, cherries, plums, and other fruits in abundance there, "how happy I should be, and how healthy you would be the other things being eaquel."[35]

Yet if the sojourn at Battle Creek had been necessary for Martha's own well-being, it had also meant another lengthy separation from her daughter Mabel, now almost ten years old and well able to express her feelings. "I have written in my journal every day since you went a way," she told her mother not long after she left. "I hope you are well and like the place. It is very lonesome here without you I have to sleep all alone and we dont have any body to give baked russets to."[36] This letter certainly seems to indicate that Martha and Mabel had grown close again after Martha came back from Colorado; interestingly, in her memoir Mabel mentions nothing about Martha's stay at the institute and implies that her mother was absent from her life again during most of the 1860s when in fact she was not.[37] Two faded documents in the Maxwell Papers, the phrenological charts for Martha and Mabel prepared in Baraboo on January 7, 1865, by "Prof. C. S. Powers," testify further to the association of mother and daughter, as does a photograph taken of them about that time.[38]

In any event, Martha returned to Baraboo in the spring of 1867. By this time it had been almost five years since she had left her husband James in Colorado, a period during which she had begun her lifework in science, but in which she had been taxed almost beyond endurance by the care of her husband's family as well as her own daughter. Restored to health, still she made no move to rejoin James, who was becoming well established in Boulder. Instead, evidently having reached a personal crossroads

of sorts, she gathered up her daughter and left Baraboo for the
new settlement of Vineland, New Jersey.[39]

Established in 1861 in southern New Jersey, Vineland was, if
not precisely utopian, certainly a community based on idealistic
and visionary principles. The founder, C. K. Landis, had purchased a large tract of land on which he proposed to create a society of

> happy, prosperous, and beautiful homes; to first lay it
> out upon a plan conducive to beauty and convenience,
> and in order to secure its success, establish therein the
> best of schools, —different branches which experience
> has shown to be beneficial to mankind; also manufacto-
> ries, and different industries, and the churches of differ-
> ent denominations; in short, all things essential to the
> prosperity of mankind; but at the same time, under such
> provision for public adornment, and the moral protec-
> tion of the people, that the home of every man of
> reasonable industry might be made a sanctuary of
> happiness, and an abode of beauty, no matter how poor
> he might be. In fact, I desired to make Vineland a desir-
> able a place to live in by reason of its various privileges,
> and over all to throw such a halo of beauty as would
> make people loth to leave it, and if they did so, would
> draw them back again.[40]

To this end Landis designed a model townsite in the center of the
tract, featuring broad streets lined with double rows of shade
trees. Surrounding the town were small parcels of land of five to
fifty acres adapted to fruit culture.[41]

Founded on such principles, Vineland obviously had an immediate appeal to reformers of all sorts. Feminists especially
were drawn to the congenial atmosphere; Edward Everett Hale,
the noted author and Unitarian minister, was moved to comment
in 1869 that "Vineland is the only new place I ever visited where I
have found the greater part of the women satisfied."[42] Those active in the temperance movement also came to participate in the
experiment, for the community did not permit the sale of liquor.
The first Good Templars' lodge in New Jersey, in fact, was orga-

nized in Vineland in 1866. "Vineland became known in all parts of the country as a temperance town, and noted for its enterprise and moral sentiments," wrote one local historian in 1881. "The consequence was that thousands of the best people in other States selected it as their future residence, and settled here permanently."[43]

With Martha's interest in reform, particularly temperance and feminism, it is easy to see why she found the Vineland enterprise appealing, so off to New Jersey she went with Mabel. She purchased a five-acre lot, which in 1869 sold for $150 to $200, and enrolled her daughter in school.[44] Yet Martha's stay in Vineland was short-lived, for James, having apparently reached something of a crossroads himself, took matters into his own hands. According to Felger, who undoubtedly obtained the story from Mary, James asked Martha to return to Colorado; she refused, he went to Vineland, and she consented.[45] Thus it was that the *Baraboo Republic* on January 29, 1868, carried a small notice stating that James and Martha Maxwell were expected back in their own home from New Jersey.

What adjustments or concessions James had made are not known, but obviously he had been sufficiently persuasive to induce his wife to come home. Whether or not the rapprochement would last, however, remained in question. During the years that Martha had lived apart from James she had begun her life-work in natural history and taxidermy, despite the family pressures and problems that had in part caused her to enter the health institute at Battle Creek. Afterward, with her decision to emigrate with Mabel to the temperance community of Vineland, New Jersey, one senses that she had emerged from her time of trouble stronger, more resolute, and even more determined to act on her beliefs. The decision to return to James must have been difficult, one undoubtedly made only with assurances that she could continue the activities that gave meaning to her life. In any case, some sort of accommodation had been reached, and the Maxwells were ready to begin life as a family again for the first time in several years.

This portrait of Martha Maxwell was probably taken in 1865 in Baraboo. At that time Martha had been back in Wisconsin for about three years and had embarked on her lifework preparing mounted specimens for the Baraboo Collegiate Institute. Courtesy Mrs. E. Geoffrey Cullen, St. Louis, Missouri.

This photograph of Mabel Maxwell was probably made around 1866 or 1867. Note the impish gleam in her eye; she wrote later that she "bubbled over with high spirits and an invincible lightheartedness that my mother viewed with foreboding." Courtesy Mrs. E. Geoffrey Cullen, St. Louis, Missouri.

An 1867 view of Baraboo, Wisconsin, situated on the Baraboo River. Martha
moved here with her family in the late 1840s and left permanently for Colorado
early in 1868. Courtesy Sauk County Historical Society, Baraboo, Wisconsin.

This portrait of Mabel Maxwell at about eleven years of age (c.1868–69) is of interest not only as a graphic indication of the little girl's attitude toward her mother's work but also as a very early view of Martha's taxidermic accomplishments. One copy of the photograph is identified (probably by Mary Dartt Thompson) as depicting some of the birds that were sold to Shaw's Garden in 1870. Courtesy Colorado Historical Society, Denver.

Mary Dartt Thompson, photographed in Baraboo c. 1870. Many years later Martha's daughter wrote that "as the years passed, the affection which Martha bore for her sister Mary was probably the most important relationship in her life." Courtesy Mrs. E. Geoffrey Cullen, St. Louis, Missouri.

Looking west from Thirteenth and Pearl streets in Boulder, this view shows the Dabney-Macky block where Martha established her Rocky Mountain Museum in 1874. Courtesy Colorado Historical Society, Denver.

This unidentified, unmounted stereograph from the Maxwell Papers may depict some of the collection that was sold to Shaw's Garden in 1870. The two specimens on the center branch seem to be the same ones shown in the preceding portrait of Mabel. Courtesy Colorado Historical Society, Denver.

This view of Martha Maxwell's home and workroom on Boulder Creek was taken by Joseph B. "Rocky Mountain Joe" Sturtevant, a prolific artist and photographer who arrived in Boulder about 1876. Courtesy Parsons Collection, Boulder Historical Society, Boulder, Colorado.

Made of heavy brown-and-white-checked material, a hunting outfit that belonged to Martha Maxwell is now in the collections of the Boulder Historical Society. Courtesy Boulder Historical Society, Boulder, Colorado.

This photograph is one of the earliest showing Martha Maxwell with examples of her taxidermic work. Courtesy Western Historical Collections, University of Colorado, Boulder.

One of several views showing Martha Maxwell with her gun and dressed in her hunting costume, described in *On the Plains* as "a gymnastic suit of neutral tint and firm texture." Courtesy Colorado Historical Society, Denver.

James A. Maxwell, Martha's husband and the father of her daughter, Mabel, photographed in Chicago about 1868. Courtesy Mrs. E. Geoffrey Cullen, St. Louis, Missouri.

Robert Ridgway, shown here at the beginning of his career with the Smithsonian, collaborated with Martha Maxwell on several studies and prepared a catalog of the birds in her collection. Courtesy Smithsonian Photograph Collection, Record Unit 95, Smithsonian Archives, Washington, D.C.

Rocky Mountain Naturalist

Less than a month after they returned to Baraboo, the reunited Maxwell family—James, Martha, and Mabel—left Wisconsin for Colorado.[1] Eight years had elapsed since Martha had first set out for the gold fields, years in which she had discovered her strong interest in taxidermy and natural history. Once back in the Rockies she would lose no time continuing this interest, and the next period in her life was characterized by collecting excursions into the mountains coupled with arduous, backbreaking labor mounting the specimens she obtained. It also saw the beginning of her friendship and collaboration with scientists at the Smithsonian Institution. James, now most supportive, helped out with equanimity and good humor, although Mabel was not so understanding of her mother's work. During the next five years the rift between them deepened, even as Martha attained a measure of prominence for the birds and mammals she displayed in representations of their natural habitats.

On their way to a new beginning in Colorado, Martha and her family were able to take the train as far as Cheyenne, Wyoming, the closest station on the transcontinental line to Boulder and Denver. As Mabel recalled later, the trip was a "novel experience" for her, although her father was less enthusiastic. As noted earlier, James had made a number of trips by wagon across the plains, principally between Denver and Omaha, in the 1860s (fourteen by Mabel's count), and for him, she said, "the whole pleasure of travel was ended when the railroad came into being."[2] Accompanying the Maxwells on the trip was Martha's half-sister Mary Dartt, who had been teaching school at Catharine Beecher's Milwaukee Female College following her graduation from the Baraboo Collegiate Institute.[3]

Once the party reached Cheyenne they had no choice but to take a carriage to Boulder, as the Denver-Pacific Railroad, which would link Denver to the main line, would not be completed until 1870. Named for the boulders prevalent everywhere, Boulder had grown up at the mouth of Boulder Canyon following the nearby discoveries of gold early in 1859. Farther up into the mountains were little mining settlements such as Gold Hill, Ward, and Sunshine, while Central City and Black Hawk were just "over the range." Eastward stretched the fertile Boulder Valley, while towering above were the Flatirons, great slabs of sandstone jutting into the air and catching the morning sun. Soon after she arrived, Mary Dartt, like others before and since, tried to capture the beauty of the Boulder area in words. Telling readers of the *Baraboo Republic* of the "delightful climate" and "pure and bracing atmosphere," she concluded that "to any one who is fond of the beautiful and sublime in nature . . . no place could be more attractive."[4]

Yet, as elsewhere in Colorado, growth in Boulder during the 1860s had been slow; the railroad had not arrived, and by 1868 the problem of extracting gold from the difficult "refractory" ores was just beginning to be solved. Indian problems on the plains and the dislocations of the Civil War also had played a part in retarding settlement. Even the University of Colorado, which had been authorized in Boulder by the first territorial legislature in 1861, would not open its doors for classes until 1877. Nevertheless, there were those who had seen the possibilities in Boulder as a trading and mining supply center, among them James Maxwell and his son Jim. James had not established a permanent home, however, and soon after their arrival the family rented a two-room stone house on the main street, only a few doors from the building where Martha would one day open her Rocky Mountain Museum.[5]

Shortly after their arrival in Boulder the Maxwell family moved from the little stone house on Pearl Street to a house about a mile east of town belonging to an English family planning to spend the summer in England. For Martha and Mary the new dwelling "in the country" seemed much more desirable for, as Mary later noted, "Mrs. Maxwell and I wanted to be out of doors where she could study the animal life and get specimens to mount, and I could botanize."[6] Indeed, Martha's serious study of natural history and her increasingly single-minded devotion to her work began with her second residence in Colorado. "Having comparative leisure, she was inspired with a desire to make a collection of its fauna as being the most useful and practical way in which she could embody her new enthusiasm," Mary wrote in *On the Plains*. "It seemed especially desirable this work be done, from the fact that the strange and curious animals peculiar to its plains and mountains were rapidly disappearing."[7]

At first, Martha depended primarily on the boys in the neighborhood and also on her husband to obtain the specimens for her collection. Yet she soon discovered that she would have to go after the birds and mammals herself if she were to get all that she wanted, for, in Mary's words, "was there ever a boy that could be depended upon to be in sight at a critical moment!"[8] Thus she obtained a gun and began practicing her marksmanship. Although James teased her for aiming with her left eye, he saw that she soon became fully as proficient as he with the weapon. According to a story that assumed almost legendary proportions in the telling and retelling (although there is no reason to assume that it is not based on fact), this was not the first time that Martha had handled such a firearm. Much earlier, in Wisconsin, she had taken a gun belonging to Josiah Dartt and killed a rattlesnake that was threatening to strike at her sister Mary.[9]

In order to obtain her specimens, Martha and her family made many collecting trips into the mountains, one of the first being to the area of the Hot Springs in Middle Park in August 1868. The group, which consisted of James, Martha, and Mabel Maxwell, Mary Dartt, and an unspecified number of other travelers, had plenty of company, for Middle Park was teeming with explorers, politicians, writers, and various other excursionists during the latter part of that summer. For example, Maj. John Wesley Powell and his party had spent a second season collecting and observing in the area preparatory to attempting the descent of the Colorado River the next year. On August 20 the Major and a group that included *Rocky Mountain News* editor William N. Byers set out to mount an assault on Long's Peak and reached the summit three days later, apparently the first white men to accomplish the feat.[10] At the same time, a contingent of the party headed by Schuyler Colfax, then Speaker of the House of Representatives and the Republican vice-presidential nominee, was returning from a week's stay in Middle Park.[11] As the Maxwell group proceeded up Boulder Canyon to Rollinsville, they chanced upon some of the distinguished members, in Mary's words, "sitting around a camp fire in front of a little log cabin, smoking their evening cigars." They attempted to persuade Colfax and Illinois Lieutenant-Governor William Bross to favor them with political speeches, but the men declined, pleading fatigue despite their desire to accommodate the wishes of such charming company. Even this disappointment did not dampen Mary's enthusiasm for the trip; as she remarked in a letter published later in the *Baraboo Republic*, "we have had a gay time ever since we started."[12]

Within a few days they reached Middle Park, a beautiful high mountain valley approximately seventy miles long and thirty miles wide. Ringed by mountains and anchored by Berthoud Pass to the south, the park is bisected by the Grand (Colorado) River meandering from its headwaters in Grand Lake on the eastern edge. Hot sulphur springs, considered by the Utes to have magical medicinal properties, abound, and for years Byers nurtured dreams of a grand resort and spa in the park. The native inhabitants were continuing to live there in the summer of 1868, although they had signed a treaty in March giving up all their land east of the 107th meridian, well to the west of Middle Park, and the pressures to relocate were daily growing stronger as settlers discovered the economic potential in farming, mining, and otherwise exploiting the natural resources of western Colorado.

For Martha Maxwell, Middle Park was a fine laboratory for her researches. She and Mabel spent their time "clambering over the rocks in quest of berries, in pursuit of the shy birds and squirrels, who were their only companions, and in preserving the varied fruits of their rambles."[13] Using her gun to good advantage, Martha shot specimens of the little striped mountain chipmunks ("just lightnin' on legs," an old miner had remarked to them) and some tufted-eared squirrels and captured several varieties of birds.[14]

Collecting specimens on such trips was not without its difficulties, however. The frequent mountain showers often drenched clothing, sometimes more than once a day, and as Mary noted, getting up in the morning after such a chill required some determination. "Clothes damp, boots hard and stiff, frost a quarter of an inch thick on everything outside the tent, and no hope of warmth and breakfast, till, from under sheltering rocks and logs, enough fuel can be gathered for a fire."[15] Even some eighty years later, Mabel also remembered clearly how uncomfortable she was, and how much she hated it. "I have a vivid picture of a fat, reluctant child hustling in the morning into clothes that were damp and stiff, giving the merest pat of ice water to her face and hands before taking her tin plate of food, and shivering in the thin, cold mountain air while shoes, stiff and damp, scuffed over the frost-covered ground."[16]

Rain showers and icy mountain air were not the only unpleasant aspects of such excursions. In fact, it was on the return trip from Middle Park that a tragic accident was but narrowly averted, leaving Mabel with what must have been recurring nightmares for many months afterward. Going back to Boulder, it was arranged that Martha and Mabel would each ride their own ponies, leading a third horse behind them packed with baggage. Mabel's pony, however, which she described as "a vicious beast,"[17] persisted in biting her and the other horses, and so Martha decided to put Mabel behind her on her own horse and lead the troublesome pony; Mabel was instructed to hold onto the packhorse, no matter what. Descending a steep hill a few miles above Boulder, the packhorse refused to go on, and Mabel, still clinging to the halter, was jerked backward off her mother's horse, stopped only by a stone from going over the edge.

Remounting, Martha and Mabel continued along the treacherous road. By now it was growing dark and raining, the lightning and thunder making the descent even more dangerous. Martha dismounted and went on, leading all three horses. In *On the Plains*, Mary captured the terror of one moment in Boulder Canyon in fine Victorian prose. "Once the lightning revealed a scene that thrilled the terrified mother cold with horror," she wrote. "Mabel's horse had mistaken the road, and, ignorant of this, she was urging it with all her energy into the boiling, seething flood. One moment more and they would be swept under a bridge and be dashed against the dark, pitiless rocks. Mrs. Maxwell's whole being seemed voiced in the scream that reached her child just as she discovered her danger and turned from the threatened grasp of inevitable death."[18] Fortunately, a light appeared, revealing one of Martha's stepsons standing before them with a lantern. The ordeal, if not the fear, was over.

Safely back in Boulder, Martha turned her attention to preparing a display for the third annual exhibition of the Colorado Agricultural Society, held in Denver in late September and early October 1868. "The largest collection of Colorado birds we have ever seen is now on exhibition at the Fair Grounds," reported the *Rocky Mountain News*. "They were picked up by Mrs. Maxwell, of Boulder, within six months, count over one hundred different kinds, and are arranged on two large shrubs of cottonwood with a great deal of taste." The collection, which the *News* reported was "probably the greatest attraction in the room," was one "which not only does rare credit to the skill and scientific attainments of the lady who has placed them on exhibition, but which has added much to the appearance of the room, and to the interest of the fair."[19] Her entry in the fair represents the first time that she had shown her work in public (not counting the displays in the Baraboo Collegiate Institute), at least so far as the surviving records indicate, and thus the descriptions are of considerable interest, revealing as they do the already high level of her skill and ability as well as her general approach to mounting and display.

The judges who awarded the prizes concurred with the evaluation of the *News*, stating that "too much praise cannot be awarded the ornithologist who at great labor and expense prepared this interesting collection for exhibition at the Fair." Continuing with their report, they specifically drew attention to the lifelike qualities of the specimens, commenting that "the birds, ducklings and chicks [were] arranged in such natural position as almost to deceive the eye. There were over one hundred varieties represented, from a humming bird to the mountain eagle; from the young chicken to a large hawk, so appropriately placed that they looked as if in their native homes." Impressed, the judges recommended an award of fifty dollars and a diploma, the highest honor possible, to Martha "as a partial return for the interest this display added to the Fair."[20] Although Martha would refine and improve upon this first display at the Colorado Agricultural Society fair, the main elements of her work were already in place: the display of a number of attractive and well-crafted mounted specimens, arranged in a semblance of a natural and lifelike setting.

Yet even if her artistic tendencies were well formed, Martha also realized, despite her success at the fair, that if she were to be truly successful as a naturalist she required more advanced scientific training. On the one hand, Martha had attended two coeducational colleges, Oberlin and Lawrence; on the other, she had completed neither course, and much of her work had been at the preparatory level. Moreover, neither Oberlin nor Lawrence at the time had "a single stuffed bird or mammal," and botany, she felt, was "the only natural science of which she was given even a rudimentary idea."[21]

For Martha Maxwell, the study of botany had been particularly attractive, as it combined both her love of nature and the outdoors with the intellectual pursuit of a subject. On one occasion, for example, she reported a "very pleasant ramble" in the woods near Oberlin to gather wildflowers for her class, commenting at other times that she loved best "the handyworks of nature in there *wildest* forms" and was "very fond of wild, natural scenery."[22] As Almira Hart Lincoln (a sister of Emma Willard) wrote in her popular and often-reprinted *Familiar Lectures on Botany* (1829), "Botany is not a sedentary study which can be acquired in the library; but the objects of the science are scattered over the surface of the earth, along the banks of the winding brooks, or the borders of precipices, the sides of mountains, and the depths of the forest."[23]

Botany indeed was considered an especially suitable subject for women. "The study of Botany seems peculiarly adapted to females," wrote Lincoln; "the objects of its investigation are beautiful and delicate; its pursuit leading to exercise in the open air is conducive to health and cheerfulness."[24] Lincoln did not intend for women to become scientists in their own right, however, but to use their knowledge to enhance life in the home, her views thus reinforcing rather than challenging the domestic sphere.[25] In fact, women generally were encouraged to study all areas of science, from astronomy to zoology, mostly so that they could be better teachers and better wives and mothers. They found ample opportunities in the numerous academies and seminaries that dotted the landscape and in the lyceum lectures that reflected and contributed to the popular enthusiasm for science abounding in antebellum America.[26]

Against this context, then, it is necessary to separate perception from reality and to consider Martha Maxwell's educational background both objectively and as she viewed it. Here it is interesting to compare her with Graceanna Lewis, a Pennsylvania Quaker naturalist. Ten years Martha's senior, Graceanna had embarked on scientific study at least by 1860; between 1862 and 1869 she had had the opportunity to read in the library and study specimens in the museum of the Academy of Natural Sciences in Philadelphia under the direction of the curator of birds, John Cassin. "By 1869," writes her biographer, Deborah Warner, "she was truly the best educated woman naturalist in the United States."[27]

Martha, of course, had not had an opportunity for sustained study in such a renowned institution. She had attended college (as Graceanna did not) but did not graduate; a study has shown, however, that only fifty-one percent of the male scientists active in the period 1800–1863 had a degree.[28] She did have the example and encouragement of her stepfather, Josiah Dartt, and she had later worked with Professor Hobart at the Baraboo Collegiate Institute. But even if she had had "more than ordinary educational advantages," certainly overall her background could not have equaled that of Graceanna Lewis. More to the point, Martha herself felt that "there was much to regret in this respect."[29] All in all, it was clear, at least in her mind, that she was not prepared for her self-appointed task. Thus, early in 1869, she penned a letter to the Secretary of the Smithsonian Institution in Washington, D.C.:

> Will you please tell me what textbooks upon Ornithology you use in your Inst. where they may be obtained, and their cost.
>
> I am making a collection of Colorado specimens, have something over a hundred different varieties, among them are some which seem new and strange, at least I am unable to classify them with my present light upon the subject. Is the report of your Institute upon Natural History to be obtained, and at what price? Have you all the specimens of the fauna of this Ter. that you desire, or would you like to employ a person, who can bring good references as a workman in the business, to secure specimens for you?[30]

Back came a response from Secretary Joseph Henry, informing her that the "only textbook that will serve your purpose as to the birds of Colorado" was a volume of the *Pacific Railroad Reports*, referring to the report prepared some ten years earlier by Assistant Secretary Spencer Baird. Bringing together information gathered by the parties that had surveyed various proposed railroad routes in the 1850s, the report was, as Baird pointed out in the preface, "an exposition of the present state of our knowledge of the birds of North America, north of Mexico."[31] A subsequent edition published by Lippincott in 1860, although virtually identical to the 1858 edition, featured additional bibliographical notes and some new plates. According to one advertisement, it was "the especial object of the authors and publishers to adapt it to the wants of the student and lover of nature, and to present in condensed form, and at a price within the reach of all, a reliable text-book in this favorite department of natural history."[32]

However, Henry went on, "If there are any birds in your collection that you cannot identify, and will send them to us by mail, Prof. Baird will determine them for you."[33] With this exchange of letters, Martha Maxwell thus opened up a dialogue and a line of communication with the country's premier center of scientific study. In the years to come her ties with the institution, and especially her relationship with ornithologist Robert Ridgway and, to a somewhat lesser extent, with Baird, would prove to be among the most rewarding aspects of her professional life.

From the time of her arrival in Colorado in 1868 through most of 1870, Martha continued to expand her collection of native birds and mammals. In addition to making excursions into the nearby mountains, she and James, often with Mary and Mabel in tow, also went northward into Wyoming to collect. On one occasion (probably in the fall of 1869), the family joined with that of a professional hunter in Cheyenne and decided to journey to the Black Hills in search of game. Although the trip was not as productive as they had hoped initially, Martha did manage to obtain an antelope; according to the story as told in *On the Plains*, she and two boys from the party saw a large herd feeding near a lake. Martha crept closer and closer, but still the antelope did not flee. "The secret was soon discovered. Upon the end of her ramrod fluttered a piece of bright red cloth. This was held above her as she crept forward, to excite their curiosity. In their efforts to determine what it could be, danger was forgotten; and she was within easy range when the report of her fire rang out, and a fine buck fell struggling in the grass."[34]

Apparently Martha was quickly gaining a reputation as a good taxidermist, for by 1870 she was mounting specimens for others as well as enlarging her own collection.[35] In part, at least, she seems to have undertaken such work for financial reasons. Initially James Maxwell was successful in his various business ventures, and by early 1869 the family had been able to move into a new brick home of their own. As had happened in the past, however, James again had had misfortune, perhaps partially as a result of his trusting nature. Mabel, for example, wrote later that the Methodist minister "cheated him out of nearly everything he owned," although Mary, with Victorian reticence, only referred to the Maxwells' "bad luck." At any rate, they had to move out of their new house, and Martha had to take whatever work came along as much for money as for love.[36] It was not easy; in fact, on one occasion, writing from Laramie, she confided to Mary, "I am so sick & tired of this kind of life that nothing but shere necessity induses me to stay a single day."[37]

The necessity of raising money also induced her, in 1870, to sell the collection that she had acquired at such cost. That fall she had again displayed her specimens at the Colorado Agricultural Society fair, where they had attracted the same attention and acclaim as in 1868. Reportedly, the exhibit included some six hundred specimens, "wild cats, wolves, foxes, deer, antelope, weasels, squirrels, badgers, a dozen varieties of eagles and hawks, grouse of several species, and in short, nearly every beast and bird of this country, with many of the reptiles," said one reporter.[38] For her work she was awarded two ten-dollar premiums, one for "stuffed birds and animals," the other for "stuffed reptiles, &c."[39]

Because of her success and prominence, Martha had been promised by some of the "leading men in the Territory" that if she showed her collection in Denver, they would pay for her to transport it to a fair in St. Louis.[40] Once there, she decided that because of the reversal of the family fortunes, she would sell it to Shaw's Garden, now the Missouri Botanical Garden. Modeled to some degree on the famous Kew Gardens in England, the institution, which included a library and museum, had been developed beginning in the 1850s by wealthy retired merchant Henry Shaw, a native of England.[41] According to the records of the garden, Martha was paid six hundred dollars for the specimens, "a sum," Mary noted in *On the Plains*, "insignificant compared with their cost to her."[42] Indeed, it was exceedingly difficult for Martha to part with the collection, for "so great was her attachment to her specimens, so enthusiastic had been her desire that each one should be of permanent good to natural history, that it was with the bitterest pain she thought of their disposal."[43] Nonetheless, little else could be done. The collection was sold, and it remained on display in the museum building at Shaw's Garden until sometime after Shaw's death in 1889. At that time, the specimens were found to be so damaged by insects and in such need of repair that they were stored and forgotten. By 1906, when University of Colorado Museum Curator Junius Henderson inquired about the collection, he was told that it was "in such condition now that it is of little value. . . ."[44] Thus, like Martha's later work, the specimens that were collected and mounted with such devotion ultimately were lost, having survived neither in the institution to which they had been entrusted nor in the fading memories of those who had seen them.

Some good, however, did result from the sale, for with the money the Maxwells were able to have a home of their own again. Martha bought a tract of land at the mouth of Boulder Canyon, and James moved to the site a house that had been next to his lumber mill farther up the canyon.[45] By this time Martha's other half-sister, Sarah Elizabeth, or Lizzie, as she was now generally known, had joined the group in Boulder, having arrived in the late summer of 1868.[46] Also a teacher, she had taught for a time in Central City, where she had met the dashing young mining engineer and surveyor Hal Sayre, a Fifty-niner and veteran of Sand Creek.[47] They made a handsome couple—Lizzie, said Mabel, "was beautiful, with the most perfect profile I ever saw, blue-black hair, hazel eyes, and vivid coloring"—and before long they married, on May 11, 1870.[48]

The minister who married Lizzie and Hal, Nathan Thompson of Boulder, was himself a member of the family, having married Martha Maxwell's other half-sister, Mary, on New Year's Day, 1870.[49] Born in 1837 and a graduate of Amherst College and Andover Theological Seminary in his native Massachusetts, Thompson had come to Colorado in 1865 under the auspices of the American Home Missionary Society to serve as the pastor of the Congregational church that had been organized a few miles east of Boulder in 1864. The next year services were moved to Boulder, and Thompson had spearheaded efforts to build a new brick church for the congregation.[50]

With her two half-sisters married, and having disposed of her mounted specimens in St. Louis, Martha was ready for a new challenge. Displaying the "hang-on-it-iveness" that she had once characterized as one of her traits, she started almost immediately on another collection with the duplicate skins still on hand.[51] "She was up early and late, and to say that her time was 'more than occupied,' does not express it!" wrote Mary in *On the Plains.* "Society was ignored, all superfluous articles of food and dress were dispensed with, and the large margin of time which such things demand was used, with the closest and most rigid economy in the furtherance of her plan."[52] Mabel later saw the Shaw's Garden sale as a real turning point in her mother's life. After the transaction, Mabel related, Martha "regarded taxidermy as a profession rather than a mere hobby, however engrossing it may have been, and from this time on it seemed to me that she was never at home, or if she was, that she was busy in what we called her den."[53] Or, as Mary neatly summed it up in *On the Plains*, "*Taxidermy, as a fine art, subservient to science,* became the work of her life."[54]

The setting for this work, as Mabel indicated, was the little "den" on Boulder Creek near the Maxwell house. As Mary pointed out later, the location was "an admirable one for a naturalist, as it was visited by animals from both the mountain ranges and the plains."[55] The work-house, or den, had been built especially for her, "and what a curiosity-shop it soon became!" she exclaimed.

> Wire, hemp, cotton, and hay; clay, salt, plaster, and alum; mosses, grasses, and branches of trees; bars of iron, and blocks of wood; palette, brushes, putty, and paints; nests and eggs of birds, and fresh-water shells; bottles of insects, and reptiles, glass eyes, and tools; fossils, minerals, and bones of beasts; heads and horns of buffalo, antelope, and mountain sheep; birds' skins, heads and antlers of deer and elk; guns and ammunition; in fact, something of almost every created thing that she could get in all stages of transformation and preservation![56]

How did she do it? Although little information is available, it is possible to reconstruct to some degree the procedures involved in Martha's taxidermic work from descriptions in *On the Plains* and from references scattered through various interviews and articles. For example, here is how she prepared the antelope skin obtained on the hunting expedition described earlier:

> The afternoon was passed by Mrs. Maxwell in skinning her trophy and in taking measurements of it, to assist her in building up the artificial body over which the skin was to be placed.
> Of these measurements, in large animals, from

fifteen to twenty were needed, and, aside from the length and the height, it was desirable to take them from the body after the removal of the skin. This work, together with the cleaning of such bones as it was important to preserve, was neither easy nor agreeable, but she always preferred doing it herself, as it gave her the opportunity of studying the shape and disposition of prominent muscles, etc. She considered a knowledge of the anatomy of an animal as essential in taxidermy, as in sculpture, to the finest artistic effect.[57]

As indicated, after skinning and measuring the animal, the next step was to construct a model or mannequin over which to stretch and fit the skin. Early in her taxidermic work Martha apparently used molds made of plaster of paris or clay, later developing an iron framework that was then covered by hay or various other materials. One reporter at the Centennial described the process as follows: "Instead of . . . preparing the skins by sewing them up and stuffing them, she engaged a blacksmith, who, under her direction, made light iron skeletons, which she covered over with wool, cotton or other materials, to simulate flesh, and over this body sewed the skin, using only the leg bones of the animal."[58]

Martha was thus using procedures in the late 1860s and early 1870s that were similar in principle to those that William Hornaday, the most celebrated taxidermist of the late nineteenth century, would develop a few years later. What is noteworthy about Martha's work is not the fact that a *woman* was mounting a variety of animals, large and small, but that *anyone* was employing such relatively sophisticated techniques in an isolated settlement at the edge of the Rocky Mountains in Colorado Territory. The center for taxidermic work at the time in the United States was Ward's Natural Science Establishment, founded in Rochester, New York, in the 1860s by merchant-entrepreneur Henry Ward, a one-time University of Rochester professor. Ward's dealt in natural history specimens and museum displays and served as well as the preeminent training ground for young taxidermists.[59] Yet when the eighteen-year-old Hornaday arrived in Rochester in 1873 as an apprentice, he found the taxidermists there still stuffing animal skins with straw. As Hornaday's recent biographer observes, "taxidermy was still in a primitive state when young Hornaday began his work at the Establishment, even though the best taxidermy in the United States was performed there."[60] After completing a series of worldwide collecting expeditions beginning in 1874, he returned to Ward's and by 1879 developed his technique of mounting lifelike specimens on clay-covered mannequins.[61]

No evidence has been found to indicate that Martha knew of Ward's Natural Science Establishment, nor that she had any assistance in learning how to mount animals and birds, save the knowledge she gained from examining the specimens of the German taxidermist and the help she obtained in Baraboo in the early 1860s. Her procedures, in fact, seem to have developed through a combination of trial and error, augmented by observations in the field and enhanced by her innate artistic tendencies.[62] Nor is there any indication that Hornaday knew of her work. For example, in an article published in 1922, Hornaday asserted that in 1879 "there were in America a few very good bird taxidermists, but no amount of bush-beating could scare out even one good mammal mounter."[63] Yet certainly the two were kindred spirits in many respects, and in his classic book *Taxidermy and Zoological Collecting*, first published in 1891, Hornaday would emphasize the attributes desirable in a taxidermist that Martha exemplified. "The ideal taxidermist," he wrote, "must be a combination of modeller and anatomist, naturalist, carpenter, blacksmith, and painter. He must have the eye of an artist, the back of a hodcarrier, the touch of a wood-chopper one day, and of an engraver the next." Recommending the cultivation of a "delicate and artistic touch," Hornaday concluded with the following advice:

> Do not leave a specimen looking as if a coal-heaver had
> finished it. Work at it, and keep on working at it until it
> is perfect; and then go back to it the next day, and work
> at it some more! There is no inferno too deep or too hot
> for a slovenly, slatternly taxidermist. The fault with
> such workers usually lies not so much in their lack of
> skill as in their lack of patience and the dogged stick-to-
> itiveness that conquers all difficulties, no matter

whether they come singly, in platoons, or by divisions.[64]

Without question a good deal of hard, unpleasant work was involved in mounting specimens. For example, consider Martha's attempts to deal with a turkey buzzard that was in an advanced state of decomposition when she received it. Although she took it to the creek bank, the odor still reached the house some distance away. Both Mary and Mabel urged her to give up the task, "but they counselled in vain. Too sick to endure its presence a moment longer, she would retreat for a while; but as soon as it was possible to summon the strength and resolution, go to work again."[65] It was at least a week until her appetite returned, and longer yet before the bird could be placed with the rest of her collection.

That collection soon filled the rooms of the Boulder house, and by October of 1871, less than a year after she had sold her collection to Shaw's Garden, Martha had an exhibit ready for the Boulder County Agricultural Society fair. In addition to squirrels, rabbits, weasels, snakes, and various birds, the display featured "a black bear, full grown, and represented as in life, skillfully prepared in perfect natural appearance; a young grizzly bear, two years old, and yet standing six and a half feet high. . . ." All were arranged, said a reporter describing the scene, "in tree and bush, as if [in] their native haunts."[66] For her efforts Martha was awarded a diploma for the "Best Collection Stuffed Birds Reptiles and Animals," as well as several "premiums" donated by patrons of the fair, including a shawl from a local merchant.[67] The week after the fair closed the Boulder newspaper carried Martha's card of thanks, along with her assurance that "any specimens in Natural History will be thankfully received and prepared for the inspection of donors" at the next county fair.[68]

During the early 1870s Martha also continued to make excursions into the mountains, often accompanied by her husband as well as friends and acquaintances. On these trips, as earlier, she was usually attired in a costume described in *On the Plains* as "a gymnastic suit of neutral tint and firm texture."[69] Consisting of a pair of bloomer-like or "Turkish" trousers with a medium-length overskirt, the dress bore a strong resemblance to the garment advocated by those active in the dress-reform movement. Beginning with Amelia Bloomer's much-maligned outfit of the late 1840s and early 1850s, the wearing of such a costume became a central tenet among feminists who saw it as both more convenient and healthful (no corsets, bodices, hoops, or long skirts to trail in the mud) and as a way to free women from the "tyranny of fashion." Martha had seen some of the "Turkish costumes" in 1851 at Oberlin, and similar dresses had been adopted for use at the Western Health Reform Institute where she had been a patient in the mid-1860s.[70] Notwithstanding the health-reform and feminist implications of the dress, however, such a costume obviously was practical for traveling and for mountain excursions. Julia Archibald Holmes, for example, had worn a similar outfit while crossing the Kansas plains in 1858 en route to her successful ascent of Pikes Peak and had found it to be "beyond value in comfort and convenience."[71] And as that intrepid English traveler Isabella Bird, who came to Colorado in 1873, explained about her similar "Hawaiian riding dress," it was "the 'American Lady's Mountain Dress,' a half-fitting jacket, a skirt reaching to the ankles, and full Turkish trousers gathered into frills falling over the boots, — a thoroughly serviceable and feminine costume for mountaineering and other rough traveling, as in the Alps or any other part of the world."[72]

A number of the Maxwell excursions both in the mountains and on the plains are described in *On the Plains*. Interspersed with romantic descriptions of the scenery and dialogue on the order of "Red-hot demons! there's a *snake* in this hole!"[73] are examples of Martha's proficiency and her determination to capture whatever it was she was after. "The sight of a new specimen always affected her, as the smell of alcohol is said to affect an inebriate," Mary wrote, "and she would sacrifice any amount of personal comfort, and put forth any degree of extra effort to obtain and preserve it."[74]

For instance, once Martha spied a hawk's nest at the top of a tree. "Oh, dear! must I give up that nest?" said Martha to her husband. "I don't want to, if it can possibly be helped," he replied. Although they had no ladder, Martha had an idea. She could stand on James's shoulders. He agreed and lifted her upward.

"There, how is that?" he asked as he picked her up.

"All right, thanks; only I wish you were a little tall-er," she replied, "I can only just touch the limb. Could you possibly stand on tip-toe? That's it! Hold your neck stiff now!" and putting one foot on his head, she braced the other against the inequalities of the bark and drew herself up among the branches.

"Oh! this is splendid!" she called down from among the leaves. "Now, you'll be sure to take care of the old bird! I want her, you know."

With Martha up in the tree, James went to the wagon for his gun, returning to shoot the mother hawk so Martha could gather a baby hawk and an unhatched egg. Eventually both birds were stuffed and placed in a nest like that they had first occupied, "with their little mouths open and their necks stretched up toward their mother, which, with a rabbit in her talons, was suspended over them."[75]

James Maxwell, in fact, as this portrayal indicates, seems to have been most genial and very understanding of his wife's obsession during these early collecting trips. In 1870 he and his son Jim had dissolved their business partnership, and since that time, as one biographical account put it, he had been "leading a retired life."[76] Although he took part in some civic activities (he was an officer in the Good Templars in 1870 and "President of the Day" at the 1871 Fourth of July celebration),[77] he had a good deal of time to give to Martha's work, and he was apparently exceptionally even-tempered and supportive about it in the beginning. In 1873, for example, he bought her a "No. 14 double barreled English gun" for twenty-five dollars.[78] And whatever the reality of the Maxwells' marital relationship, Mary and Martha chose to depict him in *On the Plains* as a man whose "vigor of body and equanimity of mind were seldom disturbed. If the weather was disagreeable and the roads almost impassable, he was jolly and smiling. If the team grew fractious and the harness broke—no uncommon event—he whistled, talked to the beasts, and 'tinkered the gearing. . . .' "[79] Similarly, Mabel characterized her father as having "one of the most wonderful dispositions I ever knew. . . . He had a gift for serene acceptance."[80] Indeed, even

Martha's obituary in a Boulder newspaper spoke of James's "indulgent and royal nature, inclined to afford her delight in art all facilities in his power."[81]

As has been shown earlier, however, daughter Mabel usually was far less supportive. She not only hated camping, but she also resented the time that her mother's work demanded. A lifetime later, she vividly remembered her attitude toward the specimens that Martha labored over, convinced that her mother loved them more than she did her. "Interesting as the results were," she wrote in her autobiography, "I recall clearly my own reaction. I was bitterly jealous of the animals that seemed to absorb all the interest and affection for which I longed."[82] Characterizing herself as "a small, fat child, hungry for love, longing for reassurance," Mabel was certain that "for some reason, inherent in her nature, my mother excluded me from the deep love which she had for all living things."[83]

To hear Mabel tell it, and one must keep in mind that she was writing her account when she was almost ninety years old, her childhood after the family moved to Boulder was one in which Martha neglected virtually all household and motherly duties in favor of her work. Undoubtedly exaggerated, probably overdramatized, Mabel's recollections are nonetheless chilling in their clarity. For example, Mabel remembered that when her mother was away on hunting trips without James, she endeavored to keep house for her father, with decidedly mixed results. "How I did it I can't imagine; my mother was not at all domestic and there was no one to teach me. If my father had not been the most amiable of men I do not believe he could have stood it."[84] In addition, Mabel related, she also had to make her own clothes. "I would walk into Boulder, buy a piece of calico, hack it out in some crude fashion, and sew it up. It must have looked awful but at least the dress covered me. Anyhow there was no choice. I either had to devise a dress for myself or go naked."[85]

Mabel's feelings, however, which she probably made no secret of at the time, did not deter Martha from her work of collecting and mounting birds and mammals and of learning more about them. It must be remembered, too, that Martha always felt that she was working as much for the future well-being of her daughter as she was for herself, whether or not Mabel recognized or accepted the means by which this would be accomplished. She continued to write to the Smithsonian, and in order to augment the collection and provide a source of remuneration, she took pains to acquire duplicate skins which could be sold or exchanged.[86]

By early 1873, however, Martha had come to another crossroads. In the years after the sale to Shaw's Garden the number of her specimens had grown so large that the little house and den at the mouth of Boulder Canyon could no longer contain them. Also, the Maxwell finances were still in sorry shape, as usual, and as Mary put it in *On the Plains*, "it was evident, unless her work could be made self-sustaining, much of it must be disposed of, and further work in that direction resolutely abandoned."[87] The fact that Mabel would be ready for college the next year made the financial situation even more acute. The choice was clear; either Martha must go forward with her work on a more businesslike basis, or she must give it up. In reality, of course, there was no choice, for Martha could no more have given up her lifework than she could life itself. Ultimately, the solution to her dilemma was equally clear: she would open a museum.

Thus in just a few years Martha Maxwell had both furthered and deepened her interest in taxidermy and natural history. Working with single-minded determination, she collected her specimens, used every means at her command to learn more about them, perfected her taxidermic techniques, and presented the fruits of her labor in public displays and exhibitions. By early 1873 she was ready to expand her horizons and continue working on an even higher level as she struggled to do what she thought best for her daughter and herself. That Mabel did not share Martha's commitment, however, was becoming obvious, and in time her private anguish formed a poignant counterpoint to her mother's public success.

Opening the Rocky Mountain Museum

As Martha Maxwell planned her museum, she began to envision precisely what she hoped to accomplish by opening it. First and foremost, it would be truly a scientific institution, ultimately "a kind of academy of science, perhaps an adjunct to the State university located in this place," she told Spencer Baird in the spring of 1874.[1] Further elaborating on this point in *On the Plains*, published a few years later, Mary Dartt wrote that Martha's "observations of the differences made in animal life, by climate and surroundings, had long made her wish for some museum, which, from its arrangement and classification, should enable them to be studied with greater ease and accuracy than was then possible." If she were to establish a museum to demonstrate what she had seen, she might make a contribution to scientific knowledge.[2]

Moreover, with her strong interest in learning, Martha hoped that the museum exhibits, "if artistically mounted and arranged, would interest the young, and awaken in them a love for a culture within the reach of all, in its nature wholesome and refining." Those particularly concerned with higher education, she thought, might support her plan. Finally, the museum would present "curiosities" principally for their amusement value, hoping thus to draw in members of the general public, perhaps otherwise uninterested in the exhibits, who by buying tickets would help contribute revenues to support the scientific and educational work. Yet all must be appealing in order both to educate and to entertain.[3]

Martha's conception of a museum that would be at once scientific, educational, and popular was remarkably sophisticated, particularly considering the time period and the geographical area in which she developed it. Her ideas placed her in the vanguard of museum philosophy in the 1870s, although there is no evidence that she drew upon or was influenced by what was happening elsewhere in the country. And even in the East, the movement that would see the development of large natural history museums and similar multifaceted institutions was in its infancy; the American Museum of Natural History, for example, had been chartered only a few years before, in 1869 (the cornerstone for the building on Central Park West was laid in 1874), and the United States National Museum building in Washington would not be completed until 1881.[4] George Brown Goode, the undisputed master of museum theory and management in the late nineteenth century, was just beginning his career in 1873 at the Smithsonian Institution under the tutelage of Spencer Baird. Eight years later, as assistant director of the National Museum, he would issue a document listing three functions of the museum. It should be, he wrote, a museum of record, a museum of research, and an educational museum "of the broadest type," with "descriptive labels adapted to the popular mind."[5]

There is also no indication that Martha knew of Charles Willson Peale's famous museum which had opened in Philadelphia in 1786 and existed until the mid-nineteenth century, albeit in decline after Peale's death in 1827. Featuring scientifically accurate exhibits, the museum also reflected Peale's desire to educate the public by offering published catalogs and lectures and other activities. "Far ahead of its time," writes Charles Coleman Sellers in *Mr. Peale's Museum*, "it had the triple function of a modern museum of science: actual specimens were systematically arranged and documented, research was fostered, and, above all, the 'diffusion of knowledge' was promoted by a happy process formerly known as 'rational amusement'—enjoyment while learning."[6] Thus Martha Maxwell, although she probably did not realize it, was developing a museum based on principles similar to those advocated by some of the most innovative and farsighted masters in the field. Her "Rocky Mountain Museum" would serve science and learning through exhibits that would both inform and entertain.

Now that she had decided to proceed with the museum, Martha began to work harder than ever making preparations for the opening. More collecting trips were necessary, and this time excursions were made on the plains southeast of Boulder as well as in the mountains. Her aim, as explained in *On the Plains*, was "to collect specimens of everything needful to a complete representation of the natural productions of Colorado." The trips netted snakes, skunks, ptarmigans, and "a number of varieties of petrified wood, shells, Indian curiosities, etc." as well as various adventures.[7]

In addition, Martha had decided that displays of "foreign curiosities" would be needed to attract the audience necessary for the museum to succeed. These, she concluded, should be obtained on the Pacific Coast, as she thought they would seem more exotic and appealing to the population of Colorado, which came mostly from the East and the South. Thus it was that in August of 1873, with a ticket given her by a friend, Martha set out for San Francisco on the train. With her was her sister Lizzie, traveling with her new baby Ethel; she would be joined later by her husband Hal Sayre. James Maxwell and Mabel, then entering her last year of high school, stayed at home in Boulder.[8]

By early September Martha was settled in San Francisco and was ready to begin the task of obtaining items for the museum. Not confining her search only to the city, within a month she visited the Giant Sequoia in the area now known as Calaveras Big Trees State Park. Staying in the famed Mammoth Grove Hotel, she thought that the region more than lived up to its reputation as a tourist attraction. "There is no humbug about this place," she wrote her family. "The mammoth trees are all they are said to be, and the magnificent grove over which they reign, is among the finest in the world 'tis said." Walking alone among the huge sequoia, which sometimes reached three hundred feet in height, she found to be almost a spiritual experience, one so profound that she had difficulty putting it into words. "It is to me the most enchanting place I ever visited and for once my intense love and longing for a dense, deep, dark forest, was fully gratified, not however until I had visited it alone by moon light, and no language can describe the *magnificence* of that *solitude*."[9]

Obviously pleasurable, the trip to the Big Trees was also productive in terms of acquiring objects for the museum. For example, John Perry, one of the proprietors of the hotel, gave her a section of bark and some wood from the famous tree known as the "Old Father." (Many of the trees in the grove had been given names such as "U. S. Grant" or "Longfellow"; one that was on the ground, which probably had stood some 450 feet high, was called "The Father of the Forest.") Only the size of her hotel bill (she told her family that all hotels in California "belong to the 'gross beak' family") prompted her to limit her stay to two nights. There were so many birds and squirrels she was anxious to obtain—if only she and James were camping out, she could have remained in that idyllic setting much longer.[10]

As it was, Martha returned to the city. She evidently spent a good deal of time at Woodward's Gardens, located on Mission Street not far from her lodgings. Developed in the late 1860s by hotel operator Robert Woodward and billed as "the Central Park of the Pacific, Embracing a Marine Aquarium, Museum, Art Galleries, Conservatories, Menagerie, Whale Pond, Amphitheatre & Skating Rink," the gardens by the early 1870s were one of San Francisco's premier attractions for residents and visitors alike. "The Eden of the West!," trumpeted its advertisements. "Unequaled & Unrivaled on the American Continent/Nature, Art and Science Illustrated."[11]

Martha was able to take full advantage of the resources of the institution through the kindness of the curator of the gardens, the Saxon-born taxidermist Ferdinand Gruber.[12] In fact, some of the ideas that she later implemented in her own museum evidently grew out of her observations at Woodward's Gardens, which advertised its aims as "education, recreation, and amusement," similar to those that Martha hoped to accomplish.[13] Notwithstanding its Barnum-like popular qualities, the gardens had achieved a respectable scientific reputation; in 1871, for example, Smithsonian Secretary Joseph Henry had termed the specimens "generally well classified and properly labeled."[14]

Gruber also introduced Martha to colleagues such as D. S. Bryant, an avid collector and taxidermist described in *On the Plains* as "a wealthy merchant of ornithological tastes."[15] Born in Cambridge, Massachusetts, in 1823, Bryant had arrived in San Francisco via Cape Horn in 1850. He engaged in the cattle and grain businesses, all the while avidly pursuing his hobby of hunting and mounting natural history specimens.[16]

Martha also met the famed West Coast naturalist James Graham Cooper, author of *The Natural History of Washington Territory* (1859) and a prodigious collector up and down the coast, particularly in the fields of conchology and ornithology. During the last half of 1873 Cooper was living in San Francisco while making various excursions into the surrounding area, and he and Martha apparently moved in the same circles for a time.[17]

Thus the months in San Francisco passed happily and profitably for Martha, while James and Mabel tried to manage on the home front. James, in fact, had even done some collecting on his own, including making another trip into Middle Park, then going south around Colorado Springs and into South Park.[18] As for Mabel, now growing into young womanhood, she was beginning to show signs of enjoying the active social life that would so distress her mother in later years. "May is doing finely in her Studies," James informed Martha on November 10. "Attends Singing School two nights in the week, lodge one, Church one, and complains because I restrain her from attending parties & sociables pretty much all the evenings left in the week."[19] Although James may have found it difficult at times to cope with his spirited young daughter, the task was probably made easier by the fact that Mabel's beloved grandmother, Amy Dartt, and Josiah Dartt had by this time followed the rest of the family to Colorado and were also living in Boulder.[20]

By the end of 1873 Martha was preparing to return home with her treasures. Like most collectors, she had trouble turning anything down, and by the time she was finished, her acquisitions ranged from Japanese teaware to coins to a shark's jaw.[21] Yet just as she was ready to leave she saw something else that she had to have—a suit of ancient armor. Even though she had no money left, Martha was determined to acquire it for the museum. Trading in her railroad ticket for fare on a lower-priced "emigrant train," she endured an uncomfortable ride back to Colorado—but she had the armor.[22]

Once back in Colorado, Martha set about acquiring additional items such as mineral specimens for the museum. To assist with this work she hired a man named John W. Glass. Very little is known about Glass either before or after his association with Martha Maxwell. In 1867 he had furnished some information about his background in a letter to the president of the Academy of Natural Sciences of Philadelphia, written from Cincinnati, Ohio, in his distinctive, slanted hand. At that time, he stated, he had a collection of "minerals, fossils, curiosities, antiquities, jewels, & Indian rellicks, collected during the past sixteen years in California, and other places on the Pacific Coast." He wished to dispose of these materials before returning to California and asked if the Academy would be interested in purchasing them. If such an agreement were concluded, Glass would then send additional specimens to the institution "from whatever country I may find them." The Academy has no further information on Glass, however, and efforts to trace him in California have so far proved unproductive.[23] By 1872 he was apparently in the Colorado area, as the *Rocky Mountain News* on July 21 carried a brief mention of a "prospecting tour" in southern Colorado, New Mexico, and Arizona by Glass and some seventeen other men.[24]

In any event, by early 1874 Glass was working for Martha Maxwell, and the Boulder newspaper encouraged all to cooperate with him when he visited the mines, commenting that although "collections of cabinet specimens have become a burden in some localities," the assistance of the miners would not only benefit Martha Maxwell, "who is herself public spirited," but more importantly, the success of her enterprise would be "the best advertisement of the county."[25] Glass made a collecting trip into the mountains in February, and by February 20 he was able to inform Martha that he was shipping 920 pounds of minerals to her.[26]

In addition to collecting for the museum, Martha also continued to study the natural history specimens that formed the heart of her work. However, as her knowledge increased, so did the complexity of the problems she faced, and once again she turned to her friends at the Smithsonian Institution for help. As she later remarked to Spencer Baird, "I am so far 'out of the world' that it is difficult getting textbooks upon any branch of Science or Natural History, and any assistance in this direction will be gratfully remembered."[27]

As with countless other serious but untrained collectors around the country, Baird did what he could to help. If she would let him know what books she had on natural history, he wrote, he would try to send such others as the Smithsonian could spare, upon payment of the shipping expenses.[28] Martha responded that the only reference books she had were her copies of *Birds of North America*, which she thought "invaluable," and Cooper's *Natural History of Washington Territory*. What she particularly needed, she told him, was "any work giving the deffinitions of scientific terms. Webster's Unabridged is my only assistant in my perplexing research in this direction, and it frequently fails to meet my demands."[29]

Martha was frustrated also by her attempts to comprehend on her own the available texts. "Pardon me, but I sometimes think that writers upon natural history forget that many of the most ardent lovers of Nature, are unfortunately without a classical education," she commented to Baird, "and consequently their books, without an accompany[ing] vocabulary, instead of opening up a highway to the uncharted world in which they revil, permit barriors, which only the most determined and persistent effort can remove."[30]

In response to Martha's request for help with terminology, Baird referred her to the "Glossary of Technical Terms used in Descriptive Ornithology" by Elliott Coues, one of the most prominent ornithologists of the day and the author of the highly original *Key to North American Birds* which had come out in 1872.[31] Coues's "Glossary" had just been published in Baird's *History of North American Birds*, coauthored with T. M. Brewer and Robert Ridgway. Issued in three volumes, the monumental work was a descriptive account of North American birds, including discussions of mating habits, popular nomenclature, and other aspects of their "life histories" (Baird's earlier study as part of the *Pacific*

Railroad Reports had not covered such biographical information).[32] Baird told Martha regretfully that he could not afford to send her a copy of the *History* without cost, although he could obtain it for her at a twenty-percent discount.[33] Martha was not able to buy the set at the time, but a year later she sent Baird a thirty-dollar postal order for it.[34]

Baird in turn, as with his other collectors, asked Martha for help in building up the Smithsonian collections. For example, he told her that he was "particularly desirous" of obtaining the eggs of the Rocky Mountain ptarmigan and sent her an egg drill and a blowpipe to aid in this endeavor. He also hoped to procure "well identified nests & eggs of other species, particularly of any of the jays." In return he offered to send her bird skins, perhaps from South America, for her museum. "For whatever you can supply that is of importance to our museum, we shall be glad to make return fourfold," he assured her.[35] Martha did her best to comply, and although she did not succeed in obtaining the ptarmigan eggs, she did send a box of shells and some finch skins for addition to the Smithsonian holdings.[36]

In fact, her study of the little rosy finch, commonly found in the Colorado mountains during the winter months, was of particular interest to Baird, and he quickly asked for more information—where were her specimens gathered? and at what altitude? How did they differ from the species that could be found in the summer on Mount Lincoln, Pikes Peak, and other "summits"?[37] Martha responded in detail, describing the differences among them and informing Baird that she had skinned over forty specimens, some found near Boulder, others near Idaho Springs at about 7,800 feet altitude.[38]

Also keenly interested in Martha's discoveries was the young ornithologist Robert Ridgway, a scientist of abundant enthusiasm and capable of prodigious accomplishment. Born in 1850, Ridgway had studied birds since his boyhood days in Illinois. At the age of fourteen, he had begun a correspondence with Baird that led to the opportunity in 1869 to collaborate with his mentor on the *History of North American Birds* following a stint as a zoologist with Clarence King's Fortieth Parallel Survey. In 1874 he had become a regular member of the Smithsonian staff as an ornithologist with the United States National Museum. Handsome and even considered something of a "dandy" in his early Washington years, Robert Ridgway and Martha Maxwell became fast friends and congenial colleagues.[39]

Initially, it was their mutual interest in the rosy finches that provided the first occasion for them to collaborate. Sometime in the late spring of 1874, Ridgway wrote to Martha asking for her assistance. She assured him that it would give her great pleasure to help in his investigation and offered to send all the skins he wanted.[40] The importance of her contribution can be seen in the publication resulting from Ridgway's work, which appeared the next year. Before describing the appearance and the habits of the different varieties, which he termed "among the rarest in the North American *Ornis*" until recent years, he noted that the material he had was "peculiarly rich, and entirely sufficient to decide the lines between the species and the geographical races." Most of the examples, he continued, had been sent by Charles E. H. Aiken of Fountain, Colorado, and Martha Maxwell of Boulder, "and comprised immense series of specimens, obtained at different seasons in those and contiguous localities."[41] Of the 416 specimens he studied, Aiken contributed 218 and Martha 73, with the remainder coming from the National Museum (84), several other institutions and collectors, and his own holdings (21).[42]

In addition to gathering and studying her growing collection of specimens, Martha continued to look for suitable locations for her museum. Initially she thought that Denver, which was much larger than Boulder and a crossroads for travelers besides, would be the best choice. Dr. W. D. McLeod, described in *On the Plains* as "a man of some experience as a naturalist," had been working with Glass collecting for the museum, and he investigated the possibilities in Denver, calling on former territorial governor John Evans and other businessmen to present Martha's plans. Evans, he reported, "thought well" of the endeavor; his approval, however, did not produce any concrete assistance. McLeod also quickly discovered that the available rooms for rent were either too expensive or too isolated (or both).[43] For its part, the *Boulder County News* called on all readers to help launch the museum in Boulder. "Must we allow everything to go to Denver, that is attractive to tourists and strangers, —or, rather, must we drive everything to Denver?"[44] Apparently taking such admonitions to heart, some civic-minded Boulderites offered to pay the rent on a satisfactory suite of rooms, and thus, with some reluctance, Martha decided to open her museum in Boulder. As she explained to one Denver businessman, "I have concluded to make a virtue of necessity & stay at home where my efforts are appreciated."[45]

The room that would be transformed into the Rocky Mountain Museum was located on the second floor of the Dabney-Macky Block, situated on the northeast corner of the two main streets, Twelfth (now Broadway) and Pearl. Built in 1866 by two early businessmen, Andrew J. Macky and Charles Dabney, the block was the first brick building erected in Boulder, and from time to time the second-story hall had been the site of church services, theatrical events, and school classes. For Martha Maxwell, it seemed the perfect spot for her museum.[46]

By early June of 1874, Martha was ready to allow the Boulder townspeople to see what she had accomplished. The opening was a grand affair, as the *Boulder County News* reported, "an occasion celebrated with flags and music as befitted an occurrence so significant of benefit to this country." With the strains of the Boulder Brass Band and the String Band filling the air, Martha's friends and neighbors crowded in to catch a glimpse of the exotic and unusual displays. "Why, she has everything in air, sea, earth, or under the earth, imaginable," exclaimed one enthusiastic visitor.[47]

Fortunately, what museumgoers saw during the year and a half that the enterprise was located in Boulder has been well documented both in words and in photographs. Through these descriptions and views it is possible to determine in great detail not only what specimens were displayed but also how they were arranged. For example, it is known that the collections contained all sorts of items that one correspondent termed "queer old rarities of past ages." In these "cabinets of curiosities" were coins antedating the birth of Christ, human bones from an Indian burial ground, and a German Bible printed in 1560. Here as elsewhere, however, it is apparent that Martha sought to educate rather than simply to amuse or amaze; the collection of money, said the reporter, was "so graded as to exhibit the progress in the art of money making of most nations from their first rude conception down to the present."[48]

Then, of course, there were the mineral specimens, collected in the mountains and arranged in cabinets with sliding glass doors. J. Alden Smith, a Boulder friend then serving as the Colorado territorial geologist, had helped with the displays. Shown in other cases and on the walls were items that Martha had obtained in California—reindeer hide from Alaska, war clubs from New Zealand, a tiny silk shoe from China.[49]

Central to the museum were the mounted natural history specimens—the birds perched on tree branches, the great buffalo standing in the middle of the room, the bear and the mountain lion prowling around a rocky landscape. From the descriptions and photographs that survive, it is apparent that Martha's renowned habitat groupings that created such a sensation at the Centennial were well developed in the Boulder museum, demonstrating the refinement of the ideas that she had implemented at least as early as the 1868 Boulder fair.

Among the best accounts of the animal groupings was one penned by Helen Hunt, who visited the museum in 1875. Then known primarily for her poetry and newspaper and magazine articles, often signed "H.H.," Hunt had come to Colorado Springs for her health in 1873. There she met Denver and Rio Grande Railroad promoter William S. Jackson, who became her second husband in October 1875. Six years later she published *A Century of Dishonor*, her impassioned attack on the federal government's Indian policies, which along with *Ramona* (1884) represented her greatest success.[50]

Hunt's column in the *New York Independent* entitled "Mrs. Maxwell's Museum" appeared on September 23, 1875, and was widely reprinted thereafter, drawing national attention to Martha Maxwell. Calling the habitat arrangement "the distinctive feature of the museum," Hunt described the scene for her readers:

Here are arranged mounds of earth, rocks, and pine trees, in a by no means bad imitation of a wild, rocky landscape. And among these rocks and trees are grouped the stuffed animals, in their families, in pairs, or singly, and every one in a most life-like and signifi- cant attitude. A doe is licking two exquisite little fawns, while the stag looks on with a proud expression. A bear is crawling out of the mouth of a cave. A fox is slowly prowling along, ready to spring on a rabbit. A mountain lion is springing literally through the branches of a tree on a deer, who is running for life, with eyes blood-shot, tongue out, and every muscle tense and strained. Three mountain sheep—father, mother, and little one—are climbing a rocky precipice. A group of ptarmigans shows the three colors—winter, spring and summer. A mother grouse is clucking about with a brood of chick- ens in the most inimitably natural way. . . .[51]

In another article, published later in *St. Nicholas* magazine for children, Hunt explained in detail how Martha had constructed the landscape. Again, this rare description of Martha's exhibit techniques is worth quoting at some length:

She has built up a sort of wooden frame-work, in the shape of rocks. This is covered with a coarse canvas cloth, which has been prepared with glue or some sticky substance. Over this, coarse shining sand of a dark gray color is sprinkled thick; and as the cloth is sticky, the sand remains. At a very little distance nobody would know the rocks from real rocks of dark gray stone. Then she has set real pine and fir trees among them, and little clumps of grasses, and mounds of real dirt.[52]

Perhaps even more popular than the large landscape were the small "comic groups" of three or four animals. One display, for example, showed several monkeys playing poker around a small table. "One scratching his head and scowling in perplexity and dismay at his bad cards, and another leaning back smirking with satisfaction over his certain triumph with his aces; one smoking with a nonchalant air;" wrote Hunt, "and all so absorbed in the game that they do not see the monkey on the floor, who is reaching up a cautious paw and drawing the stakes—a ten dollar bill—off the edge of the table." Another comic group, which was in fact a tableau in the large landscape, showed a squirrel and a yellow duckling coming out of a small, wooden house. "The conscious strut, the grotesque love-making of the pair is as positive and as ludicrous as anything ever seen in a German picture book," thought Hunt.[53] It is likely that Martha developed some of her ideas for these comic groupings during her visit to Woodward's Gardens in San Francisco. The 1873 catalog of the gardens, for example, in describing an exhibit of "Comical Animal Groups," listed both "two monkeys playing cards" and "gosling and chipmunk taking a walk" among the scenes shown.[54]

Not all of the animals in the museum were mounted. Two bear cubs, orphaned when their mother was killed, were given to Martha in 1875. Tame and playful, they followed visitors about and were extremely popular with children. Other live animals included a mountain grouse, squirrels, and rattlesnakes.[55]

Understandably, visitors occasionally were confused in trying to distinguish between what was real and what was a natural and lifelike illusion. Helen Hunt recalled clearly her encounter with a small terrier near the entrance to the museum. "Not until after a second or two did the strange stillness of the creature suggest to me that it was not alive. Even after I had stood close by its side I could hardly believe it," she wrote. "There was not a single view in which he did not look as alive as a live dog can when he does not stir." Such mastery of technique, she suggested, "is enough to prove Mrs. Maxwell's claim to be called an artist."[56]

By all accounts, then, Martha seems to have succeeded in her aim to develop a museum that was both entertaining and educational. The exotic curiosities, the comic tableaux, and the dramatic habitat groupings appealed to the public at large, while scientists commented on the scope and variety of the birds and mammals. When Ferdinand V. Hayden, whose survey parties had been concentrating their efforts in Colorado since 1873, paid a visit, he was quoted as declaring that the collection "excelled every other in the West . . . and that it ought surely to be connected with the University." Finding that Martha lacked some of the reports of the survey he had headed since 1867, he made arrangements to send the missing volumes to her.[57]

Establishing her museum, however, did not mean that Martha had stopped either collecting or studying, and she continued to make excursions into the mountains to obtain new specimens. In the fall of 1874, for example, she and James spent three days collecting ores, while the next year found them making a more extensive foray into Middle Park.[58]

Martha also hired a young naturalist in 1875 named J. Clarence Hersey, and he proved to be an able collector and a willing worker. A Vermont native, he had come to Colorado in 1872 and had been teaching school in Boulder and Weld counties.[59] Many years later he clearly recalled his first meeting with Martha in 1873 at her home at the mouth of Boulder Canyon. "Her enthusiastic descriptions of the specimens and of her many interesting discoveries fired my boyish imagination and opened my eyes to see, and my ears to hear, the infinite harmonies of nature surrounding us everywhere." Hersey subsequently wrote to Martha offering his services as a collector, and he spent about five months in her employ in 1875.[60] For her part, Martha was quite pleased with her young assistant (Hersey was about twenty years old at the time). "He is a *'splendid'* boy," she commented toward the end of the summer. "I never knew a more trusty, intelligent kind hearted young man."[61]

In addition to collecting for the Rocky Mountain Museum, Hersey also attempted to find more specimens to fill requests from Spencer Baird for the Smithsonian Institution. In April Baird had written to Martha asking her to use her "best efforts" to obtain "full sets of the eggs of the birds of Colorado," particularly those of the ptarmigan, jay, sparrow, and woodpecker.[62] She assured Baird that she had hired Hersey to "make a speciality of egg-gathering" and would do all she could to satisfy the request.[63] In return, Baird offered to continue to help her identify any species of birds that proved troubling, telling her that he would "take great pleasure in labeling & returning them."[64]

Thus Martha Maxwell's Rocky Mountain Museum apparently was well received both by the public and by the scientific community. Yet, as she had so often in her life, and would again,

Martha was facing one almost insurmountable problem—lack of money. From the beginning, the museum seems to have been a critical and popular success but a financial failure. Although the room rent of twenty-five dollars per month was being paid, the receipts from the sale of the twenty-five-cent tickets did not go far to meet the other expenses such as lights and fuel.[65] Moreover, tourist travel to Colorado slowed considerably after the summer months, and the population of Boulder, estimated in 1873 as 1,120, simply was not large enough to support the endeavor, particularly considering the depressed economy of the country in the mid-1870s.[66]

In order to make ends meet, Martha offered season tickets for sale and did everything else she could think of to increase business.[67] In the fall of 1874, for example, she prepared an eagle for the annual Boulder fair. In one claw it held a sign proclaiming "I am from Mrs. Maxwell's Museum don't fail to see her large collection of curiosities."[68]

Mindful that one of Boulder's prime attractions might soon be lost, the local newspaper appealed to the civic pride of readers and urged them to support the museum. Pointing out that the museum had received a good deal of favorable publicity and thus had drawn national attention to Boulder, the *Boulder County News* commented that it was "getting that reputation and appreciation abroad which is tardily accorded at home. Should we not unite to sustain an institution that is so much credit to the town?"[69]

Yet even though several prominent Boulder citizens bought the season tickets (and were duly applauded in print), the critical financial situation continued.[70] As Martha struggled to keep the museum open, she was driven not only by her personal desires for the success of the enterprise but also by the need to provide for her daughter Mabel's education. With her strong and lifelong interest in learning (indeed, one of the primary purposes of the museum was to encourage young people to find out more about natural history), Martha was determined, one might say even obsessed, that Mabel would receive the finest education possible.

Although the Maxwells were living in the town where the University of Colorado had been established, the doors of that institution were still not open to students. In any event, Martha had decided that the only place for Mabel to go to school was her own alma mater, Oberlin. Surely, she thought, Mabel would be as happy there as she herself had been some twenty years earlier. Accordingly, at the end of August in 1874, almost three months after Martha had opened the museum, Mabel left Boulder for the long journey to Ohio.[71]

Even though Martha had managed to enroll her daughter in the college (with financial assistance from her brother-in-law, Nathan Thompson), there was barely enough money to pay Mabel's expenses from one week to the next. Therefore, Martha wrote to Marianne Dascomb, the principal of the Oberlin Female Department, asking if the school would be willing to purchase natural history specimens to use for teaching purposes. The amount paid could then be credited to Mabel's tuition and board.[72] Unfortunately, Dascomb politely but firmly refused the offer. There were, she wrote, too many necessary expenses at the college that must be paid first, and, in any case, the collection would have to be seen before it could be purchased.[73]

With her hopes for that plan dashed, at least for the moment, Martha turned to other avenues to raise money. Early in 1875, she wrote to Julia Ward Howe for advice and assistance. Howe, noted as the author of "The Battle Hymn of the Republic," was then one of the leaders of the post–Civil War woman suffrage movement and a founder and editor of the influential *Woman's Journal*.[74]

In reply to Martha's initial letter, Howe wrote that she hardly knew how to advise her but suggested that it might be worthwhile, if possible, to take the collection to various cities around the country.[75] She also offered to include a notice in the *Woman's Journal*. True to her word, the February 27, 1875, issue of the weekly publication carried a brief account of Martha's work, along with a bit of editorial praise: "I consider this lady collector a marvel; without any especial training or education she has gradually taken up this line of business, and has made it a complete success. Her modesty equals her industry and skill, and her museum deserves a place in a large city."[76]

Although Martha needed money, she was loath to sell some of the specimens, as she had done in 1870. Nonetheless, she told

Howe in March that she was working up a catalog in order to advertise duplicates for sale, as she saw "no hope of making my Museum remunerative at present." She had been advised, she said, "for pecunary advantages, to conceal my sex in advertisements &c but prejudice must be overcome, and I am anxious to help in the conflict."[77]

Some way had to be found, however, for the collection and the museum to survive, and by the end of 1875 it was becoming apparent that perhaps the only solution was to move the museum to Denver. A year earlier, in the fall of 1874, Martha had again investigated the possibility of locating in the capital, encouraged by certain unnamed "Denver people."[78] The *Colorado Farmer* had also lent editorial support to such a move, admonishing Denver residents to secure it "and not leave it to struggle at starvation profits in this little mountain town" or, even worse, to be "caught up by some Eastern capitalist, who will carry it off and make a fortune in Chicago or some other large city; thus depriving our Territory of what should belong to it alone, by right."[79]

In the end, Martha concluded an arrangement with John Pickel, a businessman then living in Denver who had long been active in mining in Gilpin and Boulder counties.[80] Evidently Pickel had agreed to underwrite the venture to some extent for a year. Accordingly, the end of 1875 found Martha packing the collection for the move to Denver. Commenting on her departure, the *Boulder County News* was sad but philosophical, admitting that Boulder was not large enough to support the museum, but hoping that after the year was up "the Museum, of which our town has been so proud, may come back to us."[81]

The new Centennial year, then, found Martha Maxwell and her museum open for business at 376 Lawrence Street.[82] Again she had erected a complex habitat arrangement at one end of the room, described by one reporter as "Mammoth Cave, covered by rocks, forests and precipices, in which the animals are roving at will."[83] Martha offered further details in a letter to her sister Mary, who had recently moved to Massachusetts:

Yes, it does look more beautiful here than at B. the room
is nearly twice as high. The Mt sheeps horns touch the

cealing—there is a magnificent cave with numerous curves, sharp angles and windings—high enough for a man to walk through under the whole length of the rockwork leaning out into the back yard where we show the bears and other live animals. At one side of the room was a sink with water pipe and waste pipe this was too suggestive of bathrooms and kitchen so I filled it with rocks houseplant[s] and moss and put into it a miniature fountain which is really very pretty. In the center of the room I have a show case filled with birds nests & eggs.[84]

Satisfied that the museum was now in Denver, the *Colorado Farmer* noted that the "caves in miniature [were] a good representation of the Rocky Mountains" and applauded Martha's "taste and skill" in making the arrangement.[85] Spencer Baird, too, sent encouragement, telling her he thought she had "done wisely in removing your establishment to Denver where you will have better opportunity to make your work known."[86]

James Maxwell also had made the move to Denver, although by this time he apparently had grown less supportive of Martha's by now all-consuming venture. In fact, in 1874 he had commented to his daughter, with some resignation, that "mama is married to her museum, and I am a 'lone widdower. . . .' "[87] For her part, Martha had been anxious to have him accompany her, although she perhaps viewed him more as a source of convenient labor than of emotional and moral support. She wrote to Mabel, for example, that she and Pickel wanted him to go to Denver "as I must furnish some one in my place when I am stuffing birds &c. I think he will go, for we will give him the same wages that we would any body else but he does not like the business very well and I cannot tell whether he will go or not."[88]

James did accept whatever offer was made, and the two of them devoted all of their time to making the museum a success. Or, as Amy Dartt succinctly put it, "he does most of the work & she sticks to her business."[89] It was, in truth, a Spartan existence, requiring much dedication and self-discipline to endure. " 'How do we live in Denver?' " she wrote in answer to her sister Mary's query. "Well we don't live we only stay. We have the basement under the Museum, it is 25 by 45 ft all in one room in this we store all our heads, horns, hides (its a perfect Golgotha) manufacture my beasts, birds heads &c. cook and eat our victuals, enter[tain] company &c. . . . We have a den under the rockwork where we sleep on the floor in the museum."[90]

Sadly, however, the museum proved to be no more of a financial success in Denver than in Boulder. By the end of February Martha figured that it was six hundred dollars in debt and still was not paying expenses.[91] Thus, although she had largely realized her goal of creating a museum that would both educate and entertain, she was no farther along on the road to economic self-sufficiency. All the praise and publicity she had received from such figures as Helen Hunt, F. V. Hayden, and Julia Ward Howe, however welcome, had not been translated into financial success. At just this crucial point, however, the men in charge of Colorado's exhibit at the Philadelphia Centennial Exposition invited her to help represent the territory with an exhibit of her work. Although time was short (the exposition was to open May 10) and she was hardly settled from the recent move, after some initial misgivings Martha determined to make the most of the opportunity.

Mother and Daughter

In many respects, the Centennial in Philadelphia in 1876 was to be the high point in Martha Maxwell's life and work. It would bring her, if not happiness, at least recognition, satisfaction, and a sense of accomplishment. Before discussing her Centennial success, however, in order to fully understand the factors that motivated her, as well as her drive, discipline, and determination, it is useful first to take a closer look at the woman she had become by 1876. Fortunately, the correspondence that has survived, especially the letters she exchanged with her daughter Mabel at school at Oberlin, give glimpses both of Martha Maxwell's dreams and desires and of her relationship with her only child. These letters provide valuable insights into the nature of the relationship and of the standards and ideals that Martha held and that she tried to inculcate in Mabel. Throughout, the tone of the correspondence should be familiar to any daughter who has ever listened to her mother admonishing her to stand up straight, eat her vegetables, and always wear clean underwear lest she be involved in an accident.

One trait that Martha tried to cultivate in Mabel was her own love of learning and dedication to excellence. "In school I *always did my best*," she wrote to her daughter in December of 1874, "and this I hope you will do on every effort at composition."[1] Again, a few weeks later she wrote that she was glad that Mabel was getting along so well in Latin, while regretting her own lack of knowledge in the language, which was proving to be a hindrance in her natural history work. "Even at my age I should not flinch from attempting to master it if I *only could* command a few hours per day for study." Even so, she told Mabel, she was "not going to be too old to learn—though it will be very much harder for me than it was when I was of your age."[2]

By the time Mabel went to college, the percentage of women enrolled in institutions of higher education was over one-fifth of all students, and as the years went by a growing number were daughters of mothers like Martha who had had some training themselves in an academy or a college. Other mothers, perhaps widowed or destitute, encouraged their daughters to attend college so that they would always be able to support themselves.[3] On Martha's part, there seems never to have been any question in her mind that Mabel would go to college, nor any doubt that she would attend Oberlin, where Martha herself had been so happy. In her mind, she could give her daughter no greater gift than the same opportunity to study and learn.

Just as important as learning, and in fact a requisite for the pursuit of knowledge, was good health. Indeed, nothing could be achieved without it. Thus Martha sent her daughter a steady stream of hints and admonitions in an effort to keep Mabel on the proper path, articulating the principles that she had tried to live by from her own days at Oberlin and the sanitarium in Battle Creek. "One thing about studying evenings, be sure to have a lampshade and do not study so late evenings," she wrote shortly after Mabel had gone to Oberlin. "I fear your eyes or your health will fail. I would much rather have you give up one study and take another year for your course than that you should be overtaxed in any way."[4] Similarly, early the next year she told her daughter, "You *must have* more exercise in the open air you *must not* wear your clothes tight. You must air your room well every day."[5]

In other matters as well as in learning and health, Martha emphasized the need for both dedication and discipline. For example, she wrote on one occasion that Mabel's father had criticized her use of the words "get" and "got" in a letter. Martha concurred, commenting that such usage was "never elegant and seldom necessary" and was, moreover, indicative of the sort of carelessness that frequently happened when girls lived together.

To combat such sloppiness, Martha recommended that Mabel and her roommate "constitute yourselves a mutual improvement club and criticize each others language freely and kindly." Along these lines, Martha cautioned Mabel always to follow the Oberlin rules, however rigid she thought them and however strict the administration. "The success of every student depends upon the enforcing of these rules and I should be *sadly grieved* if my daughter in act or word should fail to respect or fail to cooperate with the oficers as much [as] possible in their efforts to have them obeyed."[6]

Finally, Martha outlined her view of the purpose of acquiring a college education. It was not, she wrote, only to pursue knowledge for its own sake, however rewarding that might be, but to prepare Mabel to do what she herself wanted to do—contribute through her work to the advancement of women. In a letter written early in 1875, she neatly summed up her position:

> You must not look upon your course of study as a *race* to be run as *soon* as *possible*; with you, the goal is *development*, let it require *more* or *less time* and the reward must be, *not* the completing of so many studies, but the *possession* of *capacity* and *ability* to *accomplish good* and *achieve honor* in some of the many fields now inviting *women's labor*. If parrot like, you could repeat all books, but fail to make them a part of your own intellectual being, all is useless. And if you succeed in this, and have no health to enable you to use your mind with all its treasures, then all is *worse than useless* for *you* are only fit to be *useless* and *miserable*.[7]

By this time, in fact, Martha had come to see her work as the best way for her to demonstrate the abilities of women and thus to support the cause of feminism. "My life is one of physical work, an effort to prove the words spoken by more gifted women," she told Julia Ward Howe. "The world demands proof of womans capacities, without it words are useless."[8] Similarly, she had confided earlier to Marianne Dascomb of Oberlin that in addition to providing for her daughter's education, "my next ambition is to build up a temple of science that shall be a credit to *our sex* and an acquisition to the world."[9]

At this point it is important to distinguish between feminism and the woman's rights movement. As historian Gerda Lerner has pointed out, "American feminism embraces all aspects of the emancipation of women," while the woman's rights movement denotes the struggle for legal rights such as the vote.[10] While Martha Maxwell was very definitely a feminist, she did not particularly focus her efforts on achieving the suffrage. Rather, she was interested in showing what women could do and in demonstrating that they need not be constrained by the limitations of their sphere. Indeed, this point was made emphatically in *On the Plains*. "I think it has been growing on the human mind ever since that little drama at the gate of Eden, that *capacity* and *ability*, rather than birth, color, sex, or anything else, should determine where individuals belong, and what they shall do," Mary Dartt wrote. "If they can use a gun, and are so inclined, what is to hinder their doing it?"[11]

Always a person who tended to "stand up and be counted" for what she believed in, from her days at Oberlin Martha had participated in causes such as moral reform and temperance that nurtured many post–Civil War women activists.[12] She had also seen firsthand the discrimination that women faced even in the progressive atmosphere of Oberlin. Ultimately, however, she came to feel that simply doing her work represented her most important contribution to feminism. Others might speak out on the lecture platform or write for the press—she would demonstrate by example and excellence. "The greatest desire of my life is to help inspire women with confidence in their own resources and abilities," she told Spencer Baird in 1875. "Talk is pure nonsense, about the matter, work, and excellence in the things wrought, will set the whole matter right."[13] It was for this very reason that she had been reluctant to sell the collection again, for with it, as she commented to Howe, "I ought to be able to do more for the cause of women than I could do with the money it would bring."[14]

As with most women, however, time was always a problem, and Martha felt that she had not been able to spend as much time as she would have liked in the struggle. In her experience in Colorado, she told Howe, she had found no clubs or associations except the "Female prayer meeting," as the women were "over-taxed with domestic cares," and help was difficult to obtain. "You see, we have not the time for united effort toward improvement that our sisters in the east can claim," she concluded.[15]

Martha may have somewhat underestimated her influence, however. For example, her friend Jennie Bartlett, an artist who had lived in Boulder at one time, wrote to her from Minneapolis in 1873, inquiring if she had seen any of the "*workers*" such as writers and lecturers Anna Dickinson and Grace Greenwood, both of whom had spoken in Colorado, and asking if she was "as great a worker as ever. How good it is that there are even a few women who are not satisfied with idleness—who devote what 'spare' time they have to something other than fine clothes."[16]

On the other hand, another artist friend, Mary Elizabeth Achey, knew only too well the obstacles faced by women who were serious about their work. Achey, the first professional woman artist to paint in Colorado, apparently came to Nevadaville with her husband and two children in 1860. While no contemporary evidence has thus far come to light indicating that she and Martha knew each other then, it is reasonable to assume that they became acquainted during those early mining-camp days. Achey later lived in Central City before moving to Napa, California, and Martha evidently visited her during her 1873 trip to San Francisco.[17] In 1875, Achey wrote to Martha that she had not been able to paint much because of her family responsibilities. "It does seem to bad that you are so much interrupted in every way, our experience is so similar in being overburdened that I know just how to sympathise with you."[18]

In considering Martha's attitudes toward education and feminism, and her attempts to persuade her daughter to continue and even surpass her own achievements, it is interesting to contrast these views with those of James Maxwell and to speculate how he may also have influenced Mabel's outlook on life. As has been seen, Mabel loved her father dearly and depended on him a great deal, particularly during her mother's absences. While James was certainly concerned about his youngest daughter's future, his views were more traditional than Martha's, his attitude more relaxed.

Although little of James's correspondence has survived, several letters that he wrote to Mabel from Colorado in the 1860s indicate something of his views. During this period, when Mabel was living with Martha in Baraboo, James told his little girl of his hopes and dreams for her, in the process revealing some of his thoughts on womanhood. For example, in one letter written in 1865 he discoursed at some length on the importance of housekeeping. He wanted, he said, for Mabel to learn to be "a *good* housekeeper, that is, to cook well, to keep the house & yourself tidy and clean." Elaborating on this theme, he told her that without attention to such details, it would be impossible for her to have a happy home life. "No amount of book learning," he continued, "can possibly make up, or atone for the lack of being a good housekeeper, because to keep house *well* lies at the very foundation of a *good home*." Warming to his subject, he gave further examples of his position. "How can we have a *home* without a house?" he asked, "and how can a house be pleasant if everything in it, is slovenly, & dirty, and out of place and the victuals we eat morning, noon and night are poorly cooked and prepared?" In conclusion, he wrote, he hoped that Mabel (who was but eight years old at the time) would "feel it a pleasure and a duty, as it must needs be your business" when she grew up to embark upon "the housekeeping part of a home" for herself and her family.[19]

Certainly James's views would have found widespread acceptance in the mid-1860s, reflecting as they did some of the points made by Catharine Beecher in her highly influential *Treatise on Domestic Economy*, which had gone through numerous editions since its first publication in 1841. In explaining how to deal with virtually all aspects of domestic life, Beecher's book had not only filled a practical need but had also raised "housekeeping" to the level of a skilled profession, one that contributed to the "intellectual and moral elevation" of the country.[20] Yet it also takes no great stretch of the imagination to infer that James might have been reflecting some dissatisfaction with his marriage to Martha in placing such an emphasis on housekeeping. Indeed, what little evidence survives on this point indicates that attention to such details was far down on Martha's list of priorities, subordinate always to her work in natural history. For example, in 1878 she wrote to her sister Mary about the difficulties of getting her washing done, commenting in passing that "ironing is unhealthy you know!"[21] Similarly, two years later she admonished Mabel, who by that time had graduated from college and was back in Boulder, to be certain that her household duties did not endanger her health. "Dont neglect to take every measure of sleep you can possibly get. . .," she told her, "and dont worry if the housework is neglected."[22]

It would not be fair to imply, however, that housework and the raising of a family were James's only concerns; although his objectives for his daughter were different from Martha's, he thought it important for Mabel to have "almost constant schooling all the way up through your youth and early womanhood because . . . you must needs be well fitted up, to be a happy, well doing, usefull woman."[23] Indeed, in a will written in 1860 while he was on the way to Colorado, James stated that in the event of his death, part of his estate (should there be any) was to be used to educate Mabel "in all the Ornamental, Scientific & Classical branches which she may choose to pursue" to the age of twenty (the three youngest daughters from his first marriage were similarly provided for).[24] He wanted, he told her on another occasion, to "send you to school and learn you work that you may be useful, and learn you to sing & play on the melodeon that you may be interesting."[25] James's overall view of true womanhood, in fact, might have been summed up best in a letter he wrote to Martha about the same time commenting on her half-sister Mary. By this time Mary had received much praise for her poetry and had high hopes for a writing career. James fretted, however, that this acclaim might "unduly elate her," might, indeed, "unstring, unnerve, and unfit her for the sterner and more important duties of life." This would be unfortunate, he concluded, for "mentally and morally, she is made up of the right kind of stuff, having a foundation Strata of *correct principles* and *right* heart & emotions, guided by good common sense, a *true* woman."[26]

It was thus with such conflicting parental advice ringing in her ears that Mabel set off for Oberlin. From the beginning she was very homesick, a natural occurrence for a young girl going so far from home. "It is terribly lonesome here, and I am *so* home-sick," she wrote to her Aunt Mary and Uncle Nathan shortly after she arrived. "I stay in my room and study wishing all the time that I was at home."[27] In fact, Mabel seems to have had an un-commonly severe attack of the disease; she commented many years later in her autobiography that she was "so homesick I could neither eat nor sleep and finally had to take to my bed."[28]

Martha, too, was lonesome for her only daughter, acknowl-edging just after she left that "I miss my baby so much that I cant refrain from writing just a word though I've nothing in particular to say."[29] Despite the distance between them, and the demands of her work, at this time in her life nothing mattered more to Martha than advising and guiding Mabel and achieving an en-during relationship, perhaps even a partnership with her. Such intimate relationships, particularly between mothers and daugh-ters, were, as historian Carroll Smith-Rosenberg has pointed out, central to the mid-nineteenth-century female world.[30] "The di-aries and letters of both mothers and daughters attest to their closeness and mutual emotional dependency," she writes.[31] At a time when the majority of women led traditionally domestic lives, daughters learned how to be good wives and mothers in an "apprenticeship system" that "tied the generations together in shared skills and emotional interaction." The hostility often pres-ent in today's mother-daughter relationships was, she states, almost wholly absent.[32]

In the relationship between Martha and Mabel Maxwell, however, the situation was somewhat different, although many of the emotions were the same. For example, Martha had seldom led a life of "traditional domesticity," yet her desire to "appren-tice" her daughter into her own chosen world of intellectual de-velopment and feminist action was no different from the desires of other women to teach their daughters the skills of housewifery and motherhood. The closeness of which Smith-Rosenberg speaks was often absent from the relationship, however, for in Mabel's view, the years of both physical and psychological separation from her mother had already taken their toll, forever preventing the forging of such a bond. Conflict born of distance, resentment, and rebellion was as much a part of the interaction between mother and daughter as was the love that was undeniably present as well.

A comment from Mabel to her Aunt Mary penned in the fall of 1875 indicates something of her feelings. "I presume you have seen that article about Mamas Museum in the last Independent," she wrote, referring to Helen Hunt's column. "It is very interesting I think if Mama dont write pretty soon I'll know more about her through the papers than from her personally."[33] Recalling her emotions many years later, Mabel was even more explicit. When her mother visited her at Oberlin toward the end of her second year, on the way to the Centennial, Mabel remembered that she was "pitifully glad" to see her, "but something fundamental had happened to our relationship because of the long separations that had extended over so much of our lives. It was too late to build a bridge of understanding; the chasm had grown too wide. So it happened that our whole relationship was built on externals."[34]

Mabel's feelings, however, did not prevent her from trying to live up to her mother's expectations, however difficult and uncongenial that task might be. "How desperately fearful I was all that year of not making good, not satisfying mother, not showing her that I was genuinely appreciative and grateful of her sacrifices!" she wrote in her memoir. "Happily, I came out well in my examinations."[35] Indeed, even though she complained on one occasion that she "*never* saw any thing *so* perfectly unlearnable" as geometry,[36] one of her instructors told Martha that Mabel was a "diligent and careful student," who showed promise that she would "come out in the end a fine scholar and a noble woman."[37] Mabel's attempts to please her mother even extended, at one point, to a short-lived notion to prepare herself to teach at the University of Colorado after graduation, a plan that Martha endorsed wholeheartedly. "I am much pleased with your idea of preparing yourself to fill some Prof's Chair in the University," she wrote. "After acquiring a thouroug[h] general education determine upon some Branch and make a speciality of that learning all that is to be known about it. As J. Alden Smith says his teacher used to tell him, 'Learn a little of all things, and all of one thing.' "[38]

Underlying the emotional issues in the relationship between Martha and Mabel, and providing in some respects the context in which they were discussed, was the ever-present question of money. Apparently Nathan Thompson had agreed to send his wife's niece the sum of $250 per year for her education, which for Mabel, at least, proved to be inadequate. With board and tuition, books, and wood for the stove in her room, she calculated at one point that she would have only $30 per term left over for everything else.[39] And to Mabel, "everything else" often meant clothes and shoes, despite her attempts to economize. "I know I spend a good deal, but you must remember when I came, I had no winter clothes to speak of, and every thing does cost so," she wrote to her mother in the fall of 1874 in tones familiar to the parent of any college student.[40] For her part, Martha urged simplicity and restraint in matters of dress, as much for philosophical as for financial reasons. "It will not do to spend anything for show," she told her, "that is, your dress must be made in the way that it cost[s] the least and be comfortable & desent."[41]

Yet despite her feelings, Martha tried to give Mabel everything she really needed, at one point borrowing twelve dollars for a cloak for her.[42] Constantly worried that the money from Nathan Thompson would be insufficient to keep Mabel in school, she tried almost anything to augment her meager income from the museum, mentioning on two occasions that she had swept the church and was sending Mabel the money thus earned.[43] Mabel's father was of little help, partly because he was himself earning no money, and partly because he was not particularly supportive of Mabel attending Oberlin. If she were to go to any school, he thought, she should go to Northwestern University in Evanston, Illinois, where she could live with one of the daughters from his first marriage and thus save on expenses.[44] And as for Mabel herself working at Oberlin, she soon found that the small sum she could earn (eight cents an hour) in the dining room was hardly worth the time, a position with which Martha agreed.[45]

Thus, despite much effort and sacrifice on the part of both Martha and Mabel, spiced with differences in temperament, philosophy, and general outlook on life, Mabel's two years at Oberlin were less than a total success. "I hated Oberlin and, most of all, I hated writing home for money," she recalled later. "Often it seemed to me that I would rather take a beating than send back another request."[46] If for Martha Oberlin had been the fulfillment of a dream, for Mabel it was just the opposite. "So much about Oberlin revolted me;" she wrote, "the thin crust of piety which covered petty grafting, the narrowness, the unreasonable restraint."[47]

Yet as Mabel's second year drew to a close, neither mother nor daughter was prepared to give up her dream: Mabel's of a conventional mother who would provide a traditional home, Martha's of a daughter who would exemplify and contribute to the advancement of women. During Martha's brief visit to Oberlin in the spring of 1876 on the way to the Centennial, which might prove to be their financial salvation, a scene occurred that mirrored all the tension, the hope, and the desperation inherent in their relationship. Here is how Mabel remembered the incident:

> I wanted fiercely to have mother make a good impression when she visited me. She was so pretty; she was more intelligent than those around me; she had accomplished more; she was on her way toward being a celebrity, though she had never sought for fame. But I was conscious that she looked different from other women. She had no personal vanity at all; her clothes were shapeless and odd; her hair was drawn back in a peculiar fashion, though that was the era of ringlets and elaborate hairdress.
>
> And mother's pleasure in seeing me was destroyed when she discovered in horror that I had had my ears pierced.
>
> "How could you do it!" she protested. "It is a relic of barbarism. Only the lowest savages mutilate their flesh."
>
> It went on and on. When she had finished, I felt beaten and flattened, my spirit broken. The rest of her visit was anticlimax.[48]

Although profoundly disturbing to Mabel, the confrontation at Oberlin, only one of many that punctuated the relationship with her mother, had been years in the making and could hardly be resolved quickly, if at all. Whether or not Martha and Mabel could ever come to terms with their differences remained in question. Thus Martha continued on to Philadelphia, hoping that her daughter would one day do what she herself was about to attempt, "to *accomplish good* and *achieve honor* in some of the many fields now inviting *women's labor.*"

"Woman's Work" at the Centennial

Arriving in Philadelphia in the late spring of 1876, Martha Maxwell was quickly caught up in the excitement of the Centennial. Here she would have a chance to show "what a woman could do" and, perhaps even more importantly, make some money to support Mabel's education. Yet for several months she would also be separated from her husband; that her absence would change their already troubled relationship, and not for the best, seemed a reasonable assumption. Once having made the decision to leave Denver, however, Martha was determined to make a success of her exhibit, joining the millions of other Americans in Philadelphia for whom the Centennial represented all that was best in the proud, confident, and optimistic America of 1876.

In the years since 1871, when the United States Congress had passed an act providing "for celebrating the One Hundredth Anniversary of American Independence, by holding an International Exhibition of Arts, Manufactures, and Products of the Soil and Mine" in Philadelphia, a magical city had appeared on the lush and verdant expanses of Fairmount Park.[1] Opened officially on May 10, 1876, by President Ulysses S. Grant and the ranking celebrity, Emperor Dom Pedro of Brazil, the exposition featured five principal buildings (the Main Building, the Machinery Hall, the Horticultural Hall, the Memorial Hall, and the Agricultural Hall), along with the United States Government Building, the Women's Pavilion, and the buildings erected by individual states and foreign governments. Extravagant and overflowing with the miracles of the age, the Centennial had something for everyone, and by the time it was over on November 10, some ten million visitors had come to gape and marvel. It was a kaleidoscope of wonders, a complex mixture of patriotism and celebration that was the event of a lifetime for all who were a part of it.[2]

No less was this true for Martha Maxwell, who over a year earlier had expressed her interest in taking part in the Centennial. In March 1875 she mentioned to Julia Ward Howe that she had written for information for exhibitors, and she also sent a letter to Elizabeth Gillespie, the driving force behind the Women's Pavilion, inquiring about the possibility of participating in that landmark display of "women's work."[3] The Women's Pavilion would have provided both a logical and a congenial setting for Martha's proposed exhibit, for the women who were planning the pavilion, unprecedented in size and scope, conceived of it as a showcase for women's accomplishments ranging from the traditional to the innovative and the unique. Altogether, the displays would demonstrate without doubt the myriad capabilities of women and thereby serve as both catalyst and inspiration in the struggle for greater political, legal, and social freedom and would as well strengthen feelings of sorority and sisterhood. The Bible quotation that the organizers chose for the inscription over the entrance said it all: "Let Her Works Praise Her in the Gates" (Proverbs 31).[4] Or, just as Martha had written to Spencer Baird, "Talk is pure nonsense, about the matter, work, and excellence in the things wrought, will set the whole matter right."

Yet Martha received no answer from Gillespie, and so she put aside any thought of going to Philadelphia and concentrated on making the Boulder museum a success.[5] She also supported the plans of the Boulder County Centennial Association; for example, in May she had offered the museum rooms as a location where specimens slated for exhibit in Philadelphia could be stored.[6] The question of a Centennial exhibit arose again, however, when she received a letter written by Spencer Baird in mid-October 1875. The Smithsonian, he wrote, was "making a special collection to illustrate the economical natural history of the United States at the Centennial." To this end, a "new series" of mammals and birds was being mounted, and he thought that Martha might be interested in showing what she could do "in the way of the artistic presentation of some animal groups." If she could make up a display ("not too large," he cautioned), the Smithsonian would pay a "fair price" and place it in the exhibit under her name. Baird also suggested that she prepare some examples of her work for the Women's Pavilion. "This department of taxidermy as practiced by yourself is one of the fine arts & requires the high qualifications of a modeller and sculptor," he told her, "& I shall be glad to have you enter the lists not only with your own sex who may take a part in the exhibition , but also with the taxidermists of the male sex."[7]

Martha was immensely encouraged by Baird's letter, and she was at no loss for ideas for Centennial displays. Her ambitions, indeed, ranged far beyond the execution of some specimens designed only to demonstrate her skills, although this was important. As she wrote to Baird, a taxidermist must be proficient in preparing "the most minute as well as the largest bird and mammal, from the young hummingbird in its nest to the Mt Eagle, and from the Shrew to the Buffalo including the varieties of work intermediate." In addition to displaying her abilities, however, she wanted to put together two historical groups, which she described to Baird in some detail. More typical of the then-current flamboyant, "theatrical" taxidermic style than of true habitat groups, one would represent the beginning of the Revolutionary War, the other the close of the conflict; each would feature three figures. "The first a fine male Lion with one foot upon the prostrate form of 'Fair Columbia', her laurel wreath upon the ground, the American Eagle attacks the lion in defence of the maid. The second group shows the Lion vanquished, Columbia sitting under the shadow of the Eagle's wing while he puts the wreath upon her head." She wanted to arrange the specimens "upon rock work among foliage" and, if there was enough space, "make a cascade of real water with a lake and live Mt. trout . . . at its foot."[8]

One can almost hear Baird's gasps as he opened her letter with its descriptions of plans he obviously thought were impractical, not to say farfetched. She should not, he wrote, "attempt so ambitious a group," but even if she went ahead she should leave out the lion, "an Old World Form [which] would be quite out of place, even if it were possible to obtain a good skin, which would be a matter of considerable uncertainty." He recommended instead the preparation of a "spirited group, showing perhaps a pack of wolves attacking a deer or antelope" and thought that the eagle and fox she had mentioned might suffice, although he cautioned her not to "attempt too much action, as the spectator becomes wearied by the delay of the denouement." Finally, she should give up any thought of a waterfall. "I fear it will be quite impossible," he worried, "to undertake the enterprise of executing the running water with the living animals in it."[9] In the end, although Martha exhibited neither in the Women's Pavilion nor in the Government Building, her display turned out to be larger and more sophisticated than the theatrical groups she had described to Baird—and it had running water.

The exhibit that brought Martha Maxwell such acclaim at the Centennial was placed in the state building that Kansas and Colorado had erected jointly near the Women's Pavilion. Constructed in the form of a cross, it was one of the few state buildings that actually contained exhibits, as most states elected to contribute displays in one of the main buildings. Colorado had been allotted one-fourth of the space on payment of one-fourth of the cost.[10] Yet because the agreement between Kansas and Colorado was not completed until March 1876, as late as February Martha was telling her sister Mary that she still had no idea whether or not she would go to Philadelphia. Apparently nothing had come of the exhibits she had discussed with Baird, and, in any case, she had just moved her museum from Boulder to Denver. Added to this was the fact that the Colorado centennial board was being reorganized and two new commissioners, a young lawyer from Pueblo named George Q. Richmond and a man with a varied and eccentric background in politics, mining, and the military known as "Commodore" Decatur, were slated to begin work on March 1. Although they were anxious to have her take part in the exhibit, she wrote to Mary, she was uncertain about accepting the offer. "I suppose I should live through the moving of it again but its dreadful to think of and I must loose so much hard work in fixing it up here," she lamented.[11]

Several factors, however, combined to influence Martha to

pack up the museum and move it to Philadelphia. She had come to realize more and more that it was not possible to make a financial success of the enterprise anywhere in the new and sparsely populated Territory of Colorado. Perhaps if she took the collection to Philadelphia and then sold it, she reasoned, she would be able to continue with the study of natural history in more comfortable circumstances. Most importantly, she might be able to earn enough money to keep Mabel in school, always the goal that was uppermost in her thoughts. Thus she made up her mind to accept the agreement offered by the Colorado Centennial commissioners and began, in Mary's words, "all the hurry and worry and work of the weeks that preceded her departure from Denver."[12]

Arriving in Philadelphia, Martha found that her work was just beginning. The Kansas-Colorado Building, in fact, was not even completed, and she had to wait until enough of the construction was finished to begin building her landscape. Colorado had been allocated the west wing of the building, and Martha was given one entire wall for her display. As soon as possible she set about making the landscape using "paste, pulverized ore, water, lime, gravel and evergreens" with only the aid of one incompetent assistant. Working virtually round the clock for two weeks, she completed her masterpiece, all the while fending off questions from inquisitive passersby.[13]

Finally the exhibit was open to the public, and from the beginning it attracted throngs of visitors who were uniformly intrigued not only by the natural, lifelike displays but also by the small woman who had prepared them. Calling her "a modern Diana," a Philadelphia reporter commented that "if there is any one person who at such a place as an international exhibition can be regarded as the observed of all observers it is Mrs. Maxwell."[14] Similarly, Nathan Meeker, a founder of the Union Colony at Greeley and the alternate United States Centennial Commissioner from Colorado, was not exaggerating when he wrote that "her Collection was what first began to be talked about in distant places, and which induced many who otherwise would not have gone, to make the journey, — & her fame increased every day to the last week and the last day."[15]

Fortunately, photographs and descriptions of the display have survived, making clear that this was a complex, comprehensive exhibit of mammals and birds of both the plains and the mountains, a more sophisticated habitat grouping than Martha had constructed either in the Boulder or the Denver museum. Arrayed against one wall was a mountain landscape of trees and boulders, down which a stream trickled into a small lake which, in Mary's words, was "peopled by aquatic creatures: fishes swimming in the lake—turtles sunning themselves on its half submerged rocks, while beavers, muskrats and water-fowl seemed at home upon its margin." Between the stream and the lake was a cave, above which were arranged Rocky Mountain animals at elevations suggesting the altitudes at which they were found: "fierce bears, shy mountain sheep, savage mountain lions or pumas, and a multitude of smaller creatures, each in an attitude of life-like action." On an area representing the plains were "huge buffaloes, elk, antelope and their native neighbors."[16] As in the Colorado museums, live animals such as prairie dogs and rattlesnakes completed the picture.[17] In front of it all was a modest placard that read "Woman's Work."

Most visitors had never seen anything like it, and they streamed in from morning until night, bombarding Martha and Mary (who came from her home near Boston for a time) with an unceasing barrage of questions: "Did she kill all these animals?"; "How did she stuff 'em?"; "Is game as thick as this all over the Rocky Mountains?"[18] Some asked about the landscape itself—was that "real Rocky Mountain soil?" wondered one tourist.[19] At least one woman viewed the whole endeavor even more literally. As reported by a newspaper correspondent who saw the episode as "another example of the idiocy of the race," the woman approached the stream with a "little tin pail; filling it with water from this stream she drank it down, filled it again and handed it to her sharp-elbowed friends who were behind me, with the request that they should 'try the Colorado water,' and then she went on to tell how she 'never drank the Schuylkill water' here if she could get anything else, for it wasn't healthy."[20]

Then there were those who poked and prodded and jabbed, curious and uncertain as to whether any of the lifelike specimens were, indeed, alive. Like Helen Hunt before him, when the Emperor of Brazil visited the exhibit and saw the small terrier he "was deceived, and tried to whistle the little favorite from a stare that proved to be only life's charming but stony counterfeit."[21] And a Philadelphia correspondent reported a similar scene. "Yesterday a stranger, one of those Vandals who delight in be-daubing statuary and poking their canes at valuable paintings, in a loud voice enough to be heard by all those near, said: 'Mariar, watch me make the critter jump.' So saying he applied his walk-ing-stick to the turtle. In another minute the joke had circulated, and the roar of laughter which ensued told the stranger of his mistake. The turtle was a stuffed one."[22]

If members of the public were entranced by the spectacle of the lifelike specimens "all a good deal occupied in preying upon each other, or being preyed upon," in the words of the *Atlantic Monthly* correspondent, they were most curious about Martha Maxwell herself.[23] "There was never an hour, through all the summer," Mary wrote later, "when there were not numbers of interesting and appreciative people eager to know all about her and her adventures, about the country where all her specimens were obtained, its climate, resources, agriculture, and mines; how the latter were worked; how the land was irrigated, etc. etc."[24] Major articles about Martha appeared in *Harper's Bazar*, the *Phrenological Journal*, and the *New Century for Women* (pub-lished by the Women's Centennial Committee), while newspa-pers from coast to coast carried reports of the "Colorado Huntress."[25] In greater or lesser detail, the correspondents out-lined the story of Martha Maxwell's life, from her early days in Pennsylvania and Wisconsin to her residence in Colorado, and analyzed not only her accomplishments but also her appearance, her motivations, and her family.

Over and over, the reporters who flocked to the Kansas-Colorado Building to interview Martha for their readers were struck by the disparity between the masculine image they thought her work suggested and the appearance of the woman herself. As they looked at her, the image that was reflected back depended as much upon the observer as on the observed and provided an indication of the variety of ways in which Victorian

America chose to view the seeming anomaly that was Martha Maxwell. "As a general rule they expect to meet an Amazon in size and strength, clad in a suit of buckskin, with murder in her eye, a Sharp's rifle in her hands, and wearing a belt stuck full of revolvers and hunting knives," ran a typical comment. "Instead, however, they find a petite little woman, dressed in a plain dark suit, slight of stature, with pleasant face, dark hair, and the manners of a thorough lady."[26] "Modest," "delicate," "chaste," "unassuming," "sweet-voiced," "unobtrusive," "quiet"— in such words did the reporters describe her.[27] If some saw her "keen, eager eye, and a countenance full of animation and intelligence," her stature indicating "a combination of activity, strength, and intrepidity," or her "resolute mouth, blue eyes, [and] an intellectual forehead,"[28] most approvingly described her as womanly and feminine, "a lady of character, chaste, modest, of respectable culture"; a "petite, refined, gentle, intelligent, warm-hearted, and thoroughly womanly woman."[29]

In addition, whatever the reality of her situation, reporters wished to see her as a woman who had attained her success without compromising her family responsibilities. "As a wife, mother, and householder she holds a well-accredited and happy record," said *Harper's Bazar*, while a Philadelphia reporter wrote that "during the ten years in which Mrs. Maxwell has been acting the role of the mighty hunter, or huntress, she has raised a family of children and attended to her household duties without assistance."[30] Another correspondent succinctly summed it all up: "The lady is a woman of education, refined and womanly, a good wife and mother, as well as a good taxidermist."[31]

Overall, Martha was not displeased with such views of herself, which, in fact, were quite consonant with her own. It is clear that while she wished to demonstrate through her work "what a woman could do," she wished also to retain her feminine qualities and identity, never appearing as the "Amazonian huntress." Giving a clue as to the ways in which she wanted to be perceived are several sentences on a scrap of paper, undated but obviously in Martha's handwriting. Possibly answering questions posed by a journalist, she jotted down her thoughts:

So far it is womans Enterprise a womans selfdenial will
and muscle [that] has brought it [the collection] to its
present status—and I am unwilling it should loose its
feminine identity by being massed to a mans ‹*capital*›
money.

I have done this work with the consciousness that
womans work is looked upon with suspicion—and I am
gratified to know that coneseurs in the art pronounce it
above criticism.

A great many of my birds and animals I have ‹*shot*› procured myself with a gun—and I am not a masculine
woman eather. My height is a little less than five feet
and I weigh 120 lbs—[32]

In addition, she wrote to her sister Mary on September 2, 1876,
that she had received a copy of a newspaper article published in
Paris:

. . . it may amuse you to know what absurd things they
say about me there. I've no duplicate copy or would
send you one. Will copy one sentence "Admirable as
the collection is in taxidermic skill and landscape
arrangement the most wonderful of all is the little rocky
Mountain woman herself, who has killed many and prepared them all. She is still young" (!!) "rather small, her
face is somewhat bronzed but not atall unpleasantly so;
her blue eyes dance with sweetness and intelligence and
the mixture of gentleness, courage, and capabilities is so
blended in her appearance as to make her very attractive" (!!) "As an illustration of what 'woman can do'
there is nothing in the womans Pavilion of such brave,
strong and really artistic completion as Mrs. Maxwell's
display in Colorado." This however it may vary from
the truth is very pretily said & helps to remove the picture of the Amazon.[33]

In this respect, Martha was much like the women who exhibited in the Women's Pavilion. As one historian of this enterprise
recently observed: "Female organizers never intended to desex
women. Instead, they hoped to mix feminine virtue with profes-

sional achievement."[34] Similarly, Anne Firor Scott has pointed out how the feminist and the "true woman" could coexist in one individual; that is, nineteenth-century women could and did hold both feminist and traditional views simultaneously.[35] Thus Martha could wish to be seen as independent and feminist on the one hand, attractive and feminine on the other and find no contradiction in the dichotomy.

Some writers, though, instead of or in addition to emphasizing her feminine qualities, cast Martha in the image of a frontierswoman who had taken gun in hand so that she might survive in the Wild West. "She wears, when hunting, the costume and trappings of the frontiersman, rides her mustang, and hunts the mountains and plains with a boldness that rivals the most daring hunter," asserted one reporter.[36] Another commented that after she moved to Colorado, "she found it necessary, in order to protect herself against the incursions of savage animals and hostile Indians, to become a proficient in the use of the rifle."[37] A third, exaggerating a common eastern conception, reported that at her homes in Mountain City and Boulder, "she frequently met Indians of the Sioux, Arapahoe, and Cheyenne tribes, but, fully understanding their treachery as well as their cowardice and vanity, was able to protect herself from harm under all circumstances."[38]

Martha's own pride in her prowess with a rifle notwithstanding, she was most anxious that her image as a "huntress" not overshadow either that of a feminine woman or of a serious naturalist. Shooting specimens was for her only a means to an end, a way to collect examples of Rocky Mountain mammals and birds for scientific and educational purposes.[39] To those who asked how she could bear to kill the specimens she mounted she had a ready reply, one that was expressed most forcefully later in *On the Plains*: "There isn't a day you don't tacitly consent to have some creature killed that you may eat it. I never take life for such carnivorous purposes! All must die some time; I only shorten the period of consciousness that I may give their forms perpetual memory; and I leave it to you, which is the more cruel? to kill to eat, or to kill to *immortalize*?"[40] (Yet on several occasions she posed for the camera in her hunting costume, complete with gun, thus reinforcing to some extent the very image that she wished to contradict.)

As the reporters and tourists continued to flock around Martha Maxwell's exhibit, recognition of her abilities came from other quarters as well. In July, in appreciation of her contributions to the success of the Kansas-Colorado Building, the Kansas and Colorado commissioners presented her with an Evans Magazine Rifle which, she was told, could be "loaded with 34 cartridges in 45 seconds and discharged in 20 seconds without removing the Hand from the Lock." As Martha accepted the gun she once again reiterated her goals. "The use of this rare gift shall be directed by a love of science," she assured the commissioners, "and in the pursuit of objects for the study of natural history it shall be my trusted companion and assistant."[41] And when the Centennial awards were given out at a ceremony in September Martha earned one of the bronze medals "for a very large and exceedingly interesting collection of wild animals and birds of the Rocky Mountain region."[42] (In a departure from tradition, only a uniform bronze medal was given, instead of first, second, and third prizes. An accompanying written report by the judges set forth the "inherent and comparative" merits of the winning displays or products, which were divided into various groups. There was no limit to the number of awards that might be given in a particular category; of some thirty thousand exhibitors, over thirteen thousand received medals.)[43]

In addition to receiving such tangible recognition, Martha also had the opportunity to increase her contacts with the scientific community. "She was made welcome at the Philadelphia Academy of Science & of Natural History," Nathan Meeker reported, "[and] learned and scientific people from every nation were glad to see her."[44] (The Philadelphia Academy of Natural Sciences, however, has no records indicating that she was made a member of that society. A few women had by that time been elected to membership on their scientific merits, notably ornithologist Graceanna Lewis.)[45]

Moreover, Ernest Ingersoll, a naturalist who had become a member of the Hayden Survey in 1874 as an assistant to photographer William Henry Jackson, prepared a listing of the land and fresh-water shells that Martha had brought to Philadelphia for exhibit. A former Oberlin student, Ingersoll had been curator of the museum there before going on to study at the Museum of Comparative Zoology at Harvard.[46] "These shells she kindly entrusted to me for examination," he wrote in the *American Naturalist*, "and they seem to me worthy of notice, as they add materially to the previously known molluscan fauna of the State."[47] Ingersoll also noted that they were of particular interest as the first collection brought east since he had gathered his specimens in 1874 for the survey, and that furthermore, Martha's shells came "from the eastern slope of the Range, where I succeeded in finding almost nothing at all near Berthoude Pass or at Colorado Springs."[48] Ingersoll had published a report on the mollusks of the area encompassing not only Colorado but the Great Plains to the east and the region to the crest of the Sierra Nevada on the west.[49] He had tabulated 138 "nominal species" in all, and with Martha's specimens he was able to add 6 new ones, all new to the whole "province" as well as to Colorado. Of one in particular, an example of an Anodon, he commented that if it "should prove to be an undescribed species, it ought certainly to be dedicated to the energetic naturalist to whose intelligence and care we are indebted for this interesting collection of Colorado mollusks."[50]

Going beyond such contemporary acclaim, what was the long-term influence of Martha Maxwell's celebrated Centennial display? Can it be shown that her work played a role in the later development of habitat exhibits in natural history museums? To answer these questions, a brief review of certain aspects of museum history is necessary. In the United States, the beginning of habitat grouping concepts, like so much else in the history of museums, can be traced to Peale's Museum in Philadelphia in the late eighteenth century. Here Peale had erected a hilly landscape with trees and rocks surrounding a glass-covered pond; stuffed fish and waterfowl were displayed on the banks, while bear, deer, and leopards stood on the mounds and birds perched in the branches of the trees. The exhibit, however, was vulnerable to damage caused by visitors who could not refrain from touching the lifelike specimens, and Peale soon devised glass-fronted cases in which small groupings were displayed against watercolor paintings of the native habitats. By the early nineteenth century, a one-hundred-foot wall in the famous "Long Room" was covered with 140 cases of birds shown against backdrops "painted to represent appropriate scenery, Mountains, Plains or Waters, the birds being placed on branches or artificial rocks, &c."[51]

Yet until the 1880s, few scientific museum displays were anything other than rows of specimens placed side by side against white backgrounds so that they could be compared with one another. The first group in the American Museum of Natural History, a theatrical depiction by French ornithologist Jules Verreaux of an Arab courier on a camel being attacked by lions, had gone on display in 1869. Frederic Webster, a taxidermist from New York who later studied at Ward's, had been mounting birds on tree limbs, sometimes against painted backgrounds, since the late 1860s, while Julius Stoerzer mounted a seal grouping in 1875 for the U.S. National Museum display at the Centennial.[52] However, as late as 1872, Elliott Coues had written that "'spread eagle' styles of mounting, artificial rocks and flowers, etc., are entirely out of place in a collection of any scientific pretensions, or designed for popular instruction. . . . Birds look best on the whole in uniform rows, assorted according to size, as far as a natural classification allows."[53]

In fact, many students of museum history, not to mention Hornaday himself, trace the beginnings of the modern habitat display to Hornaday's 1879 grouping of a family of orangutans in a tree.[54] Entitled "A Fight in the Tree-Tops," it was exhibited at a meeting of the American Association for the Advancement of Science in 1879, and Hornaday wrote some ten years later that although it might be immodest of him to say so, "I cannot help believing that the production of that group marked the beginning of an era in the progress of museum taxidermy in the United States."[55]

By 1922, when he reviewed the history of habitat groups for *Scribner's Magazine*, Hornaday was even more convinced that "the idea of scientific museum groups of large mammals, with natural or artificial accessories, was born in a forest reeking with live orang-utans and gibbons on the Sadong River, Borneo, in the glorious month of November, 1878." It was while he was in that forest, Hornaday continued, that "the first large mammal group ever produced in America ['A Fight in the Tree-Tops'] was thought out and determined upon."[56]

Nowhere in his account, entitled "Masterpieces of American Taxidermy," did Hornaday so much as mention Martha Maxwell's work, and when Mary Dartt Thompson read the article she immediately sent a letter to him drawing his attention to her sister's accomplishments. "I do not think all his statement[s] should go unchallenged," she commented to University of Colorado Museum Curator Junius Henderson. "It is not just."[57]

Just or not, Hornaday was not alone in claiming credit for originating the habitat group concept. Looking back over his career at the age of ninety-five, Frederic Webster boasted that, in 1868, he "first conceived the idea of museum 'habitat' groups" and related how he had then mounted groups of birds among natural materials and made stereoscopic views of them for sale.[58]

Certainly it is true that Webster's groups and Hornaday's "A Fight in the Tree-Tops" and an 1880 companion piece, "Orangs at Home" had considerable impact, although it is overstating the case to say that either man, or Martha Maxwell, for that matter, "invented" the idea of the habitat group. Probably, as American Museum of Natural History Director A. E. Parr stated in 1959, the concept developed "more or less simultaneously and independently," perhaps as an outgrowth of the ornamental arrangements of birds on bushes favored in Victorian homes.[59] Martha Maxwell, in fact, had devised groupings of birds and mammals in both the Dartt home in Baraboo and the Maxwell home in Boulder.[60]

Hornaday's orangutan grouping, however, seems to have had more impact than any of the earlier displays and is thus deserving of its place in museum history. While it is not surprising that Hornaday and Webster assign themselves prominent roles in developing the habitat grouping concept, it is somewhat less clear why Frederic A. Lucas, then director of the American Museum of Natural History, did not mention Martha Maxwell's exhibit in his 1914 survey entitled "The Story of Museum Groups," even though he was familiar with her work. In 1923, for example, he wrote to Mary Dartt Thompson thanking her for letting him borrow some photographs of Martha's groups and telling her that she was "in error in supposing that I never heard of her because I happened to see these very specimens at the Centennial."[61]

Hornaday also had visited the Centennial between collecting expeditions,[62] but Martha Maxwell's exhibit, if indeed he saw it, seems not to have left a lasting impression on him. Probably it is too easy to speculate that Martha Maxwell was denied recognition as a "pioneer" in the art of habitat grouping because of her sex. Just as likely an explanation is the fact that her death occurred in 1881 at the moment when taxidermy, like many other fields, was becoming professionalized; a year earlier the Society of American Taxidermists had been organized with Webster as president, Hornaday as secretary, and Lucas as treasurer.[63] Had she lived, it is conceivable that she might have joined the group (women as well as men were members) and enjoyed the benefits of collaboration and friendship. Yet prejudice, as she might have said, cannot be denied, and Lucas's failure to include her work in his history does not alleviate suspicion in this direction.

Despite such lack of recognition, however, given the abundant documentary and pictorial evidence of Martha Maxwell's museum displays in Colorado and at the Centennial, one must agree with the evaluation of Junius Henderson, who wrote in 1915 that her work represented "one of the earliest efforts in America to exhibit the animals of a large area in an imitation of their natural environment." Although as a Boulderite and friend of Mary Dartt Thompson he was not a disinterested observer, Henderson's summation seems judicious, sympathetic, and fair: "Without any attempt at demonstration, ore can scarcely doubt that such an exhibit at such a time must have at once stimulated work upon modern habitat groups. The extent of its influence upon modern methods there is no way of accurately measuring, but even those who never heard of the estimable lady are perhaps to a greater or less extent reaping the results of her stimulating example."[64]

While Martha would have been gratified to know that Henderson, at least, would regard her work so favorably, and while she was pleased with the contemporary recognition she was receiving, she never lost sight of her goal to earn enough money so that her daughter could continue in school. Unfortunately, however, in this as in other instances concerning money, she soon ran into problems that threatened her relatively modest hopes for financial success. As part of her agreement, the Colorado commissioners were to pay the expenses of packing and shipping the collection to Philadelphia and returning it to Colorado, as well as Martha's expenses from the time she left Denver until the close of the exhibition and her return to Colorado, if she wished. In order to remunerate her for her time, she was to have the right to sell photographs of herself and the exhibit as well as duplicate specimens.[65]

The Centennial Photographic Company, however, held a monopoly on views of the exhibition, and because Martha's exhibit was so popular, the firm was not able to supply her with as many photographs as she could sell. Finally, toward the end of the summer she took matters into her own hands and arranged herself to have copies made; from September 30 to October 20 she sold 5,610 photos, in addition to all the views that the company could furnish. As soon as the company discovered that she was acting on her own she was ordered to stop selling the copies altogether or risk having her stands closed, and she had no alternative but to comply.[66] "I was never so anoyed in my life about a little thing as about these pictures," she wrote to Mary on September 2.[67]

Despite such obstacles, Martha kept on with her work from morning to night, estimating at the end of September that she had saved enough money to keep Mabel in school for the next two years, regardless of whether her father contributed toward her expenses or whether the collection was sold. Martha was encouraged also by the visits she had had at Oberlin and during the summer with Mabel, who had spent a two-week vacation in Philadelphia with a schoolmate. If Mabel remembered the encounter at Oberlin as one filled with recrimination and misunderstanding, Martha had come away with a much different view. She had been, she told Nathan Thompson, "delighted" with Mabel's "progress, appearance, and asperations." She had feared that

Mabel might be growing tired of school, but she had obtained the impression instead that her daughter was anxious "to *commence* a *longer* and more *thorough* course" at the University of Michigan at Ann Arbor. "Of course my ambition for her knows no bounds," she commented to her brother-in-law, and at this juncture, Martha pronounced herself pleased that what she had seen of Mabel "strengthened my faith in her and my hopes for her future."[68] (Again, Mabel's later view of that summer visit was quite different. "We tried hard to rebuild the kind of relationship that we both wanted," she wrote, "but the visit left us mutually dissatisfied and longing for the kind of communion that we had missed.")[69]

At the moment, though, Mabel's expressed wish to transfer to the University of Michigan set off another round of family discussion about her education. Writing to Nathan Thompson, who thus far had been paying most of Mabel's expenses, Martha wondered if her daughter should go to Oberlin, Ann Arbor, or Cornell. Despite her strong feminist views, Martha had enjoyed her coeducational experience at Oberlin and was not in favor of Mabel attending a women's college at this time. "I've observed students from Vasser and other female schools," she commented to Thompson. "They seem awkward in mixed society, which is an additional reason for disliking such schools."[70] James Maxwell continued to hold out for Northwestern, refusing to contribute any support unless she attended the Illinois school. In the end, Mabel's desires prevailed. "Nothing gives me so much pleasure as to know that you are determined to have a thorough education and to assist you in obtaining it," Martha wrote in giving her permission to go to Ann Arbor. "Only *do not* permit your health to be injured."[71] Although Martha was worried about expenses, despite the money she had set aside, she cautioned Mabel that if she would be "as economical as possible," she would spare no effort to keep her in school. "I care nothing for any personal pinching or self-denial," she told her. "I am used to it, but I wish to give you all the study you can have for the money at command."[72]

With Mabel's immediate future taken care of, Martha then began considering what she would do with the collection once the Centennial Exposition closed on November 10. She had achieved more fame and prominence than she had thought possible, and she hoped to build on her accomplishments to achieve financial stability, continue with her study of science, and advance the cause of feminism. "I feel that my life is but just commenced!!" she exclaimed to Mary, "and I want to use it to the best advantage in all ways."[73] Thoughts of taking the collection to the Paris Exposition in 1878 crossed her mind, and other opportunities might be available in the wake of her Centennial success. Who could tell? Perhaps, after years of hard work and sacrifice, the brighter days for which she had yearned were at hand.

Certainly Spencer Baird was encouraging. Writing shortly after the exposition ended to Nathan Meeker, he observed that Martha possessed "a most excellent knowledge of natural history" and that her specimens were "extremely well prepared"; he hoped that the exhibit would be retained and made available elsewhere.[74]

In fact, after the close of the Centennial, Martha made an agreement with two men named Alvin O. Buck and John Gardiner to exhibit the collection in Washington, D.C. They would pay the expenses of shipping it from Philadelphia, and as soon as it opened would pay her one hundred dollars per month until February 1, 1878. For her part, she agreed to superintend the arrangement and maintain it in good condition; Buck and Gardiner would keep the admission fees, but she would be free to sell "objects of Natural History &c."[75] By December 1 she was in Washington, and on December 21 "Mrs. Maxwell's Colorado Centennial Exhibit" opened to the public at 930 Pennsylvania Avenue.[76] The display apparently was similar to that in Philadelphia, according to one newspaper report: "The various animals are very naturally arranged upon the declivities of a section of the Rocky Mountains, down which a stream descends, losing itself at one point to issue again in a beautiful fountain. The mountain side is covered with a thick growth of evergreens and mosses. A beautiful grotto is a noticeable feature, and the animals are most life-like."[77]

Although the *Washington Gazette* urged all those in the capital to visit the exhibit, saying that "no one should fail to see this work of ingenious skill and untiring labor,"[78] business was terrible from the beginning. "Times are most fearfully dull," Martha lamented to Mabel on December 28. "We opened the Museum rooms a week ago but as yet there is no custom and no sales. I fear the whole thing will be a failure, and that it will trouble me to get my pay."[79] Early in the new year she wrote to her sister Mary that her fears were being realized. "Business here is perfectly dead," she told her, and to make matters worse, Gardiner had failed in his own endeavors.[80] A month later she informed Mabel that the museum still was bringing in no money, and that she had to pay the expenses that had been incurred—indeed, at that moment she was being sued for the nonpayment of a sixty-five-dollar debt. Truly she was at a loss to see how to extricate herself from the situation. She cautioned her daughter, however, not to mention the dilemma to James Maxwell or Nathan Thompson; "I've troubles enough without being sensured or derided for doing the best I can."[81]

Not that her stay in Washington was completely devoid of pleasure. She roomed with Mary Sherman, who had written the article about her in the *New Century for Women* and was helping her with the French lessons that Martha was taking presumably in preparation for the Paris Exposition.[82] She was making some "good acquaintances," she told Mary, and had been invited by the Hutchinson Family, whom she had first seen at Oberlin, to accompany them to their concert early in January.[83] She and Mary Sherman also took a trip to Mount Vernon.[84] Yet despite such diversions, the immediate outlook seemed bleak. "I'm disgusted with myself," she confided to Mary, "because I'm accomplishing nothing everything is so uncertain."[85]

Adding to her uncertainty was the fact that she was having a great deal of difficulty collecting the money she had been promised as part of her agreement with the Colorado commissioners. Despite the bargain they had made with her, she had received no money since June of 1876; she calculated, in fact, that they still owed her a total of $733.80.[86]

Even as Martha's finances grew more troubled, however, she continued to send money to Mabel for her schooling at Ann Arbor. On December 28 she sent her ten dollars, another ten dollars on January 2, fifty dollars on January 23, and another fifty dollars on February 7.[87] "It does seem a very expensive place where you are," Martha commented, "but I suppose it can't be helped. Is there any way to economize?" Perhaps, she suggested, Mabel's washing cost more because she wore "more white shirts and collars than is necessary." She herself wore "for common the cheap ruffles which I get for 22 cts per doz. and two last me a week & my work soiles them faster than yours. Can you get them there? Would you like some sent from here?" Yet when Mabel suggested leaving school because of the lack of money, Martha would not hear of it. "Ever since you were born it has been my ambition to realize in you my own disappointed hopes for education and usefulness," she told her. "So long as there is the least probability for success I cannot give it up."[88]

Nor should Mabel feel that she was taking money that belonged to her father. "I know your father is getting old, but he is in good health and has never permitted himself to be injured by care or over work," she told her with some asperity. "He has money . . . which he will not use for your schooling or for building a house, he has nobody but himself—and the church—to support. . . ." Thus, she concluded, "I do not feel that I am to be sensured in his account, or that you are using what he has a right to claim."[89]

Still, there were times now, as there had been in the past, when Martha Maxwell was not so certain that her chosen life had been the most beneficial for her daughter. A short time before she penned her assurances to Mabel, she commented, in one of her regular appeals to Mabel's discipline and good judgment, that if "any evil" should befall her, "all our Oberlin friend[s] and Colorado friends will blame you and your crazy, ambitious mother. . . ."[90] And a year earlier, she had confided that "I often think it would be much better for you if my aspirations and tastes led me to nothing beyond the washtub for I should be far more independent in Money matters than now." James had agreed, she said, and "Mr. T[hompson] has told me that I'd better be raising chickens—so you see I have not only hard work and poverty to contend with, but a lack of sympathy at home."[91]

On the brighter side, Mabel was doing well at the University of Michigan, saying later that "I was happier there than I had ever been in my life." She took a scientific course, partly to please Martha and also because she liked mathematics. She studied hard, made good grades, and enjoyed being one of the few women in an overwhelmingly male institution (the university had first admitted women in 1870).[92] In contrast to her two years at Oberlin, which had been marked by homesickness and rebellion against the Oberlin way of life, Mabel apparently came into her own at Ann Arbor. If Martha was moving heaven and earth to keep her there, the money and sacrifice were not in vain.

Still, for Martha Maxwell the direction her life would take in the aftermath of her Centennial triumph was far from clear. "The great query with me now is how can I best utilize in the future, this notoriety that has come to me unsaught," she had written to Mary from Philadelphia. "It should result in pecuniary good as well as in pretty words—at least the pretty words of the present should put me in better communication with people's pockets in future."[93]

Back in Colorado, James Maxwell also found the future "clouded & dark." The "elephant," as he referred to the collection, was requiring ever more of Martha's time and attention, while on the horizon loomed either more success at the Paris Exposition or "the possible poor house or mad house." Echoing Martha's views, he wrote that surely she ought to be able to realize some financial gain from her fame; if that could not be accomplished "with the vast amount of notoriety you and your work have recd., then pray tell me, what is notoriety worth?" What would please him best, he concluded, would be for Martha to "sell out, swap off, give away, or leave" the collection and return to Colorado, there to set about obtaining money from the legislature to cover the Centennial expenses and provide funds with which to prepare a new collection for the university while making a home for him and Mabel after she finished her education.[94]

Rejecting that alternative, at least for the moment, Martha sought help from an expert, master showman P. T. Barnum, who had seen her collection at the exposition. Remarking that by this time he was "pretty well out of the Museum business," he had told her that "it wont pay *anywhere* to show alone by itself," although exhibiting the collection in conjunction with a store or business might be financially feasible.[95]

Certainly Barnum's prediction seemed to be coming true so far as the Washington exhibition was concerned. Thus on the one hand Martha Maxwell had received acclaim from press and public as well as from the scientific community that she could scarcely have imagined when she had left Denver a few months before. Her exhibit, moreover, would later be recognized as having made a significant contribution to the development of habitat groups in natural history museums. Nonetheless, as she moved beyond her Centennial triumph, Martha found, as often before, that instead of having achieved some security and stability in her personal life, she was facing even more conflict, change, and uncertainty. That the problems in her relationship with her husband and daughter appeared to be rooted in the basic, unalterable differences between her needs and expectations and theirs made them no less difficult or painful to resolve. Whatever the ultimate outcome, however, Martha was determined at the moment to continue to try to find the money somewhere to support her work and help with Mabel's education. Finally, two solutions appeared that promised at least some degree of hope. She and Mary would produce a book, a "sketch" of Martha's life and accomplishments, and she would exhibit her collection again in Philadelphia.

"On the Plains"

During the first two years after the close of the Philadelphia Centennial Exposition, Martha Maxwell, then in her mid-forties, continued to struggle with the dilemma of finding a way to keep on with her work and to derive enough money from it to enable her daughter to finish college. For reasons that may have been entirely clear only to her, she came to feel that it was impossible to return to Colorado and resume living with her husband James. With Mary now residing near Boston she did have some family in the East, and there were undoubtedly more chances for financial success and personal fulfillment there than in the still remote and sparsely settled West. Thus from Philadelphia Martha had gone directly to Washington, and it was while she was in the capital exhibiting the collection that the idea for a book began to take shape.

By early 1877 it appears that Mary was busily writing the "sketch," while Martha was arranging for catalogs of the birds and mammals to be prepared.[1] In fact, initially a "catalogue and history of the exhibit" was to have been published as part of the agreement Martha made with Buck and Gardiner to show the collection in Washington—the men would pay half the expenses of publication, Martha the other half, with proceeds to be shared in the same proportion.[2] Plans fell through quickly when Buck could not come up with the money, and although there seemed to be little demand for the work at the time, Martha encouraged Mary to continue with her part "and we will see what we can do with it."[3]

Martha saw the proposed book not only as a project that promised financial salvation but also as one that would help her sister Mary through a difficult period in her life and might launch a significant writing career for her as well. As early as 1865 Mary had been contributing long, narrative poems to the Baraboo newspaper, and she had thereafter written accounts in verse and prose on a variety of subjects. Such a level of literary activity was not in the least unusual for mid-nineteenth-century women, writing being acceptable both as a means of self-expression and as a source of income.[4]

Although separated in age by ten years, Martha and Mary remained close friends and lifelong confidantes, bound by the emotional ties that so typified nineteenth-century sisterly relationships.[5] As Smith-Rosenberg writes, "Sisterly bonds continued across a lifetime. . . . Such women, whether friends or relatives, assumed an emotional centrality in one another's lives. In their diaries and letters they wrote of the joy and contentment they felt in one another's company, their sense of isolation and despair when apart. The regularity of their correspondence underlines the sincerity of such words."[6] For example, Martha told Mary in 1876, "You know and understand me better than anyone living," while Mary wrote on another occasion, "I have thought of you daily and hourly & wished we had a telephone so that we could talk back & forth without stoping our respective works."[7] Indeed, ample evidence exists to support the assertion Mabel made many years later that "as the years passed, the affection which Martha bore for her sister Mary was probably the most important relationship in her life."[8]

Evidently Mary was going through a difficult time in her marriage early in 1877; "you know she and Nate are not happy together," Martha confided to Mabel, "and I doubt if they ever will be. Its too bad she's a darling and deserves a congenial companion."[9] Concerned, Martha attempted to cheer her sister up. "Do please write me that you are in better spirits, that is if you are," she wrote from Washington. "It grieves me to think that my dear affectionate little sister is sick and unhappy. Wish I could be with you you would then forget your own troubles in sympathizing with me in mine."[10]

While Mary struggled with her problems and continued to work on the manuscript, Martha arranged with Robert Ridgway of the Smithsonian to prepare a catalog of the birds in her collection. Since Martha had been in Washington she and Ridgway had become personal friends as well as colleagues, and Martha had become better acquainted with Mrs. Ridgway and the other members of the family. Something of the warmth and closeness of their relationship is indicated in an exchange of letters after the birth of the Ridgways' son Audubon Whelock Ridgway in May 1877. "He is a young ornithologist, but does not take very much interest in birds yet, his chief amusement being sleeping, exercising his lungs, and cramming his fist in his mouth," the proud father informed Martha. "He is (*of course*) a fine baby."[11] Martha was delighted with the news. "Yes, I know '*he*' is an 'ornithologist' and an artist too, for a strong trait in the character of father and mother too, must be reproduced. I only wish it were '*she*' for there are more boys than girls now, possessing such gifts. How I wish I could see this bird of all birds and his mother. Please remember me with warmest love to her and the other members of your family."[12]

Ridgway had finished the catalog in April and had arranged to have it printed as a separate pamphlet; it also appeared in the May, June, and July numbers of *Field and Forest*.[13] Having helped Martha with this project, Ridgway then turned to ask her for assistance with one of his own concerning the rosy finches about which he had written earlier. He now wished to determine more precisely the "amount of difference usually observable between the two sexes," having been "forced into" a debate about the birds with Joel A. Allen, the noted ornithologist who was then curator of birds at the Harvard Museum of Comparative Zoology. "Very naturally," Ridgway told her, "[I] want to prove to every one's satisfaction that I am right—as I most undoubtedly am."[14] Martha quickly replied, and in thanking her Ridgway told her that the notes she sent were "just what I want."[15] This was not Ridgway's first brush with controversy within the ornithological fraternity; in fact, he had been involved in a dispute in 1873 with Elliott Coues, who had accused him of giving Allen insufficient credit in an article to the point of plagiarism. Coues's criticism was unduly harsh and without adequate foundation, and the two men soon smoothed over their differences for the time being. Allen himself had not suggested that Ridgway was guilty of misappropriating his work, and the whole episode was unfortunate as well as unnecessary.[16]

It was thus somewhat ironic that the man Martha Maxwell chose to write up the mammals in her collection was none other than Elliott Coues. Martha probably knew nothing of his disagreement with Ridgway, nor should it have made any difference in his association with her; in any event, Coues was eminently qualified for the assignment and undertook it with enthusiasm. Much more than a typical army surgeon, Coues by 1877 had achieved a place of considerable prominence in natural history. Collecting specimens and making observations during tours of duty in Arizona Territory, the Carolinas, and Maryland and with the Northern Boundary Commission, Coues had written an amazing number of books and articles, including the *Key to North American Birds* published in 1872; still to come were many more publications and the editions of the journals of Lewis and Clark, Zebulon Pike, and other explorers that would establish his reputation as a historian as well. Even more to the point, Coues had just returned from Colorado, where he had been assigned as secretary and naturalist with the Hayden Survey. Arriving in Cheyenne in August 1876, he had traveled into North Park and Middle Park, over Berthoud Pass, and then north back to Cheyenne, returning to Washington in October.[17] This, of course, was exactly the area in which Martha had done much of her collecting, and Coues was delighted to have an opportunity to examine her exhibition while it was in Washington. His "repeated visits," he commented, "afforded me both pleasure and instruction," and by May of 1877 he had completed his catalog of the mammals in the collection.[18]

While Ridgway and Coues were working on their catalogs, Martha closed the exhibit in Washington and returned in late March to Philadelphia, where she had made arrangements to participate in the "Permanent Exhibition" in the Main Building that had evolved from the Centennial.[19] Although some of the Centennial buildings were to remain in Fairmount Park, at least for a time, the breathtakingly large Main Building (1,880 feet long and 464 feet wide) originally was slated to be torn down. Toward the end of the exposition, however, the International Exhibition Company was organized, money was raised from cash donations and stock subscriptions, and the building was purchased from the Centennial Board of Finance.[20]

Traversing the full length of the Main Building was a 120-foot-wide center aisle, and it was along this "Main Avenue" that Martha had secured space for her exhibit. Apparently she constructed a landscape much like the one in the Kansas-Colorado Building, featuring a cave and a stream of running water. "On the rocks are seen bears, deers, wolves, foxes, panthers and catamounts; rabbits, hares and partridges appear in great naturalness; a camp of prairie dogs; a large black bear and deer and two fawns fill the foreground," read one typical description.[21]

As in 1876, Martha Maxwell's exhibit brought the same favorable notices from the press and the same attention from the public. For example, take the woman who brought her small child into the exhibit and later recounted the experience. Seeing "a nice little animal just high enough for his feet to touch the ground when he sat upon it," she related, "I lifted him onto it and said: 'Jump, Georgie Porgie, ridie pidie on the bearie wearie.' I didn't think she heard me, but she turned round like a house afire and cried 'Good gracious, Madam! don't teach your child such erroneous notions of natural history; that is a panther.'"[22]

With all the acclaim, however, Martha soon discovered that her display in the Permanent Exhibition was bringing her no more financial success than did the previous exhibits.[23] To make matters worse, she was embroiled in a controversy again over the right to be exempt from the photographic monopoly and sell her own pictures. She had thought the matter settled when her application for space containing the request for the exemption had been accepted, but apparently such was not the case. To have to fight this battle all over again plunged her into despondency. "I am indeed sorry to find you so lowspirited and discouraged but to tell the truth Im too nearly in the same condition to do you any good," she wrote to Mary on May 1. "In fact I feel that there's but little to hope for."[24]

Yet whatever problems she faced, it was difficult for Martha to remain discouraged for long, for there was always some new project on the horizon that promised either financial salvation or personal fulfillment or both. For example, during the summer of 1877 she received a pamphlet describing the "Woodruff Scientific Expedition Around the World," an ambitious two-year journey planned to begin in October. Combining classes and lectures with opportunities to collect specimens in various exotic locales, the expedition could accommodate three hundred persons, "including 20 ladies," who would each pay $2,500 for the once-in-a-lifetime experience.[25] "As the schoolgirls say [I] 'am dying' to join it," she told Ridgway. "But that 'missing link' money, so necessary to connect the present with our hopes in the future, will, I fear, continue to be missing." Perhaps he knew of someone who would buy her collection or otherwise furnish the necessary funds, in return for what she could collect during the expedition. "The pleasure of working in such a field, with such company, and what I could see and learn would be ample compensation for my time," she continued. "If you can suggest anything that will throw light on the vexed question of 'ways and means' you will confer a great favor."[26] Besides giving her a seemingly unparalleled opportunity for study, the expedition also might serve as a chance to introduce Mabel to the field of natural history, for the idea was beginning to take shape in Martha's mind that her daughter would follow in her footsteps. "If I only dared hope that we can both go with the Expedition how happy I should be," Martha wrote her. "I shall not go unless I can get money enough to take us both & I fear there is no hope of this."[27]

Martha's plans to go on the expedition never materialized (nor, ultimately, did the expedition itself),[28] and as the summer of 1877 wore on her financial situation, instead of improving, was steadily deteriorating. Indeed, no matter in which direction she turned, she was faced with nothing but bad news. For one thing, not only had the museum cases and boxes of household items she had left in Denver been broken into, but she was expected to pay two hundred dollars in taxes, and there was a claim as well of about six hundred dollars which she had thought would be paid by some "prominent citizens of Denver" but which still remained unpaid.[29] Back taxes also were due on some property she owned in Boulder, her stepfather Josiah Dartt informed her, and her name had appeared in the newspaper in the delinquent tax list.[30] Small wonder, then, that she renewed her efforts in September to obtain the money she felt was owed her by virtue of her agreement with the Colorado Centennial commissioners. Recounting the terms to Secretary of State William M. Clark, she pleaded with him to intercede and support her position. She had fulfilled her part of the contract at the Centennial—her success was ample proof of that—and now the state should pay what was justly her due. Receiving the funds, she told him, would enable her to visit Colorado "and perhapse save something from the wreck there or at least have the pleasure of paying my debts."[31]

What to do? Martha was having no success collecting the money from Colorado, and another solution, that the new university at Boulder would make an agreement with her and buy the collection, also did not materialize, although Josiah Dartt and James Maxwell had presented such a request to the regents.[32] Perhaps the 1878 Paris Exposition would provide the answer, but here again, Martha's hopes were dashed. In early September she went to New York to see Richard McCormick, the former journalist and governor of Arizona Territory who was serving as commissioner general for the United States to the exposition, and initially was encouraged by his interest in the collection. Toward the end of their conversation, however, McCormick informed her that should she participate in the exposition, *"no sales were to be made"*—a considerable obstacle to success, as she well knew.[33] Still not giving up entirely on the possibility of going to Paris, she wrote to Colorado Senator Henry M. Teller on October 18, asking him to use his influence to secure space for her within that allotted to the United States as well as financial assistance.[34]

Yet it was becoming apparent that her dream of going to Paris would remain just that, and with the Permanent Exhibition closing during the winter months, not to mention her severe financial problems, Martha was in a quandary. If she didn't go to Paris, she had asked Mary a few months earlier, "What shall I do? go to Colo. and raise cabbages and potatoes by your leave, Lords

Grasshoppers & Potato Bug[s]."[35] In truth, signs were beginning to appear indicating that even if Martha was financially able to go to Colorado, she was reluctant to do so in the wake of her slowly deteriorating relationship with her husband James. For example, hints of discord were apparent in a letter she wrote to Mabel from Philadelphia in April. Asking if Mabel had written to her father, Martha commented that she had received "several *unpleasant* letters" from him and warned her daughter not to suggest that she continue such correspondence. "Im tired of such letters," she concluded, "and all I can say dont satisfy him."[36]

Thus, instead of going back to Colorado, Martha went to Boston, where early in 1878 she enrolled in classes in the Woman's Laboratory of the Massachusetts Institute of Technology (MIT). "Here I am a prospective school girl!!" she enthused, "only think of it!"[37] The laboratory was the project of Ellen Swallow Richards, a remarkable woman who had been graduated from Vassar in 1870 at the age of twenty-eight with an A.B. degree. Anxious to pursue chemistry as a lifework, she had persuaded the Massachusetts Institute of Technology to accept her as a special student in 1871. Two years later MIT awarded her an S.B. degree — the first to a woman. She remained at MIT (although without a regular position) and married Prof. Robert Hallowell Richards in 1875, with whom she had a long and mutually productive relationship.[38]

By late 1876 Richards had managed to secure support from the Boston Woman's Education Association to start the Woman's Laboratory, where women, mostly schoolteachers, could undertake "the study of Chemical Analysis, of Industrial Chemistry, of Mineralogy, and of Chemistry as related to Vegetable and Animal Physiology."[39] (Women were not admitted to MIT as regular students until 1878.) Officially in the charge of MIT professor John M. Ordway, the laboratory was directed by Richards on a day-to-day basis until 1883, when it was consolidated with the regular classes. Finally, in 1884, Richards was appointed to the MIT faculty as an instructor in sanitary chemistry. Remaining there until her death in 1911, she went on to achieve renown in establishing the field of home economics.[40] To Martha Maxwell, able to take advantage for a short time of the opportunities she had made possible at MIT, Ellen Richards was simply "a darling—my ideal woman."[41]

Anticipating being a student again, Martha was fairly brimming over with joy. "I never looked forward to anything with such satisfaction, yes, *positive pleasure,* as the next few months," she told Mary the day before classes began. "I only wish they might be years."[42] She was not disappointed. "My studies are a delight," she wrote to her sister about a week later. "You would be captivated with the study of Biology. I am bound to have a large microscope and perhapse can spend a part of next summer with you showing you the wonderful things which it reveals for instance—the moving protoplasm in the plant and the beating of the heart in the egg of a snail."[43]

Indeed, it is apparent that Martha's love for learning had hardly diminished since she had been a student at Oberlin more than twenty-five years earlier. If anything, her avid interest in the pursuit of knowledge was burning more brightly than ever, as she revealed in an introspective letter to her stepfather, Josiah Dartt, who had always both shared and supported her desires. What she was attempting to do, she told him, was "to learn how I can accomplish the most for science with the greatest benefit to myself, mentally I mean, financially I have no ambition beyond a living, which I always expect to work for & I wish such work to be in a field for mental improvement." Truly, there were "so many wonderful discoveries to be made in science especially in its connection with the R[ocky] M[ountains]," she wrote. Referring to Louis Agassiz (1807–1873), the Swiss scientist who had done so much to popularize the study of natural history in America, she continued. "Agazzes says 'The education of a naturalist now consists chiefly in learning how to compare.' This cannot be learned without the habit of *close* observation, which you always tried to teach me—and which I tried to learn, but I find I never did, and I doubt if one ever can without the discipline which the microscope gives." Looking back over the years, she now concluded that she should have "collected less and have studied what I did collect more." Her "genius," she decided, consisted of "the ability and the will for *hard work,* and had I known how to use this genius I should have done more work for science, art, and myself and less for the moths. . . ."[44]

Fortunately, now she had the opportunity to do so, and she took classes in chemistry, assaying, and mineralogy, as well as biology.[45] She was "charmed" by Prof. Alpheus Hyatt, a noted paleontologist and zoologist who taught one of her classes.[46] Apparently she did well in her studies; on one occasion, for example, Hyatt told her that she owed it to herself to stay at least another winter and said that she might "add a great deal to the world's scientific knowledge."[47] Such praise, coming from a man who was an important theorist of evolution, added further confirmation of Martha's innate talents and abilities.[48] Another time several groups of legislators visited the laboratory. "I am said to have distinguished myself . . . by exhibiting the lobster which I was dissecting and teaching them about its ears stomach heart &c &c," she told Josiah. " 'Technology egotism so soon' you say— perhapse so, but a breath of Col[orado] air will dry it up."[49]

All in all, Martha concluded that her experiences at the Woman's Laboratory were providing the answers she had sought. "I am becoming daily more an[d] more *convicted* upon the subject of Natural History," she wrote to Mary, "and in the success of that I can read the answer to the question 'What must I do to be saved' not only for myself but for you too."[50] The laboratory was ideal. "Here everyone has absolut[e] freedom all are ambitious without emulation, in their studies and all are happy—but ah me!" she sighed, "it costs lots of money."[51] To make ends meet and afford the eighty-dollar tuition fee, she gave taxidermy lessons and continued to live her usual ascetic lifestyle in a bare attic room, cooking and serving her own food on tin dinnerware.[52]

Life in Boston for Martha was not only study and work, however. One Saturday she visited art classes at a Boston school, telling Mary afterward that "my old love for the art again haunts me" and that she would like to study further in that field, for "in fact as natural history is now taught a ready command of chalk and the blackboard is as assential as for mathematics besides there is often no way of expressing ones observations in study except by the pencil."[53] Jennie Bartlett, the former Boulder artist, also was in Boston, and Martha enjoyed spending time with her.[54] And one time she met Lucy Stone and Henry Blackwell on the street. "We were all in a great hurry," she wrote Mary, "but they expressed a great desire to see me again & told me to make the [Woman's] Journal rooms my office."[55]

More importantly, Martha had the opportunity to become acquainted with some of the members of the New England Woman's Club, founded in 1868 and presided over by Julia Ward Howe during most of the period from 1871 to 1910. Among the most powerful and influential of such organizations, the club was particularly interested in woman suffrage and other reform movements such as dress reform.[56] Regular meetings were held on Monday afternoons, and not long after Martha had arrived in Boston she was invited to talk about her collection. "I was as frightened as a school girl," she confided to Mary, "but thought it would look ungrateful to refuse and thought to put them off with a few words upon the objects &c of the Col. but I soon found myself unmersifully pelted with questions such as only a company of women resolved to know the bottom of a thing can only ask." Despite her initial reservations, she ended up having a grand time, telling her sister that everyone had been "charming" and that the "congratulations & handshakings seemed like old times." The women, she thought, were "intellectual and brilliant," and they invited her to come again.[57]

Thus, despite her ever-present financial worries, Martha was caught up in the Boston social and cultural whirl and seemed to be enjoying every minute of it. Even better, her sister Mary and her family were close by in West Acton, and Mabel had transferred to Wellesley, the new women's college founded in 1870. Having been, in her words, "supremely happy" at Ann Arbor, Mabel had come to Wellesley only because Martha had insisted, her desire to have her daughter near (perhaps to make up for past absences) overriding her previous objections to women's colleges. Mabel longed to stay in Michigan, and James Maxwell had written earlier to say that he thought that she should either continue in school there (but only if he and Martha could support her without help, which was impossible at the time) or return to Boulder and attend the university.[58] Martha won out, but the change proved to be something of a mixed blessing, for Mabel hated Wellesley as much as she had Oberlin, and many years later she still remained rather dramatically unreconciled to the change. "Wellesley it was to be," she wrote in her autobiography. "Nothing that had ever happened to me in my life hurt as this did."[59]

Still in question, however, was the status of Martha's marriage to James Maxwell. While she was enjoying her studies in Boston, James was becoming more and more lonesome, frustrated, and anxious for her to come home. "The Museum has had its day & several at least," he wrote early in 1878, recommending that she dispose of it and return to Boulder "and show me that your fame hasn't ruined you for a model little woman wife & mother." Another summer, he continued, "is all I can give for *Skylarking*. Years have been spent on it & another ought to suffice and wind it up and turn you in heart & mind, and will homeward."[60]

By July, with no change in sight, he seemed resigned to the inevitable. "You are married to your idol," he told her, "& I suppose I had but let you alone."[61] The next month, however, he made one last attempt, urging that she dispose of the collection as best she could and come home. "You should be here, and in *any* event and under *no* circumstances is it the right & proper thing for a wife & mother to settle herself . . . in a distant city or country among utter strangers away from her husband & home," he wrote, "at least until she utterly ignores such relationship with the duties & obligations that grow out of it." It had been two and a half years since he had had a wife "upon whom to lean an aching head or heart or *vice verse*," and he had endured the situation as long as he could. If she would only come home, even if she had no money to show for the collection but was willing "heartily to enter into the plans & labors and duties that make a home pleasant and happy," he would "express no regrets for the past" but would work cheerfully "to consummate that which I esteem worth more than forty Museums."[62]

Unhappily for James, Martha was unmoved by his entreaties. "With me the ratio between past labor on the Col[lection] & the happiness expected at home is not such as to warrant such a result," she wrote to Mary in September. "Besides I think any one with my advantages & the spunk of a grasshopper on a frosty morning even—would be an idiot to do such a thing."[63] Even a report that James was evidently paying attention to another woman did not cause Martha to rethink her position. Learning that he was "playing the gallant to her very extensively carrying her to Denver Golden Georgetown & probably to Estes Park," Martha remarked that this was "all very well—if he can *afford* it."[64]

Unable fully to resolve the conflicts in her life, however, Martha had sought help from Harriet Clisby, a woman doctor recommended by Mary. Dr. Clisby, who along with three other doctors advertised in the *Woman's Journal*, provided "just the medicine I liked," Martha told Mary. "Says I must let nobody hinder me in the work that is given me to do. If they will not help me I must go on without them, that my experience has already proven that I have a work to do for the world that neither my obligation to May or Mr. M must be permitted to interfear with." Martha had a "good cry," she related, but was cheered by Dr. Clisby's advice to take life one step at a time, "and the light which shows this step will show the next." Thus Martha had decided to return to Philadelphia to reopen her exhibit in the Main Building for the summer season. "What then I don't know," she concluded. "Wish you could help the light to dawn on the next step."[65]

One offer, at least, Martha did well not to accept. Early in June, just after she arrived in Philadelphia, she received a letter from Nathan Meeker, the former alternate U.S. Centennial commissioner from Colorado who was currently the Indian agent at the White River Agency in northwestern Colorado. "I am now located among the Indians lonely enough for any body," he wrote. "If I should get things in the shape I wish by next spring I think I would like you here as teacher & civilizer." The salary, he continued, would be about seven hundred dollars a year, and company would be provided by his wife and daughter, who were expected soon. "How would you like it? Let me hear from you."[66] The next year Meeker and many of the employees at the agency were killed by the Utes who rebelled against his "civilizing" methods in an uprising known as the Meeker Massacre; Mrs. Meeker and daughter Josie were captured but later set free.[67]

Turning down Meeker's suggestion, Martha continued to oversee her exhibit for another summer in the Main Building and to cling to the hope that she would either be able to recover the money still due her from her agreement with the Centennial commissioners or sell the collection to the University of Colorado, or both. Yet no one in Colorado seemed able to help with either of her objectives, and she wrote to Mary on September 1 that "I've lost faith in Colo. so far as my interests are conserned."[68] Many years later a comment from her one-time associate, J. Clarence Hersey, emphasized how disappointing this failure must have been. "Mrs. Maxwell *longed so earnestly* to have her marvelous collection go to the university," he wrote to Mary in 1908, "and would gladly have given it to the state, if she could just be assured of enough to eat—of the essentials to live the simple life,—while she might continue to perfect it as the complete and representative collection of the Rocky Mountain region, the centennial state, she loved so much."[69]

In addition to the disappointing news from Colorado, business at the Permanent Exhibition continued in the doldrums; on October 18, for example, Martha commented to Mary that "there is no business at the Main Building and I dont see how Im to get along."[70] Yet however bleak the situation seemed, Martha had by no means given up. If she could not obtain money from Colorado, perhaps the book about her life and work might prove to be the answer.

All during the period 1877–78, when Martha was alternately in Washington, Philadelphia, and Boston, Mary was working on the book that would eventually be published as *On the Plains, and Among the Peaks; or, How Mrs. Maxwell Made Her Natural History Collection*. By mid-1877 the manuscript was substantially complete—over four hundred handwritten pages—and Martha set about trying to find a publisher, a task that proved to be almost as difficult as developing the collection in the first place.[71] Yet with Martha's continuing financial problems, the book seemed to provide the only ray of hope. "In case the Picture business fails," she wrote to Mary from Philadelphia during the spring of 1877, "we *must* make a success of the sketch."[72]

Thus Martha began canvassing eastern publishing firms, with results that were anything but encouraging. For example, she left the manuscript at Harper's, and when she inquired about it, the representative informed her that it was taking its "regular course," explaining that three readers were analyzing it, and that the decision whether or not to publish would be made by the two who agreed. "I asked as you probably do 'are they men or women,' " she wrote to Mary, " 'all men' he said, and he said there was no possibility of hurrying them."[73] Martha also planned to submit the work to Scribner's, but by the end of 1877 the manuscript still had not been accepted.

By the spring of 1878 Martha had decided to send "the poor unfortunate" to Charlotte Fowler Wells, who had headed the publishing firm of S. R. Wells following the death of her husband Samuel in 1875.[74] Beginning in the 1830s, Wells, her two brothers, Orson S. Fowler and Lorenzo N. Fowler, and her husband had played leading roles in popularizing phrenology, then considered a scientifically valid method of determining character traits and abilities based on various cranial types. Their publishing concern—Fowlers and Wells after Samuel joined the family in 1844, S. R. Wells after the brothers sold their interests in 1855—issued numerous pamphlets and manuals not only on phrenology but also on reform topics ranging from temperance to the water cure.[75] Wells also published the *Phrenological Journal*, which had carried a lengthy article about Martha during the Centennial, and Charlotte Wells wrote that she was happy to hear from her again. The manuscript, she told her, was "well written," and she thought that Mary showed "considerable genius as an author." She would like very much to publish the book, she continued, but did not have the financial means to do so.[76]

Less encouraging was the response from editors at Appleton, who reported on May 10 that they were "unable to avail" themselves of the work. "There appears from our reader's report to be some interest in the work, if only from the fact of a lady becoming a taxidermist;" the spokesman, J. Milner, continued, "but we fear it would not command a sufficient number of readers to make the venture profitable, and the long continued depression of the publishing business makes us more than usually cautious in undertaking new work."[77]

Finally, on September 21, 1878, a contract was signed between Martha Maxwell and Mary Dartt Thompson, the "parties of the first part," and the Philadelphia firm of Claxton, Remsen and Haffelfinger. Described by publishing historian John Tebbel as "one of the largest book publishing and book distributing firms in the United States at its peak," the company had been founded in 1868 by Charles C. Haffelfinger, John A. Remsen, and Edward Claxton, all of whom had been active in Philadelphia publishing for many years. The house was known for its scientific books but also carried works on history, religion, and education on its list.[78]

Instead of turning over the manuscript to the publisher, however, Martha instead had given Claxton the stereotype plates and the engravings that she had had prepared under her direction during the summer, for it was still common procedure for authors to bear part of the expense of publishing their works by paying for the plates. With the plates in hand, Claxton agreed to print the book, paying royalties to Martha and Mary of six and two-thirds cents for each paper copy sold at fifty cents and thirteen and one-third cents for each cloth copy sold at one dollar. (By comparison, in 1879 Helen Hunt Jackson was offered a twelve-and-one-half-percent royalty on a novel retailing at a dollar and a half.) The royalties would be paid on all copies sold—an advantage, since some publishers exempted a certain number until their costs were recovered. Martha and Mary would be allowed to purchase as many copies as they wished for eighteen cents each (paper) and thirty cents each (cloth); on these the publisher would pay no royalties.[79] "I must hasten to inform you that the world moves—those 'letter press plates' *are at the publishers*!!" Martha jubilantly wrote her sister's family on September 6. About two weeks later, she continued, an edition of five hundred copies "will be ready for the world."[80]

Thus the book that had at one time been entitled "A Novel

Career: How Mrs. Maxwell Made Her Centennial Collection" issued forth from the presses of Claxton, Remsen and Haffelfinger. Bibliographically the book presents an interesting puzzle. Of nine copies examined, five list "second edition" below Mary Dartt's name on the title page, four do not; in all cases the publication date is given as 1879, the copyright date 1878. The binding is variously maroon, green, or brown, with gold stamping. The nature of the front matter before the first page of text varies considerably; copies marked "second edition" contain an engraved portrait of Martha Maxwell lacking in the others, while two of the second edition have, in addition, a photographic portrait tipped in. (Mary Dartt Thompson gave both of these copies to the Colorado Historical Society, one in 1922, the other in 1924.) Despite the differences, it appears that all copies were printed from the same plates, except for the front matter, and that the "second edition" is what would be called today a "second printing."[81]

Carrying the byline of Mary Dartt (not, it should be noted, Mary Dartt Thompson), the 237-page volume presented an account of Martha Maxwell's life through the Centennial, ostensibly to answer the questions raised by those who had crowded around as Mary was attempting to explain the exhibit in the Kansas-Colorado Building:

I had not finished assuring the large fat man in the white hat that I was by no means the person who had performed the work he saw before him, when the tall woman in the linen duster, and the short one in the white finger-puffs, and the young one in the idiot fringe, and the old gentleman with the gold-headed cane, and the man with the blue cotton umbrella, and the rough with the battered felt, and—I couldn't possibly begin to tell who else—all began at once to ask:

"Is she a young woman?"

"Is she married?"

"Where is she at?"

"Did she kill all these animals?"

. . . .

"Is she a half-breed?"

"Is she an Indian?" and as that crowd surged by,

another wave continued the inundation of like questions!

I kept hold of my departing senses with an effort, and leaned forward to catch the words of some dear old Quaker ladies. They were asking in soft, confiding voices: "Will thee be so kind as to tell us something of the history of this collection?"

Blessings on their sweet, motherly faces! I would have attempted anything for them!

Gentlemen of scientific proclivities echoed the request—people of all kinds repeated it with an emphatic "Do tell us who she is, and how she did it!"

The promise was made, and, though it is rather late, here is its fulfillment![82]

Of considerable interest, of course, is the extent to which the book can be used as a factual, reliable source for the events of Martha Maxwell's life. Most of the episodes can be verified independently, and the persons mentioned, usually as "Dr. Mc——" or "Miss E——," can be identified. Also, since the project obviously was a joint endeavor, it would be useful to know exactly how much Martha contributed to the actual composition of the manuscript. Some pages, in fact, are written in her hand, although it is impossible to know which passages Martha may have drafted herself and which she may have merely recopied. One can only conclude that both women contributed to the form and the substance, in undetermined proportions, and that the final draft represented what both wished to say about Martha Maxwell.

In general, On the Plains followed and amplified the outline of Martha's life that had been given to the reporters at the Centennial. Her prowess with firearms was traced back to the episode on the Wisconsin frontier when she had shot a snake that was about to attack her sister Mary. The story then continued with an account of the work she did with Professor Hobart at the Baraboo Collegiate Institute, the journey to Colorado, the sale of the collection to Shaw's Garden, the various collecting trips in the mountains, the journey to California, and the opening of the Boulder museum in 1874. Much of the article by Helen Hunt was included, as was an item from the Boulder newspaper on the museum opening.

Throughout, the book painted a portrait of Martha Maxwell as a feminine and artistic woman devoted to the study of natural history:

> In introducing Mrs. Maxwell to those who have never seen her, it may be well to premise that she is neither an Indian, nor half-breed, nor an Amazon, despite the title of "Colorado Huntress," which many newspapers have given her, one who, thirsting for notoriety, seized deadly weapons and went out on a crusade against the animal kingdom.
>
> On the contrary, she is a wee, modest, tender-hearted woman, lacking one inch of five feet in height, and "as shy as one of her own weasels!"
>
> She simply has a passion, not unknown in the history of science, for all living creatures—an irresistible desire to study their habits and relations, together with a taste for the expression of beauty in form, that would have made her a sculptor had she been placed in circumstances to have cultivated it.[83]

At the end of the book, Mary (and Martha) expressed the hope that "if this story of her adventures shall stimulate any one to a deeper love of her favorite study, whatever her future may be, she will deem her past a success."[84] Martha's view of herself as a scientist above all was also reinforced by the dedication that was placed at the beginning of On the Plains: "To Spencer F. Baird, The Sympathetic Friend of Nature's Friends, as well as Distinguished Naturalist, This Sketch of an Amateur's Work is Respectfully Dedicated."[85] Baird appreciated her thoughtfulness and graciously responded to her gift of a copy. "Of course I cannot but feel flattered at your remembrance of me," he wrote, "& can only hope that the work may be a source of pecuniary advantage."[86]

Even more importantly, the book contained as an appendix the catalogs prepared by Elliott Coues and Robert Ridgway. Appearing first was Coues's nine-page "Notice of Mrs. Maxwell's Exhibit of Colorado Mammals," which he had prepared while the collection was in Washington during the winter of 1876–77. In his introduction Coues spoke warmly not only about the scientific value of the specimens themselves but also about the manner in which they were displayed, his views contrasting sharply with those he had expressed on such exhibits in 1872. He was "glad to see," he wrote, "a collection of our native animals mounted in a manner far superior to ordinary museum work, and to know that there was at least one lady who could do such a thing, and who took pleasure in doing it." It represented, he continued, "a means of popularizing Natural History, and making the subject attractive to the public; this desirable object being attained by the artistic manner in which the specimens were mounted and grouped together." Too often, he noted, "faulty taxidermy" created misconceptions and only succeeded in "rendering the study of Natural History unattractive." Only with "such skilful and faithful representation of nature" such as Martha Maxwell had achieved could the "best results" be obtained. High praise, indeed, from one whose judgment carried considerable weight in scientific circles and who appreciated and understood Martha's objectives, as he pointed out both the scientific and the artistic accomplishments of "the intelligent and enthusiastic lady-naturalist."[87]

Following the introduction came Coues's descriptions and identifications, prepared both from his conversations with Martha in Washington and his own observations in Colorado in 1876. In this respect, decidedly the most important specimens he found in the collection were those of the American or black-footed ferret (*Mustela nigripes*). First reported by John James Audubon and John Bachman in 1851, the wily animal was lost sight of for some years thereafter, and as Coues noted in his 1877 monograph *Fur-Bearing Animals*, "doubt has been cast upon the existence of such an animal, and the describer has even been suspected of inventing it to embellish his work."[88] So anxious was Coues to obtain specimens that he had advertised in 1874 in the newspapers, with the result that several ferrets had been given to the Smithsonian Institution.[89] Yet Coues himself had had no luck finding any ferrets during his 1876 Colorado tour, even though he was in an area of many prairie-dog towns, their natural habitat, and thus he was greatly surprised and pleased to discover that Martha had captured three by trapping and by drowning them out of prairie-dog holes. His long description of the ferret included as well an account of its habits based on Martha's observations.[90] Also of interest to Coues was the specimen of a river otter (*Lutra canadensis*), another mammal that he had not found during his Colorado excursion.[91] Many others in the collection, of course, as Coues noted, were both common and abundant—foxes, minks, squirrels, chipmunks, prairie dogs, rabbits. Taken all in all, however, Coues appraised the collection that Martha had shown in Philadelphia and Washington as one that was "remarkably fine,"[92] and the catalog that he prepared stands as his only work, in a bibliography that runs to some forty pages, exclusively on Rocky Mountain mammals.[93]

Just as important was the catalog of the birds that Robert Ridgway had prepared in 1877, which had been printed in *Field and Forest* and was now included as the last twelve pages of *On the Plains*.[94] Saying that the collection contained "excellently mounted specimens," Ridgway wrote that it illustrated "very fully the avian fauna of Colorado, while it bears testimony, not only to the great richness and variety which characterize the productions of the new State, but also to the success which has crowned the enthusiastic and intelligent efforts of a 'woman Naturalist.'"[95] A "systematic catalogue," the work was followed by several additional notes, one of which described an owl that henceforth would bear Martha Maxwell's name.

The little screech owl was, Ridgway determined, a new race (*Scops asio maxwelliae*). "I name this new form in honor of Mrs. M. A. Maxwell," he wrote, "not only as a compliment to an accomplished and amiable lady, but also as a deserved tribute to her high attainments in the study of natural history."[96] When Martha received a copy of the catalog with this praise she was, of course, thoroughly gratified, although a bit overwhelmed. "I see nothing about it to criticize, except the rather extravagant compliments given the owner of the birds," she told Ridgway. "I will say frankly, however, that I am *very* proud of my owl, not particularly of the 'Maxwell' but of the '*ae*' there is such a predominance of 'i' and 'ii' you know."[97] To her sister Mary she commented that the catalog was "quite as complimentary as *you* even can wish, and what is still better he names an owl after me. . . . Scops asio var. Maxwelliae or common name Mrs. Maxwells owl. So much to be remembered by hereafter."[98]

Indeed, although she had no way of knowing it at the time, the owl represented an even more significant recognition, for a recent study has shown that Martha Maxwell was in fact the first woman ornithologist to have a subspecies she herself discovered named after her.[99] For his part, Ridgway continued always to hold her work in high esteem. "Her collection was indeed a fine one," he wrote in 1911 to her would-be biographer A. H. Felger, "would have done credit to any one, and certainly was a most remarkable accomplishment for a woman."[100]

After the publication of *On the Plains* another scientific assessment of Martha's work came from Joel A. Allen in his review of the book for the Nuttall Ornithological Club of Boston, the first ornithological society in North America, founded in 1873 and for males only until the mid-1970s. Allen had collected in Colorado, Wyoming, and the Dakotas during the period 1867–76, publishing papers that included the first list of mammals from Colorado and the first local list of Colorado birds.[101] Terming the book "a very intelligent and pleasantly written account," Allen wrote that the Centennial exhibit had constituted "a startling revelation of what a woman can do in one of the most difficult fields of art. . . ." Martha Maxwell, he went on, was "something more than a successful and enthusiastic taxidermist; she is an ardent and thorough student of nature, and her explorations of the zoology of Colorado have revealed the existence of many species in that State not previously known to occur there, and contributed many new facts regarding the habits and distribution of others."[102]

The reviews in the popular media, although usually brief, also were generally positive and enthusiastic. For example, one newspaper thought that "Miss Dartt manifests no less talent and skill in her style of dressing up abstruse scientific facts than did Mrs. Maxwell in preparing her numerous subjects for their Centennial levee," while another called her style "natural and piquant." The *Boston Evening Gazette* said that the book was "written in a lively anecdotal and graphic style, and is racy and interesting reading"; *Farm and Fireside* called it "an intensely and highly instructive little work." The *Boston Sunday Globe*, however, said that "it will hardly interest the general public, and seems to have been written principally as an advertisement of Mrs. Maxwell, which could easily have been dispensed with."[103]

Collecting the clippings as they were sent from the publishers (by October 16 Claxton had mailed 107 copies to editors), Martha set about trying to sell as many books as possible.[104] A four-page circular was prepared containing the best excerpts and pointing out that the volume was "a suitable book for holiday presents" ("Illustrated. Cloth extra, gilt centre, $1.00; Fancy Paper, 50 cts.").[105] On November 28, Martha reported to Mary that she had mailed about 175 circulars, stamped with her name and address, and was planning to send out more shortly.[106]

Yet even with such positive response from both the scientific community and the general public—and even James Maxwell wrote that he thought the book was "charmingly written & the incidents mainly true to the facts"[107]—sales were disappointingly slow. By the end of November, Martha told Mary that Hartley of Claxton, Remsen and Haffelfinger "says they get but few orders, but the book is not dead."[108] Like so many other projects in which she had invested her hopes, this one too seemed destined to prove a financial, although not a critical, failure. *On the Plains*, however, did provide a permanent record of her scientific achievements and assured that she would be remembered for her contributions to natural history—the black-footed ferret, Mrs. Maxwell's owl. The book is, as well, a delightful story with an affecting charm and sincerity, one that is well worth the attention of today's readers.

Now that more than a century has passed, how should Martha Maxwell's importance in the field of natural history be viewed? Most significantly, she was the first woman field naturalist who went out as men did and obtained and prepared her own specimens, and the first woman who had a subspecies she herself discovered named after her.[109] It is also important to recognize that Martha spent some eight years collecting in the West, mainly in Colorado, a lengthy period in contrast to the shorter, intermittent forays made by many other naturalists. She was active on a continuous basis, and as a careful observer of living creatures, she had ample opportunity to observe them in their native haunts. The knowledge she gained in this manner, of course, was used to good advantage in her realistic habitat displays. Her goal was to have a complete collection of the birds and mammals of Colorado, and despite her many problems, she achieved a good deal of success. Certainly Spencer Baird thought so, writing in 1876 that she deserved "the highest credit for what she has done in the way of bringing together a complete representation of the mammals & birds of Colorado."[110] Several years later, in his review of *On the Plains,* Joel Allen also emphasized that Martha had both discovered species in Colorado "not previously known to occur there" and contributed new facts on "the habits and distribution of others."[111]

Thus four of the most noted scientists of the day—Spencer Baird, Joel Allen, Robert Ridgway, and Elliott Coues—uniformly praised Martha's work as a naturalist, offering both respect and admiration in assessing her work. If her personal circumstances had been different—if she had had more family support, more education, more money, more time (and, perhaps, if she had been a man)—she might today be as well known as they. Certainly she had both the natural gifts and the determination needed for rigorous scientific work, although these attributes were not enough to overcome entirely the handicaps of her particular place and sex and time. Regardless, she should be remembered for what she did accomplish in making her collection of Colorado birds and mammals and presenting it to the public. Many other naturalists before and since have had much less "to be remembered by hereafter."

11

Lonely and Alone

Although the publication of *On the Plains* did bring Martha Max-well additional fame as well as a measure of immortality, the book did not change her daily life materially nor give her the financial security for which she longed so desperately. In fact, for the next two and one-half years, until her death in 1881, she continued to seek both the financial success and the spiritual fulfillment that had thus far eluded her. In the process, she suffered through periods of devastating loneliness, increasing health problems, and despair over her daughter's future.

By Thanksgiving of 1878, Martha admitted that she was lonesome and homesick, but she saw no way to return to Colorado unless she sold her collection.[1] In fact, in order to make ends meet, she had, of all things, accepted temporary work in Philadelphia dressing dolls for sale at Christmas. "Glorious occupation! Intellectual! Scientific!!" she exclaimed to Mary. "I *hate* it, but must live I suppose and may be glad to do what is work."[2] As she indicated to her sister, the irony of a person with her attitude toward fashion being involved in such labor was not lost on her. "I agree with you about the value of things which make children happy—and were I preparing the innocent little babies of *our* childhood I should be *comparatively* contented," she told Mary, "but these are quite a different class—for they all represent the 'girl of the period' and must have the wasp waist—the long trail and all the fashionable follies which I detest and I can but think that I am cultivating in other womans daughters the love of just those things which I so much deplore in my own."[3]

By early 1879, however, Martha was able to make a brief trip back to Boulder, necessitated by reports of the serious illness of her mother. Amy and Josiah Dartt had been living in Boulder since the early 1870s and in 1874 had built a new house on the corner of Ninth and Arapahoe streets.[4] In the intervening years Amy had become, in her granddaughter Mabel's words, "more eccentric with age, harsher and more unrelenting in her religion, outwardly all austere crust, and beginning to develop a fierce sense of possessiveness."[5] As always, she took particular pride in her house and gardens and, as always, she was afflicted with a variety of real or imagined illnesses, despite her adherence to "health reform" principles. Word reached Martha shortly after the beginning of 1879 that her mother's condition had become even worse, and thus she made a difficult and hurried trip to Colorado. Once there, she found that the letter summoning her had been "a little more dismal than was necessary" and that her mother's health was not so precarious.[6]

The Dartts' financial situation was no better than her own, however, and Martha discovered that their house had a number of mortgages on it.[7] Josiah apparently still lacked a taste for making money, although he had engaged in surveying since late 1871. He also worked mines in Summit County on occasion in association with his son-in-law Hal Sayre.[8] Amiable as always, he preferred reading the *Scribner's* and *Harper's* that he exchanged with a neighbor and studying caterpillars and butterflies with President Joseph Sewall of the university.[9] Eventually, Hal and Elizabeth Sayre arranged to pay the Dartts' living expenses and took care of the debts that had accumulated.[10]

Little evidence survives to indicate how much contact Martha had with her husband James during this visit. Whatever the status of their relationship, their opportunities to talk were limited because James was frequently out of town on business tending to a "wood contract." One Saturday evening he did come to Boulder, Martha wrote, but he stayed at his home while Martha remained at her mother's.[11]

Returning to the East after her visit in Boulder, Martha was again at the Permanent Exhibition by the summer of 1879. That year, in a move that harked back to her days in Nevada City, she had agreed to take over the management of the Log Cabin Restaurant, which had been developed at the Centennial.[12] Presided over by guides wearing costumes from the Revolutionary period, the New England Log Cabin had contained such artifacts as John Alden's writing desk and a silver teapot used by Lafayette in Boston and had offered typical New England meals of brown bread and baked beans. Next door was the New England Modern Kitchen, juxtaposed with the cabin to show the differences between 1776 and 1876.[13] The New England Log Cabin had been one of the few exhibits in the entire exposition that had been historical or had evoked the Revolutionary era, as the overwhelming majority reflected the forward-looking America of 1876.[14]

Martha soon found that running the Log Cabin Restaurant was no easier than anything else that she had lately attempted. Business was so bad that she had to let the help go. Then, as she related to Mary, "[I] was of course obliged to do all the work myself the baking and cleaning *very* early in the morning—sweeping setting tables &c—next putting on a decent callico dress to wait on customers in then attend to the wants of any who might call with various kinds of work sandwiched in. After the building closed I washed up the dishes & shut up shop." She did hire a "Man Friday," plus extra help on big days, "but I'm a perfect drudge," she concluded, "and so uncongenial to my tasks."[15] Still, as she commented to her sister later, "there is more money in the *Eating* business than anything else—except the *drinking* business, which no amount of money could tempt me to engage in."[16]

As the end of 1879 approached it had been three and one-half years since she had been in Colorado for any appreciable length of time. Shuttling about the East Coast from Philadelphia to Boston to New York to Washington and back again, she was as unsettled as ever, working from morning to night, away from her friends and family (by her own choice) and with pitifully few financial resources. "I'm as lonesome as a stray dog," she wrote to Mary in November, "do write me a long letter soon."[17] She told her that she planned to spend the winter working on the collection; "You dont know what a piece of selfsacrifice it is to stay from you all this winter but I'm not going to cry about it although

I am so utterly alone and must spend the winter in hard disagreeable work," she wrote to Mabel on another occasion.[18] Yet the immediate alternatives seemed no more agreeable. Perhaps she might do as James urged, "dispose of everything no matter at what sacrifice and come home—& to what a home? and to what occupation?"[19] Examining the question from all sides, she could come up with no better solution than to spend another lonely winter in the East, working and hoping for better times in 1880.

For Martha did have a plan, another idea that she hoped would at last put her, and her daughter, on the road to economic self-sufficiency. Mabel had finished her studies at Wellesley in 1878 and had gone back to Boulder, where she was teaching school and living with her grandparents, since the Maxwell house at the mouth of the canyon was too far to walk.[20] As ever, Mabel's future and well-being were paramount in Martha's thinking. "If only his interest and my own were at stake I might sit down among the spiders & bedbugs at the farm & study them," she wrote to Mary discussing James's wish that she come home. "But to think of May without a home & the temptation which besets every girl to throw herself away to secure one—I *cannot* indure it. I believe she is trying to do her best—but poor child she is naturally so extravagant that she can never make a home for herself. If I only have the brains and the strength to avail myself of the opportunities which *seem* to be before me I can put a comfortable little house on the farm—and be free from debt in a very short time."[21] Thus Martha's dream at this point encompassed the very home for which Mabel had always longed and which Martha wanted her to have without marrying for it. And the opportunity? It was waiting, Martha hoped, on Rockaway Beach, Long Island.

As early as 1878, in fact, Martha had envisioned erecting a building at a seaside resort where she would combine exhibits with facilities for selling ice cream and other refreshments to tourists, the better to enhance the chances of ultimately selling the collection.

> In front should be a room for the sale of Book, pictures,
> minerals, grasses, &c. —Beyond it and entered through
> a cave—the "refreshment" room. The animals in

groups or singly placed on bits of rockwork landscape here and there about the room—some of them on the sides of shelving rocks which are supported by rustic pillars (trees with the limbs cut within a foot or two of the body and upon which vines climb and birds and squirrels play hide & seek). Between these pillars archways should be formed of grasses, vines, &c. Among the groups scattered about the room, and under the supported groups, the rustic tables should be placed.

Continuing to describe her plans to her sister, she pointed out, in her view, "what a scope there is for 'Art-taxidermy' and how attractive it might be made to those of artistic scientific & romantic tastes." Such an undertaking, she conceded, "would amount to nothing pecuniarily if the aesthetic taste only was appealed to," but combined with "the taste for the best quality of ice cream &c &c . . . where thousands of rich people congregate daily for pleasure there must be money in it." Also, she noted that the collection "so far has had only a scientific value, and in these times cannot be sold for money—but placed where it would be money producing—could without doubt, be sold to advantage."[22]

Martha considered Coney Island, Asbury Park, and a proposed resort between New York and Philadelphia, but for one reason or another none of these possibilities seemed feasible.[23] By the end of 1879, however, she had found a tract of land available for lease on Rockaway Beach, an area of popular seaside resorts on a narrow peninsula of land extending westward from Long Island, and had been able to make a deal at less than the going rate because the owner found her idea attractive. "All my friends think I have made a good 'strike,' " she told Mary, "and am confident of my success if I can only get started right which means *cash* to considerable an amount."[24]

Facing the Atlantic Ocean, and separated from Brooklyn and Queens on the other side by Jamaica Bay, the peninsula had been developing steadily since the famed Marine Pavilion had opened during the 1830s at Far Rockaway on the northeastern end. Although the hotel had been destroyed by fire in 1864, development had moved steadily westward, with many hotels and bathhouses catering to the summer tourist trade. Moreover, as 1880 dawned prospects were looking even brighter for Rockaway Beach, as a mammoth hotel, which supposedly would be the largest in the world, was being constructed, and a railroad was being built on trestles across Jamaica Bay, thereby making access from the city more convenient.[25] "Rockaway Beach seems to be fairly alive with mechanics and laborers," the *Long Island Weekly Star* reported in January, and certainly there was good reason for Martha to be optimistic about her chances for success.[26]

Thus it was that Martha packed up and left Philadelphia and moved to Brooklyn, where she found rooms on the third story of a small house in the Williamsburg section.[27] "It is a very poor dirty part of Brooklyn but it is near her [ferry] depot for Rockaway Beach & is so a more economical place for her than any other part of the city," her sister Mary, who had come for a visit, told Nathan Thompson. The apartment had four rooms, Mary continued, and Martha had a comfortable bed, a nice, cozy living room, "a room for her taxidermy & a little room for coal & to dry clothes in."[28]

Once settled, Martha turned all of her attention to her new undertaking, which was to be, Mary told Nate, "a kind of hotel— her collection to be only a secondary attraction the food & bathing the main thing."[29] She immediately began raising all the plants she could for the museum and found a dealer who could let her have a number of bathing suits at bargain prices, along with more than a thousand yards of material which she intended to make up into more suits.[30] By March she had determined that she would erect a building thirty by fifty-five feet, with three stories, a flat roof, two porches, and a lean-to on the back for a kitchen. Although she did not plan to finish all of the building at once, when completed it would have ten rooms.[31]

In order to do the work, Martha made a financial arrangement with DeWitt C. Littlejohn, a politician and businessman from Oswego who was heavily involved in Rockaway Beach development. Noted for his oratory when he was a member of the New York Assembly, Littlejohn had also served a term in Congress. "Tall, dark and slender, graceful in his movements, possessing a voice which was deep and resonant, he had few peers as an orator or debater," according to a local historian. He was also, in the assessment of this writer, the Oswego area's "most controversial political and financial figure in the nineteenth century, and consecutively, leader of the Whig and Republican parties."[32] To Martha, Littlejohn appeared to be a savior who would make her dreams a reality. "He *seems* to me like a strong 'big brother' who will reach down and help me up this jaggad forbidding mt side," she told Mary, "but I may be *sadly* mistaken."[33]

Certainly Littlejohn seemed both generous and genuinely interested in Martha's beachhouse-museum. She confided to Mary that he told her he thought she was "a very brave woman . . . to stay here as I do, and to try to do what I so much wish" and that he felt obliged to help her by seeing that her bills were paid up to a maximum amount of six thousand dollars.[34] Moreover, although theirs was strictly a business dealing, he hoped that he would not have to ask her for any repayment except interest for some time and assured her that he had "never foreclosed a mortgage—never took more than 7 pr ct interest never turned any one out for rent—never distressed any body in his life."[35] For her part, Martha insisted that he take a mortgage on the lease and collection as collateral.[36]

In late April and early May, Martha made another quick trip to Boulder, where again she found Amy's health not so poor as had been reported.[37] This time, however, she was able to talk with James briefly, but the discussion did nothing to improve the relationship, at least in her eyes. "I think he does not feel the slightest interest in May or me either," she wrote to her sister; "his great fear is that we shall get something *out of him*."[38] Undoubtedly James would have disputed this view, especially so far as his daughter was concerned, but no letters survive to present his side of the question. Martha's assessment, though, does indicate how little remained of the marriage by 1880.

Returning to New York, Martha had her establishment ready for the 1880 season. Much to her delight, Mabel and a friend spent their vacation from teaching helping out.[39] Yet, although the promised railroad did begin operations, the huge hotel had not opened (it was torn down a few years later after one wing opened briefly in 1881), and Martha found herself in October, as usual, with more debts than assets. Fortunately, Littlejohn paid all the bills she owed and, as she told Mary, "said he was going to see me square on my feet for another Season then if I cant get along we will have another talk."[40] Now Littlejohn held a chattel mortgage on the collection and on all Martha's household goods, the first payment coming due in two years, the second in three.[41] However, she had cleared some money in Philadelphia, where she had gone in September for a fair, and with Littlejohn helping her with her large debts, she thought that she could get along all right until spring.[42]

As she tried to make a success of her Rockaway Beach venture, Martha continued also to attempt to find a measure of peace in her spiritual and personal life. Several years earlier, in a section written for inclusion in *On the Plains* but omitted from the book, she discussed at some length the need for one to study both biology and "psychology" in order to answer "those old questions, where did we come from, why are we here, where do we go to."[43] "The truth for which we wait, in deep unrest, must come from the perfected researches of both. The subtlest investigations of both, can alone determine the relations, between mind and matter, what are the powers of each, and how they modify and influence each other," she concluded.[44]

Almost as soon as she had moved to Brooklyn she began attending Plymouth Church, which Henry Ward Beecher had served since 1848. Although somewhat past the peak of his greatest popularity, the charismatic Beecher still drew huge crowds with his emotional and dramatic sermons. In fact, Martha arrived somewhat late for the first service she tried to attend and was turned away along with hundreds of others.[45] The next week she and Mary went earlier and were able to get good seats.[46]

Martha continued to attend the Plymouth Church services regularly, and although, as she wrote to Mary, she did not "fully endorse" all the sentiments Beecher expressed, "his evident sincerity, his earnestness, his originality of thought and his happy way of expressing it make his spoken sermons sublime—they loose much in print."[47] Indeed, Martha was so impressed with Beecher that she wrote a letter to him about some of her problems and asked him to say something in his next lecture that would help her. It was a "hasty, disconnected letter," she told Mary; "I wrote as I always do without anything to indicate sex."

Much to her surprise, Beecher read the entire letter to the congregation and devoted most of an evening to it. "The reason he did so he said was because it was typical of the unsettled condition of the minds of very many thinking people," she reported to her sister. She struggled to remember all that Beecher had said, telling Mary that "the line between superstition and truth—between mythology & reality he did not attempt to draw though requested to do so." She noted that he emphasized the distinction between "intellectual and emotional religion—Said we can never enter heaven 'head first we must enter heart first,' " but that she herself disagreed, saying that the two should go together. At the end, Beecher looked at the signature and commented that he did not know anything about the writer, not even if the person was a man or a woman. After the service, as everyone was filing out and shaking the minister's hand, Martha thanked him for answering the questions. "He said, 'Was it *your* letter? I hope you will come out all right.' With 'thank you' I hurried on for fear of attracting attention."[48]

Although Martha was able to find spiritual sustenance at Beecher's church (at one point she even considered becoming a member, if she were going to be in Brooklyn for any length of time),[49] she continued to be troubled not only about her own problems but about what would become of her daughter. Until Mabel departed from Wellesley in 1878, Martha had clung to the hope that she would follow in her footsteps as a naturalist. Mabel, on the other hand, had thought that her mother would return to Boulder permanently after she had finished her course at the Woman's Laboratory at MIT. Again mother and daughter had had a confrontation, one that in Mabel's view "left scars time never healed."

> Mother was terribly disappointed. I had failed her. Over and over I made my fruitless explanations. I realized and appreciated all the sacrifices she and the family had made to educate me, but I could not make myself over. I doubted whether anyone could.

Mother did not understand. From then on, as long
as she lived, she looked upon me as an ugly duckling
hatched by a thoroughbred hen. What did I want? A
home, I told her. All my life I had longed for a home and
I had never had one. The feminist in mother protested
fiercely. What about a career? Making a home, I re-
torted, seemed to me the finest and most useful career a
woman could have. I still believe that.[50]

Mabel's views of marriage were quite the opposite of those of
many of her classmates, the students, especially in the new
women's colleges such as Wellesley, who would become known
as the first generation of "New Women." These early graduates
often placed career ahead of marriage; indeed, between the 1870s
and the 1920s, some forty to sixty percent of women college
graduates remained unmarried, in contrast to ten percent of all
American women. Opting for a life outside a traditional domestic
setting (although they often formed lifelong alliances with female
colleagues), they taught in the women's colleges or worked in
settlement houses, rejecting the marital role that gave their
mothers their principal identities. As a result, as Carroll Smith-
Rosenberg writes, "Resentful words, lingering guilt, and conse-
quent alienation divided the New Women from their mothers
and their female kin."[51] Similar resentment, alienation, and guilt
characterized the relationship of Martha and Mabel Maxwell as
well; in this instance, however, the daughter was rejecting her
mother's career *in favor* of marriage, in her view "the finest and
most useful career a woman could have."

By contrast, Antoinette Brown Blackwell (1825–1921) and her
daughters seem to have resolved such issues more amicably. Like
Martha, Antoinette had studied at Oberlin; she received a literary
degree in 1847 and then spent three years in the theological
course, although the college did not grant her a degree. In 1853
she became the first ordained woman minister in the United
States when she was ordained by the Congregational church. She
married Samuel Blackwell, brother of Elizabeth and Emily, and
they became the parents of five daughters. Antoinette felt that
women could and should combine both domestic responsibilities
and work or other interests outside the home; she did not,

however, attempt to prescribe the direction her daughters' lives would take. For example, Florence, born in 1856 and thus just a year older than Mabel Maxwell, was, like Mabel, seemingly more interested in beaux than in anything else. Antoinette did not object when Florence contemplated matrimony. "I believe she is right in thinking that she is best adapted to a home of her own;" she wrote to Lucy Stone in 1878, "and that she could learn to be a good wife, mother and housekeeper, with a good deal of energy to spare for wider outside interests." Florence, in fact, did marry, and interestingly enough, she followed in her mother's footsteps to some extent and became a lay preacher. Two other daughters became physicians. "Antoinette was as satisfied with Florence's settling into marriage—with a bit of preaching on the side—as with Edith's decision to study medicine," says a recent biographer. "She was not overly concerned either with the demands of popular etiquette or with pushing young women into a model based on professional work outside the home."[52]

For Martha and Mabel Maxwell, however, there was no such resolution, and both women were shaken by the latest disagreement; Mabel felt later that "I had hurt my mother profoundly, and in doing so, hurt myself."[53] For her part, Martha tried to smooth over the differences that existed between them. "I *did* feel a little hurt but I lay nothing up against *you* my dear," she wrote on June 6. "I know I talked very discouraging to you, it *pained* me to do so. . . . If I said anything in word or spirit that was objectionable I hope you will forgive me."[54]

Thus Mabel went back to Boulder, where she lived with her Grandmother Dartt in town and taught school in the interval between college and marriage, and Martha tried to make the best of it. If Mabel had settled on teaching as a profession, then Martha determined that she would be the best teacher possible, and she therefore bent all her efforts in that direction. Sending her daughter advice much as she had when she was at Oberlin, Martha encouraged her to excel in every way. "Perfect yourself in your profession & be prepared for a higher position than you at present occupy," she wrote in November 1879. "You can hardly imagine my anxiety for your success in your chosen field of labor."[55] A month later she informed Mabel that she would be sending her some copies of a magazine for primary teachers, and that she would subscribe to the journal for her if Mabel thought it would be worthwhile.[56] Early the next year she inquired again about Mabel's progress. "How do you like your school and are you making a success of teaching? I feel *very* anxious that you should *excell* in your chosen proffession dont let anything interfere with your efforts in that direction."[57]

Yet, as was usually the case, Mabel had more on her mind than teaching. "I bubbled over with high spirits and an invincible light-heartedness that my mother viewed with foreboding," she recalled in her autobiography. "It was obvious, even then, that I was not cut out for a life of spartan discipline like my mother's."[58] Despite her high hopes for Mabel's success as a professional woman, Martha knew only too well that Mabel's interests and attitudes were profoundly different from hers, much to her dismay. Writing to her sister Mary shortly after Mabel had returned to Colorado to teach, Martha vented her frustrations. "So May is gone. Poor dear victim of vanity and slave to fashion. Must her soul be dwarfed & her life blighted in this way. It seems unbearable—yet I am utterly powerless to prevent it. . . . Poor Child poor Child! I see nothing but unhappiness for her in future—the love of dress has ruined her."[59]

Indeed, from Martha's point of view, the worst happened—Mabel began keeping company with a Boulder doctor some eight years her senior named Charles C. Brace, who had come to Boulder in 1876 from Georgetown.[60] Not that this was easy, since she was living with her Adventist grandmother. "I have always wondered why anyone called on me more than once," she wrote later. "A man who came on Sunday was apt to find when he left that an anti-tobacco pamphlet had been slipped into his coat pocket."[61] But Brace, who in Mabel's words was "tall, good-looking, with dark hair, blue eyes, and a prominent nose," would not be deterred. "For some time I held back, uncertain whether I could cope with so forceful a nature, but nothing would swerve him—not my uncertainty, not grandmother Dartt's anti-tobacco pamphlets, not even her annoying habit of turning a hose on my callers." Probably it was this very strength that drew Mabel to young Brace, along with his views of marriage and family. "When his friends pointed out that the women of my family rarely stayed at home, he simply laughed. Not for a moment did he doubt that *his* wife would stay home."[62]

As soon as Martha got wind of Mabel's interest in Brace she tried to find out more about him, particularly during the winter of 1880–81 when the doctor was urging Mabel to accept his proposal. "What do you think of Dr. Brace? and how do you like him?" she asked Mabel's grandmother.[63] "Is he a good associate for her?" she inquired of Mary.[64] The answers she received satisfied her to some extent. "I guess he is smart and possessed of many good traits—but he occasionally takes as [sic] social glass & smokes which you know I cant abide," she commented to Mary.[65] Yet despite her efforts to come to terms with the fact that Mabel would probably soon be married, there were times when Martha could not hide her disappointment. "If he is a suitable person for her I suppose—as much as I hate it—that she had best marry," she wrote to Mary in January of 1881. "She might distinguish herself as student or a teacher. But her inordinate love of society will prevent any continued effort. She will surely marry somebody and she might do worse if she refuses the Dr. . . . You know how my ambition for her has been crushed. Now that she may marry reasonably well is all I can hope."[66]

Such views were nothing new on Martha's part. In 1875, for example, she had commented to Mabel that "the fact that woman is not allowed to *choose* who she will marry but simply to *accept* the first specimen of the biped homo that might offer for fear no other one ever would, seems to heathenish for a sivilized community."[67] By 1877 she was even more explicit. "This marrying is fearful business," she commented to her sister about a friend's marriage. "Why couldn't she have remained free."[68] And just before Mabel became involved with Charles Brace, her mother cautioned against marrying anyone until it was absolutely necessary. Recounting a wedding she had attended in Philadelphia, Martha wrote that "it made my heart ache to think of the days and nights of pain and care that she was entering upon, and that the lovely face would so soon be faded & furrowed—and I prayed that my darling might put off the evil day for many years at least."[69]

Such negative assessments were not atypical of at least some post–Civil War feminist thought. For example, as William Leach discusses, New York Sorosis founder Jane Croly, in *For Better or Worse* (1876), described "in painful detail the dreariest features of contemporary marriage: girls forced by circumstances to marry for bed and board and economic security, or worse, brilliant and resourceful women condemned by marriage to dependence, seclusion, intellectual sterility, and even madness. The picture is so bleak that marriage, even on feminist terms, emerges as a risk too dangerous to be taken."[70] If Croly painted her view of marriage in words, Martha Maxwell conveyed hers in exhibits. For example, she wrote once that she had decided to illustrate "connubial bliss" at Rockaway Beach with two owls, one red, the other "gray with defiant blue eyes and the broom in one claw— the other has a horse whip in one of his and vengence in his eyes."[71] It can be surmised, however, that Martha's feelings perhaps owed as much to the deteriorating state of her own union with James Maxwell as to any abstract philosophy.

By this time, in fact, if the Maxwells were not divorced, they might as well have been. In analyzing the marriage, two separate but interrelated questions need to be considered. First, why did Martha Dartt marry James Maxwell in the first place, and second, how and why did her later career affect the relationship (and vice versa)?

To begin, it seems obvious that Martha did not really love James, not in the way she apparently loved the Oberlin student with whom she had had an "understanding." By the middle of the nineteenth century, the ideal of romantic love and affection, rather than economic or political considerations, had become accepted as the basis for marriage;[72] Martha, however, had chosen her husband for almost every reason other than love. As the years went by, this intrinsic lack of deep emotion might have assumed greater importance.

Moreover, it is possible that the difference in age between Martha and James (almost twenty years) was in itself sufficient to argue against a long-term happy relationship. James's expectations of marriage and the place of women seem to have owed much to the Cult of True Womanhood, which had been developing during the first part of the nineteenth century. Martha, however, had never accepted "woman's sphere" as her lot in life; moreover, she had reached the full flowering of her potential during the Civil War and afterward, when women increasingly began to challenge such assumptions. Thus if James was not particularly sympathetic to her work, especially as it became all-consuming, neither was Martha sympathetic to his desire to have his wife remain in the home. "Irreconcilable differences" indeed, rooted in backgrounds too different for either to overcome.

While Martha and James did not actually divorce, if they had filed for legal action they would have been taking an increasingly common remedy for marital unhappiness; between 1870 and 1880, for example, the number of divorces grew one and one-half times as fast as the population.[73] Their reasons also would have been consistent with trends becoming apparent in the years between 1870 and 1900. "Men sought the remedy of marital dissolution when they found women becoming too independent," writes Carl Degler; "women petitioned for divorce when they found their desire for autonomy and self-identification within marriage thwarted by men's insistence upon their subordination to the family."[74] So it might have been with the Maxwells.

It can be argued further that Martha Maxwell perhaps should not have married at all, given her strong dedication to her work and the difficulties of combining it with marriage. During the latter part of the nineteenth century, even as greater opportunities were opening up for women, it seemed almost axiomatic that if a woman wanted a career, she must either forgo marriage or deal with unending conflict. Statistics on the marital status of women college graduates reflect this assumption; moreover, by 1890 over fifty percent of women physicians were single, and of women who earned the Ph.D. degree between 1877 and 1924, three-fourths were unmarried.[75]

To take a few specific examples of women with aspirations comparable to Martha's, Graceanna Lewis remained single, in part, because she recognized the difficulties of combining marriage and family, as did Maria Mitchell (1818–1888), the noted professor of astronomy at Vassar and probably the best-known woman scientist of her day.[76] Somewhat later, the reformer Charlotte Perkins Stetson Gilman (1860–1935), struggling with such conflicts, told her second husband, "Dear, if I had to choose to-day between you and my work—two hearts might break, and I might die of the breaking, but I could not choose other than the one way."[77]

Yet in Martha Maxwell's case, it is hard to see that her drive to have her own career was sufficiently developed by 1854 for her even to consider the alternatives. Certainly her Lawrence class-mate, Francena Buck, had seen "no knowledge of her slumbering talent."[78] The choice simply was not there to be made. One must then ask if she pursued her career because of her innate drive, and therefore had an unsuccessful marriage, or if she channeled her energies into her work *because* she had an unhappy marital relationship. Put another way, if she had married the Oberlin stu-dent, would she have had any desire to have a career? Given Martha's activist nature, it seems obvious that she would not have been content to remain exclusively in the home; she might, however, have devoted herself to reform activities more compati-ble with marriage. In any event, however one relates cause to effect, the result was still the same; by 1880 James Maxwell was living in Colorado, while his wife was laboring half a continent away in New York.

All in all, as Martha remained in her rooms in Brooklyn dur-ing the bitterly cold winter months, preparing for another season with her bathhouse-museum on Rockaway Beach, she was as lonely and discouraged as she had ever been in her life, but she held on with stoic perseverance. "Never see any one to speak with—imagine myself shipwrecked but you know I care but little for the society of any except my dear ones who are far away," she wrote to Mabel.[79] Still, she was able to use the long winter eve-nings to study bookkeeping, and she had more bathing suits to make or to mend.[80] To keep warm she had a lounge fixed up in the kitchen. "Of course there is nothing very cheerful or agree-able about it," she told Mary, "but while I meet nothing *un*indur-able in life, I suppose I've no reason to complain."[81]

Yet, although she did not fully realize it, Martha's difficulties stemmed as much from physical as from psychological problems. As early as mid-1878 she was including references about her poor health in letters to Mary and Mabel, usually coupling such information with assurances that she was overcoming her difficulties through sheer determination and an exercise of will. After one severe bout of illness in Philadelphia, she wrote to Mary and her family that "my reason told my will it *must hang on*—there was work to be done. So Ive been hanging—now Ive pretty good footing and shall climb out of this just as fast as I can."[82] A few months later, however, she gave in to dejection. "I must say my health is miserable," she told her sister, "and I am obliged to work so hard that I am exhausted and discouraged."[83]

Martha attributed her difficulties to the menopause, but instead of improving as the months went by, she grew steadily weaker. By November 1880 she was "quite dangerously bad," she told Mabel; her sister, she continued, had been "looking up my care in a doctor book" and had sent her "about two pages of quotations."[84] No such remedies seemed to help; it seems obvious that she should have been under a physician's care, rather than relying on self-help measures. Lack of money and time, as well as her persistent belief in the efficacy of willpower, evidently prevented her from seeking competent medical assistance.

Thus Martha's health continued to decline. "If I can only get over this annoying, disgusting, debilitating & discouraging infermaty I should have but little fear of failure," she wrote to Mary from Brooklyn in December 1880. "What does your Author say about its continuance. When is there any hope of its stopping?"[85] The next month she told her mother that she had been "dangerously ill" and in February wrote to Mary that she was "never worse—but am better now can sit up without fainting and by tomorrow morning can probably walk straight."[86] By March of 1881 she felt "perfectly worthless—have lost all energy & ambition—wonder what will become of me—perhapse a big wave will come and stir me up—am sure I hope something will happen."[87]

Not only did Martha's health continue to decline, but she received word that her beloved stepfather, Josiah Dartt, had died in Boulder in April.[88] Since the latter part of 1880 he had been in poor health, as he had written to his daughter Mary, and she had traveled to Colorado to be with him.[89] Naturally, Martha was upset that she was unable to be with the family, but the newspapers they sent, she told her brother-in-law, Nathan Thompson, "have cheered my exile more than you can guess. . . ."[90]

Within weeks, however, she was no longer alone, for her condition grew so precarious that Thompson hurried to her bedside from Massachusetts, and Mabel was summoned from Colorado.[91] When she arrived, Mabel found that her mother was only partly conscious. She immediately called a doctor, who informed her that her mother was dying from an ovarian tumor. Nothing could be done, but mother and daughter were reunited at last, and all their differences, for the moment, faded into insignificance. "Mother was so pitifully glad to see me that it almost broke my heart," Mabel recalled later.[92] Martha Maxwell died in her daughter's arms early on the morning of May 31, 1881.[93] She was not quite fifty years old.

Grief-stricken and completely alone, Mabel made arrangements to bury her mother (James had wired from Boulder that she was to do whatever she thought best).[94] She located a cemetery at nearby Woodsburgh, and there, two days later, Martha Maxwell was laid to rest with a brief Episcopal burial service. "I can never tell you the bitterness of today, the long eight miles of rough road—the sobbing and wailing of the surf as it broke on the sand," Mabel wrote Mary afterward. "I thought my life would go when I heard the clods of earth thrown in on my darling Mamma."[95]

Despite her sorrow, Mabel remained on Rockaway Beach throughout the summer, attempting to salvage something of her mother's dream. If there were times that she had resented Martha's commitment to her work, now all that mattered to her was to save the collection.[96] Working almost round the clock, Mabel bent all her efforts toward this goal. "I am willing to give years of my life to do it, if it can be done, and God will give me the strength, I trust," she wrote to her Aunt Mary shortly after Martha's death. As alone as her mother had been, Mabel struggled to finish the bathing suits and prepare for the tourist season. "A dozen times a day I put my head down on the machine and give up to my grief. Then comes the thought 'Is this the way you show your love for your Mother in useless grief when you might work for her.' Then I go on but Oh it is a very hard task."[97]

Mabel's perseverance paid off, and by the end of the summer she was able to retire her mother's most pressing debts and realize a surplus of some eight hundred dollars.[98] Although she had been successful in raising the mortgage, she had no money to remove the collection from Rockaway. Remembering that Elliott Coues had shown a great interest in her mother's work, she turned to him for advice. "It is my great desire to have it placed where its scientific value will be appreciated," she wrote. "I cannot bear the thought that my mothers life and work should be wasted and destroyed now." Perhaps, she thought, the Smithsonian would be interested. Passing along Mabel's letter to Joel Allen, Coues commented that although he doubted that the Smithsonian would buy the collection, perhaps the American Museum of Natural History would like it. "You know [it] is a splendid on[e] in taxidermy, and important as faunal," he wrote. "It would be a pity to have it broken up."[99]

No agreement was reached with either institution, however, although in the fall Martha's benefactor, DeWitt Littlejohn, conveyed to Mabel for one dollar "all the stuffed animals and birds and all the minerals and all fixtures belonging to the same and which belonged to the late Martha A. Maxwell, and which are now in the building known as the Rocky Mountain House at Rockaway Beach in Queens County State of New York." The property was to be removed by April 1, 1882.[100]

With the collection legally hers, Mabel left it in storage in New York for the time being and returned to Colorado. On December 1, 1881, she was married to Dr. Charles C. Brace.[101] "It was a simple wedding, with few guests, and there was no time for a honeymoon," she wrote later.[102]

Thus ended the life of Martha Maxwell. Combining her love of nature, her thirst for knowledge, and her desire for artistic expression, she had pursued her own vision wherever it might lead, and whatever the cost. Influenced first by her grandmother Abigail, who took her on excursions into the woods near their Pennsylvania home, and later by her academically minded stepfather Josiah, Martha embarked on an odyssey that eventually encompassed both public acclaim and private despair. "She had a deep love for all animal life, a passion for beauty, and an unsatisfied and unfocused need for self-expression in some form," her daughter wrote many years later. "To all of these traits taxidermy made a strong appeal."[103] J. Clarence Hersey, who as a young man had fairly idolized her as he assisted with her work, later summed up his impressions like this: "Indeed she was an artist whose ability must express itself, and whose very life was always reaching out for the true and the beautiful. Her powers of perception were keen and quick; her mind alert and rational, and all her sympathies with scientific truth."[104]

During the course of her brief life, Martha Maxwell was by turns (and sometimes simultaneously) a collector of natural history specimens, a popularizer, and a student who aspired to pursue science in a professional, academic manner.[105] If her relationship with Spencer Baird was one of student and mentor, that with Robert Ridgway was more nearly one of collegial equality between peers. Both had nothing but praise for her accomplishments—Baird said that she possessed "a most excellent knowledge of natural history" and Ridgway named an owl for her "as a deserved tribute to her high attainments in the study of natural history." Similarly, Elliott Coues called her collection of mammals "remarkably fine," and Joel A. Allen termed her "an ardent and thorough student of nature."

The general public, too, was aware of the accomplishments of the "lady taxidermist" via countless articles in newspapers and magazines published from coast to coast during the Philadelphia Centennial Exposition, as well as through the book *On the Plains*. Earlier, the widely read author Helen Hunt had told of the Rocky Mountain Museum in Boulder, and Julia Ward Howe had published an endorsement in the *Woman's Journal*. In addition, shortly before her death the story of her life was preserved in the *History of Clear Creek and Boulder Valleys*—a biography that covered almost four pages (substantially longer than any of the male subjects) and called her "one of Colorado's most prominent and enterprising ladies."[106]

Yet many of her accomplishments were either soon forgotten or, indeed, not acknowledged at all, seemingly as fragile as the mammals and birds whose lifelike recreation had been the work of her own life. As the years went by seldom was she given recognition as a "pioneer" in the art of habitat grouping, as Junius Henderson called her, and almost never were her specimens preserved in any museum or collection.

Moreover, in personal terms one might question whether the achievement was worth the cost. What really drove Martha Maxwell to devote uncounted hours in her workroom beside Boulder Creek? Why did she spend the last five years of her life going from pillar to post with no settled home and usually no family nearby? What was she searching for? Often she was lonely, yet never did she allow thoughts of home and family to deter her from her chosen path. "A pretty strong hang-on-it-ive trait of charactor," she once described it, and hang on she did, until the end. From time to time she gave her own answers: she was working to advance the cause of feminism; to make money and thereby provide an education for her daughter; to leave a legacy to the University of Colorado.

Today Martha Maxwell deserves to be remembered for her contributions as a field naturalist, especially for Mrs. Maxwell's owl, and to the development of habitat groups in museums. Even more, her life offers an example of a relationship between a mother who wanted nothing more than for her daughter to surpass her accomplishments and a daughter who could write many years later that she had "grown up, believing more and more intensely that there is no woman's work comparable to the making of a home, to the raising of happy and healthy children, to a marriage which is a real partnership."[107] The problems that Martha Maxwell faced in her relationships with her husband and daughter are neither new nor unique; Carl Degler, after all, entitled his book published several years ago *At Odds: Women and the Family in America from the Revolution to the Present.*[108] At odds they were, and perhaps mothers and daughters more than a century later may learn from them.

In the end, it seems appropriate to allow Martha to have the last word. "I am condemned for having an ambition to be something more than the common lot of mortals," she once wrote in the back of a small diary. "Well I have a desire to live for something more than the gratification of those who cannot appreciate the sacrifice. Yes I would do something which shall follow me doing good to others after I am gone."[109]

Epilogue

THE COLLECTION

What happened to Martha Maxwell's collection after her death? As with many episodes during her lifetime, the story is convoluted and the outcome disheartening. After Mabel returned to Colorado and married, the expense of keeping the collection in storage in New York was too great, and thus she accepted the suggestion of a friend of her husband to place it in the hands of a man named J. P. Haskins of Saratoga Springs, New York.[1] On March 20, 1882, an agreement was made with Haskins whereby he would care for the collection and exhibit it in Saratoga Springs. He also had the right to sell the collection with the consent of the Boulder friend who was acting in Mabel's behalf; one-quarter of the proceeds would go to Mabel.[2]

For some years thereafter Mabel and Mary heard nothing more of the fate of the collection. In 1893, however, Mary decided to find out what had happened to her sister's lifework. In a paper written over thirty years later and presented to the Colorado Historical Society, she recounted the saga. Here, in part, is the story in her words:[3]

What Became of Mrs. Maxwell's Natural History Collection?
by Mary Dartt Thompson

. . . The Columbian exhibition commemorating the discovery of America, was to be held in Chicago, but not until the summer of 1893. During the preceding winter a request was received from the committee in charge of the Woman's Exhibit for Mrs. Maxwell's collections of animals, to form a part of it. Rumors had reached us that evil days had fallen upon Dr. Haskins, and, as no satisfactory report could ever be had concerning the collection, Mrs. Brace, who was living in Denver, asked me to go from my home in Baltimore to see about it and find out whether the proposition was feasible.[4]

I did not announce my coming, but learning at the station at Saratoga that Dr. Haskins made his home at a certain hotel, went directly there. From the proprietor I learned that the collection was then stored in a barn, that the doctor had had it at various times on exhibition and had, when the receipts at the door ceased to pay, taken the specimens to some barn where they remained until some occasion came to bring a crowd to the Springs, then he would rent a place and get them out again.[5]

The careless way in which they had been handled had awakened indignant comment from many of the citizens of Saratoga. The next morning I made myself known to the doctor, and asked to be shown my sister's collection. He was profuse in apologies for having them where they were, after the shock of seeing me was over. The barn was a small two-story building, and the larger mammals filled the lower floor completely. The smaller ones were set upon the timbers of the frame work. They looked natural but so dusty and neglected that it made me heartsick. I can never forget a lynx that was on a beam above the window, he looked alive and his eyes followed me with such a fierce reproachful look that I could hardly bare to leave him. The birds were upstairs, a pitiful few of them in a most dreadful condition. It was a sad comment upon the way they had been handled.

Dr. Haskins did not look kindly upon the idea of their going to Chicago, but I was in no mood to talk with him. My one thought was to get what was left of them away from there and in some place where their value would be appreciated and they would be preserved. On my way home I stopped in New York City and visited the Natural History Museum. I knew its curator, Mr. [Joel A.] Allen, had known Mrs. Maxwell and admired her work. He was grieved at my report, said she had given the world a great object lesson in the possibilities of artistic taxidermy, and he wished her collection could appear at the exposition, but it would mean a great deal of work to make it look as it should, and no little expense.

I knew there was no hope in that direction. There was no money to do with even could we find anyone with the skill to repair the specimens and group them effectively, and take charge of them during the time of their stay in Chicago.[6]

Yale University was at that time erecting the Peabody Museum that would be an appropriate home for them, and Mrs. Brace, after some correspondence gave them a deed of gift for the collection.[7] They sent men to Saratoga to examine it and estimate the cost of its removal and repair, but they encountered unexpected difficulties. Dr. Haskins would not give it up without payment of what they considered an exorbitant sum for its keeping.[8] It was useless to argue with him or to appeal to Mrs. Brace who was living in Denver. He would go to law about it before he would take less or part with the collection. The college felt it could not pay the sum nor could it take a law suit on its hands, so it remained in his possession and for our peace of mind, we resolved to strive to forget it. This was in 1893.[9]

In the autumn of 1919, one of those incidents we read of in stories and consider an ingenious creation of the author's imagination occurred. My daughter, who is in the main Library of the Department of Agriculture,[10] took up a newly received book to catalogue; from it fell a letter. In glancing at its contents to see what disposition should be made of it, her eye fell on these lines: "I saw the remains of the Maxwell collection of Colorado animals and birds in a stall in Saratoga. A man wanted $100 for them, but I had no use for most of them. They had been out in the weather during a severe winter and most of the birds were falling to pieces. How sad these things mean so little to most people. (Signed) H. W. Shoemaker, Restless Oaks, McElhatten, Pa." (This was September 1919).[11]

She copied them for me and returned the letter to the dealer. I wrote at once to Mr. Shoemaker and received the following letter in reply: "Dear Mrs. Thompson;—Upon returning home yesterday after a weeks absence on business, I found your unusual letter of October 8th, which I hasten to answer. I first heard of the

Maxwell collection through Mr. S. N. Rhoads of Philadelphia, who had seen it at the Centennial in 1876.[12] I saw the collection first at Saratoga in 1911, it being exhibited there by Prof. J. P. Haskins, who charged 25c admission to view it. I saw it on a number of occasions in Saratoga as I went there nearly every summer. On returning there this summer, I found that Prof. Haskins had died, and that it was now owned by H. Hubbard [E. Hammond], Sporting Goods Dealer, Broadway, Saratoga Springs. I saw what was left of the collection and offered him sixty dollars for all of it except the bison and elk, (for which I have no room here), but he wanted me to pay the freight about $40.00 more, so we broke off negotiations after I had agreed to pay half the freight. In my opinion all of the animals in the collection can be restored by a good taxidermist, that is, all that remains. The best specimens are missing, no doubt carried off during the winter following Prof. Haskins death when his museum was demolished and the specimens set out in the snow in a vacant lot in the cold winter of 1917 and 1918. Had I gotten to Saratoga last year (I was in the army) I might have been able to see more of it. I am, Yours very truly. (Signed) Henry W. Shoemaker."[13]

Hope immediately sprang to life. The State University of Colorado was now in a position to care for the specimens and I felt sure would gladly have them. Upon writing to the curator of their museum [Junius Henderson] whom I knew to be deeply interested in Mrs. Maxwell's work as a pioneer naturalist, I learned they had some years before (1906) looked into the matter and had some correspondence with the Peabody Museum at Yale which offered to transfer all claims to them if they could get it away from Dr. Haskins. They had sent Dr. [Francis] Ramal[e]y, of their faculty, to examine it without giving Dr. Haskins an idea or any reason beyond general interest in such work. He did not think the condition of the specimens would permit their removal. They had had too much exposure and neglect so the matter had been dropped.[14] Prof. Henderson on the receipt of my letter and Mr. Shoemaker's, replied that Dr. Ramal[e]y was a naturalist and not a taxidermist and if I wished to send an approved taxidermist there to examine and report on them they would be very glad to cooperate with me in rescuing what remained. I sent the man who does the work of that kind for the State of New York. His report was not very favorable, although he sent me a list of the specimens which with skill and much care could be made good.[15] There were so few of them and they were so out of connection with their former groups that it was decided by Prof. Henderson and myself that they might represent, were they repaired, specimens of the taxidermic art, but could not embody the distinctive idea for which Mrs. Maxwell stood in her work.[16]

The story of Mrs. Maxwell's Collection is ended.

Her fate and its destruction are depressing tragedies, but, in the economy of the Universe nothing is ever wholly lost. The visible embodiment of an idea may perish but the object lesson once seen is rarely forgotten.

Thousands of people at the Centennial were shown the artistic possibilities of taxidermy and the greater beauty as well as the educational value of giving specimens natural surroundings.

In a very short time a complete change took place in museums in the exhibition of animal life and in less than nine years, clubs were formed for its culture as an acknowledged department of real art.[17]

THE FAMILY

What happened to Martha Maxwell's family? The following accounts sketch briefly the lives of Martha Maxwell's husband, daughter, and other close relatives after her death.

JAMES A. MAXWELL remained in Boulder until his death, residing during the last part of his life at the home of his son Charles Alonzo (Lon). "His was an insatiable mind whose love for reading and whose mental curiosity continued until his death," wrote his daughter Mabel. "At seventy-six he received a diploma for taking Chatauqua [*sic*] courses."[18] Early on the morning of January 23, 1891, he failed to appear for breakfast and was discovered sitting upright in his chair, where he had quietly passed away, an open book still in his hand.[19]

MABEL MAXWELL BRACE and her husband, Dr. Charles C. Brace, had two children, Mabel, born in 1885, and Maxwell (1889). In 1893 Brace went into practice with a Denver doctor, and the family moved to the capital. Brace later acquired an interest in the manufacture of antiphlogistine, used to treat tuberculosis, and became president of the Denver Chemical Manufacturing Company. The Braces ultimately relocated to the East Coast and settled permanently at Tarrytown, on the Hudson River.[20] Active to the last, Mabel Maxwell Brace published her family reminiscence, *Thanks to Abigail*, in 1948. She died just a few months short of her one-hundredth birthday in 1957 in Irvington, New York.[21]

AMY SANFORD DARTT died in Boulder on February 11, 1901, at the age of ninety-six. "The venerable lady had enjoyed excellent health until Wednesday, the 6th instant, when she was taken with the grip, which caused her death," reported the *Boulder Daily Camera* in a front-page obituary.[22]

MARY DARTT THOMPSON lived to be almost one hundred years old. "Up to the time of her death she was alert and interested in everything," remembered Mabel Maxwell Brace. When Mary visited Mabel and her husband, her niece continued, "she would sit at the table, as thin as a rail, with burning eyes, eat like a sparrow and talk about everything under the sun."[23] During her later years she helped found the Laurel, Maryland, free public library, the woman's club in Laurel, and the Prince George's County Federation of Women's Clubs. She and Nathan Thompson were the parents of three children, a son, Clarence, who died in infancy, and two daughters, Mary Florence (Dot) and Helen Morton. Mary Dartt Thompson died in East Falls Church, Virginia, in 1940. Nathan Thompson died in 1917 in Laurel, Maryland.[24]

SARAH ELIZABETH DARTT SAYRE died in Denver in 1939. From Central City she and her husband, Hal Sayre, moved to Denver, where she was active in social circles. The Sayres had three children, Hal, Jr., who died in an accident in 1902, Ethel, and Robert.[25] Hal Sayre died in Denver in 1926, one of the last of the Fifty-niners.[26]

EMMA MAXWELL married Henry Howard Potter in Baraboo in 1856. They had five children: Carrie V., Ida A., Kate W., Mary B., and Howard H.[27]

JAMES P. MAXWELL continued his activities in Colorado business and politics well into the twentieth century. In addition to serving in the territorial legislature and the state senate during the 1870s, he was the mayor of Boulder (1878–80) and county treasurer (1880–82). From 1888 to 1893 he served as state engineer, and he was again elected to the senate in 1896. From the turn of the century onward he devoted himself mainly to surveying and mineral engineering and to serving as president of the First National Bank of Boulder. He also had extensive business interests in the Steamboat Springs area. When he died at the age of ninety in 1929 he was said to be the oldest living graduate of Lawrence University. He and his wife Francelia had three sons, Clint, Mark, and Ray, and two daughters, Maria and Helen.[28]

CHARLES ALONZO MAXWELL died in 1911 in Boulder. After his initial gold-mining endeavors in Colorado in the 1860s he had gone back to Baraboo, where he had a stroke attributed to the effects of the mercury used in extracting gold. He recovered and returned to Boulder, where he resumed mining. In 1872 he married Mary A. Davis at Laramie, and they had five children.[29]

CAROLINE OPHELIA MAXWELL married George W. Rust, the commercial editor of the *Chicago Times*, in 1865. The Rusts, who later moved to Boulder, had three children, Caroline and twins Melvin and Nellie. Nellie Rust (1868–1939) became a well-known Boulder businesswoman.[30]

ELLEN C. MAXWELL married William Hill of Prairie du Chien, Wisconsin, in 1865. Hill, for many years editor of the *Baraboo Republic*, later was involved in banking in Neodesha, Kansas.[31]

AUGUSTA MAXWELL married James N. Pierce and became the mother of three sons. Noted throughout her life for her musical ability and excellent voice, she died in Berkeley, California, in 1910.[32]

Otus asio maxwelliae, a subspecies of eastern screech owl named for Martha Maxwell by Robert Ridgway "as a deserved tribute to her high attainments in the study of natural history." This recent example is from the collections of the Smithsonian Institution. Courtesy Division of Birds and U.S. Fish and Wildlife Service, National Museum of Natural History, Smithsonian Institution, Washington, D.C.

Only a few examples of Martha Maxwell's work survive in any form. These study skins, specimens of gray-crowned rosy finches, were sent by Martha to the Smithsonian Institution. Courtesy Division of Birds and U.S. Fish and Wildlife Service, National Museum of Natural History, Smithsonian Institution, Washington, D.C.

In this illustration from *On the Plains*, Martha Maxwell, James Maxwell, and Dr. W. D. McLeod, on a collecting trip for the Boulder museum, watch J. Clarence Hersey deal with a rival for a bird's nest. From *On the Plains*, opp. p. 140.

CHLOROFORMING A SNAKE.

A number of photographs, mostly stereographs, of Martha Maxwell's Colorado museum have survived, forming a significant documentary record of her museum work. These two images of the Boulder museum were published as "Rocky Mountain Stereoscopic Views" by Alexander Martin, who maintained a studio in Boulder from 1874 to 1878. Courtesy Western Historical Collections, University of Colorado, Boulder.

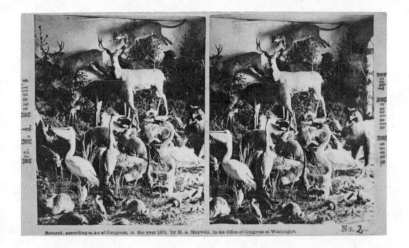

Apparently beginning in late 1875 or early 1876, the prolific Denver photographer William G. Chamberlain offered for sale a collection of stereographs entitled "Mrs. Maxwell's Rocky Mountain Museum Series." Although almost all of the Chamberlain stereographs carry on the reverse information implying that the displays pictured were in the museum at 376 Lawrence Street in Denver, other evidence strongly suggests that these exhibits were in the Boulder museum. This image gives an overall view of one of Martha Maxwell's dramatic habitat groupings. Courtesy Western History Department, Denver Public Library, Denver, Colorado.

The Chamberlain stereographs included the comic group of card-playing monkeys. Courtesy Western History Department, Denver Public Library, Denver, Colorado.

Another comic tableau in the Chamberlain series showed a squirrel and a duckling emerging from a small wooden house. Courtesy Western History Department, Denver Public Library, Denver, Colorado.

Martha Maxwell's display at the Philadelphia Centennial Exposition was situated against one wall in the Colorado wing (left) of the Kansas-Colorado Building. Courtesy Colorado Historical Society, Denver, Colorado.

Martha Maxwell and her exhibit of "Woman's Work" at the Philadelphia Centennial Exposition. Enthusiastic visitors bombarded her with questions from morning until night, causing her to escape occasionally into her "cave." Courtesy The Historical Society of Pennsylvania, Philadelphia.

Mabel Maxwell at Wellesley College, 1878. Although Mabel had been "supremely happy" at the University of Michigan, where she had transferred after two
years at Oberlin, her mother wanted her to attend school in the Boston area,
where Martha was spending much of her time and where Mabel's aunt Mary
Dartt Thompson lived. "When I arrived, feeling abandoned and forlorn, I did
not fit in anywhere," she wrote later in her memoir. From *Thanks to Abigail*, opp.
p. 110.

This portrait of Martha Maxwell was probably made at the time of the Centennial or soon thereafter. It appears as an engraving in some copies of *On the Plains*. Courtesy Mrs. E. Geoffrey Cullen, St. Louis, Missouri.

Appendix A

Notice of Mrs. Maxwell's Exhibit of Colorado Mammals by Elliott Coues*

I had the pleasure of inspecting Mrs. Maxwell's collection of the animals of Colorado, while the exhibit was in Washington during the winter of 1876–7.

My repeated visits afforded me both pleasure and instruction. I was glad to see a collection of our native animals mounted in a manner far superior to ordinary museum work, and to know that there was at least one lady who could do such a thing, and who took pleasure in doing it. While the collection embraced several specimens of high scientific interest, I regarded it as one of the most valuable single collections I had seen—for beyond the scientific value which any collection of the animals of a locality may possess, it represented a means of popularizing Natural History, and making the subject attractive to the public; this desirable object being attained by the artistic manner in which the specimens were mounted and grouped together. Faulty taxidermy has a great deal to do with creating misconceptions of nature in the public mind, and with rendering the study of Natural History unattractive. The best results may be hoped for when such skillful and faithful representation of nature, as these of Mrs. Maxwell's, come to be recognized as a means of public instruction.

*On the Plains, and Among the Peaks, 217–25.

With Mrs. Maxwell's kind permission I made for my own benefit some notes on the species of mammals contained in the collection, and I take pleasure in furnishing a list of the specimens, which she is at liberty to use in any way she may see fit. My identifications of the species are supplemented by some remarks partly based upon my own observations in Colorado in 1876, partly derived from my conversation with the intelligent and enthusiastic lady-naturalist herself.

Family FELIDÆ.
THE COUGAR, OR AMERICAN PANTHER.
Felis Concolor—Linn.

The collection contains two full-grown specimens of this great cat, sometimes called "the Californian lion," and much dreaded for its depredations upon live-stock. One was killed near Boulder by poisoning the carcass of a young horse which the panther had destroyed. The other was shot.

The cougar appears to be rather common in the mountainous portions of the State, where two or three are usually killed each year, but is only rarely seen on the prairie.

THE MOUNTAIN LYNX.
Lynx Canadensis?

The most common Lynx of the Rocky Mountains in this latitude appears to be a modification of the Canada Lynx, *L. canadensis* of authors, and is perhaps entitled to varietal designation as a geographical race of that species. It may be named var. *montanus.* I have seen similar specimens from elevated portions of California. These Lynxes do not seem to be specifically separable from *L. canadensis,* but they are distinguishable at a glance from the *Lynx rufus,* which also occurs in the same locality. They are much more abundant than the *L. Rufus,* and numbers are shot or trapped each year. Several well-prepared specimens are contained in the collection.

THE COMMON OR BAY LYNX.
Lynx Rufus—Raf.

One specimen of the ordinary lynx of the United States—which, as just intimated, is not so common in Colorado as the preceding species—was shot on Câche-Le-Poudre creek at the eastern base of the mountains.

Family CANIDÆ.

THE GREAT GRAY WOLF.

Canis Lupus Occidentalis—Rich.

One specimen, full grown, and in fine order. This animal is much less numerous than the following species.

THE PRAIRIE WOLF, OR COYOTE.

Canis Latrans—Say.

A very abundant animal in Colorado as in most other parts of the West, and occurring in the mountains as well as on the plains.

THE RED FOX OF THE PLAINS.

Vulpes Macrurus—Bd.

Numerous specimens of this species, differing much in color, but all apparently referable to the animal described by Baird in 1852. It runs into many color varieties, as the cross and silver-gray, and in one case of which I learned the animal was pure black, with a white tip to the tail. One of the specimens in the collection is re-markably light-colored.

THE SWIFT OR KIT FOX.

Vulpes Velox—Say.

This is a common animal in Colorado, living in burrows on the prairie.

THE GRAY FOX.

Urocyon Cinereo-Argentatus—Coues.

Apparently rare in Colorado.

Family MUSTELIDÆ.

THE WOLVERENE, OR CARCAJOU.

Gulo Luscus—Sab.

It is only of late years that the presence of this remarkable animal so far south has been known. It ranges chiefly in the high north, where it is the most serious annoyance with which the trapper has to contend. The specimen in the collection was captured with a steel trap near Boulder. The animal resides in the mountains, and does not appear to be very rare.

THE AMERICAN MARTIN OR SABLE.
Mustela Americana—Turton.

Though not represented in the collection, I enumerate this species as one of the known animals of the State.

THE LONG-TAILED WEASEL.
Putorius Longicauda—Bd.

Several specimens of this interesting species, believed to be perfectly distinct from the common ermine, are contained in the collection. These illustrate very fairly the specific distinctions from *P. erminea*, being rather dark-colored, especially on the head, with the under parts decidedly tawny, instead of sulphury-yellow, abruptly defined against the white of the chin, and the black tip of the tail restricted to the terminal pencil. The species turn perfectly white in winter in this latitude, as well as farther north.

THE LEAST WEASEL.
Putorius Vulgaris—Griff.

One specimen of this pretty little creature was procured near Boulder.

THE MINK.
Putorius Vison—Gapp.

This common animal is represented by several specimens.

THE AMERICAN FERRET.
Putorius Nigripes—Aud. & Bach.

Mrs. Maxwell's collection contains several specimens of this extremely interesting animal, unknown to naturalists until within a few years. It was originally described by Audubon and Bachman; but subsequently lost sight of until recently, when a few specimens reached the Smithsonian from different localities in the West. It appears to be not at all rare in some portions of Colorado, especially about the plains at the foot of the mountains, where it lives among the prairie-dogs and feeds upon them. Two individuals were captured by being "drowned out" of prairie-dog holes, and another was trapped. Mrs. Maxwell kept one alive for some time. It became quite tame, readily submitting to be handled, though it was furious when first caught. It was kept in a wire cage and fed on beef. When irritated, it hissed and spat like an angry cat. It used to hide by covering itself over with the material of which its nest was composed, but at times, especially at night, it was very active and restless.

THE COMMON SKUNK.

Mephitis Mephitica—Bd.

This animal is far too numerous in Colorado, especially about the settlements in the foot-hills and on the prairie.

THE LITTLE STRIPED SKUNK.

Mephitis Putorius—Coues.

Rather common in the mountains and foot-hills, but less so than the last.

THE BADGER.

Taxidea Americana—Bd.

In the specimens examined in Mrs. Maxwell's collection the white stripe runs down over the shoulders, showing an approach to the condition seen in the var. *berlandieri*. The species is abundant in the open portions of the State.

THE OTTER.

Lutra Canadensis—Cuv.

The otter appears to be a rare animal in Colorado. I did not find any sign of its presence during my tour in that State in 1876, and the single specimen in the collection was the only one of which Mrs. Maxwell had known.

Family URSIDÆ.

THE BEARS.

Ursus ———?

These formidable animals are represented by a fine group of several specimens, in which three varieties may be recognized. One of the largest is a true grizzly bear, which was shot about forty miles from Denver. Others belong to the variety known as the "cinnamon" bear, and form an interesting group of two cubs crying over their dead mother. Another specimen is the black bear, perhaps of an entirely different species from the rest.

Family BOVIDÆ.

THE AMERICAN BISON, OR BUFFALO.

Bison Americanus—H. Smith.

The mounted buffaloes of this collection represent both the

ordinary species of the plains, and what is known as the "mountain buffalo," by some erroneously supposed to be a different species. The latter are decidedly darker and more uniformly colored than the former, and were shot in September, 1873, near Whitely's Peak, Middle Park.

In 1876 a small band of buffalo still lingered in North Park.

THE MOUNTAIN SHEEP.

Ovis Montana—Cuv.

A family group consisting of both male and female, and a lamb, shot on the main range near Boulder.

Family ANTILOCAPRIDÆ.

THE ANTELOPE.

Antilocrapra Americana—Ord.

I have nowhere else found antelope so abundant as they were in North Park during the summer of 1876. They were almost continually in view, and thousands must breed in that locality.

In one of the finely mounted specimens in Mrs. Maxwell's collection the points of the horns curve inward toward each other; the two together making a heart-shaped figure.

Family CERVIDÆ.

THE AMERICAN ELK.

Elaphus Canadensis—De Kay.

Represented by a fine pair shot near Whitely's Peak.

THE BLACK-TAILED DEER.

Cervus Macrotis—Say.

This is the most abundant of the Cervidæ in Colorado, and is represented by a fine group of two bucks, a doe and two fawns.

THE WHITE-TAILED DEER.

Cervus Virginianus—Bodd.

One specimen, a doe from Câche-Le-Poudre creek. It is far less numerous in Colorado than the last-named species.

Family SCIURIDÆ

The family of the squirrels is very numerously represented in Colorado, both in species and individuals. No less than eight different species are contained in the collection.

THE TUFT-EARED SQUIRREL.
Sciurus Aberti—Woodh.

This large and beautiful squirrel, equalling in size the cat and fox squirrels of the East, is common in the pine-covered mountains of Colorado. It is in this region peculiarly subject to melanism, this state being more frequently observed, than the normal coloration. Several specimens examined are uniform deep brownish black, while only one is of the ordinary grey color, with the black stripe on the side.

FREMONT'S CHICKAREE.
Sciurus Hudsonius var. *Fremonti*—Allen.

Very abundant in all the woods of the high mountains.

FOUR-STRIPED CHIPMUNK.
Tamias Quadrivittatus—Wagn.

An exceedingly abundant little animal everywhere in the mountains and parks.

SAY'S CHIPMUNK.
Tamias Lateralis—Allen.

Common in the pine timber, especially in rocky places of the higher ranges.

LARGE GROUND SQUIRREL.
Spermophilus Grammurus—Bachm.

This is a large and conspicuous species, with its long, bushy tail looking much like a regular tree-squirrel. It is common in rocky places on the foot-hills.

THIRTEEN-STRIPED GROUND-SQUIRREL.
Spermophilus Tridecemlineatus—Aud. & Back.

Very common in open places.

THE PRAIRIE-DOG.
Cynomys Ludovicianus—Baird.

One of the commonest and best known animals of the country, the colonies of which dot the prairie on every hand.

THE YELLOW-BELLIED MARMOT.
Arctomys Flaviventris—Aud. & Backm.

Apparently confined to the foot-hills and mountains, where it is common.

Family MURIDÆ.

ROCKY MOUNTAIN RAT.

Neotoma Cinerea—Bd.

Found in abundance in the mountains of Colorado. They often come about the house and take up their residence, proving very mischievous and undesirable from their propensity to steal and hide everything they can get hold of and carry off. Among the articles which Mrs. Maxwell has found in their retreats, are bushels of weeds of various kinds, chips of wood, cow-manure, old stockings, tent-blocks and ropes, pieces of crockery, knives, forks and a broken doll.

THE BUSH RAT.

Neotoma Floridana—Say & Ord.

This species also occurs, and comes about the houses like the others, but the two do not seem to get along well together.

THE WHITE-FOOTED OR WOOD-MOUSE.

Hesperomys Leucopus var. *Sonoriensis*—Coues.

A common species of general distribution in the West.

THE MEADOW MOUSE.

Arvicola?

A large species, and resembling *Arvicola riparius*, if not the same.

THE MUSKRAT.

Fiber Zibethicus—Cuv.

Very abundant in suitable places in Colorado.

Family ZAPODIDÆ.

THE JUMPING MOUSE.

Zapus Hudsonius—Coues.

One specimen captured near Boulder.

Family SACCOMYIDÆ.

THE KANGAROO MOUSE.

Dipodomys Ordi—Woodh.

One specimen taken near Denver.

Family GEOMYIDÆ.

THE POCKET GOPHER.

Geomys Bursarius—Rich.

One specimen. The species is said to be abundant on the plains and adjoining foot-hills.

Family CASTORIDÆ.

THE BEAVER.

Castor Fiber var. *Canadensis*—Coues & Yarrow.

A group of several individuals, with specimen of large stump—about three feet in diameter and perfectly sound—cut by them. The beaver is still very abundant on many of the waters of the State.

Family LEPORIDÆ.

THE MOUNTAIN RABBIT.

Lepus Americanus var. *Bairdi*—Allen.

Known also as "Snow-shoe" and "Maltese rabbit." This species is confined to the mountains and turns white in winter. In a specimen examined the roots of the hairs showed plumbeous, then a pale salmon or fawn color. The ears sometimes retain a blackish tipping or edging.

COMMON JACK RABBIT.

Lepus Campestris—Bach.

Very abundant on the prairies and parks of the State, but not found in the woods. This species is identical with that from the northerly parts of the West, but entirely distinct from the following.

SOUTHERN JACK RABBIT.

Lepus Callotis var. *Texanus*—Allen.

Said to occur in the southern part of the State as far north as the vicinity of Greeley. With the size and general appearance of *L. Campestris*, it may be distinguished by having the top of the tail black instead of white as in the foregoing species.

THE SAGE RABBIT.

Lepus Sylvaticus var. *Nuttalli*—Allen.

Very abundant in the sage brush anywhere.

Family LAGOMYIDÆ.
THE LITTLE CHIEF HARE.
Lagomys Princeps—Rich.
Common on the mountains above timber-line.

Appendix B

Mrs. Maxwell's Colorado Museum
Catalogue of the Birds
by Robert Ridgway*

The following is a systematic catalogue of the birds contained in the "Colorado Museum," prepared by Mrs. M. A. Maxwell, of Boulder, Colorado, and by her exhibited at the Centennial Exposition held in Philadelphia during the past summer. The collection consists of excellently mounted specimens, many of which were procured by the lady herself, while all were put up by her hands. It illustrates very fully the avian fauna of Colorado, while it bears testimony, not only to the great richness and variety which characterize the productions of the new State, but also to the success which has crowned the enthusiastic and intelligent efforts of a "woman Naturalist."

The collection embraces many species whose occurrence in Colorado was wholly unlooked for; such as *Nyctherodias violaceus, Garzetta candidissima,* and *Tantalus loculator* among southern species, and *Stercorarius parasiticus, Xema sabinei,* and *Œdemia americana* from the high north; the latter, it will be observed, is a strictly littoral species, hence, its occurrence in Colorado, the very centre of the continent, is all the more remarkable.

*On the Plains, and Among the Peaks, 226–37.

Family TURDIDÆ: Thrushes.

1. Turdus migratorius, β. propinquus, (Ridgw.) Western Robin. a, ♂ ad.; b, ♀ ad.
2. Turdus guttatus, γ. auduboni, (Baird.) Rocky Mountain Hermit Thrush. a, ♂ ad.; b, ♀ ad.
3. Turdus ustulatus, β. swainsoni. Olive-backed, or Swainson's Thrush. a, ♂ ad.
4. Turdus fuscescens, (Stephens.) Tawny Thrush; Wilson's Thrush. a, ♂ ad.
5. Galeoscoptes carolinensis, (Linn.) Cat Bird. a, ♂ ad.; b, ♀ ad.
6. Oreoscoptes montanus, (Towns.) Sage-Thrasher; Mountain Mocking Bird. a, ♂ ad.; b, juv.
7. Mimus polyglottus, (Linn.) Mocking bird. a, ♂ ad.; b, ♀ ad.
8. Harporhynchus rufus, (Linn.) Brown Thrasher. a, ♂ ad.; b, ♀ ad.

Family CINCLIDÆ: Water Ouzels.

9. Cinclus mexicanus, (Swains.) American Water Ouzel. a, ♂ ad.; b, ♀ ad.; c, d, e, f, young.

Family SYLVIIDÆ: Warblers.

10. Myiadestes townsendi, (Aud.) Townsend's Solitaire. a, ♂ ad.; b, ♀ ad.
11. Sialia sialis, (Linn.) Eastern Blue Bird. a, ♂ ad.; b, ♀ad.
12. Sialia mexicana, (Swains.) California Blue Bird. a, ♂ ad.; b, ♀ ad.
13. Sialia arctica, (Swains.) Rocky Mountain Blue Bird. a, ♂ ad.; b, ♀ ad.
14. Regulus calendula, (Linn.) Ruby-crowned Kinglet. ♂ ad.
15. Regulus satrapa, (Licht.) Golden-crowned Kinglet. a, ♂ ad.; f, ♀.
16. Polioptila cærulea, (Linn.) Blue-gray Gnatcatcher. a, ♂ juv.

Family CERTHIIDÆ: Tree Creepers.

17. Certhia familiaris, β. americana, (Bonap.) Brown Creeper.

Family PARIDÆ: Titmice or Chickadees.

18. Lophophanes inornatus, (Gamb.) Gray Titmouse. a, adult.

19. Parus montanus, (Gamb.) Mountain Chickadee. a, adult.
20. Parus atricapillus, β. septentrionalis, (Harris.) Long-tailed Chickadee. a, adult.
21. Psaltriparus plumbeus, (Baird.) Lead-colored Least Tit. a, ♂ ad.

Family SITTIDÆ: Nuthatches.

22. Sitta carolinensis, β. aculeata, (Cass.) Slender-billed Nuthatch. a, ♂ ad.; b, ♀ ad.
23. Sitta canadensis, (Linn.) Red-bellied Nuthatch.
24. Sitta Pygmæa, (Vig.) Pigmy Nuthatch. a, ♂ ad.; b, ♀ ad.

Family TROGLODYTIDÆ: Wrens.

25. Catherpes mexicanus, β. conspersus, (Ridgw.) Cañon Wren. a, ♂ ad.
26. Salpinctes obsoletus, (Say.) Rock Wren. a, ♂ ad.; b, ♀ ad.
27. Troglodytes ædon, β. parkmanni, (Aud.) Parkmann's Wren. a, ♂ ad.; b, ♀ ad.; c, d, e, f, g, h, young.
28. Telmatodytes palustris, β. paludicola, (Baird.) Tule Wren. a, ad.

Family MOTACILLIDÆ: Wagtails, and Titlarks, or Pipits.

29. Anthus ludovicianus, (Gm.) American Titlark. a, ♂ ad.; b, ♀ ad. [Breeding abundantly on mountains above timber-line, at an altitude of about 12,000 feet!]
30. Neocorys spraguei, (Aud.) a, ad.

Family MNIOTILTIDÆ: American Warblers.

31. Dendrœca auduboni, (Towns.) Audubon's Warbler. a, ♂ ad.; b, ♀ ad.; c, juv.
32. Dendrœca coronata, (Linn.) Yellow-rump Warbler. a, ♂ ad.; b, ♀ ad.
33. Dendrœca nigrescens, (Towns.) Black-throated Gray Warbler, a, ♂ ad.
34. Dendrœca æstiva, (Gm.) Golden Warbler; Summer Yellow Bird. a, ♂ ad.; b, ♀ ad.
35. Parula americana, (Linn.) Blue Yellow-back Warbler. a, ♂ ad.

36. Helminthophaga celata, (Say.) Orange-crowned Warbler. a, ad.
37. Helminthophaga peregrina, (Wils.) Tennessee Warbler. a, ♂ ad.; b, ♀ ad.
38. Geothlypis trichas, (Linn.) Maryland Yellow-throat. a, ♂ ad.; b, ♀ ad.
39. Geothlypis macgillivrayi, (Aud.) McGillivray's Warbler. a, ♂ ad.; b, ♀ ad.
40. Icteria virens, β. longicauda, (Lawr.) Long-tailed Chat. a, ♀ ad.
41. Myiodioctes pusillus, (Wils.) Black-cap Green and Yellow Warbler.
42. Setophaga ruticilla, (Linn.) American Redstart. a, ♂ ad.; b, ♀ ad.

Family VIREONIDÆ: Greenlets or Vireos.
43. Vireosylvia gilva, β. Swainsoni, (Baird.) Western Warbling Vireo. a, ♂ ad.; b, ♀ ad.
44. Vireosylvia olivacea, (Linn.) Red-eyed Vireo. a, ♂ ad.; b, ♀ ad.
45. Lanivireo plumbeus, (Coues.) Lead-colored Vireo. a, ad.
46. Lanivireo solitarius, (Wils.) Solitary Vireo. a, ad.

Family LANIIDÆ: Shrikes.
47. Collurio borealis, (Vieill.) Great Northern Shrike. a, ♂ ad.; b, juv.
48. Collurio ludovicianus, β. excubitoroides, (Swains.) White-rumped Shrike. a, ♂ ad.; b, ♀ ad.

Family AMPELIDÆ: Wax-wings.
49. Ampelis garrulus, (Linn.) Northern Wax-wing. a, ♂ ad.; b, ♀ ad.
50. Ampelis cedrorum, (Vieill.) Cedar wax-wing. a, ♂ ad.

Family HIRUNDINIDÆ: Swallows.
51. Progne subis, (Linn.) Purple Martin. a, ♂ ad.
52. Petrochelidon lunifrons, (Say.) Cliff Swallow. a, ad.
53. Hirundo erythrogaster, β. horreorum, (Barton.) Barn Swallow. a, ad.; b, juv.

54. Tachycineta bicolor, (Vieill.) White-bellied Swallow. a, ♂ ad.; b, c, d, juv.
55. Tachycineta thalassina, (Swains.) Violet-green Swallow.
56. Stelgidopteryx serripennis, (Aud.) Rough-winged swallow. a, ad.
57. Coltyle riparia, (Linn.) Bank Swallow.

Family TANAGRIDÆ: Tanagers.
58. Pyranga ludoviciana, (Wils.) Western Tanager. a, ♂ ad.; b, ♀ ad.
59. Pyranga æstiva, (Wils.) Vermilion Tanager.

Family FRINGILLIDÆ: Finches,
Sparrows and Buntings.
60. Pinicola enucleator, β. canadensis, (Linn.) Pine Grosbeak. a, ♂ ad.; b, ♀ ad. [Breeds on high mountains of Colorado.]
61. Loxia curvirostra, γ. mexicana, (Strickl.) Mexican Crossbill. a, ♂ ad.; b, ♀ ad. [Breeds in Colorado.]
62. Hesperiphona vespertina, (Cooper.) Evening Grosbeak. a, ♂ ad.; b, ♀ ad.
63. Plectrophanes nivalis, (Linn.) Snow Bunting. a, ♂ ad.; winter plumage.
64. Centrophanes lapponicus, (Linn.) Lappland Long-spur.
65. Centrophanes ornatus, (Towns.) Chestnut collared Long-spur. a, ♂ ad.; b, ♀ ad.
66. Rhynchophanes maccowni, (Lawr.) McCown's Long-spur. a, ♂ ad.; b, ♀ ad.; c, juv.
67. Leucosticte tephrocotis, (Swains.) Gray-crowned Leucosticte. a, ♀ ad.; summer pl.; b, ♀ ad.; summer pl.; c, ad.; spring pl.; d, ad.; summer pl.
68. Leucosticte tephrocotis, β. littoralis, (Baird.) Hepburn's Leucosticte. a, adult, winter pl.
69. Leucosticte atrata, (Ridgw.) Aiken's Leucosticte. a, ♂ ad.; winter pl.
70. Leucosticte australis, (Allen.) Allen's Leucosticte. a, ♂ ad.; summer pl.; b, ♀ ad.; summer pl.; c, ♀ ad.; winter pl.
71. Chrysomitris tristis, (Linn.) American Gold-finch. a, b, ♂ ad., summer pl.; c, ♀ ad.

72. Chrysomitris psaltria, (Say.) Green-backed Gold-finch. a, ♂ ad.
73. Chrysomitris pinus, (Wils.) Pine Gold-finch. a, b, adult.
74. Carpodacus cassini, (Baird.) Cassin's Purple Finch. a, ♂ ad.; b, ♀ ad.
75. Carpodacus frontalis, (Say.) House Finch. a, ♂ ad.; b, ♀ ad.
76. Centronyx bairdi, (Aud.) Baird's Bunting. a, ♂ ad.
77. Chondestes grammaca, (Say.) Skylark Bunting. a, ♂ ad.; b, ♀ ad.
78. Pooecetes gramineus, β. confinis, (Baird.) Western Bay-winged Bunting. a, ad.
79. Passerculus sandvichensis, γ. alaudinus, (Bonap.) Western Savanna Sparrow. a, ♂ ad.; b, ♀ ad.
80. Junco Aikeni, (Ridgw.) White-winged Snowbird. a, ♂ ad.; b, ♀ ad.
81. Junco hyemalis, (Linn.) Eastern Snowbird. a, ♂ ad.; b, ♀ ad.
82. Junco oregonus, (Towns.) Oregon Snowbird. a, ♂ ad.; b, ♀ ad.
83. Junco caniceps, (Woodh.) Gray-headed Snowbird. a, ad.; (variety; see note page 231;) b, ad.; (normal style,) c, juv.
84. Junco annectens, (Baird.) Pink-sided Snowbird. a, ad.; (normal style) b, ad.; (variety, see note on page 231.)
85. Spizella socialis, β. arizonæ, (Coues.) Western Chipping Sparrow. a, ♂ ad.; b, ♀ ad.
86. Spizella monticola, (Gm.) Tree Sparrow. a, ♂ ad.; b, ♀ ad.
87. Spizella breweri, (Cass.) Brewer's Sparrow. a, ad.
88. Spizella pallida, (Swains.) Clay-colored Sparrow. a, ad.
89. Zonotrichia leucophrys, (Forst.) White-crowned Sparrow. a, ♂ ad.; b, ♀ ad.
90. Zonotrichia intermedia, (Ridgw.) Ridgway's White-crowned Sparrow. a, ♂ ad.; b, ♀ ad.; c, juv.; in winter plumage.
91. Melospiza fasciata, γ. fallax, (Baird.) Rocky Mountain Song Sparrow. a, b, c, adults.
92. Melospiza lincolni (Aud.) Lincoln's Sparrow. a, ♂ ad.; b, ♀ ad.; c, juv.
93. Coturniculus passerinus, β. perpallidus, (Ridgw.) Western Yellow-winged Sparrow.

94. Passerella iliaca, (Merrem.) Fox-colored Sparrow. a, ♂ ad.; b, ♀ ad. [Typical *iliaca*.]
95. Calainospiza bicolor, (Towns.) Black Lark Bunting. a, ♂ ad.; b, ♀ ad.
96. Euspiza americana, (Gm.) Black-throated Bunting. a, ♂ ad.
96a. Hedymeles melanocephalus, (Swains.) Black-headed Grosbeak. a, ♂ ad.; b, ♀ ad.
97. Guiraca cærulea, (Linn.) Blue Grosbeak. a, ♀ ad.
98. Cyanospiza amœna, (Say.) Lazuli Bunting. a, ♂ ad.; b, ♀ ad.
99. Pipilo maculatus, δ. megalonyx, (Baird.) Long-clawed Ground Robin. a, ♂ ad.; b, ♀ ad.
100. Pipilo chlorurus, (Towns.) Green-tailed Ground Robin. a, ♂ ad.; ♀ ad.; c, juv.
101. Pipilo fuscus, γ. mesoleucus, (Baird.) Cañon Bunting. a, ♂ ad.
102. a, Cyanospiza cyanea, (Linn.) Indigo Bird. a, ♂ ad.

Family ICTERIDÆ: American Starlings; Hang-nests.
98. Dolichonyx oryzivorus, (L.) Bobolink. a, ♂ ad.
99. Molothrus ater, (Bodd.) Cow Blackbird. a, ♂ ad.; b, ♀ ad.
100. Xanthocephalus icterocephalus, (Bonap.) Yellow-headed Blackbird. a, ♂ ad.; b, ♀ ad.; c, pullus.
101. Agelæus phœniceus, (Linn.) Red-and-buff-shouldered Blackbird. a, ♂ ad.; b, ♀ ad.
102. Sturnella neglecta, (Aud.) Western Meadow Lark. a, ♂ ad.; b, ♀ ad.
103. Icterus bullocki, (Swains.) Bullock's Oriole. a, ♂ ad.; b, ♀ ad.; c, juv.
104. Icterus baltimore, (Linn.) Baltimore Oriole. a, ♂ ad.
105. Scolecophagus cyanocephalus, (Wagl.) Brewer's Blackbird. a, ♂ ad.; b, ♀ ad.

Family CORVIDÆ: Ravens, Crows and Jays.
106. Corvus corax, β. carnivorus, (Bartram.) American Raven. a, ad.; b, juv.
107. Corvus cryptoleucus, (Couch.) White-necked Raven. a, ad.; b, c, juv.

108. Corvus americanus, (Aud.) Common Crow. a, b, c. [Breeds in Colorado!]
109. Picicorvus columbianus, (Wils.) Clarke's Nutcracker. a, ♂ ad.; b, ♀ ad.
110. Gymnokitta cyanocephala, (Max.) Maximilian's Nutcracker. a, ♀ ad.
111. Pica rustica, β. hudsonica, (Sabine.) American Black-billed Magpie. a, ♂ ad.; b, ♀ ad.; c, juv.
112. Perisoreus canadensis, β. capitalis, (Baird.) White-headed Gray Jay. a, ♂ ad.; winter pl.; b, ♂ ad.; summer pl.; c, juv.
113. Cyanocitta macrolopha, (Baird.) Long-crested Jay. a, ♂ ad.; b, ♀ ad.; c, d, e, juv.
114. Aphelocoma woodhousii. (Baird.) Woodhouse's Jay. a, ad.

Family ALAUDIDÆ: Larks.
115. Eremophila alpestris, (Forst.) Shore-Lark. a, b, adults.
116. Eremophila alpestris, γ, leucolæma, (Coues.) White-throated Shore Lark, a, b, c, adults; d, ♀ ad.; e, juv.

Family TYRANNIDÆ: Tyrant Flycatchers.
117. Tyrannus carolinensis, (Linn.) Eastern Kingbird. a, ♂ ad.; b, ♀ ad.
118. Tyrannus verticalis, (Say.) Western Kingbird. a, ♂ ad.; b, ♀ ad.
119. Tyrannus vociferans, (Swains.) Cassin's Kingbird. a, ♂ ad.
120. Contopus borealis, (Swains.) Olive-sided Flycatcher. a, ♂ ad.; b, ♀ ad.
121. Contopus richardsoni, (Swains.) Richardson's Pewee. a, ♂ ad.; b, ♀ ad.
122. Sayornis sayus, (Bonap.) Say's Pewee. ♂ a, ad.
123. Empidonax pusillus, (Swains.) Little Flycatcher; Trail's Flycatcher. a, ♂ ad.; b, ♀ ad.; c, juv.
124. Empidonax difficilis, (Baird.) Western Flycatcher. a, ♂ ad.; b, ♀ ad.
125. Empidonax obscurus, (Swains.) Wright's Flycatcher. a, ♂ ad.
126. Empidonax hammondi, (Xantus.) Hammond's Flycatcher. a, ♀ ad.
127. Empidonax minimus, (Baird.) Least Flycatcher.

Family CAPRIMULGIDÆ: Night-jars.

128. Antrostomus nuttalli, (Aud.) Poorwill. a, ♂ ad.; b, ♀ ad.
129. Chordeiles popetue, β. henryi, (Cass.) Western Night Hawk. a, ♂ ad.; b, ♀ ad.; c, d, juv.

Family TROCHILIDÆ: Humming Birds.

130. Selasphorus platycercus, (Swains.) Broad-tailed Hummer. a, ♂ ad.; b, ♀ ad.; c, ♂ ad. With nest and two young.
131. Selasphorus rufus, (Gmel.) Rufous-backed Hummer.

Family CUCULIDÆ: Cuckoos.

132. Coccyzus americanus, (Linn.) Yellow-billed Cuckoo. a, ♂ ad.; b, ♂ ad.
133. Geococcyx californianus, (Less.) Chaparral Cock; Road-runner. a, ♀ ad.

Family PICIDÆ: Woodpeckers.

134. Picus harrisi, (Aud.) Harris's Woodpecker. a, ♂ ad.; b, ♀ ad.
135. Picus gairdneri, (Aud.) Gairdner's Woodpecker. a, ♂ ad.; b, ♀ ad.
136. Picoides americanus, β. dorsalis, (Baird.) White-backed three-toed Woodpecker. a, ♂ ad.; b, ♀ ad.
137. Sphyrapicus varius, (Linn.) Red-throated Woodpecker. a, ♂ ad.
138. Sphyrapicus nuchalis, (Baird.) Red-naped Woodpecker. a, ♂ ad.; b, ♀ juv.
139. Sphyrapicus thyroideus, (Cass.) Black-breasted Woodpecker. a, ♂ ad.; b, ♀ ad.; c, ♂ juv.; d, ♀ juv.
140. Centurus carolinus, (L.) Red-bellied Woodpecker. a, ♂ ad.; b, ♀ ad.
141. Melanerpes erythrocephalus, (Linn.) Red-headed Woodpecker. a, ♂ ad.; b, ♀ ad.
142. Melanerpes torquatus, (Wils.) Lewis's Woodpecker. a, ♂ ad.; b, ♂ ad.
143. Colaptes mexicanus, (Swains.) Red-shafted Flicker. a, ♂ ad.; b, ♀ ad.; c.
144. Colaptes "hybridus," (Baird.) "Hybrid Flicker." a, ♂ ad.; b, ♀ juv.

Family ALCEDINIDÆ: Kingfishers.

145. Ceryle alcyon, (Linn.) Belted Kingfisher. a, ♂ ad.; b, ♀ juv.

Family COLUMBIDÆ: Pigeons or Doves.

146. Columba fasciata, (Say.) Band-tailed Pigeon. a, ♂ ad.
147. Zenædura carolinensis, (Linn.) Mourning Dove. a, ♂ ad.

Family TETRAONIDÆ: Grouse.

148. Centrocercus urophasianus, (Bonap.) Sage Hen. a, ♂ ad.; b, ♀ ad.
149. Pediœcetes columbianus, (Ord.) Sharp-tailed Grouse. a, ♂ ad.; b, ♀ ad.
150. Canace obscura, (Say.) Dusky Grouse. a, ♂ ad.; b, ♀ ad., and nine chicks.
151. Lagopus leucurus, (Swains.) White-tailed Ptarmigan. a, d, adult, winter pl.; b, ♂ adult, summer pl.; c, ♀ ad.; summer pl.; and 3 chicks.

Family STRIGIDÆ: Owls.

152. Bubo virginianus, β. subarcticus, (Hoy.) Western Great Horned Owl. a, b, adults.
153. Otus brachyotus (Gmel.) Short-eared Owl. a, adult. [Apparently the typical form, and evidently different from the usual American style.]
154. Otus brachyotus, β. cassini, (Brewer.) American Short-eared owl. a, b, adults.
155. Otus wilsonianus, (Less.) American Long-eared Owl. a, b, adults; c, d, pullus.
156. Scops asio, θ. maxwelliæ, (Ridgw.) Mrs. Maxwell's Owl. a, ♂ ad.; b, ♀ ad.; c, d, pullus. [See description at end of catalogue.]
157. Scops flammeola, (Licht.) Flammulated Owl. a, adult. [Boulder, Col., March. *Iris umber brown!*]
158. Nyctale acadica, (Gm.) Saw-whet Owl. a, adult; b, c, juv.
159. Glaucidium gnoma, (Wagl.) Pigmy owl. a, ♂ ad.; b, ♀ ad.
160. Speotyto cunicularia, γ. hypogæa, (Bonap.) North American Burrowing Owl. a, ♂ ad.; b, ♀ ad.; c, d, pullus.

Family FALCONIDÆ: Falcons, Kites, Hawks and Eagles.

161. Falco saker, γ polyagrus, (Cass.) Prairie Falcon. a, "♀" ad.;
b, "♂" juv. (2nd yr.); c, "♀" juv. (2nd yr.)

162. Falco richardsoni, (Ridgw.) Richardson's Merlin. a, ♀ (?
ad.)

163. Falco sparverius, (Linn.) American Kestril. a, ♂ ad.; b, ♀
juv.

164. Pandion haliætus, β. carolinensis, (Gm.) American Osprey.
a, b, juv.

165. Circus hudsonius, (Linn.) Marsh Hawk. a, ♂ ad.; b, ♀ juv.

166. Nisus cooperi, (Bonap.) Cooper's Hawk. a, ♂ juv.; b, ♀ juv.

167. Nisus fuscus, (Gm.) Sharp Skinned Hawk. a, ♂ juv.; b, ♀
juv.

168. Astur artricapillus, (Wils.) American Gos-hawk. a, ♂ ad.; b,
♀ ad.; c, juv.; d, e, pullus.

169. Buteo borealis, β. calurus, (Cass.) Western Red-tailed Buzzard. a, b, ad.; c, d, juv.

170. Buteo swainsoni, (Bonap.) Swainson's Buzzard. a, ♂ ad.; b,
♀ ad.; c, ♀ juv.

171. Archibuteo lagopus, β. sancti-johannis, (Gmel.) American
Rough-legged Buzzard. a, ad.; b, c, juv.

172. Archibuteo ferrugineus, (Licht.) Ferruginous Rough-legged
Buzzard; "California Squirrel Hawk." a, ♂ ad.; *melanistic*; b,
♀ ad.; c, d, pullus.

173. Aquila chrysætos β. canadensis, (Linn.) American Golden
Eagle. a, ad.; b, juv., in 2nd or 3rd year; c, juv. in 1st year.

174. Haliætus leucocephalus, (Linn.) Bald Eagle. a, ad.

Family CATHARTIDÆ: American Vultures.

175. Rhinogryphus aura, (Linn.) Turkey Vulture. a, ad.

Family LARIDÆ: Jaegers, Gulls, and Terns.

176. Stercorarius parasiticus, (Brunn.) Parasitic Jaeger. a, juv.
[Boulder; December.]

177. Rissa tridactyla, (Linn.) Kittiwake Gull, winter pl. [Boulder:
December.]

178. Xema sabinii, (Prev. et des Murs.) Sabine's Gull. a, juv.
[Boulder: December.]

Appendix B / 226

179. Chrœcocephalus Philadelphia, (Ord.) Bonaparte's Gull. a, juv., transition pl.
180. Larus delawarensis, (Ord.) Ring-billed Gull. a, adult; b, juv., transition pl.; c, juv., first yr.

Family CHARADRIIDÆ: Plovers.
181. Squatarola helvetica, (Linn.) Black-bellied Plover. a, juv.
182. Ægialitis montanus, (Towns.) Mountain Plover. a, ♂ ad.; b, ♀; c, pullus.
183. Ægialitis vociferus, (Linn.) Killdeer Plover. a, b, adult; c, d, pullus.

Family RECURVIROSTRIDÆ: Avocets and Stilts.
184. Recurvirostra americana, (Gmel.) American Avocet. a, adult.
185. Himantopus mexicanus, (Muller.) American Stilt.

Family PHALAROPODIDÆ: Phalaropes.
186. Steganopus wilsoni, (Sabine.) Wilson's Phalarope. a, ♀ ad.

Family ARDEIDÆ: Herons.
187. Ardea herodias, (Linn.) Great Blue Heron. a, ♀ ad.; b, juv.
188. Garzetta candidissima, (Jacq.) Snowy Heron. a, ad., breeding plumage.
189. Nyctherodias violaceus, (Linn.) Yellow-crowned Night Heron. a, ad., breeding plumage.
190. Botaurus minor, (Gmel.) American Bittern. a, b, adults; c, juv.

Family TANTALIDÆ: Ibises.
191. Tantalus loculator, (Linn.) Wood Ibis. a, juv.
192. Falcinellus guarauna, (Linn.) Bronzed Ibis. a, juv.

Family SCOLOPACIDÆ: Snipe, Sandpipers, etc.
193. Macrorhamphus griseus, (Gmel.) Red-breasted Snipe. a, b, adult, summer plumage.
194. Tringa alpina, β. americana, (Cassin.) American Dunlin. a, adult, winter plumage.
195. Tringa maculata, (Vieill.) Pectoral Sandpiper. a, adult.
196. Tringa bairdi, (Coues.) Baird's Sandpiper. a, juv.
197. Tringa minutilla, (Vieill.) Least Sandpiper. a, juv.

198. Ereunetes pusillus, (Linn.) Semipalmated Sandpiper. a, juv.
199. Totanus melanoleucus, (Gmel.) Greater Tell-tale. a, adult.
200. Totanus flavipes, (Gmel.) Yellow-legs. a, juv.
201. Totanus solitarius, (Wils.) Solitary Sandpiper.
202. Tringoides macularius, (Linn.) Spotted Sandpiper. a, b, ad.; c, d, juv.
203. Actiturus bartramius, (Wils.) Bartram's Tattler. a, ♂ ad.; b, ♀ ad.
204. Numenius longirostris, (Wils.) Long-billed Curlew. a, ♂ ad.

Family RALLIDÆ: Rails, Gallinules, and Coots.
205. Rallus virginianus, (Linn.) Virginia Rail. a, ♂ ad.
206. Porzana carolina, (Linn.) Sora Rail. a, ad.
207. Fulica americana, (Gmel.) American Coot. a, ad.; b, c, pullus.

Family ANATIDÆ: Swans, Geese and Ducks.
208. Cygnus americanus, (Sharpless.) Whistler Swan. a, b, adults.
209. Branta canadensis, (Linn.) Canada Goose. a, b, adults.
210. Anser gambeli, (Hartl.) White-fronted Goose. a, adult.
211. Anser albatus, (Cassin.) Lesser Snow Goose. a, b, adults.
212. Anas boschas, (Linn.) Mallard. a, ♂ ad.; b, ♀ ad.; c, d, e, pullus.
213. Chaulelasmus streperus, (Linn.) Gadwall. a, ♂ ad.
214. Mareca americana, (Gmel.) Baldpate. a, b, ♂ adult.
215. Querquedula discors, (Linn.) Blue-wing Teal. a, b, ♂ ad.; c, ♀ ad.
216. Nettion carolinensis, (Gmel.) Green-wing Teal. a, b, ♂ ad.; c, ♀ ad.
217. Dafila acuta, (Linn.) Pin-tail. a, ♂ ad.; b, ♀ ad.
218. Spatula clypeata, (Linn.) Shoveller. a, b, ♂ ad.; c, ♀ ad.
219. Aythya americana, (Eyton.) Red-head. a, ♂ ad.
220. Aythya vallisneria, (Wils.) Canvas-back. a, ♂ ad.
221. Bucephala clangula, β. americana, (Bonap.) American Golden-eye. a, ♂ ad.
222. Bucephala albeola, (Linn.) Butter-ball. a, ♀ ad.; b, ♂ ad.
223. Fulix affinis, (Eyton.) Lesser Black-head. a, ♀ ad.; b, ♂ ad.

224. Fulix collaris, (Donov.) Ring-bill. a, ♀ ad.
225. Edemia americana, (Swains.) American Black Scoter. a, ♂ ad.; [*Perfect adult plumage!*]
226. Erismatura rubida, (Wils.) Ruddy Duck. a, ♂ ad.
227. Mergus merganser, β. americanus. (Cass.) American Buff-breasted Sheldrake. a, ♂ ad.
228. Mergus serrator, (Linn.) Red-breasted Sheldrake. a, ♂ juv.; transition pl.
229. Lophodytes cucullatus, (Linn.) Hooded Sheldrake. a, ♂ ad.; b, ♀ ad.

Family PELECANIDÆ: Pelicans.
230. Pelecanus erythrorhynchus, (Gmel.) American White Pelican. a, juv.

Family GRACULIDÆ: Cormorants.
231. Graculus dilophus, (Swains.) Double-crested Cormorant. a, juv.

Family COLYMBIDÆ: Loons.
232. Colymbus torquatus, (Brunn.) Great Northern Diver. a, juv.

Family PODICIPITIDÆ: Grebes.
233. Podiceps auritus, β californicus, (Lawr.) California Grebe. a, ad.; b, juv.
234. Podilymbus podiceps, (Linn.) Thick-billed Grebe. a, ad.; b, ♀ ad.; c, d, e, pullus.

NOTES.

Archibuteo Ferrugineus, (Licht.)—The collection contains a melanistic specimen of this species, which is a fact of very great interest, since this condition is very rarely assumed by the species; indeed, this example is the first I have ever seen, although very numerous specimens in normal plumage have been examined by me. The following is a description of this remarkable specimen:

General color very dark chocolate-brown, nearly uniform above, where faintly relieved by rufous spots, these most

conspicuous on the inner lesser wing-coverts; occipital feathers
snow-white at the base, those of the nape conspicuously edged
with ferruginous; upper tail-coverts irregularly spotted with
white and pale rufous; secondaries crossed by wide but indistinct
bands of silvery plumbeous; outer webs of primaries bright sil-
very-gray, more obscure on the inner quills. Tail, pearl-gray, (the
middle portion of each feather whitish, the inner webs chiefly
white,) finely sprinkled at the end and toward base with darker
gray; the shafts pure white for their whole length. Entire head,
throat, jugulum and breast quite uniform dark chocolate-brown,
or soot-color, the feathers white at extreme bases; whole abdo-
men, sides and lining of wings ferruginous-rufous, with shaft-
streaks and variously formed spots and bars of dusky; flank-
plumes similar, but with the dusky markings prevailing; tibiæ
dusky, the longer plumes variegated with ferruginous; tarsel
feathers uniform dusky; lower tail-coverts with exposed ends
pale ferruginous, the concealed portion whitish. Whole under
surface of primaries anterior to the emarginations, pure white,
immaculate; under surface of tail also uniform white. Wing, 18.80;
tail, 10.50; culmen, 1.10; tarsus, 3.25; middle toe, 1.50.

In general aspect, this specimen bears a close resemblance to
the rufous-chested examples of melanistic *Buteo borealis* (β. *calurus*,) the tail being the only very obvious difference so far as colors
are concerned, though close inspection soon reveals other
marked discrepancies, most important of which are the bright silver-gray of the outer surface and the immaculate snow-white of
the under surface of the primaries. There is little resemblance to
the melanistic examples of *A. lagopus* (β. *sancti-johannis*,) the
general color being much too rufous, while the tail is conspicuously different. The great breadth of the gape and other pecu-
liarities of structure only recognizable in *A. ferrugineus*, also immediately refer this specimen to that species.

Scops asio, ε. *maxwelliæ*, Ridgway, MSS.—Mrs. Maxwell's
collection contains a number of specimens of what is evidently a
local form of the common North American *Scops asio*, represent-

ing the opposite extreme from var. β. *kennicotti,** and quite as strongly marked as that form. These specimens and others that I have since seen, all agree in possessing with unusual uniformity the distinctive characters of the race, there being apparently much less of individual variation than in other forms of the species. This new race is a mountain bird, and possesses the distinctive features of alpine or boreal races in general, the size being larger and the colors very much paler than in the low-land races, even from much higher latitudes. In the colors, there is in all specimens an entire absence or but faint indication of any rufous tints, while the rufous phase of other forms is never assumed, as indeed, curiously enough, seems to be the case with the species throughout the western half of the continent, even where (as in California) the gray birds cannot be distinguished from individuals in corresponding plumage from the Atlantic States.

From its allies, *Scops maxwelliæ*, may be distinguished as follows:—Ch.—Ground-color above pale gray or grayish brown, relieved by the usual ragged mesial streaks of black, and irregular mottlings or vermiculations of lighter and darker shades; the ground-color, however, never inclining strongly to reddish, and no darker in shade than a *very light* ash-gray or brown. The white spots on the outer webs of the primaries frequently confluent along the edge of the feathers, the darker spots being in extreme cases hardly visible on the basal portion of the quills when the wing is closed. Face grayish white, with faint vermiculations of darker grayish. No rusty gular collar, but in its stead, sparse, narrow bars of brown or rusty, on a white ground. Lower parts with white very largely predominating. Wing, 6.80–6.90; tail, 3.90–4.10; culmen, .60; tarsus, 1.45–1.50; middle toe, .80–.85.† Hab.-

---

* Naming the several marked geographical races of this species in the order of their date of publication, they may be arranged in the following sequence: *a. asio* (*Strix asio*, Linn., S. N., 1758, 92,) *B. kennicotti* (*Scops kennicotti*, Elliot, Pr. Phila. Acad. 1867, 69;) γ. *floridanus* (*Scops asio*, var. *floridanus*, Ridgway bull. Essex Inst. & Dec. 1873, 200;) γ. *enano* (*Scops asio*, var. *enano* Lawr., Bull. Essex Inst., Dec. 1873, 200,) and ε *maxwelliæ*, nobis.

† Before me are three specimens of the typical form (*a. asio*) in gray plumage which are so much alike that if the labels were removed they could scarcely be distinguished. Two of these, a pair, are from the coast of California; the other, an

Mountains of Colorado (Mus. Mrs. Maxwell; also collection of R. Ridgway.) I name this new form in honor of Mrs. M. A. Maxwell, not only as a compliment to an accomplished and amiable lady, but also as a deserved tribute to her high attainments in the study of natural history.

Junco caniceps, (Woodh.)—A very remarkable specimen of this bird is in the collection. It differs from the usual, and we may say almost constant, plumage of the species, in having two well-defined bars of white on the wings, and in having a conspicuous tinge of bright rufous on the pileum, the plumage being other-wise normal. None of the species of *Junco* now known are characterized, even in part, by having rufous on the crown; but several tend in their variations to the other character, *i. e.* the white wing-bars; this feature being almost constant in *J. aikeni*. We have frequently seen this variation in *J. annectens*, and an adult male of *J. oregonus* in our own collection exhibits the same remarkable feature. The fact that this barring of the wings has become a permanent feature of one species, while it occasionally, but very rarely, occurs in three or more others, suggests the question of whether we do not see in this evidence of the present genesis of species; and whether these characters, now unstable, may not through accelerated hereditary transmittal become permanent, thus characterizing, in due time, new forms.

Junco annectens, (Baird.)—An adult specimen, probably a female, since it is smaller than the males in the National Museum and other collections, differs from typical examples in having the pinkish of the sides invading the whole breast and strongly tinging the throat. In other respects, however, it does differ from ordinary specimens. Its measurements are as follows: Wing, 3.20; tail, 2.80; bill, from nostril, .35; tarsus, .78.

---

adult ♀, is from Virginia. Their measurements compare as follows:

♀	Fairfax Co., Va.	6.50.	3.70.
♂	Nicasio, Cal.	6.30.	3.50.
♀	" "	6.60.	3.65.

Notes

PREFACE

1. Quoted in "Centennial Letter," *Boulder County News*, September 9, 1876.

2. Mary Dartt, *On the Plains, and Among the Peaks; or, How Mrs. Maxwell Made Her Natural History Collection* (Philadelphia: Claxton, Remsen and Haffelfinger, 1879 [1878]).

3. Floyd and Marion Rinhart, "Martha Maxwell's Peaceable Kingdom," *American West* 13 (September/October 1976):34–35, 62–63; "A Colorado Huntress Who Immortalized Her Prey," Joan Swallow Reiter, *The Women*, The Old West Series, vol. 23 (Alexandria, Va.: Time-Life Books, 1978), 182–83.

4. Maxine Benson, "Colorado Celebrates the Centennial, 1876," *The Colorado Magazine* 53 (Spring 1976):145–48.

5. Dartt, *On the Plains*, 158.

6. Junius Henderson, "A Pioneer Venture in Habitat Grouping," *Proceedings of the American Association of Museums* 9 (1915):87–91.

7. Carroll Smith-Rosenberg, "The Female World of Love and Ritual: Relations Between Women in Nineteenth-Century America," *Signs: Journal of Women in Culture and Society* 1 (Autumn 1975), reprinted in *Disorderly Conduct: Visions of Gender in Victorian America* (New York: Alfred A. Knopf, 1985), 53–76.

8. Carroll Smith-Rosenberg, "Hearing Women's Words: A Feminist Reconstruction of History," in ibid., 32–33.

9. Mabel Maxwell Brace, *Thanks to Abigail: A Family Chronicle* (N.p.: Privately Printed, 1948).

CHAPTER 1

1. Brace, *Thanks to Abigail*, 2.

2. The story of the duck is related in a five-page autobiography written by Martha covering her life through June 1851. Although clearly datelined Baraboo [Wisconsin], November 21, the year is impossible to decipher with absolute certainty; it could be 1852 or 1858. Internal evidence and the chronology of her life, however, suggest 1852 as the more plausible date. The account, hereinafter cited as Martha Dartt, Autobiography, is in the Maxwell Papers, Colorado Historical Society, Denver, for which a calendar is available.

3. Martha's reply is contained in a letter to her sister Mary (September 2, 1876, Maxwell Papers), in which she discussed the questions posed by the editor of the *Phrenological Journal*. The article was subsequently published as "Martha A. Maxwell, the Colorado Huntress and Naturalist," 38 (November 1876):349–53; see p. 350 for the editor's account of Martha's relationship with her grandmother and "all the little wild folk of the forest."

4. "Remarkable American Women: Mrs. Martha A. Maxwell the Colorado Naturalist," *Chimney Corner*, January 26, 1878, Martha Maxwell Scrapbook, 105. This scrapbook, which apparently was put together by Martha and her sister Mary, later came into the hands of A. H. Felger, who attempted to write a biography of Martha (see note 65 below). The Felger family subsequently gave the scrapbook to Hugo Rodeck, for many years director of the University of Colorado Museum, and he presented it to the Colorado Historical Society, where it is part of the Maxwell Papers. Hereinafter cited as Maxwell Scrapbook.

5. The booklet, which was "Stereotyped, Printed and Sold by H. & E. Phinney," is in the Maxwell Papers.

6. Carlton E. Sanford, *Thomas Sanford, the Emigrant to New England: Ancestry, Life and Descendants, 1632–4: Sketches of Four Other Pioneer Sanfords and Some of Their Descendants in Appendix, with Many Illustrations*, 2 vols. (Rutland, Vt.: Tuttle Co., 1911), 1:76, 438; Brace, *Thanks to Abigail*, 1–3.

7. *History of Tioga County, Pennsylvania*, 2 vols. (N.p.: R. C. Brown and Co., 1897; reprint Evansville, Ind.: Unigraphic, Inc., 1976), 1:24–29, 46, 360–69. The settlement was also called "Dartt Settlement."

8. Note dated April 7, 1897, by Mary Dartt Thompson accompanying letter from Spencer Dartt to Jared Sanford, March 12, 1833, and Mary Dartt Thompson to Florence Thompson, March 7, 1897, both in Maxwell Papers (unless otherwise stated, all correspondence or other manuscripts cited are from this collection). See also "Recollections: Connecticut to Baraboo, Wisconsin," p. 2, one of two reminiscences by Mary

Dartt Thompson apparently written in 1928. Along with another type-script entitled "Pennsylvania to Skillet Creek, Wisconsin," it is in the collections of the Sauk County Historical Society, Baraboo, Wisconsin.

9. Reminiscence by Mary Dartt Thompson headed "East Falls Church Va. Mar. 26/34," Maxwell Papers. Unpaginated, this account will be cited hereinafter as 1934 Mary Dartt Thompson Reminiscence. See also Martha Dartt, Autobiography. Two letters survive that place Amy in Litchfield; one from Asenath Sanford to Amy, February 8, 1821, and another from Amy to Asenath, February 17, 1823. On tailoring, see Elisabeth Anthony Dexter, *Career Women of America, 1776–1840* (Francestown, N.H.: Marshall Jones Co., 1950), 163.

10. Quoted in Dexter, *Career Women of America*, 163.

11. From entries in Amy's autograph album one can infer that she was in New Marlborough at least from September 1826 through September 1827; the first entry signed from Wellsboro is dated June 27, 1828. Amy Sanford Dartt, autograph album, Hal Sayre Papers, Western Historical Collections, University of Colorado Libraries, Boulder, Colorado.

12. Mary Dartt Thompson to Florence Thompson, March 7, 1897; undated reminiscence, probably by Mary Dartt Thompson, Maxwell Papers.

13. Undated letter from Jared Sanford to Abigail Sanford, quoted in Brace, *Thanks to Abigail*, 5 (original not in Maxwell Papers).

14. Jared Sanford to Spencer Dartt, August 4, 1831 (reproduced in part in Brace, *Thanks to Abigail*, 4).

15. Undated letter from Joseph Sanford to Jared Sanford, quoted in Brace, *Thanks to Abigail*, 6; undated letter from Amy Sanford Dartt to Jared Sanford, quoted in ibid., 7 (originals not in Maxwell Papers).

16. Spencer Dartt to Jared Sanford, March 12, 1833, also quoted in Brace, *Thanks to Abigail*, 8.

17. Undated letter from Joseph Sanford to Jared Sanford, quoted in Brace, *Thanks to Abigail*, 6. See also undated letter from Amy Sanford to Jared Sanford, quoted in ibid., 7 (originals not in Maxwell Papers).

18. Thaddeus Lincoln Bolton, *Genealogy of the Dart Family in America* (Philadelphia: Cooper Printing Co., 1927), 3, 50. Hereinafter cited as *Dart Genealogy*.

19. Ibid., 20; *History of Tioga County, Pennsylvania*, 1:362, 2:699.

20. Amy's assessment was recalled many years later by Mary Dartt Thompson in "Recollections: Connecticut to Baraboo," 1. See also Bolton, *Dart Genealogy*, 20. According to this work, the last letter of the Colonel's name was misread as "t" rather than "e" during his military ser-

vice, with the result that he and his descendants used the spelling "Dartt" rather than the more common "Darte." The name is also spelled "Dart" and "Dorte."

21. Polly Dartt (born 1783) died in 1819; thereafter Justus married two more wives and had four additional children (letter and note from George S. Dartt to Mary Dartt Thompson, October 13, year unknown; Bolton, *Dart Genealogy*, 50). The first husband of Irene Dartt, born in 1790, was Siah Wilson (Bolton, *Dart Genealogy*, 20).

22. Martha Dartt, Autobiography; Bolton, *Dart Genealogy*, 54.

23. Spencer and Amy Dartt to Jared Sanford, June 4, 1831; Mary Dartt Thompson states that Martha was born on Spencer's farm, but Martha writes that she was about four months old when she and her parents moved there (Mary Dartt Thompson, "Pennsylvania to Skillet Creek," 4; Martha Dartt, Autobiography).

24. Mary Dartt Thompson, "Pennsylvania to Skillet Creek," 2, 3.

25. Spencer Dartt to Jared Sanford, March 12, 1833, quoted in Brace, *Thanks to Abigail*, 9 (original in Maxwell Papers).

26. Carroll Smith-Rosenberg, "The Hysterical Woman: Sex Roles and Role Conflict in Nineteenth-Century America," *Social Research* 39 (Winter 1972), reprinted in *Disorderly Conduct*, 197.

27. Samuel Ashwell, *A Practical Treatise on the Diseases Peculiar to Women* (London: Samuel Highley, 1844), quoted in ibid., 193. Smith-Rosenberg dates Ashwell's comment as 1833 in the text, although the publication information given for his book in the citation is a decade later.

28. Smith-Rosenberg, "The Hysterical Woman," 202, 207–8. Large numbers of nineteenth-century women considered themselves ill, as Ann Douglas Wood discusses in " 'The Fashionable Diseases': Women's Complaints and Their Treatment in Nineteenth-Century America," *Journal of Interdisciplinary History* 4 (Summer 1973):25–52.

29. Martha Dartt, Autobiography. See also Mary Dartt Thompson, "Pennsylvania to Skillet Creek," 3.

30. Mary Dartt Thompson wrote many years later that she dimly remembered playing in the cradle, "long enough for mother to lie in," which she believed had been made during Amy's long illness ("Pennsylvania to Skillet Creek," 2).

31. Martha Dartt, Autobiography; Mary Dartt Thompson, "Recollections: Connecticut to Baraboo," 2. Spencer's obituary, clipped from an unidentified newspaper, is in the Maxwell Papers and is also reproduced in Brace, *Thanks to Abigail*, 11–12.

32. Martha Dartt, Autobiography.

33. Amy Sanford Dartt to James Sanford, February 3, 1835.

34. Martha Dartt, Autobiography.

35. Amy Sanford Dartt to Asenath Sanford, December 1, 1835, with postscript by Jared Sanford, Maxwell Papers; also reproduced in Brace, *Thanks to Abigail*, 13–18 (the quoted passage is on 17).

36. Martha Dartt, Autobiography.

37. Ibid.

38. Rosella Kingsbury to Amy Sanford Dartt, September 22, 1872.

39. Josiah Dartt was the son of James G. Dartt, the third son of Col. Justus Dartt (Spencer's father, Justus Dartt, was the eldest). See Bolton, *Dart Genealogy*, 20, 55.

40. Martha Dartt to Josiah Dartt, September 29, 1852; Martha Dartt, Autobiography.

41. Although Josiah Dartt's birthdate is given in Bolton, *Dart Genealogy*, 55, as August 29, 1813, which would be more reasonable in view of Amy's age, the *Sanford Genealogy*, 2:793, lists the year as 1818. This date is confirmed, moreover, by information included in his obituary in the *Boulder News and Courier*, April 22, 1881, and in his biography in *History of Clear Creek and Boulder Valleys, Colorado* (Chicago: O.L. Baskin and Co., 1880; reprint Evansville, Ind.: Unigraphic, 1971), 632. The year 1818 is also listed on his tombstone (Columbia Cemetery inscriptions in Arapahoe Chapter [Boulder, Colorado] D.A.R., "Cemetery Records Copied, 1937–1940," unpaginated typescript, Genealogy Department, Denver Public Library, Denver, Colorado. Finally, the U.S. Census, 1880, Boulder County, Colorado, 524, lists Amy's age as seventy-five and Josiah's as sixty-three—slightly inaccurate but still indicating a birthdate closer to 1818 than 1813.

42. 1934 Mary Dartt Thompson Reminiscence; Josiah Dartt obituary, *Boulder News and Courier*, April 22, 1881; *Clear Creek and Boulder Valleys*, 632–33.

43. Mary Dartt Thompson, "Pennsylvania to Skillet Creek," 10.

44. Lewis O. Saum, *The Popular Mood of Pre–Civil War America*, Contributions in American Studies, No. 46 (Westport, Conn.: Greenwood Press, 1980), 29; see also 27–54.

45. Mary Dartt Thompson, "Pennsylvania to Skillet Creek," 10.

46. Mary Dartt Thompson, "Recollections: Connecticut to Baraboo," 3. Many years later Amy Dartt showed her granddaughter Mabel a passage from the Bible which she had "interpreted . . . as a Divine command to marry him." Mabel, however, thought it "more ambiguous than an ancient oracle" (Brace, *Thanks to Abigail*, 24).

47. Martha Dartt, Autobiography; Bolton, *Dart Genealogy*, 55.

48. Mary Dartt Thompson, "Pennsylvania to Skillet Creek," 4.

49. Martha Dartt, Autobiography.

50. Ray Allen Billington, *Westward Expansion: A History of the American Frontier*, 3d ed. (New York: Macmillan Co., 1967), 509–33; John D. Unruh, Jr., *The Plains Across: The Overland Emigrants and the Trans-Mississippi West, 1840–60* (Urbana: University of Illinois Press, 1979), 28–61; Lillian Schlissel, *Women's Diaries of the Westward Journey* (New York: Schocken Books, 1982), 19–46. Westward immigration has been estimated as 1,000 in 1843 (the year of the "great migration"), increasing to 2,000 in 1844 and 5,000 in 1845 (Merrill J. Mattes, *The Great Platte River Road: The Covered Wagon Mainline Via Fort Kearny to Fort Laramie* [Lincoln: Nebraska State Historical Society, 1969], 23).

51. Mary Dartt Thompson, "Recollections: Connecticut to Baraboo," 3.

52. As Schlissel points out (*Women's Diaries*, 74 n. 22), John Faragher in *Women and Men on the Overland Trail* (New Haven: Yale University Press, 1979) views women as passive participants in the westward experience, while Julie Roy Jeffrey in *Frontier Women: The Trans-Mississippi West, 1840–1880* (New York: Hill and Wang, 1979) stresses a more active role for women in the decision to emigrate. Summarizing these interpretations, Schlissel states: "The debate on the participation of women in the decision to go West is an important one insofar as it presents a major testing of the relationship between husband and wife in America at mid-century." Schlissel herself views the women who went west as unenthusiastic at best, going only because they had to follow their husbands and fathers (*Women's Diaries*, 150–55). See also Sandra L. Myres, *Westering Women and the Frontier Experience, 1800–1915* (Albuquerque: University of New Mexico Press, 1982), 10–11, who emphasizes that no one stereotype can fit all women's experiences, as does Glenda Riley in *Frontierswomen: The Iowa Experience* (Ames: Iowa State University Press, 1981), viii, xi–xiii.

53. Myres, *Westering Women*, 252.

54. Joseph Sanford to Amy Sanford Dartt, July 4, 1841; *Portrait and Biographical Album of Ogle County, Illinois* (Chicago: Chapman Brothers, 1886), 503–5, 654–55.

55. Martha Dartt, Autobiography. Schlissel, *Women's Diaries*, 35, 152–53, points out that pregnancy, in itself, was not a barrier to immigration and cites figures from her study indicating that fourteen of seventy-three married women were pregnant at some point in their journey (160 n. 3).

56. At least he was in Byron when Joseph Sanford wrote to Amy

Sanford Dartt on July 4, 1841; see also Martha Dartt, Autobiography.

57. Martha Dartt, Autobiography. See also Mary Dartt Thompson, "Recollections: Connecticut to Baraboo," 3.

58. Martha Dartt, Autobiography; Bolton, *Dart Genealogy*, 55.

59. Martha Dartt, Diary, December 2, 1851, Maxwell Papers. Jared Sanford died October 12, 1845, in Byron; his wife Abigail had died on August 3, 1845. *Sanford Genealogy*, 1:438.

60. Mary Dartt Thompson, "Recollections: Connecticut to Baraboo," 4.

61. See Richard N. Current, *The Civil War Era, 1848–1873*, vol. 2 of *The History of Wisconsin* (Madison: State Historical Society of Wisconsin, 1976), 42–48, 53–59; the figures are from a table on 76.

62. Robert C. Nesbit, *Wisconsin: A History* (Madison: University of Wisconsin Press, 1973), 149.

63. *History of Dane County, Wisconsin* (Chicago: Western Historical Co., 1880), 899–900, 1214; obituary of James D. Sanford (died July 5, 1902) from an unidentified newspaper in the Maxwell Papers.

64. Mary Dartt Thompson, "Recollections: Connecticut to Baraboo," 4.

65. Martha Dartt, Autobiography; Mary Dartt Thompson, "Recollections: Connecticut to Baraboo," 4 and "Pennsylvania to Skillet Creek," 5; see also Mary Dartt Thompson note to A. H. Felger, "Biography of Mrs. M. A. Maxwell, Pioneer Naturalist of Colorado, Containing the Story of Colorado's Natural History Exhibit at the Centennial Exposition, Philadelphia, 1876," 5, typescript in Maxwell Papers. A. H. Felger, a biology teacher at the North Side High School in Denver, labored on a biography of Martha Maxwell for some years in the early twentieth century, but in the end produced only a partial manuscript that covers her life to 1868 (a sixty-one-page typescript survives, but it appears that some succeeding pages may have been lost). However, Felger did have access to all the notes of Junius Henderson, curator of the University of Colorado Museum (1903–33) and author of a significant article on Martha Maxwell entitled "A Pioneer Venture in Habitat Grouping," *Proceedings of the American Association of Museums* 9 (1915):87–91. Felger also obtained much information from Mary Dartt Thompson, including details that can be found nowhere else, and in answering Felger's questions Mary made notes on the typescript that are extremely useful in clarifying the details of Martha's early life. For example, in an eight-page letter to Mary of December 10, 1911, Felger posed nineteen questions on Martha's early life (collection of Harold B. Scott, Palm Beach, Florida). See also Felger to Mary Dartt Thompson, April 13, May 25, and December 4, 1908; Hender-

son to Mary Dartt Thompson, October 23, 1919; and Mary Dartt Thompson to Mabel Maxwell Brace, November 7, 1907.

66. Mary Dartt Thompson, "Recollections: Connecticut to Baraboo," 4 and "Pennsylvania to Skillet Creek," 5, 8. According to the law, in order to qualify to purchase his land under the preemption act, a settler not only had to build a house but also had to live in it as his exclusive home.

67. Mary Dartt Thompson, "Pennsylvania to Skillet Creek," 11.

68. Ibid., 6–8. Although it is difficult to determine precisely the chronology of the family's moves during the 1840s, it appears that this was the winter of 1847–48.

69. Mary Dartt Thompson, "Recollections: Connecticut to Baraboo," 5.

70. Mary Dartt Thompson, "Pennsylvania to Skillet Creek," 8.

71. Martha Dartt, Autobiography; Mary Dartt Thompson, "Recollections: Connecticut to Baraboo," 9.

72. Martha Dartt, Autobiography; *The History of Sauk County, Wisconsin* (Chicago: Western Historical Co., 1880), 792; Mary Dartt Thompson, "Pennsylvania to Skillet Creek," 10 and "Recollections: Connecticut to Baraboo," 8.

73. Mary Dartt Thompson, "Pennsylvania to Skillet Creek," 12.

74. "Early Visits to Sauk County," in *History of Sauk County*, 448–49.

75. Mary Dartt Thompson, "Pennsylvania to Skillet Creek," 15–16. See also "Recollections: Connecticut to Baraboo," 8, 10.

76. Mary Dartt Thompson, "Pennsylvania to Skillet Creek," 15.

77. Ibid.

78. Mary Dartt Thompson, "Recollections: Connecticut to Baraboo," 10.

79. Mary Dartt Thompson, "Pennsylvania to Skillet Creek," 25. The Adventist church developed in the mid-1840s in the wake of the predictions of William Miller (1782–1842), who prophesied the second coming of Christ. Amy apparently continued as a member of the Methodist church into 1849, as evidenced by a membership ticket in the Methodist Episcopal Church dated March 1849 (Amy Sanford Dartt autograph album, Sayre Papers).

80. Notes appended to Martha Dartt diary by Mary Dartt Thompson dated November 12, 1928, Maxwell Papers, hereinafter cited as Mary Dartt Thompson Diary Reminiscence. Josiah Dartt's business card in the Baraboo newspaper announced "J. Dartt: Surveyor, Engineer, Land Agent" (*Sauk County Standard*, Baraboo, August 28, 1851).

81. Josiah Dartt to Martha Dartt, April 26, 1852.

82. Amy Sanford Dartt to Martha Dartt, September 4, 1851, continuing letter of September 1. See also Mary Dartt Thompson, "Pennsylvania to Skillet Creek," 3.

83. Mary Dartt Thompson, "Pennsylvania to Skillet Creek," 7.

84. Ibid., 22.

85. Ibid., 32.

86. Josiah Dartt to Martha Dartt, October 4, 1851.

87. S. A. Dwinnell in "Early Visits to Sauk County," *History of Sauk County*, 448. Cochran had first visited Baraboo in August 1847 and organized the First Congregational Church the following December (*History of Sauk County*, 534).

88. Mary Dartt Thompson, "Recollections: Connecticut to Baraboo," 11.

89. Ibid., 11–12.

90. The by-now classic exposition of the Cult of True Womanhood is Barbara Welter, "The Cult of True Womanhood, 1820–1860," *American Quarterly* 18 (Summer 1966):151–74.

91. Josiah Dartt to Martha Dartt, October 4, 1851. Contrast this with Gerda Lerner's assertion that in the nineteenth century "for girls the subduing of the will, the acceptance of self-abnegation, and the development of excessive altruism were the desired educational goals. Fathers . . . all strove to mold their daughters into this pattern" (Gerda Lerner, *The Female Experience: An American Documentary* [Indianapolis: Bobbs-Merrill Co., 1977], 3).

CHAPTER 2

1. Barbara Miller Solomon, *In the Company of Educated Women: A History of Women and Higher Education in America* (New Haven: Yale University Press, 1985), 14–26, 50. See also Thomas Woody, *A History of Women's Education in the United States*, 2 vols. (New York and Lancaster, Pa.: Science Press, 1929), 1:329–459.

2. Quoted from the *First Annual Report of the Oberlin Collegiate Institute* (1834), in Robert Samuel Fletcher, *A History of Oberlin College, From Its Foundation Through the Civil War*, 2 vols. (Oberlin: Oberlin College, 1943; reprint ed. in one vol., New York: Arno Press and the New York Times, 1971), 1:130. Exhaustive in detail but still placing Oberlin within the context of nineteenth-century society and thought, this one-thousand-page work is both fascinating and indispensable for any study of Oberlin during this period. It has an excellent bibliography. On Finney, see William G. McLoughlin, Jr., *Modern Revivalism: Charles Grandison Finney to Billy Graham* (New York: Ronald Press Co., 1959), 11–121.

3. For an extensive discussion of the components of Oberlinism, see Fletcher, *History of Oberlin*, 1:205–426. Helpful general perspective is provided in Ronald G. Walters, *American Reformers: 1815–1860* (New York: Hill and Wang, 1978), especially 21–37.

4. Fletcher, *History of Oberlin*, 1:291, 373–82; Ronald W. Hogeland, "Coeducation of the Sexes at Oberlin College: A Study of Social Ideas in Mid-Nineteenth-Century America," *Journal of Social History* 6 (Winter 1972–73):160–76; Jill K. Conway, "Perspectives on the History of Women's Education in the United States," *History of Education Quarterly* 14 (Spring 1974):5–7. For general background on coeducation see Woody, *History of Women's Education*, 2:231–47.

5. "The Ever-Widening Circle: The Diffusion of Feminist Values from the Troy Female Seminary, 1822–72," reprinted in *Making the Invisible Woman Visible* (Urbana: University of Illinois Press, 1984), 64.

6. Lucy Stone received an A.B. degree in 1847 upon completing the Collegiate Course, while Antoinette Brown was graduated in that same year from the three-year literary course in the Ladies' Department. Brown stayed on to study theology for three more years, although she was not allowed to receive a degree. In 1878, however, Oberlin awarded her an honorary A.M. degree, followed by an honorary D.D. in 1908. For more on Brown's Oberlin years, see Elizabeth Cazden, *Antoinette Brown Blackwell: A Biography* (Old Westbury, N.Y.: The Feminist Press, 1983), 21–52. See also Carol Lasser and Marlene Merrill, eds., *Soul Mates: The Oberlin Correspondence of Lucy Stone and Antoinette Brown, 1846–1850* (Oberlin: Oberlin College, 1983).

7. Fletcher, *History of Oberlin*, 2:534. Another black girl, Lucy Stanton, had earlier been graduated from the Ladies' Course (1850). Ibid., 2:533–34.

8. Lori D. Ginzberg, "Women in an Evangelical Community: Oberlin 1835–1850," *Ohio History* 89 (Winter 1980):78–88, especially 85–86.

9. Fletcher, *History of Oberlin*, 2:508–9, 537–45. By the spring of 1852 the Toledo, Norwalk and Cleveland Railroad was being constructed which provided a direct rail connection with Cleveland. Ibid., 2:545–46.

10. Martha Dartt to parents, May 4, 1851.

11. Ibid.; Fletcher, *History of Oberlin*, 2:549–71.

12. Reminiscence of Oliver L. Spaulding, typescript, file 16/ 5/"S," Oberlin College Archives, Oberlin, Ohio.

13. Tappan Hall was named for abolitionist Lewis Tappan's brother Arthur, a businessman and also an abolitionist, whose substantial financial gifts and loans to the college included most of the funds for the con-

struction of the hall. Fletcher, *History of Oberlin*, 1:179–80, 187; *General Catalogue of Oberlin College, 1833–1908, Including an Account of the Principal Events in the History of the College, with Illustrations of the College Buildings* (Oberlin: Oberlin College, 1909), p. Int. 74; Bertram Wyatt-Brown, *Lewis Tappan and the Evangelical War Against Slavery* (Cleveland: The Press of Case Western Reserve University, 1969), 130.

14. *General Catalogue*, p. Int. 76.

15. Martha Dartt to parents, May 4, 1851; Fletcher, *History of Oberlin*, 2:594–95; *General Catalogue*, p. Int. 70.

16. Martha Dartt to parents, July 7, 1851; *Triennial Catalogue of the Officers and Students of Oberlin College, for the College Year 1851–52* (Oberlin: James M. Fitch, 1851), 38. Martha's college record (student enrollment card number 8286) shows her as a preparatory student during the 1851–52 school year (copy from the Oberlin College Archives). The courses in the Young Ladies' Preparatory Department, as given in the 1851–52 catalog, were Adams' Arithmetic, Colburn's Arithmetic, Brown's English Grammar, Modern Geography, and Andrews and Stoddard's Latin Grammar and Reader (38). Greenleaf's Arithmetic is not listed; possibly it was a substitute.

17. *Triennial Catalogue. . . 1851–52*, 26.

18. Fletcher cites figures from the period 1852–54 compiled from 490 students whose ages were given in the record books. Eleven were twenty-six or older, while there were thirty-nine aged sixteen, thirty-seven aged fifteen, and twenty-four under fifteen. The youngest was eleven, the oldest thirty-six. Fletcher, *History of Oberlin*, 2:507.

19. Lasser and Merrill, eds., *Soul Mates*, 2.

20. Josiah Dartt to Martha Dartt, June 23, 1851.

21. Ibid.

22. Martha Dartt to parents, July 7, 1851.

23. *Triennial Catalogue. . . 1851–52*, 40; Fletcher, *History of Oberlin*, 2:634–35.

24. Fletcher, *History of Oberlin*, 2:620–21; *Triennial Catalogue. . . 1851–52*, 39–40.

25. Martha Dartt to parents, July 7, 1851. The college estimated that women would receive "from three to four cents per hour, according to their efficiency." *Triennial Catalogue. . . 1851–52*, 40.

26. Amy Sanford Dartt to Martha Dartt, September 1, 1851.

27. Josiah Dartt to Martha Dartt, October 4, 1851.

28. *Laws and Regulations of the Female Department of the Oberlin College* (Oberlin: Fitch's Power Press, 1852).

29. Keith E. Melder, *Beginnings of Sisterhood: The American Woman's Rights Movement, 1800–1850* (New York: Schocken Books, 1977), 20, 21.

30. *Laws and Regulations of the Female Department*, 10–12. Study hours were 8:00 a.m. to 12:00 m. and 2:00 to 5:00 p.m. from March 20 to September 20, changing in the afternoon from 2:00 to 4:00 the rest of the year. Evening study hours were after 8:00 p.m. from March 20 to September 20, and after 7:30 p.m. otherwise.

31. Ibid., 11.

32. Martha Dartt to parents, July 7, 1851.

33. *Laws and Regulations of the Female Department*, 12.

34. Martha Dartt to parents, September 16, 1851 (continues September 15 letter).

35. Martha Dartt Maxwell to Mabel Maxwell, October 20, 1875.

36. Martha Dartt to parents, July 7, 1851.

37. Martha Dartt to parents, August 17, 1851.

38. Martha Dartt to parents, September 15, 1851; *Order of Exercises, Commencement, Ladies' Department, August 26, 1851*, program, Oberlin College Archives, Oberlin, Ohio.

39. Martha Dartt to parents, September 15, 1851.

40. Solomon, *Educated Women*, 28–29.

41. Fletcher, *History of Oberlin*, 1:291–95.

42. Martha Dartt Maxwell to Mabel Maxwell, October 20, 1875.

43. Martha Dartt to parents, August 17, 1851. Although grades were not given at all during the early years, they were later assigned for daily recitations and oral examinations, ranging from a low of "0" to a high of "6." Fletcher, *History of Oberlin*, 2:736–37. (Teachers sometimes gave grades when the institution did not.)

Mrs. Mary Cook Sumner Hopkins served as principal of the Female Department between 1850 and 1852. Little is known of her life; married first to Harlow L. Street and then to Augustus Hopkins, by whom she had two children, she died on March 7, 1897, at the age of eighty-seven in Rochester, New York. *General Catalogue*, p. Int. 153; *Union and Advertiser*, Rochester, March 8, 1897 (copy provided by Rochester Public Library); letter from Gertrude Jacob, Oberlin College Archives, October 31, 1978.

44. Martha Dartt to parents, August 17, 1851.

45. Ibid.

46. Fletcher, *History of Oberlin*, 2:760–61, 781–82; *General Catalogue*, p. Int. 74; *Oberlin Evangelist*, July 16, 1851, 119; entry for June 30, 1851, Union Literary Society, Constitution and Minutes (1850–55), file 19/3/4, Oberlin College Archives, Oberlin, Ohio.

47. Martha Dartt to parents, July 7, 1851.

48. Martha Dartt to parents, January 2, 1852 (continues January 1 letter).

49. Martha Dartt, diary, January 10 [1852], Maxwell Papers. This small diary covers portions of Martha's college years and the period immediately afterward; the brief entries, however, are generally far less informative than her letters home.

50. Fletcher, *History of Oberlin*, 2:784–96, *passim*.

51. Martha Dartt, diary, March 8, 1852.

52. Ibid., March 13 [1852]; Martha Dartt to parents, September 11, 1852; Fletcher, *History of Oberlin*, 2:796–97.

53. Martha Dartt to parents, September 11, 1852; Oberlin Female Moral Reform Society Minutes, 1835–57, p. 96, file 31/6/11, Oberlin College Archives, Oberlin, Ohio.

54. Fletcher, *History of Oberlin*, 1:297–315, *passim*.

55. Martha Dartt to parents, November 3, 1851.

56. Martha Dartt to parents, July 7, 1851; Josiah Dartt to Martha Dartt, July 11, 1851; Martha Dartt to parents, September 16, 1851 (continues September 15 letter). Among the several "phonetic journals" published during the late 1840s and the 1850s was *Type of the Times: A Journal of the Writing and Spelling Reform* (Cincinnati, 1848–59). The running title was variously *Tip of de Timz, Fonetic Advocat*, and *Wecli Fonetic Advocat*. Frank Luther Mott, *A History of American Magazines, 1850–1865* (Cambridge, Mass.: The Belknap Press of Harvard University Press, 1967), 212; *Union List of Serials*, 3d ed., 5:4284.

57. Martha Dartt to parents, May 4, 1851.

58. Martha Dartt to parents, September 16, 1851 (continues September 15 letter). Ohio Congressman Joshua R. Giddings (1795–1864), an antislavery advocate, tried to work within the existing political system for reform based on religious and ethical principles during his tenure in the House of Representatives (1831–59). See James Brewer Stewart, *Joshua R. Giddings and the Tactics of Radical Politics* (Cleveland: The Press of Case Western Reserve University, 1970).

59. Martha Dartt to parents, July 7, 1851. George Thompson, who had studied at Oberlin and had been ordained by the Council of the American Missionary Association in 1848, was preparing to go back to the Mendi Mission on the west coast of Africa, founded in the early 1840s as part of the return of the "Amistad Captives" to their homeland. Taken into slavery in 1839, the Africans, members of the Mendi tribe, had mutinied aboard the schooner *Amistad* and ended up captured and jailed in New Haven. Ordered freed by the Supreme Court, they were transported back to Africa in 1841, accompanied by missionaries who hoped

to establish an outpost for Christianizing the continent. *Oberlin Evangelist*, July 2, 1851, 11, November 10, 1852, 178–79; Wyatt-Brown, *Lewis Tappan*, 205–25; Fletcher, *History of Oberlin*, 1:258–60.

60. Martha Dartt to parents, July 7, 1851. The singing Hutchinson Family—originally the quartet of John, Judson, Asa, and their sister Abby—toured America with great success beginning in the early 1840s. "Combining songs of sentiment and humor with songs of social comment and current events, they would alternately play on the emotions of their audience, then amuse and delight them. They developed a unique 'sound,' consisting of close, balanced harmony and beautiful vocal qualities." James Morris, introduction to *There's a Good Time Coming and Other Songs of the Hutchinson Family as Performed by the Smithsonian Institution* (recording; Washington, D.C.: Smithsonian Institution, 1978), 1, 3; the quotation is from p. 3.

61. Martha Dartt to parents, September 11, 1852.

62. Martha Dartt to parents, August 17, 1851.

63. Fletcher, *History of Oberlin*, 2:710–11, 716–17, 722; *Triennial Catalogue. . . 1851–52*, 34–38.

64. See Martha Dartt to parents, September 11, 1852; this inference is also based in part on her description of the classes she attended.

65. Fletcher, *History of Oberlin*, 2:734–35; *Triennial Catalogue. . . 1851–52*, 40. I thank Oberlin Archivist W. E. Bigglestone for this clarification.

66. Martha Dartt to parents, December 20, 1851.

67. Josiah Dartt to Martha Dartt, March 13, 1852.

68. Martha Dartt to family, April 12, 1852.

69. Josiah Dartt to Martha Dartt, March 13, 1852.

70. Josiah Dartt to Martha Dartt, April 26, 1852.

71. Martha Dartt to family, April 12, 1852.

72. Josiah Dartt to Martha Dartt, April 26, 1852.

73. [Josiah Dartt] to Martha Dartt, July 3, 1852. The first passage is adapted from Lucretius, *De Rerum Natura* (2.289–91) and translates as follows: "Lest the mind itself have an internal compulsion in all that it does, and be forced, as if it were conquered, to suffer and endure." (One word is misspelled: "quiasi" should be "quasi.") The second passage reads: "To see God as more present through trackless cliffs, wild ridges, craggy slopes, amid sounding waters and the woodland dark." According to Stanley Lombardo, associate professor and chairman of the Classics Department of the University of Kansas, this passage "is written in an approximation of one of Horace's meters (the Alcaic stanza) but it contains several metrical errors. It may be the author's own composition"

(letter, October 23, 1984). I am grateful to Professor Lombardo for generously furnishing the translations and additional information.

74. Martha Dartt to parents, June 12, 1852; *Triennial Catalogue. . . 1851–52*, 36, 38; Martha Dartt to parents, September 11, 1852. Taylor's Manual of Ancient History and Manual of Modern History were offered for second-year students in the Young Ladies' Department, those pursuing the first year of the Teachers' Course, and for the senior class in the Preparatory Department. Nevin's Biblical Antiquities was a first-year offering in the Young Ladies' Department and was part of the "Shorter Course" in the Theology Department. The study of geometry began in the first year of the Classical, Scientific, Ladies', and Teachers' courses and continued into the second (*Catalogue of the Officers and Students of Oberlin College for the College Year 1852–53* [Oberlin: James M. Fitch, 1852], 40–45). Martha was listed in the 1852–53 catalog as a member of the second-year class of the Young Ladies' Department (*Catalogue. . . 1852–53*, 29).

75. Josiah Dartt to Martha Dartt, September 18, 1852.

76. Josiah Dartt to Martha Dartt, October 4, 1851, April 26, 1852.

77. Josiah Dartt to Martha Dartt, March 13, 1852, April 26, 1852.

78. Amy Sanford Dartt to Martha Dartt [June? 11, 1852].

79. Martha Dartt to parents, September 11, 1852; Josiah Dartt to Martha Dartt, September 18, 1852.

80. Josiah Dartt to Martha Dartt, September 18, 1852.

81. See the following letters: Josiah Dartt to Martha Dartt, July 11, 1851, March 13, 1852, July 3, 1852; Amy Sanford Dartt to Martha Dartt, October 6, 1851, January 9, 1852, [June? 11, 1852]; Martha Dartt to parents, April 12, 1852, July 12, 1852.

82. Martha Dartt to parents, September 11, 1852.

83. Martha Dartt to Josiah Dartt, September 29, 1852.

84. Martha Dartt, diary, [May] 28, [1852].

85. Martha Dartt to parents, November 3, 1851.

86. Martha Dartt, diary, July 5, 1853.

CHAPTER 3

1. Myres, *Westering Women*, 248.

2. Polly Welts Kaufman, *Women Teachers on the Frontier* (New Haven: Yale University Press, 1984).

3. Martha Dartt to family, June 12, 1852.

4. Certificate dated November 10, 1852, Maxwell Papers; Martha Dartt, diary, November 10, 1852; *History of Sauk County*, 513.

5. Martha Dartt, diary, November 15, 1852.

6. Martha Dartt, diary, November 22, 23, 27, December 18, 1852; January 29, 1853.

7. Mary Dartt Thompson, "Pennsylvania to Skillet Creek," 24–25. The name "Pewit's Nest" apparently was given by early settlers to a workshop dug in the walls of a canyon by an "ingenious excentric mechanic" who lived there. "The shop could not be seen from the mouth of the canyon, or from the top, or from any direction but one. Hence, by the early settlers, it was dubbed 'Pee-Wee's Nest.' " William S. Canfield, *Guide Book to the Wild and Romantic Scenery in Sauk County, Wisconsin* (Baraboo: Republic Book and Job Print, 1873), 3. Mary later wrote a poem entitled "The Pewit's Nest" (ibid., 3–4).

8. Mary Dartt Thompson, "Pennsylvania to Skillet Creek," 25.

9. Mary Dartt Thompson, Diary Reminiscence.

10. On the understanding, see Mary Dartt Thompson, Diary Reminiscence; also James A. Maxwell to Martha Dartt, October 7, 1853. Emma Maxwell was born in 1837, James P. Maxwell in 1839. William H. Canfield, *Outline Sketches of Sauk County, Wisconsin, Including It's [sic] History From the First Marks of Man's Hand to 1891 and Its Typography, Both Written and Illustrated. Volume Second — Baraboo: Ninth Sketch* (N.p., 1891), 20.

11. For biographical information on James A. Maxwell (1812–1891) and Col. James Maxwell (1789–1869) see *History of Sauk County*, 424–25; Albert Clayton Beckwith, *History of Walworth County, Wisconsin*, 2 vols. (Indianapolis: B. F. Bowen and Co., 1912), 1:541–42; *Clear Creek and Boulder Valleys*, 653–54, 660–61; Canfield, *Outline Sketches of Sauk County. . . Baraboo: Ninth Sketch*, 18–19. The elder Maxwell's title of "Colonel" probably stemmed from his service in the Black Hawk War (*Walworth County*, 1:541).

12. Susan Maxwell's date of death is given as August 2, 1853, in Canfield, *Outline Sketches of Sauk County. . . Baraboo: Ninth Sketch*, 19. James A. Maxwell and Susan Clark were married on May 5, 1836. Miriam Luke, "Fountain County, Indiana, Marriage Records, Book I, 1826–1839" (Danville, Ill.: Illiana Genealogical Publishing Co., n.d.; mimeographed typescript, Genealogy Department, Denver Public Library).

13. Charles Alonzo was born in 1841, Caroline in 1843, Ellen in 1845, and Augusta in 1847. Canfield, *Outline Sketches of Sauk County. . . Baraboo: Ninth Sketch*, 20. See also Jennie Stewart, "Boulder County Pioneers" (mimeographed typescript published by Arapahoe Chapter D.A.R., Boulder, c. 1948), 148–49.

14. *Appleton Crescent*, August 6, 1853.

15. Initially known as the Lawrence Institute, the school became Lawrence University in 1849. From 1913 to 1964 it was known as Lawrence College, then again as Lawrence University after consolidation with Milwaukee-Downer College. There is no history of Lawrence comparable to Fletcher's *History of Oberlin*. For an overall view see Samuel Plantz, "Lawrence College," *Wisconsin Magazine of History* 6 (1922–23):146–63. Details of the early years can be found in *Lawrence College Alumni Record, 1857–1922* (Appleton: N.p., n.d.), 9–41. On the campus and the buildings, see Marguerite Ellen Schumann, *Creation of a Campus: A Chronicle of Lawrence College Buildings and the Men Who Made Them* (Appleton: Lawrence College Press, 1957); see pp. 5–12 for accounts of the first two buildings.

16. *Appleton Crescent*, August 6, 1853; Plantz, "Lawrence College," 156–57, 159; *Lawrence College Alumni Record, 1857–1922*, 156. While the 1853 catalog presents the course descriptions for the Collegiate, Female Collegiate, and Preparatory departments, the students are listed merely under the headings of "Gentlemen" and "Ladies." *Fourth Annual Catalogue of the Corporation, Faculty and Students of the Lawrence University, Appleton, Wis. December, 1853* (Appleton: Crescent Print, 1853), 7–11. William H. Sampson, the first principal of the Lawrence Institute, states: "At the annual meeting in 1854 the Board of Trustees elected a faculty to meet the wants of college classes, and the catalogue for that year gives the names of twenty-eight Freshmen and four Sophomores, and an attendance in both college and preparatory departments during the year of 333." "Brief Sketches of the Early History at Lawrence University," *Lawrence College Alumni Record, 1857–1922*, 19.

17. *Fourth Annual Catalogue*, 17. See pp. 18–19 for the Preparatory Department, pp. 13–15 for the Collegiate Department, and pp. 16–17 for the Female Collegiate Department. See also the advertisement for Lawrence dated June 30, 1853, and printed in the *Appleton Crescent*, July 23, 1853 (and other dates).

18. Register of Students of Lawrence University, 1853–1864, p. 5, Lawrence University Archives, Appleton, Wisconsin.

19. James A. Maxwell to Martha Dartt, November 6, 1853.

20. Martha Dartt to James A. Maxwell, November 13, 1853; Register of Students, 1853–1864, p. 9.

21. Martha Dartt to James A. Maxwell, November 13, 1853; *Appleton Crescent*, February 8, 1854. At one time Mary Dartt Thompson had a copy of *The Casket* containing an article by Martha which she sent to the Lawrence University Archives (Mary Dartt Thompson to Henry Wriston,

president of Lawrence College, February 13, 1929 [carbon]). Unfortunately, the journal could not be located when I visited the archives in 1982.

22. Francena M. Kellogg Buck, "Lawrence in 1850–1860," *Lawrence College Alumni Record, 1857–1915* (Appleton: N.p., n.d.), 59.

23. James A. Maxwell to Martha Dartt, October 7, 1853. Assuming that the date of death given in Canfield, *Outline Sketches of Sauk County . . . Baraboo: Ninth Sketch*, is correct, James's proposal came only six weeks after the death of his first wife. No additional verification of Susan Maxwell's date of death has been found; her name does not appear in the volumes of Sauk County cemetery inscriptions collected so far in the Baraboo Public Library, and no Baraboo newspaper is available for this date. Letter from Jeanne Chickering, Baraboo Public Library, April 12, 1984.

24. James A. Maxwell to Martha Dartt, November 6, 1853.

25. Martha Dartt to James A. Maxwell, November 13, 1853.

26. Ibid.

27. James A. Maxwell to Martha Dartt, Thanksgiving Day 1853.

28. James A. Maxwell to Martha Dartt, January 1, [1854].

29. Martha Dartt to James A. Maxwell, January 14, 1854.

30. James A. Maxwell to Martha Dartt, January 29, 1854. Amy urged her daughter to give the deed to her instead of to Josiah, saying "it is quite as necessary for me to have my property secured to me as for you to have yours secured to you. . . ." Amy Sanford Dartt to Martha Dartt [March? 1854]. Amy, of course, had shared in the ownership of the farm in Pennsylvania left by Spencer Dartt.

31. Mary Dartt Thompson, Diary Reminiscence.

32. Martha Dartt to James A. Maxwell, January 14, 1854.

33. James A. Maxwell to Martha Dartt, February 16, 1854.

34. James A. Maxwell to Martha Dartt, February 17, 1854.

35. Martha Dartt to James A. Maxwell, March 3, 1854.

36. James A. Maxwell to Martha Dartt, February 16, 1854.

37. Marriage certificate, March 30, 1854, Maxwell Papers; notice in *Appleton Crescent*, March 30, 1854.

38. Mary Dartt Thompson, Diary Reminiscence.

39. Mary Dartt Thompson to Henry Wriston, February 13, 1929 (carbon).

40. Martha Dartt to James A. Maxwell, January 14, 1854.

41. Mary Dartt Thompson, Diary Reminiscence.

42. Ibid.

43. Ibid.

44. Mary Dartt Thompson to Henry Wriston, February 13, 1929 (carbon); Mary Dartt Thompson, Diary Reminiscence.

45. Carl N. Degler, *At Odds: Women and the Family in America from the Revolution to the Present* (New York: Oxford University Press, 1980), 302–3; Nancy Woloch, *Women and the American Experience* (New York: Alfred A. Knopf, 1984), 105, 167–97; Solomon, *Educated Women*, 27, 30.

46. Canfield, *Outline Sketches of Sauk County. . . Baraboo: Ninth Sketch*, 17–18; Harry Ellsworth Cole, ed., *A Standard History of Sauk County, Wisconsin*, 2 vols. (Chicago: Lewis Publishing Co., 1918), 1:426–27.

47. Canfield lists Martha Maxwell among the six women who appeared in court. It is not clear, however, whether the fine or the damages were paid. Canfield says that the women were fined five hundred dollars for rioting and set free for six weeks, after which the county judge declared them not guilty. The men then agreed to pay damages of two hundred dollars to the vendors, "which we have understood never was paid" (*Outline Sketches of Sauk County. . . Baraboo: Ninth Sketch*, 18). The *Standard History of Sauk County*, however, says that the women were taken to Lower Sauk, then held for trial in the Circuit Court. Released on their own recognizance, ultimately they were "assessed total damages at $150, which was immediately paid by the husbands and other male sympathizers of the raid" (1:427). It was common in such episodes for fines to be dismissed or for the men to pay token penalties. See Ian R. Tyrrell, "Women and Temperance in Antebellum America, 1830–1860," *Civil War History* 28 (June 1982):144.

48. Tyrrell, "Women and Temperance in Antebellum America," 143–52; see also Barbara Leslie Epstein, *The Politics of Domesticity: Women, Evangelism, and Temperance in Nineteenth-Century America* (Middletown, Conn.: Wesleyan University Press, 1981), 93–94.

49. *Baraboo Republic*, May 31, 1856.

50. Ibid., October 11, 1856, September 29, 1859.

51. Ibid., October 25, 1856.

52. Mary Dartt Thompson, Diary Reminiscence. Judge Clark, whom Mary considered the prime instigator of the match between her sister and James Maxwell, was the brother of Susan Clark, James's first wife. Clark's wife Celestia was apparently James Maxwell's sister. Clark had served for a time as a Sauk County probate judge. See Mary Dartt Thompson, Diary Reminiscence; *Baraboo Republic*, November 8, 1856; *History of Sauk County*, 348.

53. Brace, *Thanks to Abigail*, 33.

54. *Baraboo Republic*, April 19, 1856. For another good description of Baraboo in the 1850s, see the *Baraboo Republic*, September 2, 1858.

55. *History of Sauk County*, 514; *Baraboo Republic*, May 26, 1855, September 8, 1855, July 12, 1856, October 28, 1858, December 1, 1859.

56. *Lawrence College Alumni Record, 1857–1915*, 156. He continued to serve on the board until he left for Colorado in 1860.

57. Mary Dartt Thompson to Henry Wriston, February 13, 1929 (carbon).

58. James A. Maxwell to Martha Dartt, March 8, 1854.

59. *Baraboo Republic*, January 24, 1857, November 3, 1859, November 10, 1859; 1934 Mary Dartt Thompson Reminiscence.

60. *Baraboo Republic*, January 6, 1859.

61. Ibid., February 10, 1859.

CHAPTER 4

1. The literature on the Pikes Peak gold rush is extensive, ranging from popular secondary accounts to guidebooks, letters, diaries, and other contemporary sources. The various general histories of Colorado recount the landmark events; see, for example, Carl Ubbelohde, Maxine Benson, and Duane A. Smith, *A Colorado History*, 5th ed. (Boulder: Pruett Publishing Co., 1982), 59–70; Robert G. Athearn, *The Coloradans* (Albuquerque: University of New Mexico Press, 1976), 7–19; and Carl Abbott, Stephen J. Leonard, and David McComb, *Colorado: A History of the Centennial State*, 2d. ed. (Boulder: Colorado Associated University Press, 1982), 50–69. Each has helpful bibliographies. Still valuable is the detailed account in Jerome C. Smiley, *History of Denver, with Outlines of the Earlier History of the Rocky Mountain Country* (Denver: Times-Sun Publishing Co., 1901; reprint ed., Denver: Old Americana Publishing Co., 1978), 177–292. Agnes Wright Spring summarized the events in "Rush to the Rockies, 1859," *The Colorado Magazine* 36 (April 1959):83–120. This special centennial edition of the journal also included "Rush to the Rockies Articles, Bibliography, Published in *The Colorado Magazine*" (126–29).

2. *Baraboo Republic*, January 27, 1859.

3. See, for example, the *Baraboo Republic*, March 3, March 10, March 17, March 24, March 31, April 14, May 26, June 2, June 9, 1859. The Greeley-Richardson-Villard statement was carried by the paper on June 30, 1859.

4. Ibid., March 8, 1860.

5. Ibid., February 23, 1860. Martha recorded the departure in a small diary she kept from February 21 through May 31, 1860. As with her earlier diary, however, the entries are far less informative than the letters she wrote during the same period. The diary is now in the possession of Mrs. E. Geoffrey Cullen, St. Louis, Mo., Martha's great-great-

granddaughter, along with other materials that were somehow separated from the Maxwell Papers (hereinafter cited as Cullen Collection).

6. Mary Dartt to Martha Dartt Maxwell, October 6, 1860 (part of joint family letter).

7. Felger, "Biography of Mrs. M. A. Maxwell," 10–11, probably working from information supplied by Mary Dartt Thompson, gives the names of those in the group. J. Max Clark, in a letter recalling his pioneering experiences some forty years later, said that there were nine in the party when they reached Denver. Letter from J. Max Clark, Greeley, December 2, 1899, printed in the *Daily Rocky Mountain News*, Denver, December 5, 1899.

8. Felger, "Biography of Mrs. M. A. Maxwell," 10–11. Caroline Maxwell, James Maxwell's sister, had married Experience Estabrook (1813–1894), who had been attorney general of Wisconsin (1852–53), attorney general of Nebraska Territory from 1855 to 1859, and a delegate to the Thirty-sixth Congress from March 1859 to May 1860. *Biographical Directory of the American Congress, 1774–1971* (Washington, D.C.: Government Printing Office, 1971), 919. See also unidentified newspaper clippings of Caroline Estabrook's obituary in Emma Maxwell Potter's "Heart Book," now in the Lawrence University Archives, Appleton, Wisconsin.

9. Letter from J. Max Clark, December 2, 1899, in the *Daily Rocky Mountain News*, Denver, December 5, 1899.

10. Martha Dartt Maxwell to parents and sisters, March 11, 1860.

11. Martha Dartt Maxwell to Mary Dartt, March 17, 1860.

12. Martha Dartt Maxwell to parents and sisters, March 11, 1860.

13. Ibid.

14. Martha Dartt Maxwell to sisters, April 8, 1860, May 6, 1860; Felger, "Biography of Mrs. M. A. Maxwell," 11.

15. Martha Dartt Maxwell to mother, [April] 13, 1860. Generally the War Department did not allow camping within the military reservation where Fort Kearny was situated, although the specific restrictions varied from time to time. Mattes, *Great Platte River Road*, 202–4.

16. Martha Dartt Maxwell to sisters, May 6, 1860.

17. Mollie Dorsey Sanford, *Mollie: The Journal of Mollie Dorsey Sanford in Nebraska and Colorado Territories, 1857–1866*, ed. Donald F. Danker (Lincoln: University of Nebraska Press, 1959; reprint, Bison Books, 1976), 120–21 (entries for April 26 and April 29).

18. Letter of Samuel Mallory from O'Fallon's Bluff, Nebraska, June 3, 1860, "Overland to Pikes Peak with a Quartz Mill: Letters of Samuel Mallory," *The Colorado Magazine* 8 (May 1931):112.

19. "Across the Plains and in Denver, 1860: A Portion of the Diary of

George T. Clark," *The Colorado Magazine* 7 (July 1929):133. Clark (1837–1888) left Wisconsin on April 24. Later he became mayor of Denver (1865–66) and was active in banking in Denver, Central City, and Georgetown (ibid., 131).

20. Louise Barry, ed., "Albert D. Richardson's Letters on the Pike's Peak Gold Region," *Kansas Historical Quarterly* 12 (February 1943):22, 20.

21. Sanford, *Mollie*, 120.

22. Martha Dartt Maxwell to sisters, May 6, 1860. For a discussion of such trades between immigrants and Indians, see Unruh, *The Plains Across*, 166–67. Martha's humorous response was not untypical; see Glenda Riley, *Women and Indians on the Frontier, 1825–1915* (Albuquerque: University of New Mexico Press, 1984), 132–33.

23. Martha Dartt Maxwell to sisters, May 6, 1860. On this aspect of the changing relationship between Indians and emigrants, see Unruh, *The Plains Across*, 156–200; Schlissel, *Women's Diaries*, 118–44; and Riley, *Women and Indians on the Frontier*, 153–54.

24. Martha Dartt Maxwell to sisters, May 6, 1860. Martha recorded her first view of the mountains, in almost the same words, in a diary entry dated May 2, 1860. Martha Dartt Maxwell, diary, Cullen Collection.

25. Martha Dartt Maxwell to sisters, May 6, 1860.

26. Martha Dartt Maxwell, diary, Cullen Collection.

27. Richardson, letter of June 12, 1860, in Barry, ed., "Albert D. Richardson's Letters," 27.

28. For details on Denver in 1860 see Smiley, *History of Denver*, 331–50. Lyle W. Dorsett, *The Queen City: A History of Denver* (Boulder: Pruett Publishing Co., 1977), 27–32, emphasizes the negative aspects of life in Denver in the early 1860s.

29. Quoted in Dorsett, *The Queen City*, 28.

30. Martha Dartt Maxwell to sisters, May 7, 1860 (continuing letter of May 6).

31. Richardson, letter of June 16, 1860, in Barry, ed., "Albert D. Richardson's Letters," 28.

32. Sanford, *Mollie*, 131.

33. Letter from J. Max Clark, *Daily Rocky Mountain News*, Denver, December 5, 1899; Felger, "Biography of Mrs. M. A. Maxwell," 14–15. Felger states that Lon Maxwell was associated with William N. Byers in Omaha in the offices of the *Omaha Bee* before Byers came to Denver and started the *Rocky Mountain News* on April 23, 1859, and that he assisted later in putting out a newspaper in Mountain City. It is known that he served as the Mountain City agent for the *Western Mountaineer* of Golden City (see issue of December 7, 1859).

34. "Nevada District Mining Laws: Gilpin County, Colorado," *The Colorado Magazine* 36 (April 1959):131; Caroline Bancroft, *Gulch of Gold: A History of Central City, Colorado* (Boulder: Johnson Publishing Co., 1958), 42–45. Documents relating to early mining activities in the area are collected in Thomas Maitland Marshall, ed., *Early Records of Gilpin County, Colorado, 1859–1861*, University of Colorado Historical Collections, vol. 2: Mining, vol. 1 (Boulder: University of Colorado, 1920).

35. Martha Dartt Maxwell to sisters, August 20, 1860.

36. Martha Dartt Maxwell to mother, June 10, 1860; Bette D. Peters, *Denver's Four Mile House* (Denver: Published by the Junior League of Denver for Four Mile Historic Park, 1980), 14–16; Peters and Carrie Scott Ellis, "Woman's Work: The Story of Two Pioneer Women on the Colorado Mining Frontier, 1860," *Four Mile Express* 6 (July/August/September 1985):15; letter from Peters, February 1, 1984. Martha's reference to Cawker in her May 7 diary entry seems clearly to indicate a prior association. Martha Dartt Maxwell, diary, Cullen Collection.

37. Conveyance of lot from Charles W. Jones to Mary Cawker and Martha A. Maxwell, signed at Central City, May 22, 1860, Eureka District, Book C, Record of Claims (January 1860–September 1860), p. 183, Gilpin County Mining Records, Colorado State Archives and Records Service, Denver (microfilm). Sid Squibb, a Central City historian, has tentatively located the lot "on the site of or near the main parking lot in Central City proper, along the road which takes the visitor to the ghost town of Nevadaville two or three miles farther west." Peters and Ellis, "Woman's Work," 16.

38. Martha Dartt Maxwell to mother, June 10, 1860.

39. "Is Mrs. Maxwell a Naturalist and Huntress?," unidentified clipping, c. 1877, Maxwell Scrapbook, 76.

40. Martha Dartt Maxwell to mother, June 10, 1860. Martha recorded in her diary that they actually moved on May 31 into the house "without windows doors floor or roof except a small portion of roof & chamber floor." Martha Dartt Maxwell, diary, Cullen Collection.

41. Martha Dartt Maxwell to mother, June 10, 1860.

42. Susan Armitage, "Women and Men in Western History: A Stereoptical Vision," *Western Historical Quarterly* 16 (October 1985):390.

43. Martha Dartt Maxwell to mother, June 10, 1860; Lynn I. Perrigo, "A Social History of Central City, Colorado, 1859–1900" (Ph.D. diss., University of Colorado, 1936), 43.

44. Mary Cawker moved onto the Four Mile House property on September 20, 1860 (Peters, *Four Mile House*, 14–16). The log house had been built as a home in 1859 by Samuel Brantner. Located on a heavily

traveled stage route, it was four miles from a measuring point that today is the intersection of Broadway and Colfax in Denver. With two later additions, Four Mile House is now a museum (ibid., 3, 6, 9, 32). Cawker sold Four Mile House to the Levi Booths in 1864 but continued to be active in real estate and business. She moved to California in the mid-1880s and died in Los Angeles in 1908 (Peters and Ellis, "Woman's Work," 21–22). I am indebted to Nancy Markham and Bette D. Peters of the Four Mile House staff for making the connection between the Mary Cawker of Four Mile House and the woman who was briefly Martha Maxwell's partner.

45. Martha Dartt Maxwell to sisters, August 20, 1860. Apparently Martha concluded the transaction a month later; the indenture made between the two on September 19, 1860 (recorded January 4 of the following year) conveyed the property to her free and clear for $300. Nevada District, Book E, Record of Claims (December 1860–July 1862), p. 15, Gilpin County Mining Records, Colorado State Archives (microfilm). The original document is in the Cullen Collection.

46. Letter of Samuel Mallory, Nevada City, July 8, 1860, in "Overland to Pikes Peak with a Quartz Mill," 115.

47. Martha Dartt Maxwell to sisters, August 20, 1860.

48. Martha Dartt Maxwell to mother, June 10, 1860. A description of mining activities in Lump Gulch was printed in the *Daily Rocky Mountain News*, Denver, December 18, 1860. Marshall, ed., *Early Records of Gilpin County*, 175–76.

49. Martha Dartt Maxwell to sisters, August 20, 1860. This letter includes a good lengthy description of the differences between lode mining and gulch or placer mining. The extant records show that the lodes claimed by the men in the Central District, where Lump Gulch was located, between June 15 and July 13 included portions of the Sweet Ellen, Sauk County, Lawrence, Kansas, and Ethan Allen lodes. Central District, Book A, Record of Claims (April 1860–May 1863), pp. 32, 35, 36, 56, 62–63, 72, 73, 75, Gilpin County Mining Records, Colorado State Archives (microfilm).

50. Martha Dartt Maxwell to sisters, August 20, 1860.

51. See Myres, *Westering Women*, 258; Catherine Clinton, *The Other Civil War: American Women in the Nineteenth Century* (New York: Hill and Wang, 1984), 108–9.

52. Nevada District, Book E, Record of Claims (December 1860–July 1862), pp. 225, 152, 94.

53. Nevada District, Book D, Record of Claims (July 1860–December 1860), p. 199; Nevada District, Book E, pp. 59, 80, 97, 175, 182. The prac-

tices in the various districts varied considerably. The miners of the South Boulder District resolved on August 18, 1860, that "aney man having a Wife Shall have the privaledge of Staking for her a Claim on a quarts Load witch she may hoald as real astate. Likewise one yong woman over 18 years of age Shall have the same privalege," while those in the Russell District resolved on July 28, 1860, that "Females shall have the same rights as men." In the Silver Lake District, however, the motion passed on January 1, 1861, "that no woman shall hold Claims in the District." Marshall, ed., *Early Records of Gilpin County*, 66, 147, 263.

54. Martha claimed on the Kansas lode on July 30, 1860 (Central District, Book A, Record of Claims, p. 91; see pp. 72–73 for the other claims). She claimed on the Sweet Ellen, Central District, July 28, 1861 (certificate, Cullen Collection), which Lon, James A., and James P. Maxwell had claimed on July 9, 1860 (Central District, Book A, pp. 62–73); on the Sauk County Lode, Central District, July 20, 1861 (certificate, Cullen Collection), which James A. and James P. had claimed on June 20, 1860 (Central District, Book A, pp. 35–36); and on Elk Creek, Pine Creek District, June 10, 1861, which James also claimed on that date (certificates, Cullen Collection).

55. Martha's other claims, recorded on certificates or notes in the Cullen Collection, were as follows: Silver Mountain Lode, Cumberland District, September 4, 1860; Tipton Lode, Wisconsin District, December 13, 1860; Prairie Sunshine Lode, Wisconsin District, December 13, 1860; Lafayette Lode, Wisconsin District, December 18, 1860; Union Lode, Wisconsin District, December 19, 1860; No. Two Lode, Wisconsin District, December 22, 1860; Stone Lode, Wisconsin District, December 22, 1860; Fair View Lode, Union District, March 1, 1861; Garvin Lode, Union District, March 18, 1861. She also claimed on the Lord Byron Lode, August 25, 1860 (Central District, Book A, p. 118) and on the Olive Branch Lode, January 5, 1861 (Eureka District, Book E, Claims and Lode Index, p. 1).

By 1864 James Maxwell was planning to sell all of the claims the family had amassed, if he could, and he asked Martha for a power of attorney to permit this transaction. James A. Maxwell to Martha Dartt Maxwell, April 17, 1864.

56. Hiram A. Johnson, "A Letter from a Colorado Mining Camp in 1860," *The Colorado Magazine* 7 (September 1930):194. Johnson, who was a law partner of Henry M. Teller in Illinois, practiced law in Central City until the mid-1860s. Later he opened offices in New York and London to sell interests in Colorado mines.

57. Letter of Samuel Mallory, Nevada City, July 8, 1860, in "Over-

land to Pikes Peak with a Quartz Mill," 114.

58. Martha Dartt Maxwell to sisters, August 20, 1860.

59. Ibid.

60. Ibid.

61. Martha Dartt Maxwell to mother, October 3, 1860.

62. *Daily Rocky Mountain News*, Denver, October 15, 1860.

63. Martha Dartt Maxwell to mother, October 3, 1860.

64. Quit Claim Deed from John Denney to Martha Dartt Maxwell, March 30, 1861, Arapahoe County, Colorado Territory, Cullen Collection.

65. Felger, "Biography of Mrs. M. A. Maxwell," 18–19; Martha Dartt Maxwell to James A. Maxwell, February 27, 1861; see also Martha Dartt Maxwell to sisters, June 10, 1861. The account of the ranch in Felger has details which presumably were obtained from Mary and which are not found in contemporary sources. The legal description is as follows: the west half of the northeast one-fourth; the northeast one-fourth of the northeast one-fourth; and the southeast one-fourth of the northwest one-fourth of Section 17, Township 2, South, Range 67 West. Casefile 91681 for the property in the Homestead Records and Casefiles, National Archives, contains no documents dated before 1863, although a cover notation confirms the date given in Felger, "Biography of Mrs. M. A. Maxwell," 19, of June 20, 1861, when settlement officially began.

66. *Baraboo Republic*, March 14, 1861; Amy Sanford Dartt to brother (unnamed), February 16, 1862.

67. Armitage, "Women and Men in Western History," 385.

68. Martha Dartt Maxwell to mother and sisters, February 28, 1861.

69. Martha Dartt Maxwell to Mary Dartt, July 5, 1861.

70. Martha Dartt Maxwell to sisters, August 20, 1860.

71. Martha Dartt Maxwell to mother and sisters, June 10, 1861.

72. *Daily Rocky Mountain News*, Denver, March 6, 1861.

73. Ibid., April 25, 1861.

74. *Clear Creek and Boulder Valleys*, 251; Perrigo, "A Social History of Central City," 247; *Daily Rocky Mountain News*, Denver, March 27, 1861; Tyrrell, "Women and Temperance in Antebellum America," 151; Duane A. Smith, *Rocky Mountain Mining Camps: The Urban Frontier* (Bloomington: Indiana University Press, 1967), 190.

75. Martha Dartt Maxwell to Mary Dartt, July 5, 1861; Smith, *Rocky Mountain Mining Camps*, 206–7.

76. *Daily Rocky Mountain News*, Denver, November 7, 1861; Ovando J. Hollister, *The Mines of Colorado* (Springfield, Mass.: Samuel Bowles and Co., 1867), 118. See also *Daily Rocky Mountain News*, Denver, November

6, 1861; Bancroft, *Gulch of Gold*, 119; and Felger, "Biography of Mrs. M. A. Maxwell," 20.

77. Martha Dartt Maxwell to family, January 1, 1862.

78. Felger, "Biography of Mrs. M. A. Maxwell," 20.

79. Martha Dartt Maxwell to family, January 1, 1862.

80. Ibid. In the Cullen Collection is a single sheet setting forth the judgment of the three arbitrators who found in favor of Martha Maxwell. Report signed by Isaac H. August, Jonas Brantner, and John Rowe, December 30, 1861, Arapahoe County, Colorado Territory.

81. [Caroline Estabrook to Colonel Maxwell], July 21, 1862; Felger, "Biography of Mrs. M. A. Maxwell," 20.

82. Mary Dartt to Martha Dartt Maxwell, September 27, 1862.

83. Mary Dartt described her mother's ailment as "being principaly the dyspepsia" (ibid.), while Howard Potter, Emma Maxwell's husband, told James that "she is quite low with Diahrea . . . she has been sick so long that she is very much reduced." Howard [Potter] to James Maxwell, September 7, 1862.

84. Mary Dartt to Martha Dartt Maxwell, September 27, 1862.

85. Felger, "Biography of Mrs. M. A. Maxwell," 27; *Baraboo Republic*, November 26, 1862; Amy Sanford Dartt to brother (unnamed), February 15, 1862.

86. 1934 Mary Dartt Thompson Reminiscence.

87. Brace, *Thanks to Abigail*, 41–42.

CHAPTER 5

1. Mary Dartt to Martha Dartt Maxwell, May 11, [1860], continuing letter from Sarah Elizabeth Dartt to Martha Dartt Maxwell of April 24; Amy Sanford Dartt to brother, February 15, 1862; 1934 Mary Dartt Thompson Reminiscence.

2. Woody, *History of Women's Education*, 1:378; Melder, *Beginnings of Sisterhood*, 14.

3. Minerva Brace Norton, *A True Teacher, Mary Mortimer: A Memoir* (New York: Fleming H. Revell Co., 1894), 188–225. Later joined with Downer College to become Milwaukee-Downer College (now associated with Lawrence University), the Milwaukee Female College was Catharine Beecher's primary educational project during the early 1850s. See Grace Norton Kieckhefer, *The History of Milwaukee-Downer College, 1851–1951* (Milwaukee: Milwaukee-Downer College, 1951), 5–19, and Kathryn Kish Sklar, *Catharine Beecher: A Study in American Domesticity* (New Haven: Yale University Press, 1973; paperback, New York: W. W. Norton and Co., 1976), 217–26.

4. *Baraboo Republic,* November 5, 1857, June 17, 1858; Mary Dartt Thompson Diary Reminiscence.

5. Mary Dartt to Martha Dartt Maxwell, May 11, [1860].

6. Cole, *Standard History of Sauk County,* 1:436.

7. *Baraboo Republic,* February 26, 1862.

8. Ibid., July 9, 1862; Deborah Jean Warner, "Science Education for Women in Antebellum America," ISIS 69 (March 1978): 58–67.

9. *Baraboo Republic,* May 6, 1863.

10. Ibid., March 16, 1864.

11. Mary Dartt, *On the Plains, and Among the Peaks; or, How Mrs. Maxwell Made Her Natural History Collection* (Philadelphia: Claxton, Remsen and Haffelfinger, 1879 [1878]), 17. For an extended discussion of this work, see chapter 10.

12. Ibid., 17.

13. Ibid., 17–20.

14. Report of arbitration committee, December 30, 1861, Cullen Collection. A. H. Felger interviewed a number of Martha's associates and reported in 1911 that Mac Clark (evidently home from the army) and Lon Maxwell "both helped oust the German taxidermist but neither remembered his name." Felger to Mary Dartt Thompson, December 10, 1911, collection of Harold B. Scott, Palm Beach, Florida.

15. Martha Dartt Maxwell to family, January 1, 1862.

16. Felger, "Biography of Mrs. M. A. Maxwell," 29–30. With respect to what became of the specimens, Felger reported some years later that he had written to a "correspondent in Baraboo" who told him that nothing was known of them. I found no references to Martha's early work for the institute in the contemporary accounts of the school's activities in the *Baraboo Republic.*

17. Dartt, *On the Plains,* 21. See also Hobart's eloquent plea for funds to purchase scientific apparatus in the *Baraboo Republic,* March 16, 1864.

18. *Baraboo Republic,* August 5, September 30, 1863.

19. Woloch, *Women and the American Experience,* 222–23.

20. All four men gained a good deal of prominence in Boulder, and extensive biographical information is available. See the following accounts in *Clear Creek and Boulder Valleys:* James A. Maxwell, 653–54; James P. Maxwell, 660–61; Nelson K. Smith, 682–83; and Clinton M. Tyler, 687–88. For Smith and Tyler's Baraboo business, see *Baraboo Republic,* January 20, 1859. For the Colorado business enterprises, see *Clear Creek and Boulder Valleys,* 393–94; Phyllis Smith, *A Look at Boulder from Settlement to City* (Boulder: Pruett Publishing Co., 1981), 36–37; John B.

Schoolland, *Boulder in Perspective: From Search for Gold to the Gold of Research* (Boulder: Johnson Publishing Co., 1980), 208–9, 219, 220, 318–21.

21. Felger, "Biography of Mrs. M. A. Maxwell," 18; James A. Maxwell to Martha Dartt Maxwell, January 18, 1863.

22. Martha had deeded the land to her stepfather, Josiah Dartt, in September 1861; before he went back to Baraboo later that fall he appointed James A. Maxwell his attorney to lease or sell the property as he saw fit. Conveyance signed October 15, 1861, by Josiah Dartt in the Clinton Tyler Papers, Western Historical Collections, Norlin Library, University of Colorado, Boulder. On December 23, 1863, James conveyed the property to his son Lon for $200; Lon subsequently filed a homestead claim on December 30. Casefile 91681, Homestead Records and Casefiles. Then, according to Felger, "Biography of Mrs. M. A. Maxwell," 27–28, Alonzo Maxwell sold the property to a neighbor for $2600. James then invested part of this money in the sawmill. No records in the casefile substantiate these latter transactions, however.

23. Stewart, "Boulder County Pioneers," 148–49; *Clear Creek and Boulder Valleys*, 688.

24. *Baraboo Republic*, January 11, 1865; March 29, 1865; July 5, 1865.

25. Colonel Maxwell to James A. Maxwell, August 14, 1865.

26. James A. Maxwell to Martha Dartt Maxwell, April 17, 1864.

27. Amy Sanford Dartt to sister (unnamed), August 6, 1866; Felger, "Biography of Mrs. M. A. Maxwell," 32; undated note in Mary Dartt Thompson's handwriting.

28. Barbara J. Berg, *The Remembered Gate: Origins of American Feminism: The Woman and the City, 1800–1860* (New York: Oxford University Press, 1978), 118.

29. Ibid., 118–19.

30. *Health Reformer*, Battle Creek, 1 (December 1866):64 (microfilm, National Library of Medicine, Bethesda, Maryland).

31. Ibid., 1 (August 1866):opp. p. 1. For information on the founding and early years of the institute, see Alan R. Beebe, "History of the Battle Creek Sanitarium, 1866–1903" (unpublished paper, Kalamazoo College, 1949, copy in Michigan Historical Collections, Bentley Historical Library, University of Michigan, Ann Arbor), 1–8; *The Battle Creek Sanitarium Book* (Battle Creek: N.p., n.d.), 14–16; and Berenice Bryant Lowe, *Tales of Battle Creek* (N.p.: Published by the Albert L. and Louise B. Miller Foundation, Inc., n.d.), 76–80.

32. Martha Dartt Maxwell to sisters, August 20, 1860; Martha Dartt Maxwell to Mary Dartt, March 17, 1860. William Leach, *True Love and Per-*

fect Union: The Feminist Reform of Sex and Society (New York: Basic Books, 1980), 64–69, discusses the relationship of health reforms such as the water cure to feminist thought.

33. Amy Sanford Dartt to Martha Dartt Maxwell, July 4, [1852].

34. Undated note in Mary Dartt Thompson's handwriting; Felger, "Biography of Mrs. M. A. Maxwell," 32. Few contemporary records have survived concerning Martha's stay at the institute; all sanitarium files from the early years were destroyed in a 1903 fire (letter from Joni Wildman, medical records director, Battle Creek Sanitarium Hospital, April 5, 1982). The Maxwell Papers do contain a letter Martha wrote from the sanitarium dated March 1, 1867, and a photograph album from the period is now in the Sauk County Historical Society, Baraboo, Wisconsin. The carte-de-visite album, consisting mostly of unidentified portraits, has a penciled note on the title page which reads "To Mrs. M. A. Maxwell Christmas 1864" and includes portraits of Dr. H. S. Lay, a doctor at Battle Creek, and Mrs. Lay. It was given to the historical society in 1938 by Mary Dartt Thompson.

35. Martha Dartt Maxwell to sister [Mary Dartt], March 1, 1867.

36. Mabel Maxwell to Martha Dartt Maxwell, [November] 17, 1866.

37. Brace, *Thanks to Abigail*, 45.

38. "Phrenological Character" of "Miss May Maxwell" and "Mrs. M. A. Maxwell," January 7, 1865. The photograph is reproduced in Brace, *Thanks to Abigail*, opp. p. 20; the original has so far not come to light.

39. Undated note in Mary Dartt Thompson's handwriting; Felger, "Biography of Mrs. M. A. Maxwell," 32.

40. Charles K. Landis, *The Founder's Own Story of the Founding of Vineland, New Jersey* (Vineland: Vineland Historical and Antiquarian Society, 1903), 7. Landis's account apparently was written in 1882.

41. Ibid., 7–13. See also Lucius Q. C. Elmer, *History of the Early Settlement and Progress of Cumberland County, New Jersey, and of the Currency of This and the Adjoining Colonies* (Bridgeton, N.J.: George F. Nixon, Publisher, 1869), 86–89.

42. Excerpt from *Sybaris and Other Homes* (Boston, 1869), quoted in *Vineland Historical Magazine* 1 (January 1916):29. See also Leach, *True Love and Perfect Union*, 87.

43. B. F. Ladd, *History of Vineland, Its Soil, Products, Industries, and Commercial Interests* (Vineland: Evening Journal Book and Job Printing Establishment, 1881), 19.

44. There are three tax notices, dated 1869, 1870, and 1871, in the

Maxwell Papers. According to a note Mary attached to them, Martha was not able to sell the property for some time after she left Vineland. For the land prices, see the 1869 Vineland promotional leaflet *Vineland. To All Wanting Farms: New Settlement of Vineland*, bound with A. G. Warner, *Vineland and the Vinelanders* (Vineland: Printed by F. P. Crocker, 1869), copy in Long Island Historical Society, Brooklyn, New York.

45. Felger, "Biography of Mrs. M. A. Maxwell," 33.

CHAPTER 6

1. *Baraboo Republic*, February 26, 1868.

2. Brace, *Thanks to Abigail*, 45.

3. After Mary Mortimer returned to the Milwaukee Female College in 1866 she asked Mary to join her staff, and thus Mary had gone to Milwaukee early in 1867, returning later that year to teach in Baraboo. Mary Dartt Thompson Diary Reminiscence; *Baraboo Republic*, January 2, 1867, November 13, 1867. She is listed as one of Mary Mortimer's three assistants in the 1866–67 catalog. *Annual Catalogue and Circular of the Milwaukee Female College, Milwaukee, Wis. 1866–1867: Chartered as a College in 1854* (Milwaukee: Daily New Steam Book and Job Print, 1867), listing in front.

4. Letter from Mary Dartt to editor from Boulder, April 4, 1868, printed under the title "Colorado Correspondence" in the *Baraboo Republic*, May 13, 1868. The classic early history of Boulder is Amos Bixby, "History of Boulder County," in *Clear Creek and Boulder Valleys*, 380–433. There is no completely satisfactory modern history of Boulder, but see John B. Schoolland, *Boulder Then and Now*, rev. ed. (Boulder: Johnson Publishing Co., 1978) and *Boulder in Perspective: From Search for Gold to the Gold of Research* (Boulder: Johnson Publishing Co., 1980) and Phyllis Smith, *A Look at Boulder from Settlement to City* (Boulder: Pruett Publishing Co., 1981).

5. Felger, "Biography of Mrs. M. A. Maxwell," 35; Brace, *Thanks to Abigail*, 47; "Rev. Thompson Carried Hod in Building of Pioneer Church," *Boulder Daily Camera*, July 25, 1955, clipping, Maxwell Papers. The article is the second in a three-part series in the *Camera*, which printed portions of a reminiscence by Mary Dartt Thompson probably written in 1909. The manuscript, some of which has evidently been lost since it was given to the Boulder Historical Society in 1955, is in the society's collections; citations will be to the more complete printed version.

6. "High School Classes in Pioneer Days Met in Church Basement," *Boulder Daily Camera*, July 26, 1955, clipping, Maxwell Papers (part three of manuscript cited above). Felger, "Biography of Mrs. M. A. Maxwell,"

35–36, states that the house was located on the left (north) bank of Boulder Creek and would have been "situated on the east side of Walnut St., between 27th and 28th Sts., if these three streets were opened up."

7. Dartt, *On the Plains*, 23.

8. Ibid., 24. See pages 35–38 for a description of her dealings with one of the boys, "a genuine frontier lad, nearly six feet in height and sixteen years of age" (p. 35).

9. Ibid., 25–26. Many years later Mary described exactly how the snake looked and her reaction to it in "Pennsylvania to Skillet Creek," 5.

10. Wallace Stegner, *Beyond the Hundredth Meridian: John Wesley Powell and the Second Opening of the West* (Boston: Houghton Mifflin Co., 1954), 30–34; Richard A. Bartlett, *Great Surveys of the American West* (Norman: University of Oklahoma Press, 1962), 226–34; Robert L. Perkin, *The First Hundred Years: An Informal History of Denver and the Rocky Mountain News* (Garden City: Doubleday and Co., 1959), 299–302, 327–28; Robert C. Black III, *Island in the Rockies: The History of Grand County, Colorado, to 1930* (Boulder: Published for the Grand County Pioneer Society by the Pruett Publishing Co., 1969), 60–61.

11. Samuel Bowles described the Middle Park trip in *A Summer Vacation in the Parks and Mountains of Colorado* (Springfield: Samuel Bowles and Co., 1869), 54–92. Immediately after returning from Middle Park the group embarked on an excursion to South Park and the Arkansas Valley, accompanied by the women in the party who had stayed behind in Denver. Colorado Territorial Secretary Frank Hall, who went with them part way and who later married one of the young ladies, provides some details in Frank Hall, *History of the State of Colorado*, 4 vols. (Chicago: Blakely Printing Co., 1889–95), 1:453–56, as does Bowles, *A Summer Vacation*, 92–144. See also "Seventy Years Ago—Recollections of a Trip Through the Colorado Mountains with the Colfax Party in 1868, as Told by Mrs. Frank Hall to LeRoy R. Hafen," *The Colorado Magazine* 15 (September 1938):161–68.

12. Mary Dartt's letter, dated August 20, 1868, was published in the *Baraboo Republic*, October 14, 1868; a second letter continuing her description of the trip appeared on October 21, 1868.

13. Dartt, *On the Plains*, 79.

14. Ibid., 80–81.

15. Ibid., 82.

16. Brace, *Thanks to Abigail*, 55.

17. Ibid., 54.

18. Dartt, *On the Plains*, 89. See also Brace, *Thanks to Abigail*, 56–57.

19. *Daily Rocky Mountain News*, Denver, October 2, 1868.

20. *Proceedings of the Third and Fourth Annual Exhibitions of the Colorado Agricultural Society, Held at Denver, September 29th and 30th, and October 1st, 2d and 3d, 1868, and September 22nd, 23d, 24th and 25th, 1869* (Central City: Printed by David C. Collier, at the Register Office, 1870), 43. Martha also won a "first premium" for a pine cone hanging basket, reminiscent of the work she had exhibited earlier at fairs in Baraboo. Ibid., 40; *Daily Rocky Mountain News*, Denver, October 3, 1868.

21. These quotations are taken from a section in the manuscript version (p. 46) of *On the Plains* that was largely omitted from the book. Entitled "A Novel Career: How Mrs. Maxwell Made Her Centennial Collection," the manuscript is now held by the Boulder Historical Society, Boulder, Colorado; I am indebted to Laurence T. Paddock for his help in making it available to me.

22. Martha Dartt Maxwell to family, June 12, 1852; April 12, 1852.

23. Quoted in Emanuel D. Rudolph, "How It Developed that Botany Was the Science Thought Most Suitable for Victorian Young Ladies," *Children's Literature* 2 (1973):92.

24. Quoted in ibid.

25. Margaret Rossiter, *Women Scientists in America: Struggles and Strategies to 1940* (Baltimore: The Johns Hopkins University Press, 1982), 7.

26. Lois Barber Arnold, *Four Lives in Science: Women's Education in the Nineteenth Century* (New York: Schocken Books, 1984), 6–7; Deborah Jean Warner, "Science Education for Women in Antebellum America," *ISIS* 69 (March 1978):58–67.

27. Deborah Jean Warner, *Graceanna Lewis, Scientist and Humanitarian* (Washington, D.C.: Published for the National Museum of History and Technology by the Smithsonian Institution Press, 1979), 53.

28. Barber, *Four Lives in Science*, 127.

29. "A Novel Career," 46.

30. Martha Dartt Maxwell to Secretary, Smithsonian Institution, January 8, 1869, Record Unit 26, Office of the Secretary (1863–1879), Incoming Correspondence, vol. 82, p. 78, box 19, Smithsonian Archives, Washington, D.C. See also Dartt, *On the Plains*, 157.

31. Spencer F. Baird, with the co-operation of John Cassin and George N. Lawrence, *Birds*, vol. 9 of *Reports of Explorations and Surveys, to Ascertain the Most Practicable and Economical Route for a Railroad from the Mississippi River to the Pacific Ocean, Made Under the Direction of the Secretary of War, 1853–6* (Washington, D.C.: Beverly Tucker, Printer, 1858), xiii.

32. For complete bibliographical information on the Lippincott edi-

tion, see George Brown Goode, *Bibliographies of American Naturalists, I: The Published Writings of Spencer Fullerton Baird, 1843–1882*, No. 20, *Bulletin of the United States National Museum* (Washington, D.C.: Government Printing Office, 1883), 87–89; the quoted advertisement is on p. 88. For biographical details see Dean C. Allard, "Baird, Spencer Fullerton" (1823–1887), *Dictionary of Scientific Biography*, 16 vols. (New York: Charles Scribner's Sons, 1970–80), 1:404–6.

33. Joseph Henry to Martha Dartt Maxwell, February 1, 1869, Record Unit 33, Office of the Secretary (1865–1891), Outgoing Correspondence, vol. 13, p. 184, box 4, Smithsonian Archives.

34. Dartt, *On the Plains*, 108–9.

35. See Martha Dartt Maxwell to Mary Dartt Thompson, March 6, 1870, written from Laramie, Wyoming.

36. "High School Classes in Pioneer Days Met in Church Basement," clipping, Maxwell Papers.

37. Martha Dartt Maxwell to Mary Dartt Thompson, March 6, 1870.

38. *Daily Central City Register*, October 4, 1870; see also *Boulder County News*, October 5, 1870.

39. *Transactions of the Fifth and Sixth Annual Exhibitions of the Colorado Agricultural Society, Held at Denver, September 27th, 28th, 29th, and 30th, and September 19th, 20th, 21st, 22d and 23d* (Denver: The Denver Tribune Association Print., 1872), 74.

40. Dartt, *On the Plains*, 112.

41. Ibid.; for accounts of Shaw and the garden, see James Neal Primm, "Henry Shaw: Merchant-Capitalist," *Gateway Heritage* 5 (Summer 1984):2–9 and William Barnaby Faherty, S.J., "The Missouri Botanical Garden Through 125 Years," *Gateway Heritage* 5 (Summer 1984):10–19.

42. Dartt, *On the Plains*, 112; letter from Barbara L. Mykrantz, archivist, Missouri Botanical Garden, August 23, 1982.

43. Dartt, *On the Plains*, 112.

44. Letter from Barbara L. Mykrantz; Junius Henderson to Mary Dartt Thompson, October 9, 1906.

45. Brace, *Thanks to Abigail*, 59.

46. For Lizzie's account of her trip and early years in Colorado, see Elmer R. Burkey, interview with Elizabeth Dartt Sayre, January 11, 1934, typescript in Elmer R. Burkey Papers, Colorado Historical Society, Denver. See also *Baraboo Republic*, August 25, 1868; "High School Classes in Pioneer Days Met in Church Basement"; Elizabeth Dartt Sayre obituary, June 5, 1939, clipping in biographical file, Library, Colorado Historical Society.

47. Born in 1835, Hal Sayre (who in his younger days affected the spelling "Sayr"), lived to be ninety-one, dying in 1926. Although there is no full-scale biography of Sayre, a number of articles and reminiscences detail aspects of his flamboyant life. See, for example, A. B. Sanford, "How Prospectors of '59 Lived," *The Trail*, vol. 18, no. 7 (December 1925):10–19; Robert F. Sayre, "Hal Sayre — Fifty-Niner," *The Colorado Magazine* 39 (July 1962):161–77, and, with Gertrude B. Sayre, *Born Pioneers* (Denver: Privately Printed, 1963), 86–87; and Lynn I. Perrigo, ed., "Major Hal Sayr's Diary of the Sand Creek Campaign," *The Colorado Magazine* 15 (March 1938):41–57. The Western Historical Collections, University of Colorado Libraries, Boulder, holds an extensive collection of Sayre papers; see Doris Mitterling, comp., "Guide to the Hal Sayre Papers, 1859–1925" (Boulder: Western Historical Collections, 1976). Elizabeth Sayre's later diaries, dealing primarily with the Sayres' European trips, are included in the collection.

48. Brace, *Thanks to Abigail*, 66; *Boulder County News*, May 18, 1870.

49. *Boulder County News*, January 4, 1870.

50. See Nathan Thompson, *Ten Years as First Pastor of the Congregational Church of Boulder, Colorado, 1865–1875* (N.p., n.d.), 5–13; the copy in the Nathan Thompson Papers, Western Historical Collections, University of Colorado Libraries, has biographical notes and other information added by Mary Dartt Thompson. See also Sanford Charles Gladden, *Letters from the Rev. Nathan Thompson* (Boulder: By the Author, 1976), 1–4 and "Widow of First Pastor of Boulder's Congregational Church Wrote of His Career and Experiences in Boulder," *Boulder Daily Camera*, July 21, 1955, clipping in Maxwell Papers (part one of reminiscence cited above).

51. Dartt, *On the Plains*, 113.

52. Ibid., 113–14.

53. Brace, *Thanks to Abigail*, 60.

54. Dartt, *On the Plains*, 158.

55. Ibid., 113.

56. Ibid., 117–18.

57. Ibid., 109.

58. Anne E. McDowell, "Women's Department," *Sunday Republic*, August 13, 1876, clipping in Maxwell Scrapbook, 74. For other mentions of the use of iron frames, see "The Museum of Mrs. Maxwell, of Boulder, Colorado," *Philadelphia Times*, undated clipping, Maxwell Scrapbook, 59, and "Is Mrs. Maxwell a Naturalist and Huntress?," *Sunday Times*, undated clipping, Maxwell Scrapbook, 76. Helen Hunt describes Martha's practice of molding an animal of plaster and then stretching the skin over

it in one of her articles on the Boulder museum ("A Colorado Woman's Museum," *St. Nicholas* [October 1876], Maxwell Scrapbook). I have been unable to confirm statements made in two of these articles ("Women's Department" and "Is Mrs. Maxwell a Naturalist and Huntress?") that Martha patented the iron frame. Her name does not appear in *Women Inventors to Whom Patents Have Been Granted by the United States Government, 1790 to July 1, 1888* (Washington, D.C.: Government Printing Office, 1888) nor in the "Reference List of Women Inventors at the Centennial," compiled by Deborah Warner in her "Women Inventors at the Centennial," in Martha Moore Trescott, ed., *Dynamos and Virgins Revisited: Women and Technological Change in History* (Metuchen, N.J.: Scarecrow Press, 1979), 110–19.

59. For information on Ward's Establishment, see James Andrew Dolph, "Bringing Wildlife to Millions: William Temple Hornaday, the Early Years: 1854–1896" (Ph.D. diss., University of Massachusetts, 1975), 36–51; Sally Gregory Kohlstedt, "Henry A. Ward: The Merchant Naturalist and American Museum Development," *Journal of the Society for the Bibliography of Natural History* 9 (1980):647–61; and Frederic A. Lucas, *Fifty Years of Museum Work: Autobiography, Unpublished Papers, and Bibliography* (New York: American Museum of Natural History, 1933), 9–15.

60. Dolph, "Bringing Wildlife to Millions," 52.

61. William T. Hornaday, *Taxidermy and Zoological Collecting: A Complete Handbook for the Amateur Taxidermist, Collector, Osteologist, Museum-Builder, Sportsman, and Traveler* (1891; 7th ed., New York: Charles Scribner's Sons, 1921), 112. For a description of Hornaday's techniques see 140–218. See also Dolph, "Bringing Wildlife to Millions," 282–366.

62. Helen Hunt mentioned in "Mrs. Maxwell's Museum" that Martha took "several courses of instruction from taxidermists," but I have found nothing further on this point. Reprinted from the *New York Independent*, September 23, 1875, in *Boulder County News*, October 15, 1875, Maxwell Scrapbook, 10–11.

63. William T. Hornaday, "Masterpieces of American Taxidermy," *Scribner's Magazine* 72 (July 1922):3.

64. Hornaday, *Taxidermy and Zoological Collecting*, 108, 114.

65. Dartt, *On the Plains*, 114–15.

66. *Caribou Post*, October 14 [1871], clipping in Maxwell Papers.

67. Diploma dated October 6, 1871, Maxwell Papers; *Boulder County News*, October 13, 1871.

68. *Boulder County News*, October 13, 1871.

69. Dartt, *On the Plains*, 43.

70. Martha Dartt to parents, August 17, 1851; *Health Reformer* 2 (January 1868):105–7; (March 1868):129–30. The "reform dress" at the institute called for straight, not gathered or "Turkish" trousers. For an informative discussion of the dress-reform movement, see Leach, *True Love and Perfect Union*, 243–51.

71. Letter from Julia Archibald Holmes, January 25, 1859, in Agnes Wright Spring, ed., *A Bloomer Girl on Pike's Peak, 1858: Julia Archibald Holmes, First White Woman to Climb Pike's Peak* (Denver: Western History Department, Denver Public Library, 1949), 16.

72. Author's note to second edition, November 27, 1879, in Isabella L. Bird, *A Lady's Life in the Rocky Mountains*, intro. by Daniel J. Boorstin (Norman: University of Oklahoma Press, 1960), 10, n.3.

73. Dartt, *On the Plains*, 141.

74. Ibid., 137.

75. Ibid., 69–73.

76. *Clear Creek and Boulder Valleys*, 654.

77. *Boulder County News*, May 11, 1870; June 17, 1871.

78. James A. Maxwell to Martha Dartt Maxwell, October 13, 1873.

79. Dartt, *On the Plains*, 106–7.

80. Brace, *Thanks to Abigail*, 58–59.

81. *Boulder News and Courier*, June 10, 1881.

82. Brace, *Thanks to Abigail*, 52.

83. Ibid., 50.

84. Ibid., 61.

85. Ibid., 62.

86. See Martha Dartt Maxwell to Smithsonian (undated; received February 2, 1871), Record Unit 26, Office of the Secretary (1862–1879), Incoming Correspondence, vol. 100, p. 311, box 32; Joseph Henry to Martha Dartt Maxwell, February 3, 1871, Record Unit 33, Office of the Secretary (1865–1891), Outgoing Correspondence, vol. 22, p. 778, box 7, Smithsonian Archives; Dartt, *On the Plains*, 111. There are several fragmentary lists of specimens in Martha's handwriting in the Maxwell Papers, as well as brief exchanges of correspondence detailing these transactions. See, for example, C. W. Hawkins, Kansas City, to W. D. McLeod, January 8, 1874, and Hawkins to Martha Dartt Maxwell, March 25 and April 10, 1874.

87. Dartt, *On the Plains*, 136.

CHAPTER 7

1. Martha Dartt Maxwell to Spencer Baird, April 2, 1874, Record Unit

52, Assistant Secretary (Spencer F. Baird), 1850–1877, Incoming Correspondence, vol. 7, p. 137, box 34, Smithsonian Archives.

2. Dartt, *On the Plains*, 137.

3. Ibid., 137–38.

4. See Edward P. Alexander, *Museums in Motion: An Introduction to the History and Functions of Museums* (Nashville: American Association for State and Local History, 1979), 50–53. The Smithsonian museum building opened in 1881 to house carloads of artifacts from the Philadelphia Centennial Exposition as well as natural history specimens collected by the institution. Located next to the Castle, it is now known as the Arts and Industries Building; the National Museum for Natural History is across the Mall.

5. George Brown Goode, *Circular No. One of the United States National Museum*, quoted in G. Carroll Lindsay, "George Brown Goode," in Clifford L. Lord, ed., *Keepers of the Past* (Chapel Hill: University of North Carolina Press, 1965), 132–33. Goode (1851–1896) was a volunteer collector for the United States Commission of Fish and Fisheries in 1872, becoming assistant curator in the United States National Museum in 1873 (*Guide to the Smithsonian Archives* [Washington, D.C.: Smithsonian Institution Press, 1983], 26). See also Edward P. Alexander, *Museum Masters: Their Museums and Their Influence* (Nashville: American Association for State and Local History, 1983), 278–305.

6. Charles Coleman Sellers, *Mr. Peale's Museum: Charles Willson Peale and the First Popular Museum of Natural Science and Art* (New York: W. W. Norton and Co., 1980), 1. See also Alexander, *Museum Masters*, 44–77, and Brooke Hindle, "Charles Willson Peale's Science and Technology," in *Charles Willson Peale and His World* (New York: Harry N. Abrams, 1983), 106–69.

7. Dartt, *On the Plains*, 138–39; the quote is from p. 138.

8. Mary states that the ticket was given to Martha "through the kindness of a friend," and that she had also "come into possession of some property she had inherited" (*On the Plains*, 138). Mabel, however, states that it was Lizzie who was planning to go to San Francisco, and that Martha seized the opportunity to accompany her (*Thanks to Abigail*, 75). See also Martha Dartt Maxwell to Amy Sanford Dartt, September 2 [1873].

9. Martha Dartt Maxwell to James A. Maxwell and Mabel Maxwell, October 5, 1873. The Sierra Redwood or Giant Sequoia grow along the West Slope of the Sierra Nevada, while the Coast Redwood are found along the Pacific Coast. The Mammoth Grove Hotel, operated by John Perry and James Sperry, was one of California's most famous resort

hotels in the early 1870s. See Joseph H. Engbeck, Jr., *The Enduring Giants* (Berkeley: University Extension, University of California, Berkeley, 1973), 25, 80–83.

10. Martha Dartt Maxwell to James A. Maxwell and Mabel Maxwell, October 5, 1873; "Description of the Mammoth and South Park Groves," information on Mammoth Grove Hotel stationery used by Martha.

11. Charles Lockwood, "Woodward's Natural Wonders," *California Living Magazine,* November 20, 1977, 41–45; back cover, *Illustrated Guide and Catalogue of Woodward's Gardens, Located on Mission Street, bet. Thirteenth and Fifteenth Streets, S.F.* (San Francisco: Francis and Valentine, Book and Job Printers, Engravers, Etc., 1873), copy in Bancroft Library, University of California, Berkeley.

12. Dartt, *On the Plains,* 172. Ferdinand Gruber (1830–1907) was listed in the 1873 *Illustrated Guide and Catalogue of Woodward's Gardens* as the curator of the museum. One of the leading taxidermists in San Francisco during the 1870s, he also served for a time as curator of birds for the California Academy of Sciences. Joseph Ewan, "San Francisco as a Mecca for Nineteenth Century Naturalists," in *A Century of Progress in the Natural Sciences, 1853–1953* (San Francisco: California Academy of Sciences, 1955), 28–29.

13. Back cover, *Illustrated Guide and Catalogue of Woodward's Gardens.*

14. Quoted in F. Gruber, comp., *Illustrated Guide and Catalogue of Woodward's Gardens Located on Mission Street, Bet. 13th & 15th Sts. San Francisco, California* (San Francisco: Valentine and Co., 1880), 85, copy in Bancroft Library, University of California, Berkeley.

15. Dartt, *On the Plains,* 172.

16. *An Illustrated History of Sonoma County, California* (Chicago: Lewis Publishing Co., 1889), 383–84. Bryant and Martha kept in touch and exchanged specimens for at least a year; see his letter to her of September 4, 1874, which mentions her letter of June 28.

17. See Martha Dartt Maxwell to Spencer Baird, April 2, 1874, Record Unit 52, Assistant Secretary (Spencer F. Baird), 1850–1877, Incoming Correspondence, vol. 7, p. 137, box 34, Smithsonian Archives. When Bryant wrote Martha in Colorado the next year, he mentioned that he often saw Cooper, who wanted to be remembered to her (Bryant to Martha Dartt Maxwell, September 4, 1874). On Cooper, see Ewan, "San Francisco as a Mecca for Nineteenth Century Naturalists," 7, and Eugene Coan, *James Graham Cooper: Pioneer Western Naturalist* (Moscow, Idaho: A Northwest Naturalist Book, the University Press of Idaho, a Division of the Idaho Research Foundation, 1981), 134–35.

18. James A. Maxwell to Martha Dartt Maxwell, September 1, 1873.

19. James A. Maxwell to Martha Dartt Maxwell, November 10, 1873.

20. In late 1870 or early 1871, Amy Dartt had suffered a bad fall from her carriage when her horse ran away, and Martha had returned to Baraboo for a time to be with her. Shortly thereafter, Amy and Josiah moved to Boulder. See Brace, *Thanks to Abigail*, 78; undated letter from Martha Dartt Maxwell to Mary Dartt Thompson.

21. Dartt, *On the Plains*, 172. There are several receipts or bills in the Maxwell Papers itemizing the purchases that Martha made in San Francisco; see, for example, the invoice for goods totaling $16.70 from W. & F. Deakin, Dealers in Japanese Goods, dated December 24, 1873, and Martha's undated "List of Articles bought for Museum."

22. Dartt, *On the Plains*, 172–74. An undated receipt in the collection from W. R. Frink shows that Martha paid $30 for the armor with headdress, sword, and "navigator's helmet."

23. John W. Glass to President, Academy of Natural Sciences of Philadelphia, Collection 567, Academy of Natural Sciences, Philadelphia; copy and additional information furnished by Carol M. Spawn, Manuscript/Archives Librarian, September 17, 1984. I am indebted to Prof. Joseph Ewan of Tulane University for this reference; Glass does not appear in Joseph and Nesta Dunn Ewan, *Biographical Dictionary of Rocky Mountain Naturalists: A Guide to the Writings and Collections of Botanists, Zoologists, Geologists, Artists and Photographers, 1682–1932* (Utrecht/ Antwerp: Bohn, Scheltema and Holkema, 1981).

24. "Letter from Arizona," *Rocky Mountain News*, Denver, July 21, 1872.

25. *Boulder County News*, January 23, 1874.

26. J. W. Glass to Martha Dartt Maxwell, February 20, 1874. See also Glass to W. D. McLeod, February 26, 1874.

27. Martha Dartt Maxwell to Spencer Baird, April 15 [1875], Record Unit 52, Assistant Secretary (Spencer F. Baird), 1850–1877, Incoming Correspondence, vol. 198, p. 461, box 51, Smithsonian Archives. Martha dated the letter 1874, clearly an error, as the Smithsonian receipt stamp is April 21, 1875; internal evidence also confirms that the correct year is 1875.

28. Spencer Baird to Martha Dartt Maxwell, March 21, 1874, Maxwell Papers. For an account of Baird's relationship with his "collectors," see William A. Deiss, "Spencer F. Baird and His Collectors," *Journal of the Society for the Bibliography of Natural History* 9 (April 1980):635–45.

29. Martha Dartt Maxwell to Spencer Baird, April 2, 1874, Smithsonian Archives.

30. Ibid.

31. Spencer Baird to Martha Dartt Maxwell, May 13, 1874, Maxwell Papers; Paul R. Cutright and Michael J. Brodhead, *Elliott Coues: Naturalist and Frontier Historian* (Urbana: University of Illinois Press, 1981), 130–33. Coues's *Key* featured various "keys" to enable the student or amateur "to determine the taxonomic order to which a particular bird belonged, and . . . to aid in finding the specific family, genus, and species" (Cutright and Brodhead, *Elliott Coues*, 130).

32. Coues's "Glossary" was published in *History of North American Birds*, 3:535–60 (Cutright and Brodhead, *Elliott Coues*, 453). See also Goode, "Published Writings of Spencer Fullerton Baird," 230–31.

33. Spencer Baird to Martha Dartt Maxwell, May 13, 1874, Maxwell Papers.

34. Martha Dartt Maxwell to Spencer Baird, May 6, 1875, Record Unit 52, Assistant Secretary (Spencer F. Baird), 1850–1877, Incoming Correspondence, v. 198, p. 462, box 51.

35. Spencer Baird to Martha Dartt Maxwell, May 13, 1874, Maxwell Papers.

36. Martha Dartt Maxwell to Spencer Baird, April 15 [1875], Smithsonian Archives; Spencer Baird to Martha Dartt Maxwell, March 21, 1874, Maxwell Papers. Her donations during the year were recorded in the *Annual Report of the Board of Regents of the Smithsonian Institution, Showing the Operations, Expenditures, and Condition of the Institution for the Year 1874* (Washington, D.C.: Government Printing Office, 1875), 58.

37. Spencer Baird to Martha Dartt Maxwell, March 21, May 13, 1874, Maxwell Papers. For details on the finches, see Richard G. Beidleman, *Guide to the Winter Birds of Colorado*, Leaflet No. 12, October 1955, University of Colorado Museum, Boulder, 42–43, and Alfred M. Bailey and Robert J. Niedrach, *Birds of Colorado*, 2 vols. (Denver: Denver Museum of Natural History, 1965), 2:766–74.

38. Martha Dartt Maxwell to Spencer Baird, April 2, 1874, Smithsonian Archives.

39. *Guide to the Smithsonian Archives*, 305; Harry Harris, "Robert Ridgway, with a Bibliography of His Published Writings and Fifty Illustrations," *Condor* 30 (January-February 1928):15–16, 21.

40. Martha Dartt Maxwell to Robert Ridgway, June 21, 1874, Record Unit 105, Division of Birds, circa 1854–1959, folder 6, box 22, Smithsonian Archives.

41. Robert Ridgway, "A Monograph of the Genus Leucosticte, Swainson; or, Gray-Crowned Purple Finches," *Bulletin of the United States Geological and Geographical Survey of the Territories*, No. 2, Second Series (Washington, D.C.: Government Printing Office, 1875), 57.

42. List of specimens, ibid., 72–74, 76. C. E. H. Aiken (1850–1936) collected principally in the Colorado Springs vicinity, southern Colorado, and New Mexico. In the summer of 1874 he served as a naturalist with one of the Wheeler Survey parties (Ewan and Ewan, *Biographical Dictionary of Rocky Mountain Naturalists*, 2). Martha noted that a few of the skins she sent belonged to a friend, J. Martin Trippe, who had helped her collect the specimens (Martha Dartt Maxwell to Robert Ridgway, June 21, 1874, Smithsonian Archives). Ewan and Ewan identify "T. Martin Trippe" as probably the T. Trippe who was a "resident of Howardsville, San Juan Co., Colo., interested in ornithology" (*Biographical Dictionary of Rocky Mountain Naturalists*, 224).

43. Dartt, *On the Plains*, 176; W. D. McLeod to Martha Dartt Maxwell, March 11, 1874. I have been unable to identify McLeod further, beyond locating his name in the "Advertised Letters," *Rocky Mountain News*, Denver, March 3, 1872, and the "List of Unclaimed Newspapers," *Rocky Mountain News*, Denver, September 11, 1873. He is not included in Ewan and Ewan, *Biographical Dictionary of Rocky Mountain Naturalists*.

44. *Boulder County News*, March 13, 1874.

45. Reply from Martha drafted on letter from the Miners Association of Colorado, April 19, 1874.

46. "The First Brick Business Building in Boulder, Colorado," *Boulder Genealogical Society Quarterly* 4 (February 1972):21–22. See also *Boulder County News*, April 7, 1874.

47. *Boulder County News*, June 5, 1874. This account can be found also in *On the Plains*, 177–78.

48. "The Boulder Budget," clipping dated October 5, 1875, Maxwell Scrapbook, 11. See also *Boulder County News*, July 30, 1875; "Boulder and Sunshine, Two of Colorado's Most Beautiful Cities," letter from correspondent to *Kansas City Journal* dated July 7, 1875, Maxwell Scrapbook, 8; "What a Woman Can Do," undated clipping, *Colorado Farmer*, Maxwell Scrapbook, 2.

49. Dartt, *On the Plains*, 177; "The Boulder Budget"; "Boulder and Sunshine." Smith, born in Kentucky in 1830, had come to Colorado in 1864 and had been active as an assayer in Gilpin County before his appointment as superintendent of the American Mine in Boulder County in 1874. He had been named territorial geologist following the creation of that office in 1872 (*Clear Creek and Boulder Valleys*, 678–79).

50. Thurman Wilkins, "Jackson, Helen Maria Fiske Hunt," *Notable American Women, 1607–1950: A Biographical Dictionary*, ed. Edward T. James, Janet Wilson James, and Paul S. Boyer, 3 vols. (Cambridge: The Belknap Press of Harvard University Press, 1971), 2:259–61.

51. The article can be found in the *Boulder County News*, October 15, 1875 (Maxwell Scrapbook, 10–11), and (partially) in Dartt, *On the Plains*, 10–15.

52. "A Colorado Woman's Museum," *St. Nicholas* (October 1876):781–84, copy in Maxwell Scrapbook, 13; the quote is from 781–82. This article is illustrated with several engravings from photographs taken of the Boulder museum and thus provides an excellent means of identifying positively a number of otherwise unidentifiable views. See clipping entitled "Mrs. Maxwell's Museum Illustrated," *Boulder County News*, November 17, 1876, Maxwell Scrapbook, 58. Martha's procedures were not dissimilar from those described by Hornaday in *Taxidermy and Zoological Collecting*. Hornaday, however, thought that cloth was "poor stuff to use in making rockwork." See "How to Make Imitation Rocks," 228.

53. Hunt, "Mrs. Maxwell's Museum."

54. *Illustrated Guide and Catalogue of Woodward's Gardens*, 13.

55. Dartt, *On the Plains*, 179–90; "Boulder and Sunshine"; *Boulder County News*, August 13, 1875; Martha Dartt Maxwell to Mabel Maxwell, August 27 [1874], November 15, 1874.

56. Hunt, "Mrs. Maxwell's Museum."

57. "The Museum," unidentified clipping, Maxwell Scrapbook, 9. The Hayden Survey spent four seasons in Colorado (1873–1876) and produced a monumental atlas of the state, published in 1877, as well as such noted accomplishments as William Henry Jackson's famed Mesa Verde and Holy Cross photographs. See Bartlett, *Great Surveys*, 74–120.

58. James A. Maxwell to Mabel Maxwell, November 1874 (no day given); Dartt, *On the Plains*, 186–204; *Boulder County News*, October 1, 1875.

59. L. Ray Hersey, "The Frontier Legion," *Wray Gazette*, December 24, 1936, clipping, Biographical File, Colorado Historical Society. L. Ray Hersey was the son of J. Clarence Hersey's brother.

60. J. Clarence Hersey to Mary Dartt Thompson, July 15, 1908. Hersey's wife's copy of *On the Plains*, with his annotations, is now in the Sutro Library, San Francisco. There is a brief biography of Hersey in Ewan and Ewan, *Biographical Dictionary of Rocky Mountain Naturalists*, 103. A communication from Hersey, "The Little White Egret in Colorado," was published in "General Notes: Zoology," *American Naturalist* 10 (July 1876):430.

61. Martha Dartt Maxwell to Mabel Maxwell, September 26, 1875.

62. Spencer Baird to Martha Dartt Maxwell, April 21, 1875, Maxwell Papers.

63. Martha Dartt Maxwell to Spencer Baird, May 20, 1875, Record Unit 52, Assistant Secretary (Spencer F. Baird), 1850–1877, Incoming Correspondence, v. 198, p. 463, box 51, Smithsonian Archives.

64. Spencer Baird to Martha Dartt Maxwell, April 21, 1875, Maxwell Papers.

65. Exactly how the citizens of Boulder supported the museum is unclear; Martha, for example, wrote on one occasion only that "my townspeople pay my houserent" (Martha Dartt Maxwell to Marianne Dascomb, November 15, 1874, file 28/1, box 320, Oberlin College Archives). For further details see *Boulder County News*, May 28, 1875, and July 30, 1875.

66. Martha Dartt Maxwell to Marianne Dascomb, October 26, 1874, file 28/1, box 320, Oberlin Archives. The population estimate is given in *Boulder County News*, January 9, 1874.

67. *Boulder County News*, May 28, 1875; July 30, 1875.

68. Described in Martha Dartt Maxwell to Mabel Maxwell, October 4, 1874.

69. *Boulder County News*, July 30, 1875.

70. Ibid., May 28, 1875.

71. Martha Dartt Maxwell to Mabel Maxwell, August 27 [1874].

72. Martha Dartt Maxwell to Marianne Dascomb, October 26, 1874, Oberlin Archives.

73. Marianne Dascomb to Martha Dartt Maxwell, November 5, 1874.

74. Paul S. Boyer, "Howe, Julia Ward," *Notable American Women*, 2:225–29.

75. Julia Ward Howe to Martha Dartt Maxwell, February 23 [1875].

76. *Woman's Journal*, February 27, 1875, 65.

77. Martha Dartt Maxwell to Julia Ward Howe, March 15, 1875 (draft).

78. Martha Dartt Maxwell to Mabel Maxwell, November 19, 1874.

79. "What a Woman Can Do," *Colorado Farmer*, undated clipping, Maxwell Scrapbook, 3.

80. *Clear Creek and Boulder Valleys*, 674.

81. "The Museum Going to Denver," *Boulder County News*, December 3, 1875. For further mention of the arrangement, see Dartt, *On the Plains*, 205. Like some of Martha's other business transactions, however, this one apparently had a less than happy conclusion. Four years later, Martha told Mabel that she had been informed that "Mr Pickel was about attaching my Boulder property in the Denver Museum business & that I might loose them both." Such action, she continued, was "very unjust,"

and she asked Mabel to look for the agreement she had made with Pickel. Martha Dartt Maxwell to Mabel Maxwell, March 26, 1880.

82. The exact location, which is between Fifteenth and Sixteenth streets, is given in the *Boulder County News*, December 24, 1875, as well as on the back of the Chamberlain series of photographs. According to the 1887 Sanborn map of Denver in the Western History Department of the Denver Public Library, which translates the old street numbers into those presently in use, the building was situated on Lawrence Street where the Park Central complex is today (*Denver, Colorado: Published for the Denver Board of Underwriters* [New York: Sanborn Map and Publishing Co., 1887]).

83. "Mrs. Maxwell's Museum," unidentified clipping, Maxwell Scrapbook, 45.

84. Martha Dartt Maxwell to Mary Dartt Thompson, February 27, 1876. Following Nathan Thompson's resignation as pastor of the First Congregational Church the Thompsons had left Boulder in late 1875 and were living in West Acton; Thompson served as pastor of a church at nearby Boxborough for several years. Gladden, *Letters from the Rev. Nathan Thompson*, 7–11.

85. "Mrs. Maxwell's Museum," undated clipping from *Colorado Farmer*, Maxwell Scrapbook, 45.

86. [Spencer Baird] to Martha Dartt Maxwell, December 13, 1875, Record Unit 53, Assistant Secretary Spencer F. Baird, 1850–1877, Outgoing Correspondence, v. 60, p. 264, box 18, Smithsonian Archives.

87. James A. Maxwell to [Mabel Maxwell, Fall 1874].

88. Martha Dartt Maxwell to Mabel Maxwell, December 7, 1875.

89. Amy Sanford Dartt to Mary Dartt Thompson, February 21, 1876.

90. Martha Dartt Maxwell to Mary Dartt Thompson, February 27, 1876.

91. Ibid.

CHAPTER 8

1. Martha Dartt Maxwell to Mabel Maxwell, December 2, 1874.

2. Martha Dartt Maxwell to Mabel Maxwell, December 17, 1874, continuing letter of December 16.

3. Solomon, *Educated Women*, 62–68. The percentage of women students of all students enrolled in institutions of higher education was 21 in 1870 and 33.4 in 1880. Ibid., 63.

4. Martha Dartt Maxwell to Mabel Maxwell, October 4, 1874.

5. Martha Dartt Maxwell to Mabel Maxwell, February 13, 1875.

6. Martha Dartt Maxwell to Mabel Maxwell, October 12 [1874].

7. Martha Dartt Maxwell to Mabel Maxwell, January 17 [1875].

8. Martha Dartt Maxwell to Julia Ward Howe (draft), March 15, 1875.

9. Martha Dartt Maxwell to Marianne Dascomb, November 15, 1874, file 28/1, box 320, Oberlin College Archives, Oberlin, Ohio.

10. Gerda Lerner, "Women's Rights and American Feminism," reprinted in *The Majority Finds Its Past: Placing Women in History* (New York: Oxford University Press, 1979), 48–49.

11. Dartt, *On the Plains*, 25.

12. Woloch, *Women and the American Experience*, 174, 196.

13. Martha Dartt Maxwell to Spencer Baird, October 27, 1875, Record Unit 52, Assistant Secretary (Spencer F. Baird), 1850–1877, Incoming Correspondence, vol. 198, p. 465, box 51, Smithsonian Archives.

14. Martha Dartt Maxwell to Julia Ward Howe (draft), March 15, 1875.

15. Ibid.

16. Jennie Bartlett to Martha Dartt Maxwell, September 11, 1873. The *Boulder County News*, July 29, 1871, referred to her as "Miss Jennie Bartlett, a young lady artist, whose studio is at Capt. [Ira] Austin's." By 1873, when this letter was written, she was living in Minneapolis. She was later identified as a portrait painter living in Harmony, Maine (Phebe A. Hanaford, *Daughters of America; or, Women of the Century* [Boston: B. B. Russell, 1883], 286).

Anna Dickinson (1842–1932) was a popular speaker after the Civil War, for a time giving some 150 lectures per season on the emancipation of women, the rights of blacks, and other subjects (James Harvey Young, "Dickinson, Anna Elizabeth," *Notable American Women*, 1:475–76).

Sara Jane Lippincott (1823–1904), a prolific and popular author whose pen name was Grace Greenwood, had a residence in Manitou, near Colorado Springs, from 1871 to 1877 and frequently traveled around Colorado giving speeches and obtaining material for her newspaper columns (Barbara Welter, "Lippincott, Sara Jane Clarke," *Notable American Women*, 2:407–9; Marian Talmadge and Iris Gilmore, "Grace Greenwood," *1955 Denver Westerners Brand Book* [Denver: The Westerners, 1956], 224–48).

17. Undated fragment of letter from Martha Dartt Maxwell to family from San Francisco. Although most biographies of Achey state that she was in California by 1876, it is apparent from this letter and the one cited below that she was there much earlier.

Achey (1832–1886) later went to Washington Territory, where she died. Working in oil, watercolor, pen and ink, and pencil, she was perhaps the most prolific western woman artist of her period, except possibly for Mary Hallock Foote. In the late 1970s a major exhibit of her work was held in Aberdeen, Washington. Chris Petteys, "Colorado's First Women Artists," *Empire Magazine, The Denver Post,* May 6, 1979, 36–38; Phil Kovinick, *The Woman Artist in the American West, 1860–1960* (Fullerton, Calif.: Muckenthaler Cultural Center, 1976), 4; Patricia Trenton and Peter H. Hassrick, *The Rocky Mountains: A Vision for Artists in the Nineteenth Century* (Norman: University of Oklahoma Press, Published in Association with the Buffalo Bill Historical Center, 1983), 389, n. 38.

18. Mary Achey to Martha Dartt Maxwell, Napa City, February 27, 1875.

19. James A. Maxwell to Mabel Maxwell, October 7, 1865.

20. Quoted in Woloch, *Women and the American Experience,* 133. For further details, see Sklar, *Catharine Beecher,* 151–67.

21. Martha Dartt Maxwell to Mary Dartt Thompson, June 2, [1878].

22. Martha Dartt Maxwell to Mabel Maxwell, February 22, 1880.

23. James A. Maxwell to Mabel Maxwell, October 7, 1865.

24. James A. Maxwell Will, April 3, 1860, Omaha, Nebraska, Cullen Collection.

25. James A. Maxwell to Mabel Maxwell, January 31, 1864.

26. James A. Maxwell to Martha Dartt Maxwell, April 17, 1864.

27. Mabel Maxwell to Nathan and Mary Dartt Thompson, September 6, 1874.

28. Brace, *Thanks to Abigail,* 83.

29. Martha Dartt Maxwell to Mabel Maxwell, August 27 [1874].

30. Smith-Rosenberg, "Female World of Love and Ritual," 53–76.

31. Ibid., 64.

32. Ibid., 65.

33. Mabel Maxwell to Mary Dartt Thompson, portion of letter written fall 1875.

34. Brace, *Thanks to Abigail,* 90.

35. Ibid., 85.

36. Mabel Maxwell to Martha Dartt Maxwell, February 21, 1875.

37. Will H. Tibbals, Oberlin teacher, to Martha Dartt Maxwell, [c. 1875]. Tibbals (1848–1911) received his A.B. degree from Oberlin in 1875. He was probably a student teacher, as his name does not appear on the list of former faculty. Information provided by W. E. Bigglestone, Oberlin College Archives, March 22, 1985.

38. Martha Dartt Maxwell to Mabel Maxwell, September 26, 1875.

39. Mabel Maxwell to Martha Dartt Maxwell, January 24, 1875. See also Brace, *Thanks to Abigail,* 82.

40. Mabel Maxwell to Martha Dartt Maxwell, November 1, 1874.

41. Martha Dartt Maxwell to Mabel Maxwell, October 28, 1874.

42. Martha Dartt Maxwell to Mabel Maxwell, November 9, 1874.

43. Martha Dartt Maxwell to Mabel Maxwell, September 8, 1874; December 8 [1874].

44. Brace, *Thanks to Abigail*, 82. The daughter was Caroline Maxwell Rust.

45. Mabel Maxwell to Martha Dartt Maxwell, November 21, 1874; Martha Dartt Maxwell to Mabel Maxwell, December 8 [1874].

46. Brace, *Thanks to Abigail*, 83.

47. Ibid., 94–95.

48. Ibid., 90.

CHAPTER 9

Portions of this chapter were first published as "Colorado Celebrates the Centennial, 1876," *The Colorado Magazine* 53 (Spring 1976):129–52.

1. U.S., Centennial Commission, International Exhibition, 1876, *Reports*, vol. 2, *Reports of the President, Secretary, and Executive Committee*, Appendix C, 102 (hereinafter cited as Centennial Commission *Reports*). This was the official name of the event; it was commonly called either the "Centennial Exhibition" or the "Centennial Exposition." See the "Semantic Note" in John Maass, *The Glorious Enterprise: The Centennial Exhibition of 1876 and H. J. Schwarzmann, Architect-in-Chief*, History in the Arts (Watkins Glen, N.Y.: Published for the Institute for the Study of Universal History through Arts and Artifacts by the American Life Foundation, 1973), 6:6.

2. The literature on the Centennial is extensive; a good guide is Julia Finette Davis, "International Expositions, 1851–1900," *American Association of Architectural Bibliographers, Papers* (Charlottesville, Va.: Published for the American Association of Architectural Bibliographers by the University Press of Virginia, 1967), 4:74–82. Representative contemporary accounts include *Frank Leslie's Historical Register of the United States Centennial Exposition, 1876* (New York: Frank Leslie's Publishing House, 1877; reprinted New York: Paddington Press, 1974), James D. McCabe, *The Illustrated History of the Centennial Exhibition* (Philadelphia: National Publishing Co., 1876), and J. S. Ingram, *The Centennial Exposition, Described and Illustrated* (Philadelphia: Hubbard Bros., 1876). Recent works include Lynn Vincent Cheney, "1876: The Eagle Screams," *American Heritage* 15 (April 1974):15–35, 98–99 and "1876, Its Artifacts and Atti-

tudes, Returns to Life at Smithsonian," *Smithsonian* 7 (May 1976):37–47, and the excellent catalog published in conjunction with the Smithsonian Institution's recreation of the Centennial in microcosm, Robert C. Post, ed., *1876, A Centennial Exhibition* (Washington, D.C.: National Museum of History and Technology, Smithsonian Institution, 1976). Lally Weymouth, *America in 1876: The Way We Were* (New York: Vintage Books, 1976) evokes the general scene, as does Dee Brown, *The Year of the Century, 1876* (New York: Charles Scribner's Sons, 1966).

3. Martha Dartt Maxwell to Julia Ward Howe (draft), March 15, 1875; Martha Dartt Maxwell to Spencer Baird, October 27, 1875, Record Unit 52, Assistant Secretary (Spencer F. Baird), 1850–1877, Incoming Correspondence, vol. 198, p. 465, box 51, Smithsonian Archives.

4. Mary Frances Cordato, "Toward a New Century: Women and the Philadelphia Centennial Exhibition, 1876," *Pennsylvania Magazine of History and Biography* 107 (January 1983):113–35, especially 114–15. See also Warner, "Women Inventors at the Centennial," 102–3, and "The Women's Pavilion," in Post, ed., *1876, A Centennial Exhibition*, 162–73.

5. Martha Dartt Maxwell to Spencer Baird, October 27, 1875; *Saturday Mercury* (Crawfordsville, Ind.), July 29, 1876, clipping in United States Centennial Commission, Newspaper Clippings Books, 1872–1877, 16:54, Philadelphia City Archives, Philadelphia, Pennsylvania (hereinafter cited as Centennial Clippings, with volume and page number).

6. *Boulder County News*, May 14, 1875.

7. Spencer Baird to Martha Dartt Maxwell, October 19, 1875, Record Unit 53, Assistant Secretary Spencer F. Baird, 1850–1877, Outgoing Correspondence, v. 58, p. 298, box 18, Smithsonian Archives. Baird described the proposed exhibition in 1875 as one that would show, first, "all the species capable of any economical application to the wants of mankind, and, secondly, such forms as have special interest to the naturalist." *Annual Report of the Board of Regents of the Smithsonian Institution, Showing the Operations, Expenditures, and Conditions of the Institution for the Year 1875* (Washington, D.C.: Government Printing Office, 1876), 63. For a general account of the Government Building, see H. Craig Miner, "The United States Government Building at the Centennial Exhibition, 1874–77," *Prologue* 4 (Winter 1972):202–18.

8. Martha Dartt Maxwell to Spencer Baird, October 27, 1875.

9. Spencer Baird to Martha Dartt Maxwell, November 2, 1875, Record Unit 53, Assistant Secretary Spencer F. Baird, 1850–1877, Outgoing Correspondence, v. 58, p. 467, box 18, Smithsonian Archives.

10. For details on the negotiations and the agreement, see Benson, "Colorado Celebrates the Centennial, 1876," 133–34. Kansas' participation in the Centennial is described in Joseph W. Snell, "Kansas and the 1876 United States Centennial," *Kansas Historical Quarterly* 40 (Autumn 1974):337–48.

11. Martha Dartt Maxwell to Mary Dartt Thompson, February 27, 1876. On Richmond and Decatur, see Benson, "Colorado Celebrates the Centennial, 1876," 135–36.

12. Dartt, *On the Plains*, 205–6; the quotation is from p. 206.

13. Ibid., 206–9.

14. *Philadelphia Press*, August 11, 1876, Centennial Clippings, 17:208.

15. Nathan Meeker, "The Centennial of 1876," December 7, 1876, 21–22, Nathan Meeker Papers, Colorado Historical Society, Denver. The legislation that provided for the holding of the Centennial authorized the creation of the United States Centennial Commission, to consist of one delegate from each state and territory appointed by the president on nomination of the respective governors; alternate commissioners were to be appointed in the same manner.

16. Dartt, *On the Plains*, 6–7.

17. Undated clipping from *Forest and Stream*, Maxwell Scrapbook, 61.

18. Dartt, *On the Plains*, 8.

19. "The Colorado Naturalist," *New Century for Women*, undated clipping in Maxwell Scrapbook, 53.

20. *Evening Star*, Philadelphia, November 3 [1876], clipping in Maxwell Scrapbook, 65.

21. *Kansas at the Centennial: Report of the Centennial Managers to the Legislature of the State of Kansas. . . .* (Topeka: Geo. W. Martin, Kansas Publishing House, 1877), 273.

22. *Philadelphia Press*, August 19, 1876, 59.

23. "Characteristics of the International Fair:IV," *Atlantic Monthly* 38 (October 1876):500.

24. Dartt, *On the Plains*, 211.

25. "Mrs. Maxwell's Rocky Mountain Museum," *Harper's Bazar*, November 11, 1876, clipping in Maxwell Scrapbook, 49; "Martha A. Maxwell: The Colorado Huntress and Naturalist," *Phrenological Journal* 62 (November 1876):349–53; "The Colorado Naturalist," *New Century for Women*, undated clipping in Maxwell Scrapbook, 53. For examples of newspaper articles, see Maxwell Scrapbook, 49–76, and *Centennial Clippings, passim.*

26. Unidentified clipping in Maxwell Scrapbook, 72.

27. Ann E. McDowell, "Women's Department," *Sunday Republic,* August 13, 1876, clipping in Maxwell Scrapbook, 74; undated clipping from *Saturday Evening Post,* Maxwell Scrapbook, 67; undated clipping from *People's Journal,* Maxwell Scrapbook, 60; undated clipping from *Philadelphia Times,* Maxwell Scrapbook, 59; *Daily Miners' Journal,* August 4, 1876, clipping in Maxwell Scrapbook, 58.

28. Undated clipping from *Forest and Stream,* Maxwell Scrapbook, 61; *Philadelphia Press,* May 31, 1876, clipping in Maxwell Scrapbook, 61; *Weekly Alta California and San Francisco Times,* undated clipping, Maxwell Scrapbook, 50.

29. *Philadelphia Press,* August 11, 1876, clipping in Maxwell Scrapbook, 56; *People's Journal,* undated clipping in Maxwell Scrapbook, 60.

30. "Mrs. Maxwell's Rocky Mountain Museum," *Harper's Bazar,* November 11, 1876, Maxwell Scrapbook, 49; *Philadelphia Press,* May 31, 1876, Maxwell Scrapbook, 61.

31. Clipping in Maxwell Papers (not in scrapbook) identified in Martha's hand: "From Washington Chronicle."

32. Undated note, Maxwell Papers. Words italicized in angle brackets were crossed out and the following word substituted.

33. Martha Dartt Maxwell to Mary Dartt Thompson, September 2, 1876. The clipping is from the *American Register,* which had offices in Paris and London, Maxwell Scrapbook, 55.

34. Cordato, "Toward a New Century," 123.

35. Scott, "Ever-Widening Circle," 65.

36. *Philadelphia Evening Star,* June 10, 1876, Maxwell Scrapbook, 57.

37. Anne E. McDowell, "Women's Department," *Sunday Republic,* August 13, 1876, Maxwell Scrapbook, 74.

38. *Philadelphia Press,* July 11, 1876, Maxwell Scrapbook, 73.

39. See McDowell, "Women's Department," and "The Colorado Naturalist," *New Century for Women.*

40. Dartt, *On the Plains,* 118–19.

41. The presentation remarks, dated July 28, 1876, together with Martha's response, are in the Cullen Collection. She first wrote "dictated by a love of science," then changed the word to "directed." The ceremony was reported in "Presentation of a Gun to Mrs. Maxwell," letter from "Kansas" dated July 28, 1876, in *Boulder County News,* clipping in Maxwell Scrapbook, 62.

42. Centennial Commission, *Reports,* vol. 8, *Reports and Awards, Groups XXVII–XXXVI, and Collective Exhibits,* 611.

43. Centennial Commission, *Reports,* vol. 3, *Reports and Awards, Groups I and II,* iii–v; *Kansas at the Centennial,* 37; Maass, *Glorious Enterprise,* 116.

44. Meeker, "The Centennial of 1876," 23.

45. Letter from Carol M. Spawn, Manuscript/Archives Librarian, September 17, 1984; Warner, *Graceanna Lewis,* 98.

46. Ingersoll later contributed articles to *Scribner's Monthly* and wrote *Knocking Round the Rockies* (1883) and *Crest of the Continent* (1885). Ewan and Ewan, *Biographical Dictionary of Rocky Mountain Naturalists,* 113–14; Bartlett, *Great Surveys,* 105–6.

47. Ernest Ingersoll, "New Shells from Colorado," in "General Notes: Zoology," *American Naturalist* 10 (December 1876):745 (copy in Maxwell Scrapbook). The listing was also published, in less detail and with some variations, as a letter to the editor entitled "New Land Shells from Colorado," September 1, in *Forest and Stream* 7 (September 7, 1876):68 (copy in Maxwell Scrapbook).

48. Ingersoll, "New Land Shells from Colorado," 68.

49. Ingersoll, "New Shells from Colorado," 746; "Special Report on the Mollusca," *Bulletin of the United States Geological and Geographical Survey of the Territories,* no. 2, Second Series (Washington, D.C.: Government Printing Office, 1875):125–42.

50. Ingersoll, "New Shells from Colorado," 746–47.

51. Sellers, *Mr. Peale's Museum,* 26–28, 162.

52. Frederic A. Lucas, *The Story of Museum Groups,* American Museum of Natural History, Guide Leaflet Series no. 53, 4th ed. (January 1926):3–11 (reprinted from *American Museum Journal,* 1914); Dolph, "Bringing Wildlife to Millions," 306–10.

53. Coues, *Key to North American Birds,* quoted in Dolph, "Bringing Wildlife to Millions," 284.

54. See, for example, Dolph, "Bringing Wildlife to Millions," 196; Kohlstedt, "Henry A. Ward," 654.

55. Hornaday, *Taxidermy and Zoological Collecting,* 231.

56. Hornaday, "Masterpieces of American Taxidermy," 3–17; the quotation is from p. 3.

57. Undated draft of letter from Mary Dartt Thompson to Junius Henderson, accompanied by a draft of her letter to Hornaday, Maxwell Papers.

58. Frederic S. Webster, "The Birth of Habitat Bird Groups," *Annals of the Carnegie Museum* 30 (September 1945):97–111; the quotation is from p. 100.

59. A. E. Parr, "The Habitat Group," *Curator* 2 (1959):107–28.

60. Dartt, *On the Plains*, 22–23, 114–15.

61. Lucas to Mary Dartt Thompson, January 4, 1923. Lucas had been at Ward's from 1871 to 1882, then at the U.S. National Museum and the Brooklyn Institute of Arts and Sciences before serving as the director of the American Museum of Natural History (1911–23). Dolph, "Bringing Wildlife to Millions," 722.

62. Dolph, "Bringing Wildlife to Millions," 140.

63. Hornaday, "Masterpieces of American Taxidermy," 5–6; Webster, "Birth of Habitat Bird Groups," 106–7.

64. Junius Henderson, "A Pioneer Venture in Habitat Grouping," *Proceedings of the American Association of Museums* 9 (1915):89–90.

65. Martha outlined the terms of the agreement in letters to T. O. Saunders, February 6, 1877; Henry Pettit [March 1877], and to William M. Clark, September 18, 1877 (drafts or copies in Maxwell Papers). See also Martha Dartt Maxwell to Mabel Maxwell, April 19, 1876, and Meeker, "The Centennial of 1876," 22.

66. Martha Dartt Maxwell to Henry Pettit [March 1877], draft or copy. The *Philadelphia Sunday Times* also reported that a man named E. C. Norris had hired photographers to pose as workmen and thus gain access to the exhibit in order to photograph it and sell the views. Reprinted in *Denver Times*, undated clipping, Maxwell Scrapbook, 62.

67. Martha Dartt Maxwell to Mary Dartt Thompson, September 2, 1876.

68. Martha Dartt Maxwell to Nathan Thompson, September 30, 1876.

69. Brace, *Thanks to Abigail*, 93–94.

70. Martha Dartt Maxwell to Nathan Thompson, September 30, 1876.

71. Martha Dartt Maxwell to Mabel Maxwell, September 23, 1876.

72. Martha Dartt Maxwell to Mabel Maxwell, October 29, 1876.

73. Martha Dartt Maxwell to Mary Dartt Thompson, [August 1876].

74. Spencer Baird to Nathan Meeker, November 16, 1876, Cullen Collection.

75. Agreement between Alvin O. Buck and John Gardiner and Martha Dartt Maxwell, November 24, 1876, Maxwell Papers. I have so far been unable to locate further information about Buck and Gardiner.

76. Martha Dartt Maxwell to Mabel Maxwell, December 1, 1876; *Evening Star*, Washington, December 21, 1876.

77. *Chronicle*, December 20, 1876, Maxwell Scrapbook, 73.

78. *Gazette,* Washington, December 24, 1876, Maxwell Scrapbook, 98.

79. Martha Dartt Maxwell to Mabel Maxwell, December 28, 1876.

80. Martha Dartt Maxwell to Mary Dartt Thompson, January 6, 1877.

81. Martha Dartt Maxwell to Mabel Maxwell, February 7, 1876 [1877].

82. Martha Dartt Maxwell to Mary Dartt Thompson, February 18, 1877.

83. Martha Dartt Maxwell to Mary Dartt Thompson, January 6, 1877; *Evening Star,* Washington, January 3, 1877.

84. Martha Dartt Maxwell to Mary Dartt Thompson, February 18, 1877.

85. Martha Dartt Maxwell to Mary Dartt Thompson, January 6, 1877.

86. In an undated list, Martha itemized $413.80 in expenses, including $390.00 for board for six months and two weeks at $60.00 per month, and "Damage to collection in consequence of imperfect roof of K. & Co. Building $50.00." Of this, she stated that Colorado, through the commissioners, had paid her $80.00 in May and June (list with note, "Duplicate of what was sent to Jim [Maxwell]," Maxwell Papers). The finances of the Centennial Commission are difficult to unravel. I was unable to locate records in the Colorado State Archives to shed light on this issue; as Gov. John Routt pointed out in his message to the Colorado General Assembly in November 1876, the act of February 1876 "does not require the commissioners to make report of their expenditures or transactions, hence I am not officially informed in regard to what they have done (*Message of His Excellency, John L. Routt, Governor of Colorado, to the First General Assembly of the State: Delivered November 3, 1876,* 1876, 15).

87. Martha Dartt Maxwell to Mabel Maxwell, December 28, 1876; January 2, 1877; January 23, 1877; February 7, 1876 [1877].

88. Martha Dartt Maxwell to Mabel Maxwell, February 7, 1876 [1877].

89. Ibid.

90. Martha Dartt Maxwell to Mabel Maxwell, December 1876.

91. Martha Dartt Maxwell to Mabel Maxwell, October 20, 1875.

92. Brace, *Thanks to Abigail,* 95–96; Woody, *History of Women's Education,* 2:245.

93. Martha Dartt Maxwell to Mary Dartt Thompson, [August 1876].

94. James A. Maxwell to Martha Dartt Maxwell, November 22, 1876, Cullen Collection.

95. P. T. Barnum to Martha Dartt Maxwell, December 15, 1876. Barnum's visit was reported in a newspaper article entitled "Norton's Intelligencer: Centennial Jottings," undated clipping, Maxwell Scrapbook, 64.

CHAPTER 10

1. Martha Dartt Maxwell to Mary Dartt Thompson, January 6, 1877; February 18, 1877.

2. Agreement between Alvin O. Buck and John Gardiner and Martha Dartt Maxwell, November 24, 1876, Maxwell Papers.

3. Martha Dartt Maxwell to Mary Dartt Thompson, January 6, 1877.

4. A number of recent works discuss women as authors; for a summary and bibliographical guide, see Woloch, *Women and the American Experience*, 131–36, 149–50. In addition to the works by Mary Dartt cited elsewhere, for examples of her poems, see *Baraboo Republic*, July 26, 1865; August 8, 1866; December 5, 1866; December 17, 1866; June 5, 1867; September 25, 1867.

5. Melder, *Beginnings of Sisterhood*, 31–32; Smith-Rosenberg, "Female World of Love and Ritual," 62–64.

6. Smith-Rosenberg, "Female World of Love and Ritual," 62–63.

7. Martha Dartt Maxwell to Mary Dartt Thompson, September 2, 1876; Mary Dartt Thompson to Martha Dartt Maxwell, April 15, 1877.

8. Brace, *Thanks to Abigail*, 25.

9. Martha Dartt Maxwell to Mabel Maxwell, January 23, 1877.

10. Martha Dartt Maxwell to Mary Dartt Thompson, February 18, 1877.

11. Robert Ridgway to Martha Dartt Maxwell, May 28, 1877. Audubon Ridgway, the Ridgways' only child, was born on May 15, 1877. He died of pneumonia on February 22, 1901. Harris, "Robert Ridgway," 35.

12. Martha Dartt Maxwell to Robert Ridgway, May 29, 1877, Record Unit 105, Division of Birds, circa 1854–1959, Records, folder 6, box 22, Smithsonian Archives. See also Robert Ridgway to Martha Dartt Maxwell, April 24, 1877, Maxwell Papers, and Martha Dartt Maxwell to Robert Ridgway, April 26, 1877, Record Unit 105, folder 6, box 22, Smithsonian Archives.

13. "Mrs. Maxwell's Colorado Museum: Catalogue of the Birds," *Field and Forest* 2 (May 1877):195–98; (June 1877):208–14; "Mrs. Max-

well's Colorado Museum: Additional Notes," 3 (July 1877):11. See also Robert Ridgway to Martha Dartt Maxwell, April 24, 1877, Maxwell Papers; Martha Dartt Maxwell to Robert Ridgway, April 26, 1877, Record Unit 105, folder 6, box 22, Smithsonian Archives; Robert Ridgway to Martha Dartt Maxwell, May 28, 1877, Maxwell Papers.

14. Robert Ridgway to Martha Dartt Maxwell, May 31, 1877. Joel A. Allen (1838–1921) served as the curator of birds at the Harvard Museum from 1867 to 1885 and was then associated with the American Museum of Natural History (Ewan and Ewan, *Biographical Dictionary of Rocky Mountain Naturalists*, 4). Allen's comments are found in "Sexual, Individual, and Geographical Variation in Leucosticte Tephrocotis," *Bulletin of the United States Geological and Geographical Survey of the Territories*, vol. 2, no. 4 (Washington, D.C.: Government Printing Office, 1876), 345–50; Robert Ridgway's response, " 'Sexual, Individual and Geographical Variation' in the Genus Leucosticte," appeared in *Field and Forest* 2 (September 1876):37–43.

15. Robert Ridgway to Martha Dartt Maxwell, June 20, 1877.

16. Cutright and Brodhead, *Elliott Coues*, 151–55.

17. Coues's Colorado journey is described in Michael J. Brodhead, "A Naturalist in the Colorado Rockies, 1876," *The Colorado Magazine* 52 (Summer 1975):185–99. See also Cutright and Brodhead, *Elliott Coues*, 193–96.

18. Elliott Coues, "Notice of Mrs. Maxwell's Exhibit of Colorado Mammals," in Dartt, *On the Plains*, 217; Martha Dartt Maxwell to Robert Ridgway, May 29, 1877, Record Unit 105, Division of Birds, circa 1854–1959, folder 6, box 22, Smithsonian Archives.

19. Martha Dartt Maxwell to Mabel Maxwell, March 22, 1877. See also Martha Dartt Maxwell to Mary Dartt Thompson, February 18, 1877, and March 2, 1877.

20. *Frank Leslie's Historical Register*, 20; McCabe, *Illustrated History of the Centennial Exhibition*, 909–17.

21. Undated clipping from *The Exhibitor*, Maxwell Scrapbook, 97. See also additional clippings, Maxwell Scrapbook, 98–100.

22. Undated clipping from *The Exhibitor*, Maxwell Scrapbook, 98.

23. Martha Dartt Maxwell to Robert Ridgway, May 29, 1877, Record Unit 105, folder 6, box 22, Smithsonian Archives.

24. Martha Dartt Maxwell to Mary Dartt Thompson, May 1, 1877; see also Mary Dartt Thompson to Martha Dartt Maxwell, March 2, 1877, for the description of the terms she had requested.

25. *New York Times*, October 22, 1877, p. 8. The expedition had been conceived by James O. Woodruff, a native of Auburn, New York,

who had run away to sea and later gone to Indianapolis, and Daniel Macauley, a former mayor of Indianapolis.

26. Martha Dartt Maxwell to Robert Ridgway, July 1, 1877, Record Unit 105, folder 6, box 22, Smithsonian Archives.

27. Martha Dartt Maxwell to Mabel Maxwell, August 29, 1877.

28. The starting date was postponed several times, and the expedition was finally abandoned after Woodruff's death. For further details, see *New York Times*, December 2, 1878, p. 2, and July 12, 1879, p. 5.

29. Martha Dartt Maxwell to Mabel Maxwell, December 28, 1876; Martha Dartt Maxwell to William M. Clark, Colorado Secretary of State, September 18, 1877 (draft).

30. Josiah Dartt to Martha Dartt Maxwell, July 7, 1877; August 1, 1877; August 29, 1877.

31. Martha Dartt Maxwell to William M. Clark, September 18, 1877 (draft).

32. Josiah Dartt to Martha Dartt Maxwell, July 7, 1877; James A. Maxwell to Martha Dartt Maxwell, August 15, 1877, Cullen Collection. The 1877 minutes of the Board of Regents apparently contain no references to the museum (letter from Cassandra M. Volpe, Western Historical Collections and University Archives, University of Colorado Libraries, Boulder, October 17, 1984).

33. Martha Dartt Maxwell to "Dear Ones" (Mary Dartt Thompson and family), [September 8, 1877]. For biographical information on McCormick, see DAB 11:610–11.

34. Martha Dartt Maxwell to Henry Moore Teller, October 18, 1877, Henry Moore Teller Collection, Western History Department, Denver Public Library, Denver, Colorado.

35. Martha Dartt Maxwell to Mary Dartt Thompson, May 1, 1877.

36. Martha Dartt Maxwell to Mabel Maxwell, April 3, 1877.

37. Martha Dartt Maxwell to Mary Dartt Thompson, February 6, 1878.

38. Robert Clarke, *Ellen Swallow: The Woman Who Founded Ecology* (Chicago: Follett Publishing Co., 1973), 15, 43, 55–65.

39. *Massachusetts Institute of Technology, Thirteenth Annual Catalogue of the Officers and Students, with a Statement of the Courses of Instruction, 1877–1878* (Boston: Press of A. A. Kingman, 1877), 20.

40. Janet Wilson James, "Richards, Ellen Henrietta Swallow," *Notable American Women*, 3:143–46; Rossiter, *Women Scientists in America*, 67–69; Clarke, *Ellen Swallow*, 52–53.

41. Martha Dartt Maxwell to Mary Dartt Thompson, [February? 1878].

42. Martha Dartt Maxwell to Mary Dartt Thompson, February 6, 1878.

43. Martha Dartt Maxwell to Mary Dartt Thompson, February 12 [1878].

44. Martha Dartt Maxwell to Josiah Dartt, [early March 1878]. On Agassiz see Edward Lurie, "Agassiz, Jean Louis Rodolphe," *Dictionary of Scientific Biography*, 1:72–74.

45. Martha Dartt Maxwell told Josiah Dartt that she was spending "most of my time on mineralogy," while the *Boulder County News*, interviewing her the next year on a brief visit to Colorado, reported that she had taken "natural history, chemistry and assaying." Martha Dartt Maxwell to Josiah Dartt, [early March 1878]; *Boulder County News*, February 14, 1879, clipping, Maxwell Scrapbook, 103.

46. Martha Dartt Maxwell to Mary Dartt Thompson, [February? 1878].

47. Martha quoted Hyatt's comments in a letter to Mary Dartt Thompson, March 24, [1878].

48. Alpheus Hyatt (1838–1902), an 1862 graduate of the Lawrence Scientific School of Harvard, was professor of zoology and paleontology at MIT until 1888 and professor of biology at Boston University from 1877 until his death. Along with E. D. Cope, he was a leading proponent of the neo-Lamarckian theory of evolution. Stephen Jay Gould, "Hyatt, Alpheus," *Dictionary of Scientific Biography*, 6:613–14.

49. Martha Dartt Maxwell to Josiah Dartt, [early March 1878].

50. Martha Dartt Maxwell to Mary Dartt Thompson, March 24, [1878].

51. Martha Dartt Maxwell to Mary Dartt Thompson, [February? 1878].

52. Martha Dartt Maxwell to Mary Dartt Thompson, February 6, 1878; February 12, [1878]; March 24, [1878]. Martha reported the eighty-dollar figure for two days of school for eight months in an undated letter to Mary Dartt Thompson of early 1878; according to the 1877–78 MIT catalog, the tuition was two hundred dollars per year for regular students, one hundred and twenty-five dollars for one-half year or "any less fraction." Non-degree students paid the full fees, "but when a few branches only are pursued, and the time for instruction is limited, some deduction may be made." MIT, *Thirteenth Annual Catalogue*, 57.

53. Martha Dartt Maxwell to Mary Dartt Thompson, June 2, [1878].

54. Martha Dartt Maxwell to Mary Dartt Thompson, [Spring 1878].

55. Martha Dartt Maxwell to Mary Dartt Thompson, February 6, 1878.

56. Karen J. Blair, *The Clubwoman as Feminist: True Womanhood Redefined, 1868–1914* (New York: Holmes and Meier, 1980), 31–38.

57. Martha Dartt Maxwell to Mary Dartt Thompson, March 24, [1878].

58. James A. Maxwell to Martha Dartt Maxwell, August 15, 1877, Cullen Collection.

59. Brace, *Thanks to Abigail*, 98. See also Martha Dartt Maxwell to Mary Dartt Thompson, [February? 1878].

60. James A. Maxwell to Martha Dartt Maxwell, January 22, 1878, Cullen Collection.

61. James A. Maxwell to Martha Dartt Maxwell, July 28, 1878, Cullen Collection.

62. James A. Maxwell to Martha Dartt Maxwell, August 24, 1878, Cullen Collection.

63. Martha Dartt Maxwell to "Dearest Ones" (Mary Dartt Thompson and family), September 8, [1878], continuing letter of September 6.

64. Martha Dartt Maxwell to Mary Dartt Thompson [August 1878].

65. Martha Dartt Maxwell to Mary Dartt Thompson, June 2, [1878]. For an example of Dr. Clisby's advertisement, see *Woman's Journal*, January 5, 1878, p. 8.

66. Nathan Meeker to Martha Dartt Maxwell, June 24, 1878.

67. Still the best general account is Marshall Sprague, *Massacre: The Tragedy at White River* (Boston: Little, Brown and Co., 1957).

68. Martha Dartt Maxwell to Mary Dartt Thompson, September 1, [1878].

69. J. Clarence Hersey to Mary Dartt Thompson, July 15, 1908.

70. Martha Dartt Maxwell to Mary Dartt Thompson, October 18, 1878.

71. The manuscript entitled "A Novel Career: How Mrs. Maxwell Made Her Centennial Collection" is now in the Boulder Historical Society, Boulder, Colorado.

72. Martha Dartt Maxwell to Mary Dartt Thompson, May 1, 1877.

73. Martha Dartt Maxwell to "Dear Ones," [September 8, 1877].

74. Martha Dartt Maxwell to Mary Dartt Thompson, April 4, [1878].

75. Ernest Isaacs, "Wells, Charlotte Fowler," *Notable American Women*, 3:560–61; John R. Davies, *Phrenology, Fad and Science: A 19th Century American Crusade* (New Haven: Yale University Press, 1955; reprint ed. Archon Books, 1971), 53–55.

76. C. Fowler Wells to Martha Dartt Maxwell, April 25, 1878.

77. J. Milner, D. Appleton and Co., to Martha Dartt Maxwell, May 10, 1878.

78. John A. Tebbel, *A History of Book Publishing in the United States*, 4 vols. (New York: Bowker, 1972–81) vol. 2, *The Expansion of an Industry, 1865–1919*, 424–25.

79. The contract between Martha Dartt Maxwell and Mary Dartt Thompson and Claxton, Remsen and Haffelfinger is in the Maxwell Papers. Information on the publishing practices of the day is from Tebbel, *Expansion of an Industry*, 134. For details on the work of making the plates, see Martha Dartt Maxwell to "Dear Ones," dated "July-August 4," [1878] and Martha Dartt Maxwell to Mary Dartt Thompson, September 1, [1878].

80. Martha Dartt Maxwell to "Dear Ones," September 6, [1878].

81. To complicate matters further, the engraved portraits of Martha Maxwell found in some copies are of two different images. Four copies of the book are in the collections of the Colorado Historical Society, two in the Western History Department of the Denver Public Library, and one each at the Kansas State Historical Society, Topeka; the Sutro Library, San Francisco; and Smith College (available on microfilm in The History of Women Collection, Research Publications, Inc., New Haven, Conn., reel 413, no. 3007). The copy in the Sutro Library belonged to Mrs. J. Clarence Hersey and has Hersey's notes and errata. On editions see Tebbel, *Expansion of an Industry*, 134–35, who reports an 1885 interview with publisher William Lee of Lee and Shepard. Lee stated that "a thousand copies of a 400-page book was considered an edition," and that "a book would have to sell at least three editions of a thousand copies each" to turn a profit.

82. Dartt, *On the Plains*, 7–9.

83. Ibid., 15–16.

84. Ibid., 215.

85. The inscription went through at least two drafts as Martha struggled to find just the right wording. In reverse direction, across a letter dated in September 1877, she wrote: "To Spencer F. Baird the courteous gentleman as well as distinguished naturalist this sketch of an amateur's work is respectfully dedicated" and "To Spencer F. Baird the Friend of Natures Friend this sketch of an amateur's work is Respectfully Dedicated." Martha Dartt Maxwell to "Dear Ones," [September 8, 1877]. In the manuscript version of "A Novel Career" in the Boulder Historical Society, it reads: "To Spencer F. Baird, the Friend of Nature's Friends as well as distinguished naturalist this sketch of an amateur's work is Respectfully Dedicated."

86. Baird to Martha Dartt Maxwell, October 26, 1878, Record Unit 33,

Office of the Secretary (Joseph Henry, Spencer F. Baird, Samuel P. Lang-
ley), 1865–1891, Outgoing Correspondence, v. 72, p. 405, box 22,
Smithsonian Archives.

87. Coues, "Notice of Mrs. Maxwell's Exhibit of Colorado Mammals," in Dartt, *On the Plains*, 217.

88. Elliott Coues, *Fur-Bearing Animals: A Monograph of North American
Mustelidae*, United States Geological and Geographical Survey of the Territories, Miscellaneous Publications, no. 8 (Washington, D.C.: Government Printing Office, 1877), 149–50.

89. Ibid., 150–51.

90. Coues, "Notice of Mrs. Maxwell's Exhibit," *On the Plains*, 220.
For the description of the discovery of the ferrets, see *On the Plains*, 133–
35. See also Brodhead, "A Naturalist in the Colorado Rockies," 196.

Today the black-footed ferret is even more rare and has at times been
thought to be extinct. Although over the years sightings have been made
in a large region stretching from Canada to Texas and Utah to Nebraska,
in 1983 it was estimated that there may be only sixty ferrets in all of
Wyoming. More are being discovered, however, by scientists who use
radio collars to monitor the small, endangered population. Tim W.
Clark, "Last of the Black-footed Ferrets?" *National Geographic* 163 (June
1983):828–38.

91. Coues, "Notice of Mrs. Maxwell's Exhibit," *On the Plains*, 221;
Brodhead, "A Naturalist in the Colorado Rockies," 196.

92. Coues, *Fur-Bearing Animals*, 151.

93. Brodhead, "A Naturalist in the Colorado Rockies," 197. For a
bibliography of Coues's works, see Cutright and Brodhead, *Elliott Coues*,
439–80. See also Viola S. Schantz, "Mrs. M. A. Maxwell: A Pioneer Mammalogist," *Journal of Mammalogy* 24 (November 17, 1943):464–66.

94. Robert Ridgway, "Mrs. Maxwell's Colorado Museum: Catalogue of the Birds," *On the Plains*, 226–37.

95. Ibid., 226.

96. Ibid., 236; Robert Ridgway, "Mrs. Maxwell's Colorado Museum:
Catalogue of the Birds," *Field and Forest* 2 (June 1877):214. For an account
of the collection of the owls, see *On the Plains*, 132–33. See Bailey and
Niedrach, *Birds of Colorado*, 1:413–14 for further details on "Mrs. Maxwell's Owl."

Scops was the generic name in use at the time, but because it was
later pointed out that the term had been employed to refer to another
bird, around the turn of the century the generic name was changed to
Otus, which had actually predated *Scops* as a name for the screech owls.

Thus the owl, a subspecies of eastern screech owl, is now known as *Otus* (generic name), *asio* (specific or trivial name) *maxwelliae* (subspecific name). Western screech owls are now a separate species, *Otus kennicottii*. Excellent descriptions and pictures of the two species can be found in the *National Geographic Society Field Guide to the Birds of North America* (Washington, D.C.: National Geographic Society, 1983), 242–43. I am greatly indebted to Marion Jenkinson Mengel, adjunct curator of ornithology, Museum of Natural History, University of Kansas, Lawrence, for supplying detailed information on biological nomenclature (letter of November 21, 1984) and to Marianne Ainley of McGill University, Montreal, Quebec, for the reference to the *Field Guide* and for suggesting that I contact Ms. Mengel.

97. Martha Dartt Maxwell to Robert Ridgway, April 26, 1877, Record Unit 105, folder 6, box 22, Smithsonian Archives.

98. Martha Dartt Maxwell to Mary Dartt Thompson, May 1, 1877.

99. Marianne Ainley, McGill University, Montreal, Quebec, "Women in North American Ornithology During the Last Century," paper presented to the first International Conference on the Role of Women in the History of Science, Technology, and Medicine in the Nineteenth and Twentieth Centuries, Veszprem, Hungary, August 1983 (copy in author's possession).

100. Robert Ridgway to A. H. Felger, July 22, 1911.

101. Ewan and Ewan, *Biographical Dictionary of Rocky Mountain Naturalists*, 4.

102. J. A. Allen, "A Woman's Work as a Naturalist," *Bulletin of the Nuttall Ornithological Club* 4 (1879):113.

103. Undated loose clippings in the Maxwell Papers. The reviews were collected by Claxton and sent to Martha.

104. J. W. Hartley, Claxton, to Martha Dartt Maxwell, October 16, 1878.

105. Copies of the circular can be found along with the clippings in the Maxwell Papers.

106. Martha Dartt Maxwell to Mary Dartt Thompson, November 28, 1878.

107. James A. Maxwell to Martha Dartt Maxwell, November 10, 1878, Cullen Collection.

108. Martha Dartt Maxwell to Mary Dartt Thompson, November 28, 1878.

109. I am indebted to Marianne Ainley in letters of March 25 and June 23, 1985, for helping me clarify Martha's importance as a woman naturalist.

110. Spencer Baird to Nathan Meeker, November 16, 1876, Cullen Collection.

111. Allen, "Woman's Work as a Naturalist," 113.

CHAPTER 11

1. Martha Dartt Maxwell to James A. Maxwell, November 29, 1878.

2. Martha Dartt Maxwell to Mary Dartt Thompson, November 7, 1878.

3. [Martha Dartt Maxwell to Mary Dartt Thompson, November 1878], letter fragment in Maxwell Papers.

4. Sayre, "Hal Sayre—Fifty-Niner," 169; *Boulder County News*, June 5, 1874.

5. Brace, *Thanks to Abigail*, 103.

6. Martha Dartt Maxwell to "Dear Ones," February 9, 1879. See also Amy Sanford Dartt to Mary Dartt Thompson, January 22, 1879, and Josiah Dartt to Mary Dartt Thompson, February 2, 1879.

7. Martha Dartt Maxwell to "Dear Ones," February 9, 1879.

8. *Boulder County News*, October 6, 1871; October 13, 1871; November 1, 1872; Dartt, *On the Plains*, 187; Josiah Dartt to Mary Dartt Thompson, July 14, 1878; August 1, 1877.

9. Josiah Dartt to Mary Dartt Thompson, July 14, 1878.

10. Note by Mary Dartt Thompson, December 1, 1930, on an undated letter written by Mabel Maxwell from Boulder; Amy Sanford Dartt to Mary Dartt Thompson, December 16, 1879; Amy Sanford Dartt to Elizabeth Dartt Sayre, February 17, 1880.

11. Martha Dartt Maxwell to "Dear Ones," February 9, 1879. See also Martha Dartt Maxwell to Mary Dartt Thompson, February 28, 1879.

12. Martha Dartt Maxwell to Mary Dartt Thompson, July 7, 1879.

13. *Frank Leslie's Historical Register*, 87; McCabe, *Illustrated History of the Centennial Exhibition*, 722–23; Ingram, *Centennial Exposition*, 706–8.

14. Thomas J. Schlereth, "The 1876 Centennial: A Model for Comparative American Studies," in Schlereth, ed., *Artifacts and the American Past* (Nashville: American Association for State and Local History, 1980):139–40.

15. Martha Dartt Maxwell to Mary Dartt Thompson, July 7, 1879.

16. Martha Dartt Maxwell to Mary Dartt Thompson, December 3, 1879.

17. Martha Dartt Maxwell to Mary Dartt Thompson, November 19, 1879 (continuing November 2 letter).

18. Martha Dartt Maxwell to Mabel Maxwell, December 19, 1879.

19. Martha Dartt Maxwell to Mary Dartt Thompson, December 3, 1879.

20. Brace, *Thanks to Abigail*, 103.

21. Martha Dartt Maxwell to Mary Dartt Thompson, December 3, 1879.

22. Martha Dartt Maxwell to "Dearest Ones," September 8 [1878].

23. Ibid.; Martha Dartt Maxwell to Mary Dartt Thompson, September 1 [1878]; October 18, 1878.

24. Martha Dartt Maxwell to Mary Dartt Thompson, November 19, 1879 (continuing November 2 letter).

25. Alfred H. Bellot, *History of the Rockaways from the Year 1865 to 1917* (Far Rockaway, N.Y.: Bellot's Histories, 1917), 83–104.

26. *Long Island Weekly Star*, Long Island City, New York, January 23, 1880.

27. Martha Dartt Maxwell to Mary Dartt Thompson, January 12, 1880; [December 1879].

28. Mary Dartt Thompson to Nathan Thompson, January 17, 1880.

29. Ibid.

30. Martha Dartt Maxwell to Mary Dartt Thompson, [December 1879]; February 13, 1880.

31. Martha Dartt Maxwell to Mary Dartt Thompson, March 24, 1880. Along with the description she furnished a detailed diagram in the letter.

32. Charles M. Snyder, *Oswego: From Buckskin to Bustles* (Port Washington, N.Y.: Ira J. Friedman, 1968), 129, 130.

33. Martha Dartt Maxwell to Mary Dartt Thompson, March 7, 1880.

34. Martha Dartt Maxwell to Mary Dartt Thompson, March 12, 1880.

35. Martha Dartt Maxwell to Mary Dartt Thompson, April 2, 1880; see also March 7 and March 12, 1880.

36. Martha Dartt Maxwell to Mary Dartt Thompson, April 2, 1880.

37. Martha Dartt Maxwell to Mary Dartt Thompson, April 23, May 11, 1880.

38. Martha Dartt Maxwell to Mary Dartt Thompson, May 11, 1880.

39. Martha Dartt Maxwell to Cynthia [Westover], October 23, 1880.

40. Martha Dartt Maxwell to Mary Dartt Thompson, September 7 [1880]; Bellot, *History of the Rockaways*, 105.

41. Martha Dartt Maxwell to Cynthia [Westover], October 23, 1880.

42. Martha Dartt Maxwell to "Dear Ones," September 28, 1880.

43. "A Novel Career," 42. All evidence contributes to the inference that Martha composed this section (pp. 38–48 of the manuscript of *On the Plains*); it is in her handwriting and includes a number of words mis-

spelled in her own distinctive way: "consumation," "practicle," "theries."

44. Ibid., 44–45.

45. Martha Dartt Maxwell to Mary Dartt Thompson, January 12, 1880.

46. Mary Dartt Thompson to Nathan Thompson, January 17, 1880.

47. Martha Dartt Maxwell to Mabel Maxwell, February 22, 1880.

48. Martha Dartt Maxwell to Mary Dartt Thompson, February 21 [1880]; printed in part in Brace, *Thanks to Abigail*, 106–8.

49. See, for example, Martha Dartt Maxwell to Mary Dartt Thompson, March 7, 1880; October 14, 1880.

50. Brace, *Thanks to Abigail*, 101. Similarly, the daughter of reformer Frances Wright "found the moral of Fanny's life in her belief that 'the present woman's movement is tempting my sex to man's province to the neglect of its home duties & joys [and] of the rising generation.'" Celia Morris Eckhardt, *Fanny Wright: Rebel in America* (Cambridge: Harvard University Press, 1984), 290.

51. Smith-Rosenberg, "The New Woman as Androgyne," 247–57; the quote is from 257.

52. Elizabeth Cazden, *Antoinette Brown Blackwell: A Biography* (Old Westbury, N.Y.: Feminist Press, 1983), 199–211; the letter to Lucy Stone is quoted on p. 203, and Cazden's statement is on p. 211.

53. Brace, *Thanks to Abigail*, 101.

54. Martha Dartt Maxwell to Mabel Maxwell, June 6, 1878.

55. Martha Dartt Maxwell to Mabel Maxwell, November 12, 1879.

56. Martha Dartt Maxwell to Mabel Maxwell, December 19, 1879.

57. Martha Dartt Maxwell to Mabel Maxwell, February 22, 1880.

58. Brace, *Thanks to Abigail*, 72–73.

59. Martha Dartt Maxwell to Mary Dartt Thompson, November 7, 1878.

60. Born in Michigan in 1849, Brace had received a medical degree from the Hahnneman College in Chicago in 1875. J. Sherman Brace, *Brace Lineage* (Bloomsbury, Pa.: Geo. E. Elwell & Son, 1914), 31.

61. Brace, *Thanks to Abigail*, 104.

62. Ibid., 109.

63. Martha Dartt Maxwell to Amy Sanford Dartt, January 18, 1881.

64. Martha Dartt Maxwell to Mary Dartt Thompson, December 7, 1880.

65. Martha Dartt Maxwell to Mary Dartt Thompson, February 21, 1881; printed also in Brace, *Thanks to Abigail*, 110.

66. Martha Dartt Maxwell to Mary Dartt Thompson, January [1881].
67. Martha Dartt Maxwell to Mabel Maxwell, February 28, 1875.
68. Martha Dartt Maxwell to Mary Dartt Thompson, February 18, 1877.
69. Martha Dartt Maxwell to Mabel Maxwell, October 28, 1880, Cullen Collection.
70. Leach, *True Love and Perfect Union*, 184–85.
71. Martha Dartt Maxwell to Mary Dartt Thompson, December 31, 1880.
72. Carl Degler, *At Odds: Women and the Family in America from the Revolution to the Present* (New York: Oxford University Press, 1980), 14.
73. Ibid., 166.
74. Ibid., 175.
75. Ibid., 385.
76. Warner, *Graceanna Lewis*, 22–23, 80.
77. Quoted in Degler, *At Odds*, 24.
78. Buck, "Lawrence in 1850–1860," 59.
79. Martha Dartt Maxwell to [Mabel Maxwell], October 15, 1880.
80. Martha Dartt Maxwell to Mary Dartt Thompson, December 7, December 31, 1880.
81. Martha Dartt Maxwell to Mary Dartt Thompson, December 7, 1880.
82. Martha Dartt Maxwell to "Dear Ones," July 15, 1878.
83. Martha Dartt Maxwell to Mary Dartt Thompson, February 28, 1879.
84. Martha Dartt Maxwell to Mabel Maxwell, November 23, 1880.
85. Martha Dartt Maxwell to Mary Dartt Thompson, December 7, 1880.
86. Martha Dartt Maxwell to Amy Sanford Dartt, January 18, 1881; Martha Dartt Maxwell to Mary Dartt Thompson, February 22, 1881 (note appended to letter of February 21).
87. Martha Dartt Maxwell to Mary Dartt Thompson, March 2, 1881.
88. Martha Dartt Maxwell to Mabel Maxwell, May 5, 1881; obituary of Josiah Dartt, *Boulder News and Courier*, April 22, 1881.
89. Josiah Dartt to Mary Dartt Thompson, November 14, 1880, December 5, 1880; Martha Dartt Maxwell to Nathan Thompson, May 1, 1881.
90. Martha Dartt Maxwell to Nathan Thompson, May 1, 1881.
91. See letter from Nathan Thompson written from Rockaway Beach just before Martha's death and printed in the *Boulder News and Courier*,

June 10, 1881. The paper reported on May 27 that Mabel had gone to Rockaway Beach and that another teacher had taken over her classes.

92. Brace, *Thanks to Abigail*, 110.

93. Ibid., 111. Mabel states in her autobiography that Martha died at midnight, but in a postcard dated May 31, she wrote that "Mamma passed away this morning between four & five." Mary Dartt Thompson often gave the date of her sister's death as May 30.

94. Brace, *Thanks to Abigail*, 111.

95. Mabel Maxwell to Mary Dartt Thompson, [June 2, 1881]; May 31, 1881. Located at the northeastern end of the peninsula, Woodsburgh later was renamed Woodmere, to avoid confusion with similarly named towns in New York and New Jersey. Later, however, a small development was incorporated as Woodsburgh, thus perpetuating the original name. Bellot, *History of the Rockaways*, 64, 66.

Over a year earlier, Martha had written to Mary that "if some scientific or medical institution could use the cast-off tenement," she would prefer that alternative to burial. Martha Dartt Maxwell to Mary Dartt Thompson, February 21 [1880].

96. See Mabel Maxwell to Mary Dartt Thompson, June 7, June 10 [1881].

97. Mabel Maxwell to Mary Dartt Thompson, June 10 [1881].

98. Brace, *Thanks to Abigail*, 112–13. See Mabel Maxwell to Mary Dartt Thompson, June 7 [1881] for an itemization of the money owed. Part of the letter is printed in Brace, *Thanks to Abigail*, 111.

99. Mabel Maxwell to Elliott Coues, July 26, 1881, typescript furnished by the American Museum of Natural History. No record has been found of Coues's response; see Cutright and Brodhead, *Elliott Coues*, 211.

100. Conveyance signed by DeWitt C. Littlejohn, Oswego County, New York, November 11, 1881, Maxwell Papers.

101. Brace, *Thanks to Abigail*, 115.

102. Ibid., 119.

103. Ibid., 38.

104. J. Clarence Hersey to Mary Dartt Thompson, July 15, 1908.

105. Sally Kohlstedt has suggested dividing nineteenth-century women scientists of the period 1830–1880 into three "generations"— first the independents, next the disseminators or popularizers, and a third generation who chose between amateur activity and a professional career. Aspects of all three "generations" are present, it seems to me, in Martha Maxwell's life and work. See Sally Gregory Kohlstedt, "In from

the Periphery: American Women in Science, 1830–1880," *Signs: Journal of Women in Culture and Society* 4 (Autumn 1978):81–96.

106. *Clear Creek and Boulder Valleys,* 654–59.

107. Brace, *Thanks to Abigail,* 119. A psychoanalyst with the Karen Horney Clinic recently observed: "Often it's the daughter of a highly trained, successful, professional woman who doesn't want to go to college, doesn't want to prepare herself for a career, and wants nothing more than to fulfill the traditional role of her grandmother." Alexandra Symonds, M.D., quoted in Maxine Schnall, *Limits: A Search for New Values* (New York: Clarkson and Potter, 1981), 309.

108. Degler states that "the conflict between self and family, which some women in the 19th century felt and sometimes fought against, still confronted many married women well into the 20th century. In fact it remains today the central, unresolved tension in the life of a woman in the family." *At Odds,* 55.

109. Diary kept during 1860 by Martha Dartt Maxwell, Cullen Collection.

EPILOGUE

1. Haskins, who was listed in city directories as both "Josiah P." and "James P.," was identified as a geologist. His obituary in the *Saratogian,* January 3, 1916, stated that he "was a geologist and naturalist of ability and was considered an authority on such matters." Information supplied by Jean E. Stamm, Saratoga Springs Public Library, Saratoga Springs, New York, November 20, 1984.

2. Brace, *Thanks to Abigail,* 113; copy of agreement dated March 20, 1882, between J. P. Haskins of Saratoga Springs, New York, and H. N. Bradley of Boulder, the coproprietor of the Bradley and McClure dry goods store (*Clear Creek and Boulder Valleys,* 618). The agreement gave Haskins the right to exhibit the collection or offer it for sale. He was not to sell or transfer the collection, however, without obtaining Bradley's consent, and he agreed to insure the collection for at least $1,000.

3. Dated November 28, 1924, the typescript had been in the collections of the Colorado Historical Society since about that time. The account consists of a three-page introduction that briefly discusses Martha Maxwell's life and the Centennial exhibit and an eleven-page description of the fate of the collection afterward. Reproduced here is most of the second part, beginning on page 4 and continuing to the end. When the Maxwell Papers were presented to the Society in 1977, drafts of the typescript in Mary's handwriting were discovered among the letters and other documents; both are now part of that collection.

4. At the time the Thompsons were living in Baltimore, where Nathan Thompson was professor of Latin and Greek at Morgan College (1891–96). Biographical notes, probably typed by one of the Thompson daughters, Maxwell Papers.

5. When Haskins died on January 1, 1916, at the age of eighty-six, his obituary stated that he was "owner of the Saratoga County Museum of Natural History, which for many years has been an exhibit of interest here and which was to be seen in the old Waverley hotel on Broadway until that building was razed several months ago." *Saratogian,* January 3, 1916, copy supplied by Saratoga Springs Public Library.

6. In the Maxwell Papers is a letter from F. W. True, curator of the Department of Mammals at the Smithsonian, to Mary Dartt Thompson dated April 21, 1892. Responding to her request, he provided the address of the Carl E. Akeley Company, taxidermists, in Milwaukee, Wisconsin. (It is not known if she contacted Akeley.) Carl Akeley had studied at Ward's Natural Science Establishment in the 1880s and later was associated with the Field Museum of Natural History and the American Museum of Natural History. Frederic A. Lucas, *Fifty Years of Museum Work* (New York: American Museum of Natural History, 1933), 13n.

7. A copy of the agreement, signed only by Mabel Maxwell Brace, is in the Maxwell Papers. In this document, dated July 5, 1893, Mabel conveyed to Yale "all my right, title and interest in the Natural History Museum known as Mrs. Maxwell's Colorado Collection and now in charge of Dr. Haskins at Saratoga Springs, New York." In return, Mabel directed that the specimens be repaired and "suitably cased and labeled"; that the collection and each individual piece be marked as "The Mrs. Maxwell Collection"; and that all expenses for restoration, shipment, transportation, and the like be paid by Yale. If the conditions were not met, the property would then revert to Mabel.

8. Fred L. Chase (1865–1933), a Boulder native who was an assistant astronomer at Yale, was acting as a go-between in the negotiations. He reported to Mary on December 7, 1893, that Bradley had asked Haskins "what he would regard as a reasonable claim for charges against the collection." Haskins had responded that "he had been to the expense of $1216.09 but would close the matter up on receipt of $950." Fred L. Chase to Mary Dartt Thompson, December 7, 1893, Maxwell Papers. Chase had been graduated from the University of Colorado in 1886. He earned a Ph.D. from Yale in 1891 and remained there as an astronomer until 1913. He then returned to Boulder, where he died in 1933. *Who Was Who in America, I:1897–1942* (Chicago: A. N. Marquis Co., 1942), 213.

9. On December 9, 1893, Chase had given Prof. Othniel C. Marsh of

Yale a copy of the 1882 agreement between Haskins and Bradley (note penciled on copy in Maxwell Papers). Marsh (1831–1899), a Yale professor of paleontology noted for his western paleontological expeditions, had thereafter been actively involved in the negotiations; at one point, probably early in 1894, Chase reported to Mary that Marsh was ready to "push the thing as fast as he can and see what can be done." See undated letter from Fred L. Chase to Mary Dartt Thompson; see also Chase to Mary, December 7, 1893, and January 7, 1893 [1894]. However, as Mary notes, no agreement was reached; Chase thought that perhaps Yale would have moved more quickly if the agreement with Haskins had been located earlier (evidently Mary did not send it to Chase until around the first of December 1893. See undated letter from Chase to Mary Dartt Thompson, Maxwell Papers).

10. Mary Florence (Dot) Thompson was on the staff of the library of the Department of Agriculture, 1906–41; Helen Morton Thompson was a library staff member from 1902 to 1940. See typed biographical notes apparently compiled by one of the sisters, Maxwell Papers.

11. Not found in Maxwell Papers. Shoemaker was president of the *Altoona Tribune* (later the *Altoona Times Tribune*), according to the letterhead on which he wrote subsequent letters.

12. S. N. Rhoads had sent the book to Shoemaker. In a later letter, Rhoads told Shoemaker that he had bought a crossbill from Martha Maxwell at Philadelphia which was now in his collection at the Academy of Natural Sciences. See Mary Dartt Thompson's copy of letter of Rhoads to Shoemaker, October 17, 1919.

Samuel Nicholson Rhoads (1862–1952) is described in the guide to the manuscripts of the Academy of Natural Sciences of Philadelphia as a "naturalist, ornithologist, mammalogist, book dealer and businessman." He was a founder of the Delaware Valley Ornithological Club (information supplied by Carol M. Spawn, manuscript/archives librarian, September 17, 1984). The red crossbill (*Loxia curvirostra*) Rhoads purchased is still in the Academy's holdings. It was collected in Boulder; the "original number" is 895 and the Academy number is 33884 (letter from Mark Robbins, collection manager, ornithology, October 25, 1984).

13. Shoemaker's letter of October 16, 1919, along with letters of October 31, 1919; December 8, 1919; December 18, 1919; June 16, 1920; and June 26, 1920, is in the Maxwell Papers.

14. See Junius Henderson to Mary Dartt Thompson, October 6, 1906; October 13, 1906; October 23, 1919. Francis Ramaley (1870–1942) joined the University of Colorado faculty as an assistant professor of biology in 1898 and had been head of the department since 1899, a position

he held for thirty years. Obituaries of Francis Ramaley and Ethel Ramaley (died 1952) supplied by the Western Historical Collections, University of Colorado Libraries, Boulder.

15. On February 14, 1920, Clinton G. Abbott, confidential secretary and editor of the New York Conservation Commission in Albany, reported to Mary on his examination of the collection on January 21 (copy in Maxwell Papers). C. L. Palladin of Albany, a taxidermist who did work for the New York State Museum, made a separate examination at that time. Most of the collection, Abbott told Mary, was in the upper story of an outhouse at Hammond's home; the buffalo and elk were in a neighbor's horse stall some distance away. The hotel where Haskins had exhibited the collection had burned down, and the collection had been removed and left in the open; Hammond, in fact, had dug the specimens out of the snow. All told, Abbott continued, the collection was in poor shape. "Wings were off birds, bills were broken, feet gone, and the big animals were faded and unattractive. . . . My own personal advice would be that you try to forget the unfortunate history of the collection and spend no more money upon it." He added, however, that Palladin was more optimistic that the collection could be made presentable, but that the work would cost several hundred dollars (a maximum of $100 to put the birds in shape, $100 for the buffalo, and about $25 each for the other quadrupeds, in addition to renting the loft where the work would be done). See also Abbott to Mary Dartt Thompson, December 2, 1919; December 11, 1919; December 24, 1919; December 31, 1919.

16. "I believe under the circumstances the best thing would be to 'consider the incident closed,' " Henderson wrote to Mary on February 24, 1920, after receiving the news. A few months later Shoemaker proposed to buy what was left of the collection and present it to a school in Colorado, but no such deal was consummated. See Shoemaker to Mary Dartt Thompson, June 16, 1920, and June 26, 1920.

17. In fact, the Society of American Taxidermists was organized in 1880 with Frederic Webster as president, William T. Hornaday as secretary, and Frederic A. Lucas as treasurer. The group held three "very systematic competitive exhibitions" in 1880, 1881, and 1882. Hornaday, "Masterpieces of American Taxidermy," 5–6; Webster, "The Birth of Habitat Bird Groups," 106–7.

18. Brace, *Thanks to Abigail*, 117.

19. Ibid., 117–18; obituary of James A. Maxwell, *Boulder News*, January 29, 1891, clipping in Maxwell Papers.

20. Brace, *Thanks to Abigail*, 131–37; Brace, *Brace Lineage*, 31.

21. *Irvington Gazette*, August 8, 1957, clipping in Maxwell Papers.

22. *Boulder Daily Camera*, February 11, 1901.

23. Brace, *Thanks to Abigail*, 119.

24. Ibid., 118; undated biographical summary, probably prepared by Florence or Helen Thompson, Maxwell Papers.

25. Obituary, June 5, 1939, clipping, Biographical Files, Colorado Historical Society.

26. Mitterling, comp., *Guide to the Hal Sayre Papers*, 4–5.

27. Canfield, *Outline Sketches of Sauk County . . . Baraboo: Ninth Sketch*, 20.

28. Wilbur Fiske Stone, ed., *History of Colorado*, 4 vols. (Chicago: S. J. Clarke Publishing Co., 1918–19), 4:114–17; obituary of James P. Maxwell, May 7, 1929, unidentified clipping in Biographical Files, Colorado Historical Society.

29. Canfield, *Outline Sketches of Sauk County . . . Baraboo: Ninth Sketch*, 20; obituaries of Charles A. Maxwell, *Boulder Daily Camera*, January 24, 1913, and *Daily Herald*, Boulder, January 24, 1913.

30. *Baraboo Republic*, March 29, 1865; obituary of Nellie Rust, August 23, 1939, *Boulder Daily Camera*.

31. *Baraboo Republic*, January 11, 1865; Canfield, *Outline Sketches of Sauk County . . . Baraboo: Ninth Sketch*, 20.

32. Undated obituary of Augusta Maxwell, clipping in Emma Maxwell, "Heart Book," Lawrence University Archives, Appleton, Wisconsin.

Bibliography

MANUSCRIPT AND ARCHIVAL SOURCES
Academy of Natural Sciences of Philadelphia, Philadelphia, Pennsylvania
    John W. Glass, letter, 1867, Collection 567
American Museum of Natural History, New York, New York
    Mabel Maxwell, letter, 1881
Boulder Historical Society, Boulder, Colorado
    Mary Dartt, "A Novel Career: How Mrs. Maxwell Made Her Centennial Collection" (Manuscript of *On the Plains, and Among the Peaks*)
    Mary Dartt Thompson, Reminiscence, c. 1909, printed in part in *Boulder Daily Camera*, July 21, July 25, July 26, 1955.
Colorado Historical Society, Denver, Colorado
    Elmer R. Burkey Papers
    Martha Dartt Maxwell Papers
    Nathan Meeker Papers
Colorado State Archives and Records Service, Denver, Colorado
    Gilpin County Mining District Records (microfilm)
Cullen, Mrs. E. Geoffrey, St. Louis, Missouri
    Family Papers
Denver Public Library, Western History Department, Denver, Colorado
    Martha Dartt Maxwell, letter, 1877, Henry Moore Teller Collection
Lawrence University Archives, Appleton, Wisconsin
    Emma Maxwell Potter, "Heart Book," c. 1854–1910
    Register of Students, 1853–64
    Student Accounts, 1849–54
National Archives, Washington, D.C.
    Casefile 91681, Homestead Records and Casefiles

Oberlin College Archives, Oberlin, Ohio
  Robert S. Fletcher Papers
      "Record of the Proceedings of the Ladies' Board, 1851–62" (typescript), box 6
      "Young Men's Lyceum Minutes, 1849–65" (typescript), box 16
  Martha Maxwell Letters, file 28/1, box 320
  Oberlin Female Moral Reform Society Minutes, 1835–57, file 31/6/11
  Order of Exercises, Commencement, Ladies' Department, August 26, 1851
  Oliver L. Spaulding Reminiscence (typescript), file 16/5/"S"
  Union Literary Society, Constitution and Minutes, 1850–55, file 19/3/4
Philadelphia City Archives, Philadelphia, Pennsylvania
  United States Centennial Commission, Newspaper Clippings Books, 1872–77
Sauk County Historical Society, Baraboo, Wisconsin
  Martha Dartt Maxwell, photograph album
  Mary Dartt Thompson, "Recollections: Connecticut to Baraboo, Wisconsin" and "Pennsylvania to Skillet Creek, Wisconsin" (typescripts)
Scott, Harold B., Palm Beach, Florida
  Family Papers
Smithsonian Institution Archives, Washington, D.C.
  Record Unit 26, Office of the Secretary (1862–1879), Incoming Correspondence
  Record Unit 33, Office of the Secretary (1865–1891), Outgoing Correspondence
  Record Unit 52, Assistant Secretary (Spencer F. Baird), 1850–1877, Incoming Correspondence
  Record Unit 53, Assistant Secretary (Spencer F. Baird), 1850–1877, Outgoing Correspondence
  Record Unit 105, National Museum of Natural History, Vertebrate Zoology, Division of Birds, circa 1854–1959, Records
Western Historical Collections, University of Colorado Libraries, Boulder, Colorado
  James P. Maxwell Papers
  Hal M. Sayre Papers
  Nathan Thompson Papers
  Clinton M. Tyler Papers

MAJOR WORKS ABOUT MARTHA MAXWELL

Contemporary

Allen, Joel A., "A Woman's Work as a Naturalist." *Bulletin of the Nuttall Ornithological Club* 4 (1879): 113–14.

"The Colorado Naturalist." *New Century for Women*, [1876].

Dartt, Mary. *On the Plains, and Among the Peaks; or, How Mrs. Maxwell Made Her Natural History Collection*. Philadelphia: Claxton, Remsen and Haffelfinger, 1879 [1878].

H[unt], H[elen]. "A Colorado Woman's Museum." *St. Nicholas* (October 1876):781–84.

———. "Mrs. Maxwell's Museum," *New York Independent*, September 23, 1875.

Ingersoll, Ernest. "New Land Shells from Colorado." *Forest and Stream* 7 (September 7, 1876):68.

———. "New Shells from Colorado." In "General Notes: Zoology," *American Naturalist* 10 (December 1876):745.

"Martha A. Maxwell: The Colorado Huntress and Naturalist." *Phrenological Journal* 62 (November 1876):349–53.

"Mrs. Maxwell's Rocky Mountain Museum." *Harper's Bazar*, November 11, 1876.

"Remarkable American Women: Mrs. Martha A. Maxwell, the Colorado Naturalist," *Chimney Corner*, January 26, 1878.

Ridgway, Robert. "Mrs. Maxwell's Colorado Museum: Catalogue of the Birds," *Field and Forest* 2 (May 1877):195–98; (June 1877):208–14; "Mrs. Maxwell's Colorado Museum: Additional Notes," 3 (July 1877):11 (published in *On the Plains*; reproduced in Appendix B).

Later

Barker, Jane Valentine, and Sybil Downing. *Martha Maxwell: Pioneer Naturalist*. Boulder: Pruett Publishing Co., 1982 (juvenile biography).

Benson, Maxine. "Centennial Naturalist: Martha Maxwell, 1831–1881." In *A Taste of the West: Essays in Honor of Robert G. Athearn*, edited by Duane A. Smith. Boulder: Pruett Publishing Co., 1983.

Brace, Mabel Maxwell. *Thanks to Abigail: A Family Chronicle*. N.p.: Privately printed, 1948.

"A Colorado Huntress Who Immortalized Her Prey." In *The Women*, by Joan Swallow Reiter. The Old West Series, vol. 23. Alexandria, Va: Time-Life Books, 1978.

DeLapp, Mary. "Pioneer Woman Naturalist." *The Colorado Quarterly* 13 (Summer 1964):91–96.

Ellis, Carrie Scott. "A Stuffy Subject." In *1960 Denver Westerners Brand Book*. Boulder: Johnson Publishing Co., 1961.

Henderson, Junius. "A Pioneer Venture in Habitat Grouping." *Proceedings of the American Association of Museums* 9 (1915):87–91.

Peters, Bette D., and Carrie Scott Ellis. "Woman's Work: The Story of Two Pioneer Women on the Colorado Mining Frontier, 1860 [Martha Maxwell and Mary Cawker]." *Four Mile Express* 6 (July/August/September 1985):12–24.

Rinhart, Floyd and Marion. "Martha Maxwell's Peaceable Kingdom." *American West* 13 (September/October 1976):34–35, 62–63.

Schantz, Viola S. "Mrs. M. A. Maxwell: A Pioneer Mammalogist." *Journal of Mammalogy* 24 (November 17, 1943):464–66.

NEWSPAPERS AND PERIODICALS
Numerous clippings were used in this work, in addition to the publications listed below.

Appleton Crescent, Appleton, Wisconsin, 1853–54
Baraboo Republic, Baraboo, Wisconsin, 1855–68
Boulder County News, Boulder, Colorado, 1869–78, *passim*
Boulder News and Courier, Boulder, Colorado, 1878–81, *passim*
Health Reformer, Battle Creek, Michigan, 1866–67
Long Island Weekly Star, Long Island City, New York, 1880
Oberlin Evangelist, Oberlin, Ohio, 1851–52
Rocky Mountain News, Denver, Colorado, 1860–62, 1868–76, *passim*
Sauk County Standard, Baraboo, Wisconsin, 1850–52
Western Mountaineer, Golden, Colorado, 1859–60
Woman's Journal, Boston, 1875–76

ARTICLES
"Across the Plains and in Denver, 1860: A Portion of the Diary of George T. Clark." *The Colorado Magazine* 7 (July 1929):131–40.

Allen, Joel A. "Sexual, Individual, and Geographical Variation in Leucosticte Tephrocotis." In *Bulletin of the United States Geological and Geographical Survey of the Territories*. Vol. 2, no. 4. Washington, D.C.: Government Printing Office, 1876.

Armitage, Susan. "Women and Men in Western History: A Stereoptical Vision." *Western Historical Quarterly* 16 (October 1985):381–95.

Barry, Louise, ed. "Albert D. Richardson's Letters on the Pike's Peak Gold Region." *Kansas Historical Quarterly* 12 (February 1943):14–57.

Benson, Maxine. "Colorado Celebrates the Centennial, 1876." *The Colorado Magazine* 53 (Spring 1976):129–52.

Brodhead, Michael J. "A Naturalist in the Colorado Rockies, 1876." *The Colorado Magazine* 52 (Summer 1975):185–99.

Buck, Francena M. Kellogg. "Lawrence in 1850–1860." In *Lawrence College Alumni Record, 1857–1915*. Appleton, Wisc.: N.p., n.d.

"Characteristics of the International Fair: IV." *Atlantic Monthly* 38 (October 1876):492–501.

Cheney, Lynne Vincent. "1876: The Eagle Screams." *American Heritage* 15 (April 1974):15–35, 98–99.

———. "1876, Its Artifacts and Attitudes, Returns to Life at Smithsonian." *Smithsonian* 7 (May 1976):37–47.

Clark, Tim W. "Last of the Black-footed Ferrets?" *National Geographic* 163 (June 1983):828–38.

Conway, Jill K. "Perspectives on the History of Women's Education in the United States." *History of Education Quarterly* 14 (Spring 1974):1–12.

Cordato, Mary Frances. "Toward a New Century: Women and the Philadelphia Centennial Exhibition, 1876." *Pennsylvania Magazine of History and Biography* 107 (January 1983):113–35.

Davis, Julia Finette. "International Expositions, 1851–1900." In *American Association of Architectural Bibliographers, Papers*. Charlottesville, Va.: Published for the American Association of Architectural Bibliographers by the University Press of Virginia, 1967.

Deiss, William A. "Spencer F. Baird and His Collectors." *Journal of the Society for the Bibliography of Natural History* 9 (April 1980):635–45.

Ewan, Joseph. "San Francisco as a Mecca for Nineteenth Century Naturalists." In *A Century of Progress in the Natural Sciences, 1853–1953*. San Francisco: California Academy of Sciences, 1955.

Faherty, William Barnaby, S.J. "The Missouri Botanical Garden Through 125 Years." *Gateway Heritage* 5 (Summer 1984):10–19.

"The First Brick Business Building in Boulder, Colorado." *Boulder Genealogical Society Quarterly* 4 (February 1972):21–22.

Ginzberg, Lori D. "Women in an Evangelical Community: Oberlin 1835–1850." *Ohio History* 89 (Winter 1980):78–88.

Gladden, Sanford D. "'Look Pleasant, Please': Early Photographers Found Following in Boulder." *Focus, Boulder Daily Camera*, April 1, 1979.

Harris, Harry. "Robert Ridgway, with a Bibliography of His Published Writings and Fifty Illustrations." *Condor* 30 (January-February 1928):5–118.

Hersey, J. Clarence. "The Little White Egret in Colorado." In "General Notes: Zoology," *American Naturalist* 10 (July 1876):430.

Hindle, Brooke. "Charles Willson Peale's Science and Technology." In *Charles Willson Peale and His World*. New York: Harry N. Abrams, 1983.

Hogeland, Ronald W. "Coeducation of the Sexes at Oberlin College: A Study of Social Ideas in Mid-Nineteenth-Century America." *Journal of Social History* 6 (Winter 1972–73):160–76.

Hornaday, William T. "Masterpieces of American Taxidermy." *Scribner's Magazine* 72 (July 1922):3–17.

Ingersoll, Ernest. "Special Report on the Mollusca." In *Bulletin of the United States Geological and Geographical Survey of the Territories*. No. 2, Second Series. Washington, D.C.: Government Printing Office, 1875.

Johnson, Hiram A. "A Letter from a Colorado Mining Camp in 1860." *The Colorado Magazine* 7 (September 1930):192–95.

Kohlstedt, Sally Gregory. "Henry A. Ward: The Merchant Naturalist and American Museum Development." *Journal of the Society for the Bibliography of Natural History* 9 (1980):647–61.

———. "In from the Periphery: American Women in Science, 1830–1880." *Signs: Journal of Women in Culture and Society* 4 (Autumn 1978):81–96.

Lockwood, Charles. "Woodward's Natural Wonders." *California Living Magazine*, November 20, 1977, 41–45.

Miner, H. Craig. "The United States Government Building at the Centennial Exhibition, 1874–77." *Prologue* 4 (Winter 1972): 202–18.

"Nevada District Mining Laws: Gilpin County, Colorado." *The Colorado Magazine* 36 (April 1959): 131–46.

"Overland to Pikes Peak with a Quartz Mill: Letters of Samuel Mallory." *The Colorado Magazine* 8 (May 1931):108–15.

Parr, A. E. "The Habitat Group." *Curator* 2 (1959):107–28.

Perrigo, Lynn I., ed. "Major Hal Sayr's Diary of the Sand Creek Campaign." *The Colorado Magazine* 15 (March 1938):41–57.

Petteys, Chris. "Colorado's First Women Artists." *Empire Magazine, The Denver Post*, May 6, 1979, 36–47.

Plantz, Samuel. "Lawrence College." *Wisconsin Magazine of History* 6 (1922–23):146–63.

Primm, James Neal. "Henry Shaw: Merchant-Capitalist." *Gateway Heritage* 5 (Summer 1984):2–9.

Ridgway, Robert. "A Monograph of the Genus Leucosticte, Swainson; or, Gray-Crowned Purple Finches." In *Bulletin of the United States Geological and Geographical Survey of the Territories.* No. 2, Second Series. Washington, D.C.: Government Printing Office, 1875.

————. " 'Sexual, Individual and Geographical Variation' in the Genus Leucosticte." *Field and Forest* 2 (September 1876):37–43.

Rudolph, Emanuel D. "How It Developed That Botany Was the Science Thought Most Suitable for Victorian Young Ladies." *Children's Literature* 2 (1973):92–97.

"Rush to the Rockies Articles, Bibliography, Published in *The Colorado Magazine.*" *The Colorado Magazine* 36 (April 1959):126–29.

Sanford, A. B. "How Prospectors of '59 Lived." *The Trail* 18, no. 7 (December 1925):10–19.

Sayre, Robert F. "Hal Sayre—Fifty Niner." *The Colorado Magazine* 39 (July 1962):161–77.

Schlereth, Thomas J. "The 1876 Centennial: A Model for Comparative American Studies." In Schlereth, ed., *Artifacts and the American Past.* Nashville: American Association for State and Local History, 1980.

"Seventy Years Ago—Recollections of a Trip Through the Colorado Mountains with the Colfax Party in 1868, as Told by Mrs. Frank Hall to LeRoy R. Hafen." *The Colorado Magazine* 15 (September 1938):161–68.

Smith-Rosenberg, Carroll. "The Female World of Love and Ritual: Relations Between Women in Nineteenth-Century America." *Signs: Journal of Women in Culture and Society* 1 (Autumn 1975), reprinted in *Disorderly Conduct: Visions of Gender in Victorian America* (New York: Alfred A. Knopf, 1985), 53–76.

————. "Hearing Women's Words: A Feminist Reconstruction of History," in *Disorderly Conduct,* 11–52.

————. "The Hysterical Woman: Sex Roles and Role Conflict in Nineteenth-Century America." *Social Research* 39 (Winter 1972), reprinted in *Disorderly Conduct,* 197–216.

————. "The New Woman as Androgyne: Social Disorder and Gender Crisis, 1870–1936," in *Disorderly Conduct,* 245–96.

Snell, Joseph W. "Kansas and the 1876 United States Centennial." *Kansas Historical Quarterly* 40 (Autumn 1974):337–48.

Spring, Agnes Wright. "Rush to the Rockies, 1859." *The Colorado Magazine* 36 (April 1959):83–120.

Talmadge, Marian, and Iris Gilmore. "Grace Greenwood." In *1955 Denver Westerners Brand Book.* Denver: The Westerners, 1956.

Tyrrell, Ian R. "Women and Temperance in Antebellum America, 1830–1860." *Civil War History* 28 (June 1982):128–52.

Warner, Deborah Jean. "Science Education for Women in Antebellum America." ISIS 69 (March 1978):58–67.

———. "Women Inventors at the Centennial." In Martha Moore Trescott, ed., *Dynamos and Virgins Revisited: Women and Technological Change in History*. Metuchen, N.J.: Scarecrow Press, 1979.

Webster, Frederic S. "The Birth of Habitat Bird Groups." *Annals of the Carnegie Museum* 30 (September 1945):97–111.

Welter, Barbara. "The Cult of True Womanhood, 1820–1860." *American Quarterly* 18 (Summer 1966):151–74.

Wood, Ann Douglas. "'The Fashionable Diseases': Women's Complaints and Their Treatment in Nineteenth-Century America." *Journal of Interdisciplinary History* 4 (Summer 1973):25–52.

ENCYCLOPEDIA ENTRIES

Allard, Dean C. "Baird, Spencer Fullerton." *Dictionary of Scientific Biography*, 1:404–6.

Boyer, Paul S. "Howe, Julia Ward." *Notable American Women*, 2:225–29.

Gould, Stephen Jay. "Hyatt, Alpheus." *Dictionary of Scientific Biography*, 6:613–14.

Isaacs, Ernest. "Wells, Charlotte Fowler." *Notable American Women*, 3:560–61.

James, Janet Wilson. "Richards, Ellen Henrietta Swallow." *Notable American Women*, 3:143–46.

Lurie, Edward. "Agassiz, Jean Louis Rodolphe." *Dictionary of Scientific Biography*, 1:72–74.

Welter, Barbara. "Lippincott, Sara Jane Clarke." *Notable American Women*, 2:407–9.

Wilkins, Thurman. "Jackson, Helen Maria Fiske Hunt." *Notable American Women*, 2:259–61.

Young, James Harvey. "Dickinson, Anna Elizabeth." *Notable American Women*, 1:475–76.

BOOKS AND DOCUMENTS

Abbott, Carl, Stephen J. Leonard, and David McComb. *Colorado: A History of the Centennial State*. 2d ed. Boulder: Colorado Associated University Press, 1982.

Alexander, Edward P. *Museum Masters: Their Museums and Their In-*

fluence. Nashville: American Association for State and Local History, 1983.

———. *Museums in Motion: An Introduction to the History and Functions of Museums*. Nashville: American Association for State and Local History, 1979.

Annual Catalogue and Circular of the Milwaukee Female College, Milwaukee, Wis. 1866–1867: Chartered as a College in 1854. Milwaukee: Daily New Steam Book and Job Print, 1867.

Annual Report of the Board of Regents of the Smithsonian Institution, Showing the Operations, Expenditures, and Condition of the Institution for the Year 1874. Washington, D.C.: Government Printing Office, 1875.

Annual Report of the Board of Regents of the Smithsonian Institution, Showing the Operations, Expenditures, and Conditions of the Institution for the Year 1875. Washington, D.C.: Government Printing Office, 1876.

Arnold, Lois Barber. *Four Lives in Science: Women's Education in the Nineteenth Century*. New York: Schocken Books, 1984.

Athearn, Robert G. *The Coloradans*. Albuquerque: University of New Mexico Press, 1976.

Bailey, Alfred M., and Robert J. Niedrach. *Birds of Colorado*. 2 vols. Denver: Denver Museum of Natural History, 1965.

Baird, Spencer F., with the co-operation of John Cassin and George N. Lawrence. *Birds*. Vol. 9 of *Reports of Explorations and Surveys, to Ascertain the Most Practicable and Economical Route for a Railroad from the Mississippi River to the Pacific Ocean, Made Under the Direction of the Secretary of War, 1853–6*. Washington, D.C.: Beverly Tucker, Printer, 1858.

Bancroft, Caroline. *Gulch of Gold: A History of Central City, Colorado*. Boulder: Johnson Publishing Co., 1958.

Bartlett, Richard A. *Great Surveys of the American West*. Norman: University of Oklahoma Press, 1962.

The Battle Creek Sanitarium Book. Battle Creek: N.p., n.d.

Beckwith, Albert Clayton. *History of Walworth County, Wisconsin*. 2 vols. Indianapolis: B. F. Bowen and Co., 1912.

Beidleman, Richard G. *Guide to the Winter Birds of Colorado*. Leaflet No. 12. Boulder: University of Colorado Museum, 1955.

Bellot, Alfred H. *History of the Rockaways from the year 1865 to 1917*. Far Rockaway, N.Y.: Bellot's Histories, 1917.

Berg, Barbara J. *The Remembered Gate: Origins of American Feminism: The Woman and the City, 1800–1860*. New York: Oxford University Press, 1978.

Billington, Ray Allen. *Westward Expansion: A History of the American Frontier*. 3d ed. New York: Macmillan Co., 1967.

Biographical Directory of the American Congress, 1774–1971. Washington, D.C.: Government Printing Office, 1971.

Bird, Isabella. *A Lady's Life in the Rocky Mountains*. 1879. Intro. by Daniel J. Boorstin. Norman: University of Oklahoma Press, 1960.

Black, Robert C. III. *Island in the Rockies: The History of Grand County, Colorado, to 1930*. Boulder: Published for the Grand County Pioneer Society by the Pruett Publishing Co., 1969.

Blair, Karen J. *The Clubwoman as Feminist: True Womanhood Redefined, 1868–1914*. New York: Holmes and Meier, 1980.

Bolton, Thaddeus Lincoln. *Genealogy of the Dart Family in America*. Philadelphia: Cooper Printing Co., 1927.

Bowles, Samuel. *A Summer Vacation in the Parks and Mountains of Colorado*. Springfield, Mass.: Samuel Bowles and Co., 1869.

Brace, J. Sherman. *Brace Lineage*. Bloomsbury, Pa.: Geo. E. Elwell and Son, 1914.

Brown, Dee. *The Year of the Century*. New York: Charles Scribner's Sons, 1966.

Canfield, William S. *Guide Book to the Wild and Romantic Scenery in Sauk County, Wisconsin*. Baraboo: Republic Book Job and Print, 1873.

———. *Outline Sketches of Sauk County, Wisconsin, Including It's [sic] History From the First Marks of Man's Hand to 1891 and Its Typography, Both Written and Illustrated. Volume Second—Baraboo: Ninth Sketch*. N.p., 1891.

Catalogue of the Officers and Students of Oberlin College for the College Year 1852–53. Oberlin: James M. Fitch, 1852.

Cazden, Elizabeth. *Antoinette Brown Blackwell: A Biography*. Old Westbury, N.Y.: Feminist Press, 1983.

Clarke, Robert. *Ellen Swallow: The Woman Who Founded Ecology*. Chicago: Follett Publishing Co., 1973.

Clinton, Catherine. *The Other Civil War: American Women in the Nineteenth Century*. New York: Hill and Wang, 1984.

Coan Eugene. *James Graham Cooper: Pioneer Western Naturalist*. Moscow, Idaho: A Northwest Naturalist Book, the University Press of Idaho, a Division of the Idaho Research Foundation, 1981.

Cole, Harry Ellsworth, ed. *A Standard History of Sauk County, Wisconsin*. 2 vols. Chicago: Lewis Publishing Co., 1918.

Coues, Elliott. *Fur-Bearing Animals: A Monograph of North American Mustelidae*. United States Geological and Geographical Survey of the Territories, Miscellaneous Publications, No. 8. Washington, D.C.: Government Printing Office, 1877.

Current, Richard N. *The Civil War Era, 1848–1873*. Vol. 2 of *The History of Wisconsin*. Madison: State Historical Society of Wisconsin, 1976.

Cutright, Paul R., and Michael J. Brodhead. *Elliott Coues: Naturalist and Frontier Historian*. Urbana: University of Illinois Press, 1981.

Davies, John R. *Phrenology, Fad and Science: A 19th Century American Crusade*. New Haven: Yale University Press, 1955. Reprint. Archon Books, 1971.

Degler, Carl. *At Odds: Women and the Family in America from the Revolution to the Present*. New York: Oxford University Press, 1980.

Denver, Colorado: Published for the Denver Board of Underwriters. New York: Sanborn Map and Publishing Co., 1887.

Dexter, Elisabeth Anthony. *Career Women of America, 1776–1840*. Francestown, N.H.: Marshall Jones Co., 1950.

Dorsett, Lyle W. *The Queen City: A History of Denver*. Boulder: Pruett Publishing Co., 1977.

Eckhardt, Celia Morris. *Fanny Wright: Rebel in America*. Cambridge: Harvard University Press, 1984.

Elmer, Lucius Q. C. *History of the Early Settlement and Progress of Cumberland County, New Jersey, and of the Currency of This and Adjoining Colonies*. Bridgeton, N.J.: George F. Nixon, Publisher, 1869.

Engbeck, Joseph H. *The Enduring Giants*. Berkeley: University Extension, University of California, Berkeley, 1973.

Epstein, Barbara Leslie. *The Politics of Domesticity: Women, Evangelism, and Temperance in Nineteenth-Century America*. Middletown, Conn.: Wesleyan University Press, 1981.

Ewan, Joseph and Nesta Dunn. *Biographical Dictionary of Rocky Mountain Naturalists: A Guide to the Writings and Collections of Botanists, Zoologists, Geologists, Artists and Photographers, 1682–1932*. Utrecht/Antwerp: Bonn, Scheltema and Holkema, 1981.

Faragher, John. *Women and Men on the Overland Trail*. New Haven: Yale University Press, 1979.

Fletcher, Robert Samuel. *A History of Oberlin College, From Its Foundation Through the Civil War*. 2 vols. Oberlin: Oberlin College, 1943. Reprint (2 vols. in 1), New York: Arno Press and the New York Times, 1971.

Fourth Annual Catalogue of the Corporation, Faculty and Students of the Lawrence University, Appleton, Wisc. December 1853. Appleton: Crescent Print, 1853.

Frank Leslie's Historical Register of the United States Centennial Exposition,

1876. New York: Frank Leslie's Publishing House, 1877. Reprint. New York: Paddington Press, 1974.

General Catalogue of Oberlin College, 1833–1908, Including an Account of the Principal Events in the History of the College, with Illustrations of the College Buildings. Oberlin: Oberlin College, 1909.

Gladden, Sanford Charles. *Letters from the Rev. Nathan Thompson*. Boulder: By the Author, 1976.

———. *Sources for Early Boulder History*. Boulder: By the Author, 1979.

Goode, George Brown. *Bibliographies of American Naturalists, I: The Published Writings of Spencer Fullerton Baird, 1843–1882*. No. 20, *Bulletin of the United States National Museum*. Washington, D.C.: Government Printing Office, 1883.

Gruber, F., comp. *Illustrated Guide and Catalogue of Woodward's Gardens Located on Mission Street, Bet. 13th & 15th Sts. San Francisco, California*. San Francisco: Valentine and Co., 1880.

Guide to the Smithsonian Archives. Washington, D.C.: Smithsonian Institution Press, 1983.

Hall, Frank. *History of the State of Colorado*. 4 vols. Chicago: Blakely Printing Co., 1889–95.

Hanaford, Phebe A. *Daughters of America; or, Women of the Century*. Boston: B. B. Russell, 1883.

Historical Atlas of Wisconsin, Embracing Complete State and County Maps, City & Village Plats, Together with Separate State and County Histories, Also Special Articles on the Geology, Education, Agriculture, and Other Important Interests of the State. Milwaukee: Compiled and Published by Snyder, Van Vechten & Co., 1878.

History of Clear Creek and Boulder Valleys, Colorado. Chicago: O. L. Baskin and Co., 1880. Reprint. Evansville, Ind.: Unigraphic, 1971.

History of Dane County, Wisconsin. Chicago: Western Historical Co., 1880.

The History of Sauk County, Wisconsin. Chicago: Western Historical Co., 1880.

History of Tioga County, Pennsylvania. 2 vols. N.p.: R. C. Brown and Co., 1897. Reprint. Evansville, Ind.: Unigraphic, 1976.

Hollister, Ovando J. *The Mines of Colorado*. Springfield, Mass.: Samuel Bowles and Co., 1867.

Hornaday, William T. *Taxidermy and Zoological Collecting: A Complete Handbook for the Amateur Taxidermist, Collector, Osteologist, Museum-Builder, Sportsman, and Traveler*. 1891. 7th ed. New York: Charles Scribner's Sons, 1921.

Illustrated Guide and Catalogue of Woodward's Gardens, Located on Mission

Street, bet. Thirteenth and Fifteenth Streets, S.F. San Francisco: Francis and Valentine, Book and Job Printers, Engravers, Etc., 1873.

An Illustrated History of Sonoma County, California. Chicago: Lewis Publishing Co., 1889.

Ingram, J. S. *The Centennial Exposition, Described and Illustrated.* Philadelphia: Hubbard Bros., 1876.

Jeffrey, Julie Roy. *Frontier Women: The Trans-Mississippi West, 1840– 1880.* New York: Hill and Wang, 1979.

Kansas at the Centennial: Report of the Centennial Managers to the Legislature of the State of Kansas. . . . Topeka: Geo. W. Martin, Kansas Publishing House, 1877.

Kaufman, Polly Welts. *Women Teachers on the Frontier.* New Haven: Yale University Press, 1984.

Kieckhefer, Grace Norton. *The History of Milwaukee-Downer College, 1851– 1951.* Milwaukee: Milwaukee-Downer College, 1951.

Kovinick, Phil. *The Woman Artist in the American West, 1860–1960.* Fullerton, Cal.: Muckenthaler Cultural Center, 1976.

Ladd, B. F. *History of Vineland, Its Soil, Products, Industries, and Commercial Interests.* Vineland, N.J.: Evening Journal Book and Job Printing Establishment, 1881.

Landis, Charles K. *The Founder's Own Story of the Founding of Vineland, New Jersey.* Vineland, N.J.: Vineland Historical and Antiquarian Society, 1903.

Lasser, Carol, and Marlene Merrill, eds. *Soul Mates: The Oberlin Correspondence of Lucy Stone and Antoinette Brown, 1846–1850.* Oberlin: Oberlin College, 1983.

Lawrence College Alumni Record, 1857–1915. Appleton: N.p., n.d.

Lawrence College Alumni Record, 1857–1922. Appleton: N.p., n.d.

Laws and Regulations of the Female Department of the Oberlin College. Oberlin: Fitch's Power Press, 1852.

Leach, William. *True Love and Perfect Union: The Feminist Reform of Sex and Society.* New York: Basic Books, 1980.

Lerner, Gerda. *The Female Experience: An American Documentary.* Indianapolis: Bobbs-Merrill Co., 1977.

——. *The Majority Finds Its Past: Placing Women in History.* New York: Oxford University Press, 1979.

Lord, Clifford, ed. *Keepers of the Past.* Chapel Hill: University of North Carolina Press, 1965.

Lowe, Berenice Bryant. *Tales of Battle Creek.* N.p.: Published by the Albert L. and Louise B. Miller Foundation, n.d.

Lucas, Frederic A. *Fifty Years of Museum Work: Autobiography, Unpublished Papers, and Bibliography*. New York: American Museum of Natural History, 1933.

————. *The Story of Museum Groups*. American Museum of Natural History, Guide Leaflet Series No. 53, 4th ed., January 1926.

Maass, John. *The Glorious Enterprise: The Centennial Exhibition of 1876 and H. J. Schwarzmann, Architect-in-Chief*. History in the Arts. Watkins Glen, N.Y.: Published for the Institute for the Study of Universal History through Arts and Artifacts by the American Life Foundation, 1973.

McCabe, James D. *The Illustrated History of the Centennial Exhibition*. Philadelphia: National Publishing Co., 1876.

McLoughlin, William G., Jr., *Modern Revivalism: Charles Grandison Finney to Billy Graham*. New York: Ronald Press Co., 1959.

Marshall, Thomas Maitland, ed. *Early Records of Gilpin County, Colorado, 1859–1861*. Boulder: University of Colorado Historical Collections, 1920.

Massachusetts Institute of Technology, Thirteenth Annual Catalogue of the Officers and Students, with a Statement of the Courses of Instruction, 1877–1878. Boston: Press of A. A. Kingman, 1877.

Mattes, Merrill J. *The Great Platte River Road: The Covered Wagon Mainline Via Fort Kearny to Fort Laramie*. Lincoln: Nebraska State Historical Society, 1969.

Melder, Keith E. *Beginnings of Sisterhood: The American Woman's Rights Movement, 1800–1850*. New York: Schocken Books, 1977.

Message of His Excellency, John L. Routt, Governor of Colorado, to the First General Assembly of the State, Delivered November 3, 1876.

Mitterling, Doris, comp. *Guide to the Hal Sayre Papers, 1859–1925*. Boulder: Western Historical Collections, 1976.

Mott, Frank Luther. *A History of American Magazines, 1850–1865*. Cambridge: The Belknap Press of Harvard University Press, 1967.

Myres, Sandra L. *Westering Women and the Frontier Experience, 1800–1915*. Albuquerque: University of New Mexico Press, 1982.

National Geographic Society Field Guide to the Birds of North America. Washington: National Geographic Society, 1983.

Nesbit, Robert C. *Wisconsin: A History*. Madison: University of Wisconsin Press, 1973.

Norton, Minerva Brace. *A True Teacher, Mary Mortimer: A Memoir*. New York: Fleming H. Revell Co., 1894.

Perkin, Robert L. *The First Hundred Years: An Informal History of Denver and the Rocky Mountain News*. Garden City: Doubleday and Co., 1959.

Peters, Bette D. *Denver's Four Mile House*. Denver: Published by the Junior League of Denver for Four Mile Historic Park, 1980.

Portrait and Biographical Album of Ogle County, Illinois. Chicago: Chapman Brothers, 1886.

Post, Robert C., ed. *1876, A Centennial Exhibition*. Washington, D.C.: National Museum of History and Technology, Smithsonian Institution, 1976.

Proceedings of the Third and Fourth Annual Exhibitions of the Colorado Agricultural Society, Held at Denver, September 29th and 30th, and October 1st, 2d and 3d, 1868, and September 22nd, 23d, 24th and 25th, 1869. Central City: Printed by David C. Collier, at the Register Office, 1870.

Riley, Glenda. *Frontierswomen: The Iowa Experience*. Ames: Iowa State University Press, 1981.

———. *Women and Indians on the Frontier, 1825–1915*. Albuquerque: University of New Mexico Press, 1984.

Rossiter, Margaret W. *Women Scientists in America: Struggles and Strategies to 1940*. Baltimore: The Johns Hopkins University Press, 1982.

Sanford, Carlton E. *Thomas Sanford, the Emigrant to New England: Ancestry, Life and Descendants, 1632–4: Sketches of Four Other Pioneer Sanfords and Some of Their Descendants in Appendix, with Many Illustrations*. 2 vols. Rutland, Vt.: Tuttle Co., 1911.

Sanford, Mollie Dorsey. *Mollie: The Journal of Mollie Dorsey Sanford in Nebraska and Colorado Territories, 1857–1866*. Edited by Donald F. Danker. Lincoln: University of Nebraska Press, 1959.

Saum, Lewis O. *The Popular Mood of Pre–Civil War America*. Contributions in American Studies, No. 46. Westport, Conn.: Greenwood Press, 1980.

Sayre, Robert and Gertrude. *Born Pioneers*. Denver: Privately printed, 1963.

Schlissel, Lillian. *Women's Diaries of the Westward Journey*. New York: Schocken Books, 1982.

Schnall, Maxine. *Limits: A Search for New Values*. New York: Clarkson and Potter, 1981.

Schoolland, John B. *Boulder in Perspective: From Search for Gold to the Gold of Research*. Boulder: Johnson Publishing Co., 1980.

———. *Boulder Then and Now*. Rev. ed. Boulder: Johnson Publishing Co., 1978.

Schumann, Ellen. *Creation of a Campus: A Chronicle of Lawrence College Buildings and the Men Who Made Them*. Appleton: Lawrence College Press, 1957.

Scott, Anne Firor. *Making the Invisible Woman Visible.* Urbana: University of Illinois Press, 1984.

Sellers, Charles Coleman. *Mr. Peale's Museum: Charles Willson Peale and the First Popular Museum of Natural Science and Art.* New York: W. W. Norton and Co., 1980.

Sklar, Kathryn Kish. *Catharine Beecher: A Study in American Domesticity.* New Haven: Yale University Press, 1973; New York: W. W. Norton and Co., 1976.

Smiley, Jerome C. *History of Denver, with Outlines of the Earlier History of the Rocky Mountain Country.* Denver: Times-Sun Publishing Co., 1901. Reprint. Denver: Old Americana Publishing Co., 1978.

Smith, Duane A. *Rocky Mountain Mining Camps: The Urban Frontier.* Bloomington, Ind.: Indiana University Press, 1967.

Smith, Phyllis. *A Look at Boulder from Settlement to City.* Boulder: Pruett Publishing Co., 1981.

Smith-Rosenberg, Carroll. *Disorderly Conduct: Visions of Gender in Victorian America.* New York: Alfred A. Knopf, 1985.

Snyder, Charles M. *Oswego: From Buckskin to Bustles.* Port Washington, N. Y.: Ira J. Friedman, 1968.

Solomon, Barbara Miller. *In the Company of Educated Women: A History of Women and Higher Education in America.* New Haven: Yale University Press, 1985.

Sprague, Marshall. *Massacre: The Tragedy at White River.* Boston: Little, Brown and Co., 1957.

Spring, Agnes Wright, ed. *A Bloomer Girl on Pike's Peak, 1858: Julia Archibald Holmes, First White Woman to Climb Pike's Peak.* Denver: Western History Department, Denver Public Library, 1949.

Stegner, Wallace. *Beyond the Hundredth Meridian: John Wesley Powell and the Second Opening of the West.* Boston: Houghton Mifflin Co., 1954.

Stewart, James Brewer. *Joshua R. Giddings and the Tactics of Radical Politics.* Cleveland: The Press of Case Western Reserve University, 1970.

Tebbel, John A. *The Expansion of an Industry, 1865–1919.* Vol. 2 of *A History of Book Publishing in the United States.* 4 vols. New York: Bowker, 1972–81.

Thompson, Nathan. *Ten Years as First Pastor of the Congregational Church of Boulder, Colorado, 1865–1875.* N.p., n.d.

Transactions of the Fifth and Sixth Annual Exhibitions of the Colorado Agricultural Society, Held at Denver, September 27th, 28th, 29th, and 30th, and September 19th, 20th, 21st, 22d and 23d. Denver: The Denver Tribune Association Print, 1872.

Trenton, Patricia, and Peter H. Hassrick. *The Rocky Mountains: A Vision for Artists in the Nineteenth Century*. Norman: University of Oklahoma Press, Published in Association with the Buffalo Bill Historical Center, 1983.

Triennial Catalogue of the Officers and Students of Oberlin College, for the College Year 1851–52. Oberlin: James M. Fitch, 1851.

Ubbelohde, Carl, Maxine Benson, and Duane A. Smith. *A Colorado History*. 5th ed. Boulder: Pruett Publishing Co., 1982.

U.S., Centennial Commission, International Exhibition, 1876, *Reports*.
Vol. 2, *Reports of the President, Secretary, and Executive Committee*
Vol. 3, *Reports and Awards, Groups I and II*
Vol. 8, *Reports and Awards, Groups XXVII–XXXVI, and Collective Exhibits*

Unruh, John D., Jr. *The Plains Across: The Overland Emigrants and the Trans-Mississippi West, 1840–60*. Urbana: University of Illinois Press, 1979.

Vineland. To All Wanting Farms: New Settlement of Vineland. Bound with A. G. Warner, *Vineland and the Vinelanders*. Vineland: Printed by F. P. Crocker, 1869.

Walters, Ronald G. *American Reformers: 1815–1860*. New York: Hill and Wang, 1978.

Warner, Deborah Jean. *Graceanna Lewis, Scientist and Humanitarian*. Washington, D.C.: Published for the National Museum of History and Technology by the Smithsonian Institution Press, 1979.

Weymouth, Lally. *America in 1876: The Way We Were*. New York: Vintage Books, 1976.

Woloch, Nancy. *Women and the American Experience*. New York: Alfred A. Knopf, 1984.

Women Inventors to Whom Patents Have Been Granted by the United States Government, 1790 to July 1, 1888. Washington: Government Printing Office, 1888.

Woody, Thomas. *A History of Women's Education in the United States*. 2 vols. New York and Lancaster, Pa.: Science Press, 1929.

Wyatt-Brown, Bertram. *Lewis Tappan and the Evangelical War Against Slavery*. Cleveland: The Press of Case Western Reserve University, 1969.

UNPUBLISHED MATERIAL

Ainley, Marianne. "Women in North American Ornithology During the Last Century." Paper presented to the first International Conference on the Role of Women in the History of Science, Technology, and Medicine in the Nineteenth and Twentieth Centuries, Veszprem, Hungary, August 1983.

Arapahoe Chapter D.A.R., Boulder, Colorado. "Cemetery Records Copied, 1937–1940." Genealogy Department, Denver Public Library, Denver, Colorado. Typescript.

Beebe, Alan R. "History of the Battle Creek Sanitarium, 1866–1903." Kalamazoo College, 1949, copy in Michigan Historical Collections, Bentley Historical Library, University of Michigan, Ann Arbor.

Dolph, James Andrew. "Bringing Wildlife to Millions: William Temple Hornaday, the Early Years: 1854–1896." Ph.D. diss., University of Massachusetts, 1975.

Luke, Miriam. "Fountain County, Indiana, Marriage Records, Book I, 1826–1839." Danville, Ill.: Illiana Genealogical Publishing Co., n.d., copy in Genealogy Department, Denver Public Library, Denver, Colorado. Mimeographed typescript.

Perrigo, Lynn I. "A Social History of Central City, Colorado, 1859–1900." Ph.D. diss., University of Colorado, 1936.

Stewart, Jennie. "Boulder County Pioneers." Boulder, Colo.: Arapahoe Chapter D.A.R., c. 1948. Mimeographed typescript.

NONBOOK MATERIALS

There's a Good Time Coming and Other Songs of the Hutchinson Family as Performed by the Smithsonian Institution. Washington, D.C.: Smithsonian Institution, 1978. Recording.

Index

Beecher, Catharine (*continued*)
 housekeeping, 121
Beecher, Henry Ward, 181–82
Beecher, Lyman, 9
Berg, Barbara, 72–73
Bird, Isabella, 93
Birds of North America, 103
Black-footed ferret, 169–70, 208–9,
 293 n. 90
Black Hawk, Colorado, 57
Blacks, at Oberlin, 18–19
Blackwell, Antoinette Brown: at Ober-
 lin, 18–19, 21, 242 n. 6; bio-
 graphical information, 183; rela-
 tionship with daughters, 183–84
Blackwell, Elizabeth, 183
Blackwell, Emily, 183
Blackwell, Florence, 184
Blackwell, Henry, 18, 160
Blackwell, Samuel, 183
Bloomer dress. *See* Hunting outfit
Boarding House. *See* Ladies' Hall
Booth, Levi, 256 n. 44
Boston Evening Gazette, 171–72
Boston Sunday Globe, 172
Boston Woman's Education Associa-
 tion, 157
Botany, 31, 83–84
Boulder, Colorado: in 1868, 78; in mid-
 1870s, 111. *See also* Rocky Moun-
 tain Museum (Boulder)
Boulder County Agricultural Society
 fair, 92
Boulder County Centennial Associa-
 tion, 129
Boulder County News, 113
Bowles, Samuel, 264 n. 11
Brace, Charles C.: biographical in-
 formation, 185, 297 n. 60; courts
 and marries Mabel Maxwell,
 185–86, 192
Brace, Mabel (daughter of Mabel and
 Charles), 201
Brace, Mabel Maxwell. *See* Maxwell,
 Mabel
Brace, Maxwell (son of Mabel and
 Charles), 201
Bradley, H. N., 300 n. 2, 301–2 n. 8
Brantner, Jonas, 259 n. 80

Brantner, Samuel, 255 n. 44
Brewer, T. M., 103
Brooklyn, New York, 179, 181–82
Bross, William, 80
Brown, Antoinette. *See* Blackwell,
 Antoinette Brown
Brown, David, 52, 59–60
Bryant, D. S., 101
Buck, Alvin O., 145, 150
Buck, Francena Kellogg, 37, 189
Byers, William N., 80, 254 n. 33
Byron, Illinois, 10

Calaveras Big Trees State Park, 99
California, 99–102
Camping, Mabel Maxwell's attitude
 toward, 81
Cassin, John, 84
Cawker, Mary, 57–59, 255–56 n. 44
Cedar Rapids, Iowa, 52
Centennial. *See* Philadelphia Centen-
 nial Exposition
Centennial Photographic Company,
 143
Central City, Colorado, 57
Charleston Township, Pennsylvania, 3
Chase, Fred L., 301–2 n. 8, 302 n. 9
Cherry Flats, Pennsylvania, 3
Cheyenne, Wyoming, 77
Christ, Elizabeth, 60
Christ, H. J., 60
Clark, Celestia (sister of JAM), 251 n. 52
Clark, George T., 54
Clark, James A. (brother-in-law of
 JAM), 46, 251 n. 52
Clark, James Maxwell (J. Max, Mac,
 nephew of JAM), 52, 59–60, 61,
 260 n. 14
Clark, Mac. *See* Clark, James Maxwell
Clark, Susan. *See* Maxwell, Susan
 Clark
Clark, William M., 156
Claxton, Edward, 165
Claxton, Remsen and Haffelfinger
 (firm), 165–66, 172
Cleveland, Ohio, 20
Cleveland, Columbus and Cincinnati
 Railroad, 19–20
Clisby, Harriet, 162

Hale, Edward Everett, 75
Hammond, E., 200
Harper's (firm), 164
Harper's Bazar, 134
Hartford Female Seminary, 17
Harvard Museum of Comparative
    Zoology, 152, 288 n. 14
Haskins, J. P., 197–200, 300 nn. 1–2,
    301 n. 5
Hayden, Ferdinand V., 109–10, 115
Hayden Survey, 138, 153, 275 n. 57
Health, MDM's attitude toward, 117
Health reform, 73
Henderson, Junius: inquires about
    Shaw's Garden collection, 87; on
    MDM's habitat groups, 142; and
    collection after MDM's death, 200–
    201, 303 n. 16; supplies informa-
    tion to biographer, 239–40 n. 65
Henry, Joseph, 85
Hersey, J. Clarence, 110, 163, 193
Hill, William, 203
*History of Clear Creek and Boulder Val-
    leys*, MDM's biography in, 193
History of North American Birds, 103–4
Hobart, Prof. E. F., 68–69
Holmes, Julia Archibald, 93
Hopkins, Augustus, 244 n. 43
Hopkins, Mary Cook Sumner, 25–26,
    244 n. 43
Hornaday, William T.: taxidermic
    methods of, 90–92, 275 n. 52; as
    originator of habitat groups, 140–
    42; secretary of Society of Amer-
    ican Taxidermists, 142, 303 n. 17
Horticultural Hall, 128
Housekeeping, 121–22
Howe, Julia Ward, 112, 115, 118, 129,
    160
Hubbard, H. *See* Hammond, E.
Hunt, Helen: biographical informa-
    tion, 107; describes Rocky Moun-
    tain Museum (Boulder), 107–9,
    167; publishing agreement of,
    165; mentioned, 115
Hunting outfit, of MDM, 92–93
Hutchinson family, 28, 146, 246 n. 60
Hyatt, Alpheus, 159, 290 n. 48
Hysteria, 5, 13–14, 72–73, 236 n. 28

Independence Day, in Nevada City,
    63–64
Indians, MDM's encounters with, 54–
    55
Ingersoll, Ernest, 138–39, 284 n. 47
Ipswich Female Seminary, 23

Jackson, George, 50
Jackson, Helen Hunt. *See* Hunt, Helen
Jackson, William Henry, 138, 275 n. 57
Jackson, William S., 107
James, Margaret, 60
James, William, 60
Johnson, Hiram, 60, 257 n. 56

Kansas, MDM and JAM support Free-
    State cause in, 45
Kansas-Colorado Building, 131, 132,
    138
Key to North American Birds, 103, 153,
    273 n. 31
Kimball, Elizabeth, 60
King, Clarence, survey of, 104
Kinship networks, 62

Ladies' Hall, Oberlin, 21
Landis, C. K., 75
Langrishe, John, 63
Lawrence, Amos, 36
Lawrence College. *See* Lawrence Uni-
    versity
Lawrence Institute. *See* Lawrence Uni-
    versity
Lawrence University: described, 36;
    coeducation at, 36–37; James P.
    Maxwell graduate of, 203; history
    of, 249 n. 15; college classes
    offered, 249 n. 16
Lerner, Gerda, 119, 241 n. 91
Lewis, Graceanna, 84, 138, 188
Lincoln, Almira Hart, 83–84
Lippincott, Sara Jane. *See* Greenwood,
    Grace
Litchfield, Connecticut, 3, 9
Littlejohn, DeWitt C., 179–80, 181,
    192
Log Cabin Restaurant, 175–76
Long's Peak, 80
Loxia curvirostra. See Red crossbill

work, 95; social life of, 101, 185; relationship with MDM, 116–27, 143–44, 184, 194; at Oberlin, 112, 116–27; at University of Michigan, 146–48; at Wellesley, 160–61, 177; as teacher, 177, 184–85; helps at Rockaway Beach, 180; on marriage and family, 182–83, 194; courtship and marriage to Charles C. Brace, 185–86, 192; and MDM's death, 191; and MDM's collection after death, 191–92, 197, 301 n. 7; later life of, 201–2; death of, 202

Maxwell, Maria (daughter of James P.), 203

Maxwell, Mark (son of James P.), 203

Maxwell, Martha Ann Dartt: childhood interest in birds and other animals, 1–2; influence of grandmother on, 2, 6, 7; birth, 5; influence of mother, 6; death of father, 6; separation from mother, 6–7; early childhood of, 7; relationship with half-sister Mary, 9, 151; relationship with half-sister Sarah, 10; moves to Wisconsin, 11–13; musical ability of, 13; care of mother, 13–14; influence of stepfather, 14–15, 21–22, 29–31; and Cult of True Womanhood, 15–16; goes to Oberlin College, 15, 19–20; in Ladies' Hall, 21; Oberlin studies, 21, 22, 28–29, 31, 243 n. 16; opinion of Oberlin manual labor system, 22–23; opinion of Oberlin, 24; grades of, 25; social activities at Oberlin, 26–27, 28; reform activities at Oberlin, 27–28; and study of botany, 31, 83; leaves Oberlin, 32–33; on coeducation, 32–33, 144; as teacher, 34–35; courtship and marriage to JAM, 34–42; at Lawrence University, 35–37; possible Oberlin romance of, 42; as stepmother to Maxwell children, 42–44; reform activities in Baraboo, 44–45; role in Bara-

boo Whiskey War, 45, 251 n. 47; domestic activities in Baraboo, 46; and conception of child, 46; trip to gold fields (1860), 49, 51–56; separation from daughter, 52, 62, 65–66, 74; encounters with Indians, 54–55; on Denver, 56; partnership with Mary Cawker 57–59, 255 nn. 37, 40; financial arrangements with JAM, 58, 114; boardinghouse of, 59, 62, 63; acquires mining claims, 60; health principles of, 61, 73, 117; buys and lives on ranch, 61–62, 64–65, 259 n. 80, 261 n. 22; on "hang-on-it-ive" trait, 61, 88, 194; temperance activities in Nevada City, 63; Independence Day activities in Nevada City, 63–64; leaves Nevada City after fire, 64; returns to Baraboo (1862), 65, 67; encounters German taxidermist, 68–70, 260 n. 14; practices taxidermy, 70, 86, 88–89, 89–92, 260 n. 16, 268 n. 62, 275 n. 52; moves to Pewit's Nest, 70; family responsibilities in Baraboo, 70–71; Civil War activities of, 71; state of marriage to JAM, 71, 72, 156–57, 161–62, 175, 180, 186–89; health problems of (mid-1860s), 72–74; at health institute in Battle Creek, 72–74; in Vineland, New Jersey, 75–76, 262–63 n. 44; returns from Vineland, 76; goes back to Colorado (1868), 77–78; proficiency with gun, 79; on collecting trips, 79–82, 86, 93–94, 99, 110; Colorado Agricultural Society fair displays (1868), 82–83, (1870), 87; educational background of, 83–85; begins correspondence with Smithsonian Institution, 85; relationship with Robert Ridgway, 86, 104–5, 152–53, 193; relationship with Spencer Baird, 86, 193; sells collection to Shaw's Garden (1870), 87–89; buys land in Boulder Canyon, 88; "den" de-